COPYRIGHT VIGILANTES

COPYRIGHT VIGILANTES

INTELLECTUAL PROPERTY AND THE HOLLYWOOD SUPERHERO

EZRA CLAVERIE

UNIVERSITY PRESS OF MISSISSIPPI / JACKSON

The University Press of Mississippi is the scholarly publishing agency of the Mississippi Institutions of Higher Learning: Alcorn State University, Delta State University, Jackson State University, Mississippi State University, Mississippi University for Women, Mississippi Valley State University, University of Mississippi, and University of Southern Mississippi.

www.upress.state.ms.us

The University Press of Mississippi is a member of the Association of University Presses.

Portions of the introduction and chapter 1 previously appeared in *Jump Cut: A Review of Contemporary Media*, no. 57 (Fall 2016), https://www.ejumpcut.org/archive/jc57.2016/-ClaverieSuperheroIP/index.html.

Copyright © 2024 by University Press of Mississippi
All rights reserved

∞

Library of Congress Cataloging-in-Publication Data

Names: Claverie, Ezra, author.
Title: Copyright vigilantes : intellectual property and the Hollywood superhero / Ezra Claverie.
Description: Jackson : University Press of Mississippi, 2024. | Includes bibliographical references and index.
Identifiers: LCCN 2024003720 (print) | LCCN 2024003721 (ebook) | ISBN 9781496851338 (hardback) | ISBN 9781496851321 (trade paperback) | ISBN 9781496851314 (epub) | ISBN 9781496851307 (epub) | ISBN 9781496851291 (pdf) | ISBN 9781496851284 (pdf)
Subjects: LCSH: DC Comics, Inc.—Characters. | Marvel Comics Group—Characters. | Marvel Studios—Characters. | Superhero films—History and criticism. | Superhero television programs—History and criticism. | Comic strip characters in motion pictures. | Copyright—Motion pictures. | Intellectual property in motion pictures. | Duopolies.
Classification: LCC PN1995.9.S76 C53 2024 (print) | LCC PN1995.9.S76 (ebook) | DDC 791.43/652—dc23/eng/20240229
LC record available at https://lccn.loc.gov/2024003720
LC ebook record available at https://lccn.loc.gov/2024003721

British Library Cataloging-in-Publication Data available

CONTENTS

3   **Introduction**

32   **Chapter One.** Copyright Vigilantes

69   **Chapter Two.** Nolan's Batman: Criminogenic Capitalism and the (Re)Birth of a Brand

98   **Chapter Three.** Captain America and Wonder Woman: Instrumental Heroes

134   **Chapter Four.** The Adult Turn: Reproduction of the Brand

170   **Chapter Five.** *Blade* and *Black Panther*: Strategic Blackness and the Rights of Kings

205   **Coda.** Dreaming Like a Supervillain

211   **Acknowledgments**

213   **Notes**

221   **Works Cited**

238   **Index**

COPYRIGHT VIGILANTES

INTRODUCTION

PROLOGUE: FALL 1998

On August 21, 1998, New Line Cinema released *Blade*, a movie about a half-vampire vigilante who uses swords, machine pistols, and kung fu to kill vampires. Two months later, I got around to seeing *Blade* at the Wehrenberg Union Station 10 Cinema, just across the parking lot from the old Saint Louis Union Station proper, by then a hotel with an attached tourist mall. You might know Union Station from its years as a derelict shell, when John Carpenter used it as a shooting location for *Escape from New York* (1981). But buildings that seem worthless and justly neglected in one decade might later attract the eyes of investors. So can comic book characters.

The opening sequence of *Blade* introduced a handsome blond lunk on a date with a woman obviously planning to drink his blood. As she led him into a postindustrial vampire disco, the film's opening credits introduced actors, producers, and so on. But when a credit declared, "Blade and Deacon Frost characters created for Marvel Comics," I cackled in disbelief. Summer afternoons in comic shops had acquainted me with many characters from the Marvel Universe, but not these third-stringers. I knew of only two screen outings by Marvel characters: *The Punisher* (Mark Goldblatt, 1989), never released in the United States, and which I had read about in *Starlog*; and *Howard the Duck* (Willard Huyck, 1986), which even my most forgiving middle-school peers had regarded as shamefully bad. So despite my nostalgia for Marvel comic books, the sight of the company's name in *Blade*'s opening credits threw me into doubt. Had I wasted my matinee ticket?

No. Just when the handsome blond lunk seems doomed, Blade shows up and kills himself a disco full of vampires; the ensuing reels of swagger, Hong Kong–style wirework, and blood-spraying mayhem—rated a glorious R—left me wanting more. I saw *Blade* again the following week at the Avalon, a crumbling, one-screen, dollar-fifty show on South Kingshighway (long since torn down). Viewers like me helped turn *Blade* into the hit nobody expected: a midbudget, R-rated action movie with a Black star, and based on a Marvel Comics character known only to the hardest-core fans. Meanwhile, the success of *Blade* helped persuade movie producers to risk developing movies based on Marvel characters.

Two other things happened in the fall of 1998, and they had even wider consequences. In October, the United States Congress passed the Copyright Term Extension Act (CTEA), known as the Sonny Bono Copyright Term Extension Act in honor of the pop singer turned congressman who had helped draft similar legislation and had recently died in a skiing accident. Bono had campaigned to lengthen the duration of copyright stipulated by the 1976 Copyright Act.[1] Under the 1976 act, a work made by a human author received copyright for the author's lifetime plus fifty years, but a work made for hire—that is, created by the employees of a firm that received legal authorship—received copyright for seventy-five years. Bono and his colleagues regarded this as insufficient, so the CTEA extended copyright terms for another twenty years, thus freezing the public domain for two decades. Critics called the CTEA the "Mickey Mouse Protection Act," because it helped the Walt Disney Company keep its monopoly on the company's most famous cartoon character. If not for the CTEA, the early appearances of many familiar comic book characters would already have entered the public domain: Superman in 2013; Batman and the Human Torch in 2014; Robin, the Boy Wonder, and the Flash in 2015; and Captain America and Wonder Woman in 2016.[2] In the same week that Congress passed the CTEA, it also passed the Digital Millennium Copyright Act (DMCA), which criminalized even the dissemination of techniques for circumventing copy protection on media platforms like the DVD. In these two laws, Democrats and Republicans laid aside their putative differences to grant media corporations a range of boons at the public's expense.

In the two decades that followed the passage of these laws, DVDs boomed and then went bust as streaming came to replace disc media and mainland China grew into the world's second-largest theatrical distribution market, reshaping Hollywood's priorities. Meanwhile, movies and franchises based on superheroes owned by DC Comics and Marvel Comics became ubiquitous not just in American cinemas but on screens worldwide. During the two decades when the CTEA kept the public domain frozen, and when the DMCA had even teachers looking over their shoulders for cease-and-desist letters, increasing numbers of scholars began to write books about superheroes.

The covers always featured generic, off-brand characters, which signaled the books' approximate subject matter while avoiding avoid infringement lawsuits or endless runarounds with permissions offices. Many of the writers using these plausibly deniable images would argue that superhero stories tell us profound truths about the human experience or post-9/11 society, even as the same authors ignored the legal and industrial matrix from which superhero blockbusters emerged, and ignored the systems of ownership, licensing, and distribution that made superheroes both ubiquitous and profitable. *Copyright Vigilantes* offers a critical analysis of duopoly films informed by close attention to the industries that produce them.

Welcome to the book Gotham deserves.

INTELLECTUAL PROPERTY AND THE AVERSION OF APOCALYPSE

This book argues that the mode of production at America's two major comic book publishers, DC and Marvel, has shaped the narratives of the superhero films that came to dominate Hollywood's blockbuster production in the first two decades of the twenty-first century. In these films, one narrative recurs more often than all others: the villain tries to copy or capture the hero's signature powers—and this can include bodily superpowers or proprietary gadgets—and then use, distribute, or even mass-produce those powers in a scheme that threatens the lives of millions. The hero always succeeds in averting this apocalypse, restoring by force his (rarely *her*) monopoly on his superpowers. This seemingly altruistic narrative actually reflects the concerns of the brand managers, publishing and studio executives, and film producers whose fortunes depend on franchises owned by the DC-Marvel duopoly.

At the duopoly, writers and artists create works for hire, such that the firm becomes the legal author of those works. Since the 1930s, comics publishers have used work-for-hire and freelance labor to expropriate stories and characters from the workers who create them, not only so that the firms could sell magazines without paying royalties to creators, but also so that the firms could license stories and characters for other commercial uses, including adaptation into other media, again without paying royalties to creators. In the 1970s, the duopoly's revenues from licensing eclipsed their revenues from the sales of comic books (Kidman 112); both firms' business models have long depended on their ability to maintain monopoly power over the copyrighted and trademarked works that their employees created. In 1967, DC became the property of a larger conglomerate, known today as Warner Bros. Discovery Inc., and in 2009, Marvel Entertainment became the property of the Walt Disney

Company; both DC and Marvel therefore operate according to the needs of their much larger parents, providing narrative material for sister subsidiaries to develop into computer games, television shows, theme park attractions, and even comic books. When blockbuster movies based on duopoly characters obsessively rehearse the defense of IP, they reflect the concerns of the firms that benefit most from this mode of production and that stand to lose if that mode should change.

This book treats blockbuster films as nodes in a much larger industrial process, reading films allegorically for what they can help us understand about that process. Duopoly superheroes avert apocalypses, but I want to draw attention to the nature of these apocalypses as unintended allegories of the duopoly's mode of production. The word *apocalypse* comes from the Greek *apokálypsis* (ἀποκάλυψις), meaning either a literal uncovering or, in its extended sense, a revelation, as of how the world will end. Duopoly movies threaten the world with apocalypses that actually reveal the industrial processes behind these films. By showing how the duopoly's "world" could end, these apocalypses can help us understand what kinds of legal, financial, and labor arrangements make the duopoly's mode of production profitable for investors. American comic book companies have long focused on superheroes as their most profitable genre, and this genre has never gone in for endings in the dramatic sense: instead, most superhero stories have offered deferrals and never-ending battles, and publishers have turned to an infinite series of reboots, resurrections, and retreads. Likewise, superhero film franchises may show the "death" of a superhero, as in *Batman v Superman: Dawn of Justice* (Zack Snyder, 2016) or *Logan* (James Mangold, 2017), but they do so only with the promise that the character as brand can live on.

Against arguments that superhero movies satisfy some need native to audiences or reflect social fantasies, this book instead argues that film studios, especially conglomerated film studios, manufacture both these films and the demand for them, trying to maximize return on investment by selling variations on successful formulas. Since the 2000s, many writers have argued that superhero blockbusters have offered fantasies that combine mass destruction with last-minute rescues, which help Americans deal with or compensate for the September 11 attacks.[3] But in none of these films does a radical group seek to destroy a city to pressure a government to change its foreign or domestic policies, and seldom does a villain even threaten destruction for its own sake, using only his own powers. Most often, the villain threatens destruction as a side effect of copying, capturing, or spreading the hero's powers while in pursuit of some other goal. And the villain will not simply steal the hero's powers, rendering the hero a normal person, because that would give the hero a selfish reason to defend them. The genre requires that the superhero have a mission, as Peter Coogan puts it, both "pro-social and selfless" (24). So when the villain schemes to copy the hero's trade secrets or trademarks, that scheme also threatens thousands or millions or billions of citizens, giving the hero a selfless reason to protect his monopoly—a reason radically unlike the financially interested motives of DC and Marvel. Again and again, duopoly films warn of the danger of the hero's powers falling into *the wrong hands*, often using that very cliché. This book charts this narrative preoccupation over twenty years, beginning in 1998, the year *Blade* demonstrated the potential of Marvel characters at the box office. And the book ends in 2018, the year that Marvel Studios released *Black Panther* (Ryan Coogler, 2018) and began to close its main franchise with *Avengers: Infinity War* (Anthony Russo and Joe Russo, 2018).

Some might argue that we can read these films as reflections of the aspiration of creative media workers toward greater autonomy, including ownership of their work, in industries where firms constantly seek to alienate creators from their creations. If superhero stories scratch some audience itch for fantasies about the ability to bend steel or leap tall buildings in a single bound, then maybe the duopoly's blockbuster melodramas of IP defense also scratch some film industry worker's itch for a different bundle of rights. Maybe in these melodramas of IP defense, we see not the daydreams of executives, anxious to recoup investment or to protect the equity of the brands they manage, but the daydreams of filmmakers longing for different working conditions, where executives not only fail to capture what those executives cannot create, but also suffer punishment for the attempt. In these films' compulsion to punish those who challenge the superhero's monopoly, maybe we can detect filmmakers' aspiration for the moral rights (*droit moral*) more like those that artists enjoy in France, Germany, and Italy. Such rights include the right to the work's integrity, the right to choose whether or not to disseminate a work, and the right to withdraw a work from circulation (Kamina 339); unlike copyright systems, which treat such rights as alienable by contract, so-called authors' rights systems consider these rights generally "inalienable, unwaivable, and imprescriptible" (340). Filmmakers, however, do not make duopoly movies on their own initiative but do so at the behest of studios as part of much larger marketing and release strategies; duopoly films do not result from a writer-director's labor of love but by committee, on behalf of investors, and usually as part of a planned multimedia franchise. Filmmakers who want control of their work don't make duopoly movies, and if they want to make superhero movies, they invent new superheroes, either producing the films themselves or finding studios willing to develop them. Such filmmakers make superhero movies like *The Toxic Avenger* (Michael Herz and Lloyd Kaufman, 1984), *Darkman* (Sam Raimi, 1990), *The Meteor Man* (Robert Townsend, 1993), *Blankman* (Mike Binder, 1994), *Orgazmo* (Trey Parker, 1997), *The Specials* (James Gunn, 2000), *Unbreakable* (M. Night Shyamalan, 2000), *The Adventures of Sharkboy and Lavagirl in 3-D* (Robert Rodriguez, 2005), *Sky High* (Mike Mitchell, 2005), *Hancock* (Peter Berg, 2008), and *Super* (James Gunn, 2010).[4] And these films, developed outside the duopoly's regime of licensing and franchising, do not spin melodramas about the defense of superhero IP, because films made outside do not reflect that regime's structuring preoccupations.

In duopoly films, narratives about the defense of IP recur more than any other. Yet we do not see this pattern in what we might call written-for-the-screen superhero films, like those just named, nor do we see it in blockbuster franchises that have much else in common with superhero films: abundant but bloodless violence, chaste (or censor-friendly) romances by youthful characters, and presold stories adapted from other media. The Star Wars, Transformers, Harry Potter, Twilight, MonsterVerse, Hunger Games, Maze Runner, and Universal Classic Monsters franchises do not tell stories about the moral necessity of copyright protection and the punishment of unauthorized duplicators, but those franchises do not have roots in the American comics business, where publishers routinely copied competitors' successes while expropriating their own writers and artists as standard procedure. Not only does the American comics business understand how it made its fortune, but it also knows how it could lose it. Since the 1940s, writers and artists—and, increasingly, their heirs—have challenged the duopoly, filing lawsuits that keep raw both the memory of the publishers' expropriations and the threat that some judge could rule in favor of the talent, requiring publishers to pay royalties or, worse, surrender their copyrights altogether. This book analyzes some of the ways that this history of exploitation, imitation, litigation, and bad conscience manifests itself in the Hollywood blockbusters that the duopoly spawned. Instead of treating the duopoly's mode of production as either incidental or irrelevant to superhero movies, this book treats that mode of production as the chief determinant of the story that these movies blare again and again: COSTUMED HERO DEFENDS MONOPOLY, SAVES CITY.

But has the ubiquity of anticopying narratives affected popular understandings of the ethics of copying and imitation, or has it cultivated a popular reverence for monopolies? Has the duopoly convinced viewers to respect copyrights, trademarks, patents, and trade secrets that they might otherwise have mocked or violated? I will not try to answer such questions, leaving them to social scientists. Whether or not the duopoly's values have reshaped popular attitudes toward copying, originality, and the sanctity of monopolies, this book attends instead to the ways that the duopoly's values have shaped Hollywood's narratives.

Film scripts always address a potential audience of moviegoers, but they must first address an actual audience of executives who vet and shape scripts according to the needs of the studio or the related divisions of the conglomerate. Imagine a thousand screenwriters, their scripts filtered through a panel of executives working to exploit and cross-promote the company's film rights and to demonize infringers of copyright and trademark: the selective pressure of such a panel would produce the patterns that we see in the duopoly blockbusters, the managerial fantasy of a hero defending IP. The duopoly uses the virtues of the superhero to pursue the vices of the huckster and the racketeer; duopoly films interpellate the audience into rooting for the copyright vigilante, who punishes infringers outside the law.

WHY SUPERHEROES?

Changes to Hollywood's production and distribution priorities help explain why the studios turned to the duopoly's work-for-hire fictional universes. The digital video disc, first released to the North American market in 1997, offered studios an extremely profitable new platform for home video; the DVD's compactness and huge storage capacity helped it quickly supplant videotape. Between 2003 and 2007, the US media industry underwent what commentators in *Billboard*, *Retailing Today*, *Variety*, *Video Business*, and the *Wall Street Journal* called a DVD boom as retail sales of DVDs became Hollywood's largest stream of revenue. Thomas Schatz notes that this boom came about in part because of Hollywood's "decision to abandon the VHS-era rental model in favor of a conglomerate-controlled 'sell-through' strategy that returned a far greater portion of home-video revenues to the studios" (22). DC's parent, Warner Bros., led the charge. Studios that had their own home video units, as Warner did, saw great profits, in part because contractual agreements kept the revenues from home video "shielded from participations and kept captive" (Ulin 212). A home video unit didn't have to pay residuals to as many parties (e.g., stars and talent guilds); 50 percent or less of a movie's box office returned to the studio, but 60 percent or more of a movie's DVD revenue returned to the home video unit. Furthermore, during the boom, DVD retail became the "the largest source of consumer spending on filmed entertainment across all distribution channels" (McDonald 150–51). By 2007, theatrical exhibition supplied only 21.4 percent of Hollywood's revenues, while home video supplied 48.7 percent (Ulin 161). Thus potential DVD sales came to shape decisions about blockbuster filmmaking. In 2003, MGM executive Chris McGuirk called DVD "the primary market in determining whether to green light a movie or not" (qtd. in Kirkpatrick). Studios would green-light otherwise risky projects by using projected DVD profits as a "safety net" (Goldstein). Affluent young men adopted DVD early, young men bought action movies, and because a sequel boosted sales of its predecessor's DVD, studios made more sequels (Kirkpatrick). This explains the "trend among the highest selling titles" toward "fantasy-adventure franchises" (McDonald 150). But to keep DVD profits shielded from both above- and below-the-line workers, studios became more secretive about those profits (Goldstein). The studios continued to report theatrical revenues to the press, so mainstream discussion continued to focus on those numbers. Paradoxically, the DVD boom increased Hollywood's secrecy about the revenues from their most profitable sector. Even when the DVD market began to contract in 2008, this secrecy left the public largely unaware of the studios' panic, since box office figures continued to grow while bottom-line profits shrank. In 2007, Netflix had launched its streaming video service, which would erode the sell-through market for DVDs. Netflix's mail-order DVD service peaked in 2010 with 20 million subscribers; by 2015 that number had fallen to just 5.3 million, while the company's streaming service had grown to 65 million subscribers (Steel).

Yet despite the decline of the DVD market and the rise of streaming, duopoly filmmaking only gained steam, with 2008 seeing both the record-breaking box office performance of Warner Bros.' *The Dark Knight* (Christopher Nolan) and Marvel Studios beginning to release self-financed superhero films based on characters that it owned. Marvel Studios had worked before with partner studios as a glorified licensor, but with the release of the self-financed and self-produced *Iron Man* (Jon Favreau, 2008), the company established itself as what Derek Johnson called "a unique model for cinema production in the age of convergence: an independent company with expertise in a different media industry [that] drove blockbuster film content" ("Cinematic Destiny" 1). When Disney acquired Marvel in 2009, the duopoly became fully integrated into larger media conglomerates. The owners of continuity capital, once relegated to the ghetto of four-color comics, could now throw it into circulation using the machinery of media production firms as sophisticated, powerful, and far-reaching as any the world has seen. By the second decade of the twenty-first century, the duopoly's mode of production, based on work-for-hire fictional universes originally aimed at boys and young men, had become Hollywood's tentpole. According to Box Office Mojo, from 2012 to 2022, duopoly films accounted for at least four of the top ten highest-grossing films in seven different years. Over the same decade, duopoly films took first place at the domestic box office five times, and in 2021, films based on Marvel characters took five out of the top six spots ("Domestic Yearly Box Office").

At the same time, the studios began to license or to produce streaming live-action TV series not merely based on their copyrighted characters but sometimes closely tied into the narratives of their larger cinematic universes, including shows like DC's *Arrow* (The CW, 2012–20), *Supergirl* (Warner Bros. Television, 2015–21), and *Pennyworth* (Warner Horizon Television, 2019–22), or Marvel's *Agents of S.H.I.E.L.D.* (ABC, 2013–20), *Daredevil* (Netflix, 2015–18), and *Jessica Jones* (Netflix, 2015–19). Marvel Studios' "Phase Four" slate of eight new miniseries began to appear in 2021, released to Disney+ (Russell et al.). Second- and third-tier comic book characters previously known only to people who haunted the back-issue bins at comic stores now headline TV shows aimed at mass audiences, crowding the menus of streaming services.

COMIC BOOKS: MEANS TO OTHER ENDS

Since the 1970s, the duopoly has relied not on publishing but on licensing as its main source of revenue. This represents not an aberration but a continuation, even a refinement, of one of the foundational practices of the industry. Comic books appeared in the American publishing market as a means of achieving other ends, and publishers of comic books saw the licensing of stories and characters not as a secondary activity but as the basic goal of the enterprise. In 1933, the publisher Maxwell Gaines arranged licenses to repackage newspaper comic strips in a saddle-stapled booklet called *Funnies on Parade*, and Procter & Gamble would then distribute the ten-thousand-copy print run as part of a promotional campaign (Hajdu 100). In 1934, Gaines repeated this success with *Famous Funnies*, arranging more sponsors and increasing the print run to a hundred thousand, but this time, the book sold on newsstands and in department stores (100–101). The same year, the pulp writer and publishing entrepreneur Malcolm Wheeler-Nicholson set up National Allied Publishing and began to recruit freelance writers and artists to produce original stories for the aptly named *New Fun* and *New Comics* (Wright 4–5). Mark Cotta Vaz calls Wheeler-Nicholson's innovation "more practical than revolutionary: original material was cheaper than a newspaper syndicate's licensing fee of $15 a page" (24). But Wheeler-Nicholson aimed beyond mere newsstand sales, instead hoping to attract the attention of newspaper syndicates, who would pay for the rights to the stories and characters that his freelancers had created. As Wheeler-Nicholson put it, "I see these magazines more or less as brochures to interest the newspaper syndicates in an idea" (qtd. in Hajdu 20). At the genesis of the comic book as a platform, we see the duopoly's business model forming with it: a publishing firm hires talent to produce a work for hire, and that firm thereby becomes legal author of that work, and thus holder of the work's copyright, therefore entitled to license the work to others.[5] Comic books quickly attained mass popularity, but savvy publishers treated the sale of four-color magazines as a promotional activity rather than the goal of their enterprise.

Wheeler-Nicholson's business partners forced him out shortly before the company's first and greatest success: *Action Comics*.[6] When the first issue appeared, dated June 1938, its cover bore an image of a caped figure, a stylized S emblazoned on his chest, lifting a car over his head. The popularity of Superman not only established the template for a new kind of character but also demonstrated the commercial potential of comics magazines full of original stories. *Action Comics* #1 prompted a wave of new publishers to enter the field; as Shawna Kidman puts it, the popularity of Superman "helped establish the industry as an industry" (25). Writer Jerry Siegel and illustrator Joe Shuster had created the character to sell as a newspaper strip, but when they failed to find a buyer, they revised their work for the anthology format of *Action Comics*. In exchange for their Superman story, they received a check for $130 and a contract that signed all rights over to National. As Gerard Jones puts it, Siegel and Shuster "knew that was how the business worked—that's how they'd sold every creation from *Henri Duval* to *Slam Bradley*" (125). Jones points out that Siegel and Shuster had planned in terms of the industry's commercial practices even they developed Superman, drafting hyperbolic advertising slogans and making "sketches of boxes for cereal and whole wheat crackers with Superman's likeness" (115), imagining the licensing of the character even as they imagined his adventures. Nearly three decades after *Action Comics* #1, Jack Leibowitz, publisher of National, would write a letter to shareholders reaffirming the centrality of licensing to the firm's business model:

> Batman, Superman, Wonder Woman, the Flash, Green Lantern and other members of our family of fiction heroes can be molded and merchandised to suit every taste—as television performers, as illustrations for magazine advertising and point-of-sale displays, as promotional products for the ice-cream, dairy, soft drink, baking and confectionary industries, as syndicated comic strips, and as hundreds of different toy and apparel products for children and teenagers. (qtd. in Santo 69)

Timely Comics, later known as Atlas and today known as Marvel, followed National's lead. Both firms would license characters for theatrical serials like Republic's *Captain America* (1941) and Columbia's *Batman* (1943), television shows like *The Adventures of Superman* (1951–58) and *The Incredible Hulk* (1978–82), and theatrical films like *Superman* (Richard Donner, 1978) and *Howard the Duck* (Willard Huyck, 1986). Licensing played a different yet still central role in the business models of other comics publishers, like Dell, which outsold competitors by licensing familiar and successful characters from Disney, Warner Bros., and newspaper syndicates (Kidman 29). This system depended on the legal doctrine of work for hire, which treats a firm as the legal author of any works created by the firm's employees.

The practice of work for hire developed in the last two decades of the nineteenth century. It got its name in the Copyright Act of 1909 (Jaszi and Woodmansee 93). Lawmakers codified the doctrine because of firms like the Stratemeyer Syndicate, which pioneered a practice now called "book packaging," whereby the packaging firm arranges the production of a book— usually part of a series—by using freelancers, then claims the copyright in the firm's name. Edward Stratemeyer had written for magazines, producing works made for hire, and he had thus learned that "the real money in the dime-novel and story-paper industry at that time went not to the authors but to the owner of the copyright" (Greenwald 4). Between 1899 and 1909, the Stratemeyer Syndicate launched over twenty series for what publishers now call young adult readers; in 1927 Stratemeyer would launch the Hardy Boys and, in 1930, its most famous, Nancy Drew. By the 1930s, the work-for-hire doctrine had also shaped labor practices at the major newspaper syndicates, whose expropriation of the work of comic strip writers and artists provided the model for the comics business. We see here a case of the phenomenon that E. P. Thompson examines in *Whigs and Hunters*, where a mode of production depends on historically contingent and shifting legal definitions of property rights:

> What was often at issue [in early eighteenth-century England] was not property, supported by law, against no-property; it was alternative definitions of property-rights.... How can we distinguish between the activity of farming or of quarrying and the rights to this strip of land or to that quarry? The farmer or forester in his daily occupation was moving within visible or invisible structures of law.... Hence "law" was deeply imbricated within the very basis of productive relations, which would have been inoperable without this law. (261)

Work-for-hire contracts made publishers into authors by alienating legal authorship from one collective—the crew that actually created the work (usually writer, artist, editor, and other personnel)—and reassigning legal authorship to a different collective: the publishing company. The 1976 Copyright Act made it easier for writers and artists to recover copyrights that they signed away under financial pressure, and in response, publishers began to require artists not only to sign away their rights but also to promise not to try to recover them in the future. Marvel Comics used the following terms:

> MARVEL is in the business of publishing comic and other magazines known as the Marvel Comics Group, and SUPPLIER wishes to have MARVEL order or commission either written material or art work as a contribution to the collective work known as the Marvel Comics Group. MARVEL has informed SUPPLIER that MARVEL only orders or commissions such written material or art work on an employee-for-hire basis. . . . SUPPLIER expressly grants to MARVEL forever all rights of any kind and nature in and to the Work, the right to use SUPPLIER's name in connection therewith and agrees that MARVEL is the sole and exclusive copyright proprietor thereof having all rights of ownership therein. SUPPLIER agrees not to contest MARVEL's exclusive, complete and unrestricted ownership in and to the Work. ("Gary Friedrich Enterprises LLC v. Marvel Characters Inc.")

The publishers learned to dream big, requiring artists to grant them a monopoly not for the term limits decided by Congress but forever.

But in the early boom years of the comics industry, nobody thought very far ahead. Publishers needed stories to fill pages, and freelance workshops like the Eisner and Iger Studio supplied finished stories on demand and in whatever genre a publisher needed (Hajdu 24). After Superman became a hit, Siegel and Shuster set up their own studio in Cleveland, where they supervised freelancers and salaried artists, delivering the resultant work to National under the Siegel and Shuster byline while keeping their "ghost" artists anonymous (Jones 153–54). Siegel sometimes bought scripts written by ghostwriters (Gordon 106), and Shuster, whose eyesight began to fail in his mid-twenties, had "as many as five assistants" to help him with the drawing (103–4). By the mid-1940s, Siegel and Shuster earned the "highest page rate in the business" but had "six full-time assistants" (Kidman 95). Despite getting expropriated by National, Siegel and Shuster became intermediate expropriators on behalf of National.

Collaborative work makes authorship complicated, both practically and philosophically. But when a character created in a collaborative workplace gets licensed into other media, the complexity gets out of hand fast. The "creation" of a character can thus spread over time and space, as people in other industries, and working in other cities, contribute in ways unforeseen by the originators. Siegel and Shuster's Superman could not fly and had no particular vulnerability, but writers for the radio serial *The Adventures of Superman* (WOR, 1940–51) gave Superman his power of flight and his vulnerability to kryptonite. Historians of authorship have often noted that the idea of an author as a creative genius working in isolation dates only to the Romantic period; Jane Ginsburg, for example, argues that even in the French copyright system, which most commentators see as focused on the rights of the author rather than the needs of the public, "personalist doctrines" of authorship arose only after the Napoleonic era (996). Historians and philosophers may debate how to assign authorship in situations where creators have collaborated, and creators who share legal status as authors may tussle over percentages of ownership, residuals, and the like. But if a publisher believes that the work-for-hire doctrine applies, then no matter how many hands collaborated, over however many years, that publisher's attorneys have a simple answer ready: the publisher alone created the character, and the publisher alone owns it.

Work for hire renders alienable the rights of flesh-and-blood writers and artists so that firms can pay them wages instead of royalties. As Matt Stahl puts it, work for hire enables publishers to "exclude numerous creative workers from the magic circle of authorship. . . . By defining employers as authors, work for hire guarantees companies exclusive property rights, free of the claims of workers" (56). Had workers in the comics industry unionized, then they might have challenged this system. They might have created what Stahl calls "quasi-proprietary" rights (57) of the kinds enjoyed by workers in the Hollywood guilds. For example, the Screen Actors Guild established the Motion Picture Industry Pension and Health Plans, which collect residuals—profit shares—through collective bargaining agreements with the major studios. Between the Romantic fiction of the self-fashioning genius and the American capitalist fiction of the corporation as genius lies a range of possible models of collective, worker-centered authorship and ownership. In this study, however, I can only treat such models as hypothetical. In the spirit of Marvel's *What If . . . ?* series, What if comics writers and artists had formed a union and went on strike every few years? But why stop there:

What if creative workers seized control of Marvel and tried to turn it into a worker-owned cooperative? And how would investors and police respond? You see where this leads.

Anyone who studies American comics encounters a great, sometimes suffocating irony: the duopoly and its executives have always acted less like the altruistic superheroes that have made them rich and more like the racketeers whom superheroes deliver to jail. From the start, publishers copied one another's successes, making knockoff versions of any competitor's work that sold well; David Hajdu calls the comic book business "pathologically imitative" (175–76). Publishers focused on creating popular and reusable characters, easy to license into other media. As Leslie Kurtz has argued, "only a minimal amount of originality or creativity is required for a work to receive protection under copyright" (443), and many publishers did not reach even this minimum. Publishers sued each other over infringements; comics contained open threats to prosecute imitators.[7] Case law shows that characters from cartoons and comics have proved relatively easy to defend against infringement on the basis of substantial similarity. Kurtz argues that a cartoon character's "visual element . . . provides something concrete and delineated which can be the subject of objective comparisons" (450). In contrast, literary characters, whether from the pulps or the slick magazines, "do not provide a single physical image against which other characters can be compared" (451). In 1939, National sued rival Bruns Publications for infringing their copyright on Superman, and in 1941 National sued Fawcett Publications for the same, eventually winning both cases and driving their competitors from the business. Both cases hinged on side-by-side comparisons of comics panels depicting the publishers' respective characters. Judge Augustus Hand's ruling in *Detective Comics Inc. v. Bruns Publications Inc.* influenced Peter Coogan's lucid "Definition of the Superhero." Coogan argues that we can recognize the superhero genre by testing for a distinctive triad of characteristics in the protagonist: extraordinary powers, double identity, and "selfless, pro-social" mission (24). But neither the firms that produce superhero narratives nor the executives who control those firms behave in a selfless, prosocial manner. The Martin Goodmans, Jack Liebowitzes, Jenette Kahns, Ron Perelmans, and Ike Perlmutters who have controlled this wing of the culture industry have used it not to make the world, or Manhattan, or even a single firm more just but to extract surplus value from people talented enough to fill magazine pages with entertaining stories. Shawna Kidman argues that the majority of histories of American comic books treat the form as "subversive, subcultural, and resistant," while a minority of materialist histories treat comics instead as "fundamentally corporate, a dominant form" (8). Like Kidman, I see comics as a subset of the capitalist culture industries. Given the duopoly's position within larger conglomerates that seek monopolistic control over markets, I cannot read them as "resistant" against anything except competitors, regulators, and the demands of their own workers. And given this orientation, my analysis will understand duopoly movies in light of materialist critiques of the American media industries as examples of capitalist expropriation, accumulation, and expansion.

CONTINUITY CAPITAL

This book interprets duopoly blockbusters by starting from the material forces and the juridical relations of media production. My analysis places at its center the most distinctive feature of the duopoly's mode of production: the interaction of new labor with what comic book fans call *continuity*, a publisher's web of interconnected stories and characters, stretching back for decades.[8] A superhero's continuity represents not just a string of copyrighted narratives but also new means of narrative production. Eileen Meehan, in her classic political economy of *Batman* (Tim Burton, 1989), explained:

> The $30 million sunk into *Batman* is not entirely the cost of a single film. Rather, it includes the root costs of a film series. The construction of sets, the development of props, total investment, and plot presume that sequels will be shot. In the long run, WCI's investment in plant for *Batman* can be spread out across two or four other films. . . . Similarly, with the principal themes established in the orchestral soundtrack, new scoring can be limited largely to themes for villains and sidekicks, leaving WCI another chance to showcase one of its recording artists in the sequels. . . . Similarly, the sequels should provide the raw materials for novelizations and comic books. Over the long run, then, WCI's $30 million investment in *Batman* has built the basic infrastructure necessary for manufacturing a line of films, albums, sheet music, comics and novelizations. (76)

Meehan's discussion suggests that we can think of this "investment in plant" in two senses, one material and one discursive. Much as the physical infrastructure of sets and props may survive for use in sequels, so do theme music, supporting characters, and other discursive elements.

Meehan asks us to think of these investments prospectively, in terms of the firm's ability to produce sequels, yet we can also reverse our temporal orientation to think about these investments in terms of the past Batman continuity that provided what some might call the raw materials for the 1989 *Batman* film: elements like the Batman, the Joker, Commissioner Gordon, stately Wayne Manor, the murder of Bruce Wayne's parents, the Batcave, the Bat-Signal, and so on. Time Warner held the copyrights to the texts where all these elements appeared, and thus could use and reuse those elements to manufacture a new Batman film while excluding others from using them. In the first volume of *Capital*, Karl Marx writes of the way that the products of capitalist industry become tools of new production: "Though a use-value . . . issues from the labor process, yet other use-values, products of previous labor, enter into it as means of production. The same use-value is both the product of a previous process and a means of production in a later process. Products are therefore not only results, but also essential conditions of labor" (201). Furthermore, these new conditions for production

> are at once changed into means for the absorption of the labor of others. It is now no longer the labourer that employs the means of production, but the means of production that employ the labourer. Instead of being consumed by him as material elements of his productive activity, they consume him as the ferment necessary to their own life-process, and the life-process of capital consists only in its movement as value constantly expanding, constantly multiplying itself. (339)

Much as a laborer in a factory uses tools produced by other laborers in other factories, so a new artist hired by the duopoly to produce new works for hire uses narrative "tools" created by past creative labor. The Batman's gadgets, villains, *scènes à faire*, and supporting characters, all works made for hire, become means of new production. The artists and writers who created these narrative elements may have died long ago, but the corporation and its copyrights live on. As in a factory, so in the duopoly, where "the instrument of labor confronts the laborer . . . in the shape of capital, of dead labor, that dominates, and pumps dry, living labor-power" (462), and "past labor always disguises itself as capital" (666). If we accept these premises, then we can say that in the duopoly, past labor also disguises itself as comic book continuity. Continuity becomes, in Marx's terms, part of a publisher's fixed capital, the discursive counterpart to material tools like the drafting tables for drawing comics pages or the soundstages for filming movie scenes. In Marx's theory, a tool used in capitalist production transmits some of its value to each new commodity it helps produce, until the instrument of labour is worn out, its value having been distributed during a shorter or longer period over a mass of products originating from a series of constantly repeated labour-processes. But so long as they are still effective as instruments of labour and need not yet be replaced by new ones of the same kind, a certain amount of constant capital-value remains fixed in them. (160)

But unlike drafting tables, soundstages, and other tools of physical production, the stories, characters, and situations that make up continuity do not suffer wear and tear when used to tell new stories. Instead continuity functions simultaneously as a narrative brand and as a site of new production as well as new expropriation. We can therefore call a publisher's archive of copyrighted material its *continuity capital*. In this light, the Copyright Term Extension Act takes on a new significance, in that the act extended the lifetime of the duopoly's continuity capital.

Some readers may wonder why I treat the duopoly's practices as so distinctive, and why I bother with a neologism like *continuity capital* when a more familiar term like *intellectual property* might do. I have two reasons.

First, the term *intellectual property* somewhat mystifies the relations at work in the corporate manufacture of culture, because copyright—the linchpin of the system—bestows not a property right but a limited and alienable monopoly on reproduction and dissemination. Siva Vaidhyanathan usefully historicizes the term, which came into wide use only in the 1960s. He argues that the metaphor of *property* works to mystify and sacralize a bundle of rights more accurately associated with monopolies in publishing and trade (11–12). Nevertheless, at the risk of some unintended reification, I will sometimes use the term *intellectual property*, both because of its brevity compared to mouthfuls like *copyright, trademark, and patent*, and also because I often need to refer to practices more widespread than those of the duopoly.

Second, when referring to practices specific to or refined by the duopoly, I find the term *continuity capital* both necessary and appropriate because the comics industry's use of past stories as the means to produce new ones differs qualitatively from the normative practices of Hollywood. Historically, the studios did not produce movies with the intention of creating characters that would inhabit shared and persistent fictional worlds over multiple branching series. A production company like Mirisch Corporation might find that it had a breakout character like Inspector Clouseau and then use that character as the centerpiece of a film franchise; similarly, two production companies with visually iconic characters might make a crossover film like *Freddy vs. Jason* (Ronny Yu, 2003). But these exceptions do not make the rule. After the success of *Stagecoach* (John Ford, 1939), United Artists did not reuse the Ringo Kid in other westerns by having him, for example, turn up to assist the main character of the company's two dozen Hopalong Cassidy pictures. After *Shadow of a Doubt* (Alfred Hitchcock, 1943), Charlotte Newton did not continue to trap serial killers in films noirs from Universal or for any licensee. C. W. Moss, the tattooed hood who sells out the title characters of *Bonnie and Clyde* (Arthur Penn, 1967), did not show up to betray the protagonists of later films produced by Warner Bros. or directed by Arthur Penn. Poverty Row studios churned out enough parallel, serial productions that they could have had characters overlap across serials, but this would have required a degree of planning, of both scripts and marketing, absent from the serials' mode of producing ad hoc thrills. Low-budget studios could and did reuse props, sets, and back lots, but they did not draw attention to this reuse. And this kind of economizing differs fundamentally from what the duopoly did, building readerships by linking characters across multiple series: the duopoly drew attention to their reuse not of physical but of narrative materials, as they used copyrighted stories and trademarked characters as the means to soak up new creative labor. Like comics publishers, Hollywood has always used copyright to further its commercial goals, but classical Hollywood cinema favors narrative closure, while duopoly stories favor open-ended series and reboots of successful franchises—techniques that the studios would eventually adopt, but that the duopoly first refined and turned into industrial and narrative norms. The term *continuity capital* helps remind us of the distinctive contribution of the comics duopoly to the American culture industry and its relations of production.

The firms that control continuity capital use it not only to organize new production in the form of adaptations and franchises but also to attract investment. By the 1980s, Marvel Comics, underdog to the more dominant DC, still managed to earn millions in licensing fees from film production companies paying for the rights to use its characters, even though no films based on Spider-Man or the Fantastic Four appeared in theaters (Kidman 205). Herein lies the magic of licensing: even stalled productions and box office flops produce licensing fees for the licensor. The speculator Ron Perelman took Marvel public in 1991, and as *Crain's New York Business Reported*, "While an actor dressed as Spider-Man crept through the New York Stock Exchange on opening day, the stock jumped 13%" (Furman 41). This period saw Marvel become Perelman's "personal financial instrument" (Kidman 204). While his staff tried "squeezing every last dollar from his treasure trove of intellectual properties" (Furman 42), their mismanagement sent Marvel into bankruptcy court. Over three hundred Marvel employees lost their jobs to the ensuing layoffs (44), yet

Perelman only got richer. In the meantime, writers and artists at Marvel kept making new works for hire, such that Marvel accumulated continuity capital even as it hemorrhaged money and ruined livelihoods. In the 2000s, the company would open a $525 million credit line at Merrill Lynch by using some of its most popular characters as collateral (McClintock). This deal enabled Marvel Studios to launch the interconnected Marvel Cinematic Universe, the franchise that would earn the company billions. Continuity capital enters circulation and, through new infusions of creative and industrial labor, expands itself.

Continuity capital makes possible the duopoly's mode of production and its distinctive forms of exploitation. Like productive machines, continuity capital "can only develop in opposition to living labor, as hostile power and alien property" (Marx, *Grundrisse* 152). Why in opposition, and why hostile? Alienation turns past labor against present labor. Characters and stories created by work-for-hire or freelance labor generate profits for the firm, which the firm can then use to pay lawyers to oppose unionization or to draft contracts more favorable to management. A firm can also use its profits to lobby Congress to enact laws in its favor. Janet Wasko points to the 1998 Copyright Term Extension Act as "a classic example of how Hollywood clout can influence the legislative process" (*Understanding Disney* 85). Disney stood to lose *Steamboat Willie*, first appearance of Mickey Mouse, to the public domain, and the company therefore "provided campaign contributions to ten of the thirteen initial sponsors of the House bill and eight of the twelve sponsors of the Senate bill" (86). Now that Disney also owns Marvel and Lucasfilm, we can expect Disney to lobby Congress even harder to extend the company's monopolies through time. Continuity capital opposes both its own workers and the wider public.

Although I will sometimes treat continuity capital as if it were a form of machinery or a site of production, I will endeavor to treat it as Marx urged we treat capital, not as a "thing" but as "but a social relation between persons, established by the instrumentality of things" (*Capital* 839). In the duopoly, continuity capital provides a narrative, discursive version of Marx's instrumentality of things, mediating between labor and management. William G. Roy, in *Socializing Capital*, calls property "a social relationship":

> It involves rights, entitlements, and obligations not only in relation to an object itself but also in relationship to other individuals.... The owner of a factory not only has the right to decide what to use his or her factory for, a relationship of the owner to the object, but also the right of authority over others participating in using the factory. (11)

Substitute *continuity* for *factory*, and Roy's account applies to the duopoly, where past stories become the most important factor in the production of new texts. Georg Lukács warns that a dialectic method must work from the premise that "things should be shown to be aspects of processes" (179). Therefore I seek to explain both continuity capital and duopoly films as moments in the process of producing and reproducing capital, moments that reveal corporations' anxieties about ways this process could suddenly end. In *Copyrights and Copywrongs*, Siva Vaidhyanathan declares, "There is no 'left' or 'right' in debates over copyright. There are those who favor 'thick' protection and those who prefer 'thin'" (7). I argue against such a view. The Congress of the United States has repeatedly revised copyright law to benefit corporations, freezing the commons while concentrating wealth in fewer and fewer hands, and I cannot see the work of wealth concentration as anything but a right-wing project. Against the kind of radical centrism that sees class interest as epiphenomenal to law, this book sees class interest as central both to law and to the industries that the law structures.

Furthermore, this book considers exploitation as both an economic and an ethical relationship. David Hesmondhalgh notes the existence of "a strong tradition of Marxian thought that considers ethical and normative questions to be moot, and the mechanisms of the Marxian notion of exploitation to be the primary matter for consideration" (31), yet he nevertheless calls for media scholars to provide an ethical critique of capitalist exploitation, which depends on "unreciprocated flows of products from workers to capitalists" (32). The duopoly's mode of production has always embittered writers and artists. Some of the medium's most influential creators bounced from publisher to publisher, seeking the copyright to their work and, failing that, better compensation and better working conditions. In 1980, Jack Kirby met a young comics artist at a convention and, after looking over the aspirant's portfolio, warned him: "Kid, you're one of the best. But put your work in galleries. Don't do comics. Comics will break your heart" (qtd. in Horrocks). Meanwhile, publishing executives flourished. In 1985, the *New York Times* profiled Jenette Kahn, president and publisher of DC Comics. The author of the profile, Philip S. Gutis, notes that licensing and other services now account for the majority of DC's revenues, and that Kahn refers to DC not as a comic book company but as "a 'creative rights company,' whose products are providing licensing and movie revenues for other Warner divisions" (Gutis). Gutis then tells the story of Kahn's previous work for Scholastic. There, Kahn had created the magazine *Dynamite*, which became the publisher's most successful title; as she put it, "My ideas had made millions for the company, but they wouldn't pay me a fraction of what I was worth" (qtd. in Gutis). And so

Miss Kahn started a children's magazine for Xerox, under a contract that put the trademarks and copyrights in her name, and gave her a large royalty on sales. The new magazine, which she called *Smash* "because I wanted to smash *Dynamite*," never really took off. Today Miss Kahn has a six-figure salary, but memories of the unpleasant bickering with Scholastic have left her with a strong respect for the rights of creative people. In one of her first moves at DC, Miss Kahn gave the creative teams 20 percent of licensing fees for characters created since 1976. (Gutis)

But as Shawna Kidman notes, DC makes little licensing money on characters that the firm began publishing since 1976, compared to well-established characters like Batman, Superman, and Wonder Woman, so this share amounts to little more than a gesture (120). Gutis does not explain that, by default, the writers and artists at DC still made works for hire, the arrangement that Kahn found so galling at Scholastic. Nor does Gutis report the opinions of creators then working under Kahn, like Frank Miller and Alan Moore. Both Miller and Moore would leave DC in 1988, fed up with the duopoly's expropriative and exploitative business model (Lopes 114). Gutis also misses the opportunity to point out the hypocrisy of Kahn's supposed "respect" for rights that DC has always routinely denied workers as the cornerstone of their business model—as the cornerstone of the comic book industry's business model. But this book will not dwell on the hypocrisy of individual executives, since any system attracts persons eager to work within its norms.[9] This book's recurring attention to the ethical problem of exploitation will instead lead me to focus less on individual actors and more on ways that duopoly films continually remind us of the gap between the altruistic heroes on the screen and the grasping, exploitative firms that own those heroes.

ALLEGORIES AND ARCHIVES, SECRETS AND SPELLS

In its approach to film narrative, this book takes allegorical viewing as its central interpretative practice. Fredric Jameson's method of interpreting novels offers the first and most important of three models that shape my approach. Jameson treats allegory as a hermeneutic rather than ontological category, a matter of how one reads rather than what one reads, and he reads for signs of class antagonisms in novels seemingly removed from such matters. He finds patterns of meaning about the social context from which those novels emerged, and not necessarily intended by their authors: "What we formerly regarded as individual texts are grasped as 'utterances' in an essentially collective or class discourse" (11). In the production of blockbuster movies, the collective origin of the discourse becomes both more literal and more collective, because unlike novels, Hollywood blockbusters require the coordinated labor of more workers, by orders of magnitude, than novels require. As discourse, films "speak" on behalf of the executives who approve scripts and green-light projects; they do not speak on behalf of gaffers, location scouts, or makeup artists, or the nonunionized workers in studios around Asia who polish visual effects outsourced by Hollywood studios. And they do not speak on behalf of artists in the work-for-hire comics industry. Jameson seeks to infer the unacknowledged codes that shape texts in ostensibly individualist art forms produced under capitalism. In work collectively and industrially produced in the manner of a franchise blockbuster, I take individual artistic intention as, at best, secondary to the commercial objectives of the firms producing the film.

Rudolf G. Wagner's study of mainland Chinese science fiction from 1949 to 1985 offers the second model of allegorical reading. Wagner examines science fiction on either side of the Cultural Revolution (1966–76), identifying patterns that at first seem inexplicable. Although the Communist Party officially celebrates workers, peasants, and model cadres, the scientists in these stories never interact with these heroes (44); scientists travel continually but pass over populated areas, often by helicopter or narrative elision, and they never visit foreign countries (46); scientists only seem to marry other scientists, and they have children who become scientists (48–50); and the omnipresent Communist Party, its policies, and its representatives seldom get mentioned the stories (48, 51). Wagner interprets these patterns as expressions of the aspirations of scientists and popular science writers for a certain kind of life, aspirations carefully and indirectly expressed not just to the primary addressee of the fiction, the reader, but also to a more important secondary addressee: the party itself (55). To the party, these stories "present both demands and offers of compromise" (59). The stories depict scientists as assiduous in their calling and loyal to their country, and to the party that rules it; the authors show this loyalty by avoiding not just social criticism but any description of social reality, since one shades into the other. The stories therefore exclude nearly everything not directly relevant to narratives of scientific discovery, invention, or problem-solving. Scientists want the freedom to travel, but not overseas, since that might suggest the desire to defect, so "even through international travel is a much-coveted status symbol among Chinese scholars in real life" (47), the scientist-heroes do not travel internationally—except to return to mainland China from unspecified foreign countries. And most importantly, scientists solve their own problems without micromanagement by the party-state. Wagner reads these patterns as "group aspirations" in a body of fiction that portrays "how scientists would operate in the larger framework of society if their demands were met" (43). Following Wagner, we can also read the melodrama of IP defense as a reflection of the "group aspirations" of the executives who green-light duopoly films.

Jerome Christensen's work on Hollywood studios offers my third model of allegorical reading. Christensen interprets films as allegories, but he assumes intentionality; he proposes a reading of *Batman* (Tim Burton, 1989) as an "allegory contrived to accomplish corporate objectives" within the newly merged Time Warner conglomerate (Christensen, "The Time Warner Conspiracy" 591). Christensen interprets elements of the film as a deliberately coded intraconglomerate utterance from Warner Bros. executives to Time executives (591). While I take inspiration from Christensen's method, two factors limit my application of this approach. First, my project takes class as one of its fundamental categories, and it defines class in terms of control of the means of production: the duopoly's intellectual property. Therefore I look at duopoly films for expressions of the class interests that both DC and Marvel share, notwithstanding the two firms' tactical or corporate-cultural differences. After all, smart investors buy stock in both the Walt Disney Company *and* AT&T, disdaining comic-store brand loyalties. Many forms of mass culture, including the superhero film, valorize the individual while economically strengthening the collective and class-based relationship we call the corporation, and in the duopoly film's melodrama of IP defense, the cult of the exceptional individual becomes ideology in the Marxian sense of the term: a set of normative assertions purporting to benefit society but actually advancing the interests of one class at the expense of the majority. We can learn much by studying the particular histories of DC and Marvel, but the publishers' evolutions have converged such that they now occupy structurally analogous positions within publicly traded conglomerates. My approach to superhero films thus risks eliding differences both within and between DC and Marvel, as well their changing relationships with their parent firms; it also risks eliding conflicts among persons working within these firms. But by looking at what superhero films reveal about the interchangeable goals, methods, and preoccupations of these two companies, we can reveal the relationships between workers, owners, and narratives that media conglomerates work to conceal.

A second factor leads me away from a focus on inter- or intracorporation utterances of the kind that Christensen analyzes: access. Corporations and their employees keep secrets, behind passwords, nondisclosure agreements, and interpersonal relationships of trust, or fear of reprisal, or both; the most useful archive lies beyond the critical scholar's reach. Even if the conscious intentions of corporate actors appeared perfectly transparent in their internal communications, we do not have those communications. Furthermore, networks of decision and command can obscure intention: a writer for a conglomerate's magazine subsidiary may receive a suggestion to give a favorable mention to a property that the conglomerate has recently acquired, but without knowing that another division has begun preproduction on a movie.[10] In any large, opaque, and undemocratic organization, even longtime insiders have a hard time knowing who makes which decisions and why. So much harder, then, becomes the work of outsiders, who must resort to what Richard Brody calls "corporate Kremlinology."

Scholars seeking to explain patterns in the mass culture that corporations produce must therefore work in the face of corporations' deliberate concealment. Christensen notes that corporate lawyers generally try to "cover any tracks that would make a corporation's intention legible" so as to shield the client from liability (*America's Corporate Art* 315). Within the general culture of corporate secrecy, some executives, like Warner Communications CEO Steve Ross, gain reputations for "strategic opacity": Ross would move forward on a business deal only if he considered the details sufficiently difficult for outsiders to understand ("The Time Warner Conspiracy" 607–8). Outsiders constructing political economies of Hollywood must rely on the trade press, but as Janet Wasko notes, *Variety* and the *Hollywood Reporter* generally contain stories "prompted by the industry itself through the studios' extensive publicity and promotion operations" ("Critiquing Hollywood" 5). Popular journalism focuses on box office figures, but as Edward Jay Epstein argues, they only do this because studios have made a "ritual" of announcing them (22). Writing in 2000, Wasko noted that although Disney's website announces that "Disney's overriding objective is to create shareholder value," Wasko could not readily determine "who actually owns the Disney company" or "who benefits from Disney's accumulation of wealth" (*Understanding Disney* 37) beyond a small number of fabulously wealthy investors—Warren Buffet, Roy Disney, Michael Eisner—who made public their number of shares (38). The Walt Disney Company's shareholders report of January 19, 2021, invites shareholders to vote on executive compensation ratios, and it praises the "diversity" of its board of directors (one "Black," one "Latina," one "Asian & Black") (*2021 Notice* 1, 5). But the report gives detailed stock ownership figures only for the board of directors and other officers, and there we see another kind diversity. In 2021, former CEO Bob Iger owned 1,305,762 shares, while the other nine members of the board owned a mere 363,498 among them; the person with the next largest number after Iger, senior executive vice president and chief financial officer Christine M. McCarthy, owned just 156,965 shares (*2021 Statement* 78). On August 12, 2021, Disney's stock price stood at $178.24, putting Iger's stake in the company at well over $232 million, reminding us of the vertiginous extremes of wealth inequality even among the rich. But Iger and McCarthy at least theoretically work for their compensation, while most shareholders do not, and those nameless others own most of the company. Corporations release information either as required by the Securities and Exchange Commission or as strategic image management. Outsiders must therefore work with shadows and fragments.

Even media scholars attempting ethnographies of corporate media workers also run into voids and silences. Sherry Ortner reminds us that in Hollywood, "information is managed for competitive advantage" (176). She did find people who would sit for interviews, "but they were all relatively marginal in the world of Hollywood movie production. For the most part, however, people simply did not return my calls, or if they did, passed me on to other people who did not return my calls" (178). In 2017, one of my NYU Shanghai students met a Marvel executive at the Shanghai Comic-Con, and my student convinced the executive to come and speak at the university. But the executive then found himself constrained: "After checking with folks here, we kindly ask this be arranged through Disney Corporate Communications to make sure things go smoothly."[11] An agent from Disney Corporate Communications then emailed my student a boilerplate reply: "While we appreciate the opportunity and your passion for Marvel, we will need to have internal review before our executives deliver a speech at external occasions. Please understand that we could not commit . . . at this moment but surely we could build contact for future possibilities." Thinking I could help facilitate, I emailed both the agent and the executive, introducing myself as the teacher and expressing support for the student's plan. Nobody replied, to me or to the student. My subsequent email also went unanswered. Even something as anodyne as a visit to a university in mainland China's most Disney-friendly city sent the corporation into a protective retreat.[12] Every email from the Marvel executive ended with the same apotropaic boilerplate, "Nothing contained in this e-mail shall (a) be considered a legally binding agreement, amendment or modification of any agreement with Marvel, each of which requires a fully executed agreement to be received by Marvel or (b) be deemed approval of any product, packaging, advertising or promotion material, which may only come from Marvel's Legal Department."

The Disney email contained a similar incantation:

> This e-mail message and any attachment transmitted with it are confidential, intended only for the named recipient(s) above and may contain information that is privileged, attorney work product or exempt from disclosure under applicable law. Any unauthorized disclosure, copying, printing, distribution or use of this email is prohibited. If you have received this message in error, or if you are not the named recipient(s), please immediately notify the sender and delete this e-mail message from your computer.

These corporations chose silence rather than risk any utterance that might expose the company to liability or embolden anyone to make demands against them. Despite the ubiquity of Marvel and Disney advertising and commodities around Shanghai, my student and I could not even get a refusal.

Some readers may object to my focus here on the difficulty of gaining access to secretive, risk-averse media executives. Scholars used to doing research on the media industries will consider this old news and may even urge me to cultivate such access. But if I have learned anything from ethnographers of Hollywood—from Sherry Ortner to Edward Jay Epstein to Hortense Powdermaker—I have learned that a researcher's ability to get straight answers from a show business informant varies inversely with that informant's power in the business. I have never worked at DC, Marvel, or their parent conglomerates, so I have only dealt with their stonewalling permissions offices, and my attempt in Shanghai to cultivate local access led to a dead end. To readers who have not done research on the culture industries, I have a duty to highlight the strategic evasiveness of the personnel who work for companies like Marvel Studios, an evasiveness that contrasts with the welcoming, avuncular persona of Stan Lee or the curator-fanboy persona of Kevin Feige. This book seeks to help nonspecialists understand the conditions that media scholars struggle to work around.

So to explain the narrative preoccupations of duopoly movies, I seek evidence where I can most reliably find it. Following Jonathan Gray, I examine not just texts but *paratexts* (3–6): not just the films themselves but also box office data, advertising, reviews, official and unofficial public announcements, and so on. The work resembles archaeology, with corporate secrecy playing the role of time and dirt, forcing the investigator to assemble a coherent explanation from sometimes disparate and seemingly unrelated evidence. Meehan writes of the methodological difficulties that confront those who would build critical accounts of show business:

In our fascination with the highly visible show, let us not overlook the less visible business that ultimately shapes, constructs, recycles, breaks out, and distributes the show for a profit. No business means no show and doing business means constructing shows according to business needs. These are the ground rules, *recoverable* through critical analysis, from which we can safely approach the analysis of a commodified culture and the products of show business. (62; my emphasis)

This book interprets the shows based on what we can learn about the business, despite the business's best efforts to hide its workings.

OVERVIEW

Chapter 1 examines the structure and common permutations of the duopoly blockbuster's melodrama of IP defense in light of seemingly unrelated phenomena: the boom in DVD sales, the movie industry's campaigns against illicit media copying, and the invasion and occupation of Iraq. The chapter interprets duopoly films historically, not in terms of the development of special effects but in terms of comic book business practices and Hollywood lobbying, as well as the struggles between studios over film rights to particular characters. I explain the duopoly blockbuster's melodrama of IP defense, which reflects the duopoly's reliance on work for hire to exclude creators from ownership, and which extends the pro-copyright and anticopying campaigns of the Motion Picture Association of America. The chapter closes with a discussion of a hermeneutic technique for viewing films whose main characters double as iconic trademarks, brands as stars.

Chapter 2 takes as a case study the trilogy of Batman films directed by Christopher Nolan: *Batman Begins* (2005), *The Dark Knight* (2008), and *The Dark Knight Rises* (2012). Unusual for its relatively closed ending, this trilogy instantiates most of the norms of duopoly films while defying others in a deliberately auteurist direction. For each film, Time Warner threw its continuity capital into circulation, using it to produce Warner Bros. films that drove new sales for DC Comics; in each film, the Batman must defend his persona and his property against villains who would use them for their own ends. Critics have most often read the trilogy as allegorical of the so-called war on terror, but I read it instead as an allegory of the management of IP during the decade when criminal financiers wrecked the American economy and the Iraq war turned defense procurement into big business both for arms dealers and for thieves. The chapter uses the Zorro franchise, and conflicts over the film rights to Zorro, as an explanatory counterpoint to the way Warner Bros. developed its Batman films of the 2000s.

Chapter 3 compares two films, Marvel Studios' *Captain America: The First Avenger* (Joe Johnston, 2011) and Warner Bros.' *Wonder Woman* (Patty Jenkins, 2017), arguing that the historical and narrative parallels between them reveal the logic of the industry that produced them. Here the melodrama of intellectual property operates at a different level: each film introduces its protagonist as a work, a creation for specific purposes, and that work gradually attains autonomy. While many commentators adopted the studio line that these characters had "endured" since the 1940s, I argue instead that both the broader history of these characters and the specific history of these two films indicate the opposite: that the public largely forgot about these characters until two media conglomerates decided to thrust them into the public eye and build franchises around them.

Chapter 4 looks at the way some duopoly films have diverged from the coming-of-age stories typical of both superhero and non-superhero action franchises. Earlier duopoly films like *X2: X-Men United* (Bryan Singer, 2002), *Hulk* (Ang Lee, 2003), and *Batman Begins* (Christopher Nolan, 2005) had cluttered their scripts with father figures for protagonists to rebel against, but a decade later, films like *Ant-Man* (Peyton Reed, 2015), *Suicide Squad* (David Ayer, 2016), and *Logan* (James Mangold, 2017) gave us superhero fathers as protagonists. The grown-up heroes of the second half of the 2010s have grown-up responsibilities: jobs, children, and even the care of elders. These films show their protagonists growing up because the audiences of the franchises have grown up; the films diversify their respective corporate brands while giving thirtysomething viewers new points of identification. Yet even as the films show heroes "reproducing" themselves, through offspring or through the training of successors, their scripts still present the defense of IP as the superhero's highest calling. This chapter deals less with the production histories of these films and more with their strategic use of nostalgia, both for the character brand and for the corporate brand, integrating a bittersweet emotional appeal into an anticopying melodrama.

Chapter 5 considers two films headlined by Black superheroes, *Blade* (Stephen Norrington, 1998) and *Black Panther* (Ryan Coogler, 2018). These films function as rough bookends for the study, and although they emerge from very different circumstances of production, each reveals a strategic use of Blackness and its signifiers, and each revolves around melodramas of IP defense. *Blade*, based on a Marvel character, appeared after a wave of Black-themed action films, including four Black superhero films, but it has the strongest family resemblance to *Steel* (Kenneth Johnson, 1997), a flop based on a DC character. In contrast to the modestly budgeted *Blade*, *Black Panther* appeared after Marvel Studios and its cinematic universe had risen to the zenith of industry power. *Black Panther* simultaneously adds "diversity" to the range brand while offering a retrograde fantasy of absolute monarchy that helped it become the first movie to screen publicly in Saudi Arabia in more than thirty years. Both *Blade* and *Black Panther* gesture toward racism while avoiding substantive critiques of real-world injustices, instead pinning their audiences' hopes on the heroes' struggle to defend their IP from usurpers.

CHAPTER ONE
COPYRIGHT VIGILANTES

A decade after *Blade*, Marvel Studios released the film that made the studio's name synonymous not with flops but with hits: *Iron Man* (Jon Favreau, 2008). Its hero, Tony Stark (Robert Downey Jr.), has no superpowers in the strict sense, but he does have technical genius, billions of dollars, and an aerospace corporation that bears his family name. An unscrupulous executive at Stark Industries, Obadiah Stane (Jeff Bridges), envies Stark and lacks his scruples, so he reverse engineers a knockoff of Stark's prototype Iron Man armor, intending to sell it to warlords. But without Stark's miniature fusion reactor to power the knockoff, Stane's project stalls; even the research and development engineers at Stark Industries cannot duplicate the tiny reactor. Finally, Stane resorts to murder, stealing the miniature reactor that Stark wears in his chest to keep his damaged heart beating. As Stark lies paralyzed and on the verge of death, Stane looms over him, a canted framing emphasizing the betrayal. Stane exults: "Do you really think that just because you have an idea, it belongs to you? Your father, he helped give us the atomic bomb. Now, what kind of world would it be today if he was as selfish as you?" Stane's name suggests the *stain* of contamination, as does his knockoff armor: despite running on fusion, it belches dark smoke. Stane's character arc suggests that the virtuous use their natural talents to invent, while the wicked and second-rate copy, steal, and murder; his superficially prosocial rhetoric about the bomb actually undercuts his argument about sharing, for even hawkish viewers will see nuclear weapons as the limit case of the dissemination of technical knowledge. After all, the George W. Bush administration premised its invasion of Iraq on the need to stop the proliferation of weapons, which Stane takes as his goal. Stane's copying thus poses a danger not to one country but to the world.

In DC and Marvel comics, villains hatch a variety of schemes, but in the Hollywood films based on these comics, one scheme occurs more than any other: the illicit copying of the hero's powers or super-technology, always for nefarious ends. The hero resists and triumphs, and the film usually punishes the villain with death. In this chapter, I argue that the recurring melodrama of copying, defense, and punishment not only reflects the comics duopoly's dependence on the expropriation and control of intellectual property but also reflects the imperatives of Hollywood studios to sacralize IP, demonize illicit copying, and revise the law in favor of their business models. The superhero blockbuster became a dominant genre during the first decade of the twenty-first century, a period when retail sales of DVDs became Hollywood's most reliable source of revenue. Yet the ease of manufacture that made DVDs so profitable for the studios also made them profitable for bootleggers, and the growth of online peer-to-peer networks that enabled the sharing of digital files threatened to allow the noncommercial dissemination of works under copyright to the culture industries. Thus the superhero blockbuster rose toward its current hegemony during a period when Hollywood studios saw the safeguarding of their IP-based monopolies as crucial to their future, not only guaranteeing their profits on films already made, but also guiding their decisions about what films to develop and promote. Although DVD sales would begin to decline in the latter half of the 2000s, the defense of IP remained a key strategy for studios as they pivoted toward streaming.

Duopoly blockbusters used the alarmist, moralizing, anticopying rhetoric of Hollywood lobbying organizations like the Motion Picture Association of America (MPAA) as the basis for action melodramas.[1] In these melodramas, the most wicked attempt to copy or bootleg from the most virtuous, and if the virtuous do not defend their monopolies by force, whole cities may die. This genre rose to its current prominence in the years on either side of 9/11, and during the long American occupation of Iraq; but where many commentators have interpreted superhero films in terms of what they reveal about public anxieties about terrorism, war, or weapons of mass destruction, I argue instead that in their linking of copying to threats of mass destruction, these films reveal not public but corporate anxieties. Borrowing a page from the MPAA, these films assert, again and again, that illicit copying leads to mass murder, if not human extinction. This chapter treats films as corporate pedagogy, a body of discourses that seek not just to entertain but also to indoctrinate and train customer-subjects.

These films tell us little about the lives of normal people, and nothing at all about the experiences of rank-and-file workers in the culture industries, but they tell us much about how culture-industry executives want their audiences to think about intellectual property relations. Janet Wasko argues that Hollywood films "may offer engaging fantasies and convenient escape from the drudgeries of daily life, but they also offer explicit visions of the world and lessons for living in that world" (18). This chapter takes Wasko's cue, connecting the films' visions of the world back to the world that both audiences and studios inhabit, interpreting these films as "lessons for living" as media conglomerates would have us live. Against such lessons, I propose an oppositional strategy for interpreting the protagonist of such a melodrama, treating it not as a character in the conventional sense but as the anthropomorphic sign of a brand, a mask worn by continuity capital.

WONDER MEN AND CAPTAINS MARVEL

The trope of a villain who tries to copy a hero's powers did not figure prominently in superhero comics, probably because comics publishers did not fear competition from bootleggers. The logistics of printing and distributing magazines—bulky, with a low profit margin—make them unattractive to bootleggers, who can turn a quicker profit with knockoff liquor, perfume, or wristwatches. But publishers did worry about losing control of the characters that they wanted to use to generate licensing fees, and in the very first year of the superhero, the inventors of the genre published a story that made this anxiety visible. *Action Comics* #6, cover-dated November 1938, contained a story in which a dishonest marketing agent claims to represent Superman: "I have a contract from him giving me sole commercial rights to his name! . . . The cash is pouring in!" (Siegel and Shuster 71).[2] This manager approaches the *Daily Star*, offering exclusive Superman-related news, and points to evidence of his success, ranging from a billboard for a Superman-branded automobile, to a blimp trailing a banner advertising Superman gasoline, to an advertisement for a Superman radio series sponsored by a fictional breakfast cereal. The manager declares that he has licensed "Superman bathing-suits, costumes, physical development exercisers, and movie rights, to name a few—why, I've even made provisions for him to appear in the comics" (71). Reporter Clark Kent expresses skepticism. A narrative caption has already told readers of Clark Kent's secret double identity as Superman, so the scene with the manager plays on this dramatic irony. Most of the thirteen-page story consists of dialogue-heavy farce about a con artist abusing Superman's right of publicity to commit something like trademark fraud; the action promised by the magazine's title only comes ten pages in, when the manager, trying to hide his deception, tries to kill Lois Lane, who knows too much.

Even in the era before television, tales of licensing did not excite the children and adolescents who enjoyed magazines like *Action Comics*, so I find it hard to imagine many readers sticking with this one. But for the owners of trademarked characters, nothing equals the thrill of licensing, which inverts the usual dynamic of advertising: instead of the firm paying to put its trademarked or copyrighted material in public view, others pay the firm for the privilege. The licensor does need to pay for staff to handle paperwork and to manage licensees' uses of the property, but otherwise the firm can treat it as free money. Licensing thus resembles the collection of rent, minus the hassle of maintaining real estate or paying property taxes. So in the story of the fraudulent manager, we see the creators and publishers of *Action Comics* indulging in their own daydreams rather than those of their target audience. As noted in the introduction, Jerry Siegel and Joe Shuster had aimed from the start to create a character that licensees would find attractive. They saw lucrative precedents in characters that originated in comic strips, like Buster Brown and Popeye, as well as literary characters made more famous by comic strips, like Tarzan, and characters from animated cartoons, like Mickey Mouse. In 1932, Walt Disney had contracted Herman Kamen to handle the licensing of Mickey Mouse, and the combination of the mouse's visual iconicity and Kamen's firm's efforts quickly led to the character becoming, as Neal Gabler puts it, "even more popular as a brand than he was as a movie star" (197). As early as 1934, Walt Disney reported that the licensing of Mickey Mouse brought in more revenue than the animated cartoons (198). As Gabler recounts, "In his first four years Kamen had increased the licensing 10,000 percent to just under $200,000 in royalties a year. . . . Thus Disney became the first studio to recognize what would become a standard business practice in Hollywood forty years later" (198). Siegel and Shuster had hoped to interest a newspaper syndicate in a Superman comic strip so as to achieve widespread recognition of their character and concomitant licensing revenues. When no syndicate made an offer, the creators found a buyer in National Allied Publications, and a contract that allowed them a share of licensing revenues (Jones 146; Gordon 99–101). But first Siegel and Shuster had to cut up and reformat their submission for publication in magazine format (Cotta Vaz 34).[3] National then set to work not just publishing Superman but establishing a separate company, Superman Incorporated, just to manage the character's licensing. By the spring of 1940, the comics listed Superman Inc. as their publisher (Gordon 145). In February 1940, New York's WOR radio station began to air *Superman*, an adventure series sponsored by Hecker's Oat Cereal (Hayde 36). This series thus fulfilled for the publishers a law-abiding version of the fraudster's scheme from *Action Comics* #6: not only did they now have a radio program with a breakfast cereal sponsor, but they could also license that program to other broadcasters and advertisers. After the first season, Superman Inc. placed ads in trade magazines touting "195 recorded episodes available to local and regional sponsors," and demanding, "Let Superman be your super-salesman!" (qtd. in Hayde 44). But according to the terms of Siegel and Shuster's contract, together they received only 5 percent of the licensing fees for Superman (Gordon 100). Amid what Shawna Kidman calls the Superman "licensing bonanza" (27), Siegel and Shuster began to consider Superman's legitimate management almost as bad as the fraudulent manager they had invented.

Each episode of the *Superman* radio series ended with a standard, even ritual, formula. First the announcer enjoins listeners to tune in to the next episode to learn what happens. Then we hear a reprise of the sequence that begins every episode: as a whooshing sound effect signifies Superman in flight, onlookers exclaim, "It's a bird!" "It's a plane!" "It's Superman!" The whooshing fades to silence, and an announcer intones, "Superman is a copyrighted feature appearing in *Action Comics* magazine." Each episode thus ends not with the character's name or with a cliff-hanger but with a declaration of copyright, an incantation to ward off infringement. Shawna Kidman notes that the licensing of characters like Superman "reinforced the crucial role that intellectual property law was already playing in the medium's formation" (28), but in the *Superman* radio series, the end of every episode explicitly invoked that law. Unlike the fine-print copyright notices buried at the end of Hollywood blockbusters, easily ignored by viewers checking their mobile phones or pressing fast-forward, the radio show's copyright notice falls with the clarity of direct address amid silence, with no reverberation or effects on the final announcer's voice to suggest that he occupies a fictional space. That this ritual copyright declaration omits to identify Siegel and Shuster only serves to reinforce, rhetorically, National's claim to authorship.

Through the first half of the 1940s, Superman's popularity and profitability grew. By May 1940, National had sold live-action film rights to Superman to the poverty-row studio Republic Pictures; publisher Jack Liebowitz told Jerry Siegel that the serial would increase profits by "promoting the sale of licensed merchandise" (qtd. in Gordon 22–23). But as overall profits grew, Siegel and Shuster grew proportionally dissatisfied with the ways their editors at National treated them, and suspicious that Superman Inc. did not pay them their negotiated shares of licensing fees. Furthermore, Siegel believed that National had unfairly asserted ownership and creative control over the spin-off character Superboy during Siegel's military service (Gordon 108–11). In 1947, Siegel and Shuster filed a lawsuit against National, seeking recovery of the rights to Superman, $5 million in retroactive licensing payments (Jones 247), and ownership of the rights to Superboy (Gordon 109–10). Siegel and Shuster lost, but they negotiated a settlement in which National paid them $94,000 for the rights to Superboy; Ian Gordon argues that the settlement indicates that the court believed that DC had not lawfully controlled the rights to Superboy before 1947 (110). But Siegel and Shuster received only a fraction of their aim, and they had to use most of the settlement just to pay their attorney's fees (Jones 249). National fired them and went right on publishing and licensing Superman, Superboy, Lois Lane, and the rest of the characters that Siegel and Shuster had created.[4]

National used the courts to defend its monopoly on Superman. After the success of *Action Comics*, rival publisher Victor Fox had hired the Eisner and Eiger Studio, supposedly telling them, "I want another Superman" (qtd. in Jones 148). Eisner and Eiger delivered Wonder Man, blond and bulletproof in a red leotard with yellow trunks over the trousers; the cover of *Wonder Comics*, its first and only issue, cover-dated May 1939, shows Wonder Man in midair, punching in the nose of a heavy bomber aircraft. National immediately sued Fox for infringing their copyright on their car-smashing Superman. In his April 29, 1940, opinion in the case of *Detective Comics Inc. v. Bruns Publications Inc., et al.*, Judge Augustus Hand notes three ways that Wonder Man copies Superman. First, *Wonder Comics* styles its star "champion of the oppressed," as *Action Comics* styled Superman; Wonder Man possesses preternatural strength and immunity to firearms; and Wonder Man "at times conceals his strength beneath ordinary clothing" only to reveal "a skintight acrobatic costume." Hand's opinion also cites two precedents, *Sheldon v. Metro-Goldwyn Pictures Corporation* and *Nichols v. Universal Pictures Corporation*, reminding us that comics publishers and Hollywood studios have long shaped each other's fortunes, exchanging not just content to remediate but also a body of case law that helped regulate the two industries long before conglomeration brought them together. At the end of the twentieth century and the beginning of the twenty-first, when studios built blockbuster movie franchises based on duopoly characters, they built on the sedimentary layers of such precedents, laid down by cycles of innovation, duplication, and litigation.

National would challenge and defeat another publisher in the courts, but this case would take much longer, even as it ultimately led to greater rewards for National. This time, National faced not a start-up but Fawcett Publications, a well-established purveyor of magazines like *Family Circle*, *True Confessions*, and *Woman's Day*. Fawcett had entered comics not as a get-rich-quick scheme but as an expansion of the company's existing range; *Whiz Comics* #2, cover-dated February 1940, bore on its cover the red-suited, white-caped Captain Marvel, shown hurling an automobile against a brick wall. *Whiz Comics* and the subsequent *Captain Marvel Comics* sold well enough that Republic Pictures approached Fawcett to license the character for a serial it already had in preproduction; Republic needed a caped hero because National had suddenly backed out of its deal with Republic to make a Superman serial (Jones 138). When Republic released the twelve-chapter *Adventures of Captain Marvel* in 1941, National sued Fawcett for infringing its rights to Superman (*National Comics Publications Inc. v. Fawcett Publications Inc.*). The case and its appeals dragged on for more than a decade, but National prevailed, and in 1953, a defeated Fawcett ceased publishing Captain Marvel stories.[5]

A decade later, the imitativeness of the comics business brought a new complication. In 1966, M. F. Enterprises released a magazine called *Captain Marvel*; its eponymous character bore no resemblance to the red-suited Fawcett hero, and the magazine ran for only four issues. This must have attracted some attention at Marvel Comics, because in 1967 Stan Lee and Gene Colan developed their own character named Captain Marvel. But the savvy Marvel Comics not only kept the character in print but also trademarked it ("Captain Marvel. Serial Number 72283349"). Marvel's rival, National, seemed too busy to care; in 1967, National had become a subsidiary of the Kinney National Service conglomerate and had changed its name to DC Comics. In the early 1970s, when DC sought to capitalize on nostalgia for so-called Golden Age comic book characters, it licensed the original Captain Marvel from Fawcett. But Marvel Comics, with its copyrighted and trademarked character by the name of Captain Marvel, posed a new problem. DC, to avoid litigation from its current competitor, changed the name of the character that it had licensed from its former competitor: in 1973, DC began publishing a magazine featuring the old Fawcett Captain Marvel but titled *Shazam*, after the magic word that Billy Batson uses to transform into his red-suited alter ego. DC then licensed Captain Marvel to Filmation for a television series and called the series *Shazam!* to avoid litigation. In 1991, when DC finally bought Captain Marvel outright from the dying Fawcett, DC had exploited the character longer than Fawcett had, but DC had exploited it under an assumed name.

This convoluted history entered a bizarre new phase in early 2019, when Marvel Studios released *Captain Marvel* (directed by Anna Boden and Ryan

Fleck), and less than one month later, Warner Bros. released *Shazam* (directed by David F. Sandberg), films whose very titles reflect the duopoly's reliance on law to capture and exploit the works of others. In anticipation of the release of *Captain Marvel*, Marvel Characters Inc. filed a barrage of trademark claims with the United States Patent and Trademark Office. As of late 2021, Marvel had twenty-seven trademark filings related to the name "Captain Marvel" between 1967 and 2018, but eleven date from April 25, 2018. In these preemptive filings, Marvel attorney Steve Ackerman registered the exclusive right to use Captain Marvel on a vast range of commodities, like "non-medicated toiletry preparations" ("Captain Marvel, Serial Number 87893616"), "eyeglass and sunglass cases" ("Captain Marvel, Serial Number 87893623"), "decorative paper centerpieces" ("Captain Marvel, Serial Number 87893635"), and "sports bottles sold empty" ("Captain Marvel, Serial Number 87893646"). Other filings read like a tour of a down-market retailer: "Clothing, namely, bottoms, costumes for use in role-playing games, dresses, gloves, Halloween costumes, hosiery, loungewear, jackets, shirts, sleepwear, socks, sweaters, sweatshirts, swimwear, tops, underwear; footwear; headwear" ("Captain Marvel, Serial Number 87893652"). But the most hysterically elaborated filing claims exclusive rights to use the trademark in the area where Marvel Entertainment most sought to prevent competition with DC:

> Development, creation, production, and distribution of digital multimedia and audio and visual content, namely, motion picture films; development, creation, production, distribution, and rental of audio and visual recordings; production of entertainment shows for distribution via audio and visual media, and electronic means; production and provision of entertainment information via electronic communication networks; providing online computer games, websites and applications featuring a wide variety of general interest entertainment information relating to motion picture films, film clips, photographs, and other multimedia materials; entertainment services, namely, providing online non-downloadable comic books and graphic novels. ("Captain Marvel, Serial Number 87893658")

The filings reveal Marvel's determination to manufacture a blockbuster that would create demand for everything from empty sports bottles and decorative paper centerpieces bearing the likeness of their forgotten, C-list superhero. They also demonstrate Marvel's determination to deny DC any chance to generate licensing revenues by piggybacking on their new film.

The once-dominant DC Comics now treats the name of its Captain Marvel as unspeakable not just in the marketplace but even in the script of the generally charming *Shazam*. The film inadvertently highlights this with one of its better running gags. The hero's sidekick keeps spitballing names for the hero—Red Cyclone, PowerBoy, Captain SparkleFingers, and so on—but neither the sidekick nor anyone else ever calls him Captain Marvel. So *shazam*, the magic word that Billy Batson uses to transform, must now serve as both the character's name and the brand's name. As *Whiz Comics*, the 2019 *Shazam* film, and many Captain Marvel texts in between remind us, this magic acronym comprises the initials of mythological figures whose qualities Captain Marvel unites: the wisdom of Solomon, the strength of Hercules, the stamina of Atlas, the power of Zeus, the courage of Achilles, and the speed of Mercury. When Fawcett owned this reworking of public-domain figures, DC called it an infringement of Superman, but now that DC has dusted off the character for blockbuster treatment, DC treads carefully for fear of Marvel Studios.

PIRATES, BOOTLEGGERS, AND MONOPOLISTS

Like the comics business, the American movie business has long understood that laws and court decrees can make the difference between the knockoff artist and the tycoon. In his magisterial history of Hollywood's relationship to intellectual property law, Peter Decherney points out that the US film industry got its start on "forms of copying that we would now consider piracy: selling exact copies of competitors' films" and "making unauthorized adaptations of novels and plays" (12). Early film production companies made their own projection equipment and released films in proprietary formats to work only with that equipment; because they saw themselves primarily as manufacturers of hardware, many such firms "were not immediately concerned about who copied their films" (20). The 1903 breakup of the Edison Trust and subsequent standardization of projection formats shifted producers' concern away from proprietary technology and toward the films themselves. The *Ben-Hur* case of 1911 established that films could infringe works published in other media. Thereafter, books of advice for screenwriters began to warn against adapting works from the public domain, instead stressing the need to create properties original enough to copyright, since, as Decherney puts it, the studios "did not even want to adapt the classics for the screen if they could not be assured of a monopoly on the story" (56). Making and distributing bootleg copies of 35 mm film prints would cost too much to make it an attractive business, so for most of the twentieth century, film bootlegging became a background concern for Hollywood. Yet in the eighties and nineties, home video technology simultaneously offered the studios new avenues for profit as well as new vulnerabilities to what they call *piracy*.

Unlike the studios, however, I will not call it *piracy*. Pirates, in the strict sense, rob on the high seas, and they often take hostages; international law exists in part because no single nation-state can hope to thwart pirates without the help of its peers. When movie studios and record labels hyperbolically cry *piracy* when others violate their copyrights, these companies try to turn their perception of victimhood into a means to attack others.[6] So I will use either neutral terms like *copying*, which connotes no crime, or *bootlegging*, which denotes illicit manufacture but without coercion or violence.

To understand duopoly films' fixation on illicit copying as a catalyst of apocalypse, we must consider Hollywood's responses to home video, and specifically the responses of the Motion Picture Association of America, the lobbying organization of the major studios. In 1982, the development of the videocassette recorder had sent the film, television, and advertising industries into a panic as they imagined ways that the VCR might disrupt their business models. When the US Congress held hearings on the home recording of copyrighted works, Jack Valenti, president of the MPAA, used violent and even apocalyptic imagery to warn about the threats posed by the new technology. The "VCR avalanche" and its "tidal wave" of home taping would leave the studios' television markets "decimated, shrunken, collapsed" (*Home Recording* 8). Amid this "devastation," Valenti warned, studios would "bleed and bleed and hemorrhage" if Congress failed to protect them "from the savagery and the ravages of this machine" (8). "I say to you," intoned Valenti, "that the VCR is to the American film producer and the American public as the Boston strangler is to the woman home alone" (8). In the same testimony, Valenti explained why VCRs merited comparison to a serial rapist-murderer: home taping not only allowed viewers to tape films from broadcast television, in violation of studio copyrights, but even worse, it allowed viewers to fast-forward through commercials. Valenti's audience comprised attorneys, economists, industry and talent guild representatives, and one movie star, Clint Eastwood. Valenti therefore played to the room, using Eastwood in his example.

> VALENTI: You are sitting in your home in your easy chair and here comes the commercial, and it is right in the middle of a Clint Eastwood film, and you don't want to be interrupted. So, what do you do? You [fast-forward], and a one-minute commercial disappears in two seconds.
> TOM RAILSBACK (R-IL): Is that all bad?
> VALENTI: If you are watching a Clint Eastwood film it is the most cheerful thing you can do. However, if you are an advertiser who has paid $280,000

> a minute to advertise, he feels a very large pain in his stomach as well as in his checkbook because it destroys the reason for free television. . . . Indeed, when my son is taping for his permanent collection, he sits there and pauses his machine and when he is finished with it, he has a marvelous Clint Eastwood movie and there is no sign of a commercial. (9)

Valenti, a former advertising man, never lets truth or consistency get in the way of a vivid metaphor. Here, after likening VCRs to a serial killer merely because they allow viewers to fast-forward through commercials they have taped, he admits that his own son, under Valenti's roof, uses a VCR not only to fast-forward through but to erase the commercials altogether. Valenti thus accidentally reworks the old urban legend about the babysitter and the mysterious telephone caller: the police have traced the infringement back to his own house. But Valenti clarifies for the assembly that although he allows taping under his roof, he does so only because the laws currently permit it: "The plaintiffs have said they aren't going to do anything to me. I am not committing any crime" (10). Valenti may compare a machine to the Boston Strangler and worse, but that doesn't mean he won't trust it to his children.[7]

Valenti's sky-is-falling rhetoric, coupled with his disregard for truth and consistency, makes him a flashy example of what the anthropologist David Graeber calls the *goon*, a category of professional that has played a decisive role in shaping public debates about copying and copyright. In *Bullshit Jobs*, Graeber defines the job of a goon as "essentially manipulative and aggressive" and lacking any positive social value: goons "further the interests of those who employ them, even if the overall effect of their profession's existence might be considered detrimental to humanity as a whole" (36). Advertisers, marketers, and lobbyists, qua goons, deal not in truth but in manipulation, distortion, and, when safe or expedient, lies. Many goons whom Graeber interviewed disliked their jobs, but Jack Valenti seemed to relish his. Richard D. Heffner, head of the Code and Rating Administration that Valenti founded at the MPAA, said that Valenti's "power came not from dialogue with the public, but from telling the public something, conning it, not from trying to inform it" (qtd. in Vaughn 25). As Valenti himself put it in 1996, "Politicians and Hollywood are sprung from the same DNA. They both deal in illusions" (Valenti). Stephen Vaughn notes that even Valenti's critics "admired the force of his personality, which bulldozed others into accepting his point of view" (24). Valenti's bulldozer rhetoric helped set the tone for the rhetoric of other goons promoting the interests of the copyright industry, rhetoric that the duopoly films would then write into their own narratives.

After Hollywood figured out ways to profit from VCRs, the MPAA ceased comparing them to tsunamis, avalanches, and sex killers. But in the early 2000s, just as Hollywood's opposition to peer-to-peer digital file sharing rose to fever pitch, the September 11 terrorist attacks provided another set of violent metaphors and pretexts. In January 2002, the MPAA sent over fifty thousand takedown notices to internet service providers, and Valenti said of the campaign, "We're fighting our own terrorist war" (qtd. in "Black Hawk Download"). In the wake of 9/11, state agencies eager for rhetorical justifications for their power also invoked terrorism, as in November 2002, when *U.S. Customs Today* linked video bootlegging to international terrorism. The magazine argued that video bootlegging enriches networks whose agents want to "blow up a building, to hijack a jet, to unleash a plague, and to kill thousands of innocent civilians" (Millar). The same piece notes that just after the 9/11 attacks, Interpol held its first International Conference on Intellectual Property Rights, attended by a range of law-enforcement agencies, the Procter & Gamble Company, and an array of pro-industry lobbying groups: the World Intellectual Property Organization, the Motion Picture Association, the International Federation of the Phonographic Industry, the International Anti-Counterfeiting Coalition ("Protecting rights holders since 1979"), and the Global Anti-Counterfeiting Group ("Representing the voice of business in shaping an effective deterrent to counterfeiting in the UK"). None of these organizations represent workers or artists; instead they represent a sampling of what Peter Frase calls "intellectual property maximalists," rent-seeking entities that pursue the spatial and temporal expansion of intellectual property rights (81). In the wake of 9/11, the goons of corporate IP asked the world to believe that a slippery slope leads from file sharing to mass murder.

During the DVD boom of 2003 to 2007, the profitability of direct sales of DVDs led the MPAA to frame videodisc bootleggers as the kind of high-tech villains we might see in an action movie. On March 13, 2003, the House of Representatives Committee on the Judiciary held a hearing on "International Copyright Piracy: Links to Organized Crime and Terrorism." In his opening statement, Lamar Smith (R-TX) declared that a kilogram of cocaine yields 100 percent profit, while bootleg copies of *Microsoft Office 2000* would yield nine times that (*International Copyright Piracy* 9). This assertion set the hearing's tone: half prurient fascination with the profitability of video bootlegging, half horror at its technological sophistication. Smith continued:

> There is good reason why the Founders embraced the concept of intellectual property protection. They realized that if creators cannot gain from their

creations, they will not bother to create. And actors and writers and composers and singers cannot gain if their work is stolen. Would any other American industry be able to sustain its operations for long if a third of its sales were lost to theft? (9)

Smith does not note that most American actors, writers, composers, and singers do not hold the copyrights to their work, but copyright maximalists will not say this in public. Instead, they all treat copyrights as unambiguous public goods. In a prepared statement, Jack Valenti warned:

> America's crown jewels—its intellectual property—are being looted. Organized, violent, international criminal groups are getting rich from the high gain / low risk business of stealing America's copyrighted works. We don't know to what end the profits from these criminal enterprises are put. US industry alone will never have the tools to penetrate these groups or to trace the nefarious paths to which those profits are put. (*International Copyright Piracy* 47)

Valenti chooses his metaphor well: *crown jewels* conjures nationalistic pride as well as proprietary control. Twice Valenti's written statement refers to *America's* intellectual property, as if "America" held the copyrights to *Steamboat Willie* or *2 Fast 2 Furious* (John Singleton, 2003). As with the crown jewel metaphor, this possession only seems collective if we forget whose property Valenti seeks to protect.

The live portion of Valenti's testimony reveals his skill as a pitchman as he narrates a slideshow of photos taken after police raids on DVD bootlegging operations overseas.

> Our surveillance team thought it was mighty strange that no material was being shipped out of the factory until we did a raid. The enforcement team broke through the roof and then rappelled down in the place before [the bootleggers] could destroy the evidence, and found this underground tunnel. . . . [Valenti shows another slide.] This is a submersible barge. . . . When it gets underwater, fishing boats tow it. And if somebody wants to raid the fishing boat, [the smugglers] immediately cut the line to the submersible barge and then locate it by GPS positioning. . . . This next slide shows you what's in that damned barge—174,000 counterfeit DVDs were found when we made this raid. [Valenti shows a slide of seized contraband.] And finally, piracy and guns go hand in hand. . . . This is a sniper rifle, M-16, heavy weapons, as well as cocaine was there. Wherever we go, we find this connection. (46–47)

Valenti's mise-en-scène evokes adventure serials and spy movies, and his first-person-plurals—*our surveillance, wherever we go*—lend the MPAA the air of a globe-trotting anti-"piracy" commando force, somehow powerful enough to capture its enemies' underground bases and spy submarines, yet still pleading for congressional help.

In the studios' frenzy over DVD profits, the MPAA framed every illicit copy of a Hollywood film not as a disc not sold but as a disc stolen. Even worse than DVD bootlegging, peer-to-peer file sharing allowed viewers to watch Hollywood movies, but without even paying to rent DVDs, so the studios described file sharing less as a criminal racket and more as an existential threat. On September 30, 2003, the US Senate held a hearing on peer-to-peer file sharing, where Jack Valenti likened the major studios' position to that of a desperate army:

> It is said in World War I, Marshal Foch, who was a French General, later to become the Supreme Allied Commander, was in a furious battle with the Germans and he wired back to military headquarters, "My left is falling back. My right is collapsing. My center cannot hold. I shall attack." Some people say this is an apocryphal story, but I want to believe it is true because that is precisely the way I feel in confronting the assault on American movies. (*Privacy and Piracy* 18)

I want to believe it is true: listen to Valenti for long, and one starts to wonder. Like a scenery-chewing actor, he seems to believe with all his might, and this intensity, coupled with the grandiosity of his metaphors, has the charm of a B-movie poster—all *pathos*, no *logos*. Valenti asserts the collective nature of the threat, declaring the file-sharing "onslaught" not "a peculiar Hollywood problem" but "a national issue" (18). Somehow, America survived a Boston Strangler in every home, and then submersibles full of DVDs, but could America survive the file-sharing *Kaiserschlacht*? Valenti urges Congress to help, but he also recounts an array of concrete steps that the MPAA has taken, including "a public persuasion and education campaign with TV, public service announcements, trailers in theaters, and an alliance with Junior Achievement with one million kids in grades five through nine studying what copyright means and how it is of benefit to this country, and to take something that doesn't belong to you is wrong, and that no nation long endures unless it sits on a rostrum of a moral imperative, and that is being shattered" (18).

The pedagogical and propagandistic efforts of the MPAA would soon widen, in ways that mirrored the IP melodrama in duopoly blockbusters, and vice versa.

In the meantime, however, the MPAA's anticopying activism sometimes provoked backlash even from other sectors of the American film industry. The same week that Valenti likened himself to Marshal Foch, the MPAA announced its attempt to ban VHS and DVD "screeners" of Oscar-nominated films. With the help of Barry Meyer, the chairman of Warner Bros., Valenti tried to get the other major studios to agree to an MPAA ban on screeners of award-nominated films, saying the policy would help reduce bootlegging (A. Thompson). But talent guilds and smaller production companies protested that such a policy would only benefit the majors, which could afford saturation marketing campaigns that made their films inescapable. An independent production house, on the other hand, relied on screeners: "Sending out 10,000 DVDs costs only about $30,000 and gets every film to every voter" (Smith and Gordon, 56). The Screen Actors Guild immediately filed suit in federal court (Armbrust), and the Coalition of Independent Filmmakers, the Independent Filmmaker Project, and Antidote International Films brought an antitrust lawsuit against the MPAA (Kay). In December 2003, a federal judge ruled that the proposed screener ban "prohibited competition" and thereby violated antitrust rules (Wagner 10). This reminds us that ostensibly self-regulating industry bodies like the MPAA act not in the interests of "the industry" but in the interests of its most powerful members, here the conglomerated studios. Shawna Kidman, in her discussion of the 1954 crisis of the American comics industry, notes that the Comics Code Authority modeled itself on the Production Code Administration, Hollywood's self-censoring body (and precursor to the MPAA) (54). We can usefully extend Kidman's comparison here. She argues that the establishment of the Comics Code Authority allowed dominant publishers to publicly address the moral panic about comic book content while also driving smaller competitors out of the market (54, 76). In the MPAA's attempt to ban screeners, we see something similar: the MPAA invokes the danger of copying as a screen under which the leader in home video, Time Warner, can collude with the other major studios to revise industry norms in ways that will hurt smaller production companies, firms whose films make less money than the majors but win disproportionately more awards.

Pirates, bootleggers, and monopolists ultimately want the same thing: profit without the burdens of lawful participation in a market. Pirates rob others, thus obtaining goods to sell more cheaply than if they manufactured or bought those goods. Bootleggers manufacture goods, but by avoiding lawful costs of entry into the marketplace, such as licensing or import fees, bootleggers raise their own profit margins relative to legitimate competitors.

Monopolists revise laws or industry norms to exclude competitors—or they try and fail, swatted down by an antitrust ruling.

"YOU WOULDN'T STEAL A CAR..."

The MPAA's anticopying campaign found a partner in the Intellectual Property Office of Singapore (IPOS), which had launched its own campaign called "Honour IP" or "HIP" for short ("Be HIP"). The partnership between the MPAA and the IPOS resulted in the 2006 short propaganda film "Piracy: It's a Crime." Just under fifty seconds long, it shows a montage of thefts, shot with speed-ramping and breakneck zooms, while a techno score pounds. Intertitles in a distressed font harangue the viewer: "You wouldn't steal a car. You wouldn't steal a handbag. You wouldn't steal a television. You wouldn't steal a movie. [Here a shoplifter steals a DVD.] Downloading pirated films is stealing" (*Piracy: It's a Crime*). The MPAA made the film available to US DVD manufacturers, who then began putting it on discs before movies. But the manufacturers added a feature that buyers hated: viewers now could not skip "Piracy: It's a Crime," any more than they could skip the anticopying FBI warning. BBC News covered the backlash among DVD buyers, noting, "Someone really wants you to watch this" (Rohrer). Parodies of the film became an online meme, subverting the IPOS's goal of making its anticopying position hip.

But here the story lurches into farce, because not only the makers of "Piracy: It's a Crime" but also the gatekeepers of the content industries spectacularly failed to honor IP. In 2006, the film's producers had arranged to use music by the Dutch artist Melchior Rietveldt, and they had told Rietveldt and the Dutch music royalty collection agency, Buma/Stemra, that the film would run only "at a local film festival." But in 2007, Rietveldt found his music playing in "Piracy: It's a Crime" on a Harry Potter DVD (Mick). Again we recall the urban legend, only now the police have traced the piracy to the antipiracy trailer. Rietveldt then sought Buma/Stemra's help, and the agency said that it would help him seek royalties on more than seventy DVD titles where his music had appeared, but one of Buma/Stemra's agents proposed an illegal condition: Rietveldt would first transfer the rights to the song to that agent's own record label, so that the agent would receive a third of the back royalties (Solon; Sinnreich 133). The police have traced the call . . . to the police station.

"Piracy: It's a Crime" doesn't just violate the rules of the regime it promotes; it also falsely conflates copying with stealing, an equivalency promoted by nearly every intellectual property maximalist. In 2006, the MPAA's website declared, "Movie pirates are thieves, plain and simple. Piracy is the unauthorized taking, copying or use of copyrighted materials without permission. It is no different from stealing another person's shoes or stereo, except sometimes it can be a lot more damaging" ("Anti-Piracy"). Damaging how and to whom, the goons behind this page do not specify, though another page notes that illicit copying "hurts" both movie studios and below-the-line workers, "every one of the 750,000 people who get up every day in the U.S. and go to work to bring you the magic of the movies" ("Who Piracy Hurts"). Yet the site does not explain how unauthorized copying might hurt the caterers, set carpenters, or offshore CGI compositors already excluded from participation in home video profits. The site does, however, specify that the MPAA also considers file sharing a form of theft: "Whether you download a movie from an unauthorized source or sell counterfeit DVDs on the street, you are a movie thief" ("Piracy & the Law"). Visitors to the site could even complete a form that reported on people that they believed had committed infringement ("Report Piracy"). Maybe the writers intended the site for children, but its hectoring, fallacious arguments coupled with tedious minutiae about release windows would probably only convince a Jack Valenti character. Unlike the MPAA's hypothetical thief who "steals" my shoes, an unlawful copier does not deprive me of my use of the thing copied, unless by *use* I mean a monopoly that allows me to control the thing's reproduction and dissemination. Crucially, such a monopoly does not depend on my having made or thought up the thing in question, but IP maximalists leave this out. For example, Singapore's senior minister for state and former law professor Ho Peng Kee said of the "Honour IP" campaign, "Whether it is a fancy gadget, a household brand or music and movies, someone invested time and effort to create it and owns the intellectual property in it. We need to realize that it takes numerous parties working endless 18-hour days to bring to us a unique piece of movie magic" ("Be HIP"). Ho pays lip service to the labor that goes into media production while actually obscuring the legal relations that exclude most workers in capitalist enterprises—"creative" and otherwise—from any share in the profits that their work generates.

Most below-the-line media workers benefit from intellectual property laws only if they have organized to bargain for shares of residual profits. Hollywood trade unions and talent guilds have collective bargaining agreements that require studios to pay residuals from movie profits to unions, not in individual compensation but in payments to the Motion Picture Industry Pension and Health Plans ("5 Things You Need to Know about Residuals"). In the early 1950s, more than two dozen trade unions and talent guilds negotiated an agreement that established these benefits ("About"). Then, in the 1960s, the Screen Actors Guild went on strike, securing residual payments for television rebroadcasts of film (Federman). Later changes in the locations of production or the profitability of distribution platforms have prompted renegotiations of terms, as seen in the 2007 strike by the Alliance of Canadian Cinema, Television, and Radio Artists over compensation for digital media residuals with American studios (Vlessing). In late 2007, the emergence and proliferation of streaming led the Writers Guild of America to renegotiate its contract with the Alliance of Motion Picture and Television Producers (AMPTP) so that writers would get residuals for streaming and other online uses of their work. When the AMPTP failed to meet the guild's demands, twelve thousand screenwriters went on strike for a hundred days, a work stoppage that cost the California economy an estimated two billion dollars (Blickley; Ford and Rose). But most workers not represented by unions receive no share in the profits from the copyrighted works that they create, whether they work in Vancouver, Los Angeles, or Qingdao. And although cartoon animators and workers in other sectors of the US film industry formed labor unions and won better treatment through collective bargaining, writers and artists in the comics industry never did so (Lent 180–81). The great majority of comics artists have therefore worked under terms set by publishers. When the Copyright Act of 1976 took effect, it solidified the legal basis for artists to claim sole copyright, but as Paul Lopes notes, "a loophole in the act exempted 'work-for-hire' artists" (Lopes 102). In the comics industry, freelance or work-for-hire contracts strip most workers of any stake in their creations.

But sometimes even the duopoly signed contracts that it would later regret. Marvel survived the 1990s in part by licensing the film rights to characters, like those in their best-selling comic *X-Men* and its many spin-offs. In 1993, Marvel sold to 20th Century Fox the film rights to the X-Men and associated characters, as well as the term of art *mutant*, denoting a person born with superpowers powers due to a genetic mutation (*Twentieth Century Fox Film Corporation v. Marvel Enterprises Inc. US*). Although X-Men titles dominated Marvel's slate of comics throughout the 1990s, after the success of Fox's *X-Men* (Bryan Singer, 2000) and *X-Men 2* (Bryan Singer, 2003), Marvel paradoxically began reducing its output of X-titles. In 2001, X-Men titles topped the comic sales charts eleven out of twelve months, but by 2005 Marvel's reduced production and promotion led to no X-Men titles charting (Lubin). In 2014 Marvel writer Chris Claremont confirmed rumors that had circulated among fans: "The X-department is forbidden to create new characters. . . . Because all new characters become the film property of Fox"

(Claremont). In 2015, when a fan asked Tom Brevoort, Marvel's senior vice president of publishing, why the company had published no tie-in books related to Fox's *X-Men: Days of Future Past* (Bryan Singer, 2014), Brevoort evaded with another question: "If you had two things, and on one you earned 100% of the revenues from the efforts that you put into making it, and the other you earned a much smaller percentage for the same amount of time and effort, you'd be more likely to concentrate more heavily on the first, wouldn't you?" (Brevoort). The "you" here refers not to an artist or writer but to the corporate person of Marvel Entertainment.

To complicate matters, a few Marvel Comics characters, such as the superpowered siblings Quicksilver and the Scarlet Witch, lie in a gray area claimed by both Marvel Studios and Fox. The studios therefore negotiated a deal wherein Marvel could use the pair provided Marvel did not identify the siblings as mutants, a term "exclusive to the X-Men," and did not identify their father as Magneto, the recurring villain of the Fox X-Men films (Acuna). Fox's *X-Men: Days of Future Past* thus gave a prominent role to Quicksilver but cut his sister from the film. The following year, Marvel Studios' *Avengers: Age of Ultron* (Joss Whedon, 2015) gave Quicksilver and the Scarlet Witch prominent roles but never used Quicksilver's code name. Then, in the climactic battle, the film simplified things by killing Quicksilver; the man who could outrun bullets could not outrun Marvel Studios. Conglomerates share continuity capital the way bratty siblings share toys, preferring to destroy the doll rather than see the other enjoy it.

Disney's 2019 acquisition of Fox obviated the need for any further tug-of-war over Quicksilver and the Scarlet Witch and reduced the Hollywood's Big Six studios to a Big Five. But where Disney once cut off the flow of mutants to Fox, Disney now has the power to cut the flow of Fox's catalog to the world. In late 2019, exhibitors discovered that they could no longer rent films from Fox's back catalog, films as different as *All about Eve* (Joseph L. Mankiewicz, 1950), *The Sound of Music* (Robert Wise, 1965), *Alien* (Ridley Scott, 1979), *Say Anything . . .* (Cameron Crowe, 1989), and *Fight Club* (David Fincher, 1998). These films became hostage to "the long-standing 'Disney Vault' strategy of artificially creating excitement for a repertory title by keeping film prints out of theaters for years or decades, and periodically manufacturing a limited number of physical media copies" (Seitz). This kind of scarcity increases demand for the back catalog, but it also puts pressure on the few independent theaters remaining in the United States since the COVID-19 pandemic. Each theater that closes for want of programming drives more potential viewers to stay home and try streaming services like Disney+.

PEDAGOGY BY OTHER MEANS

In superhero stories, the villain functions as the true and secret protagonist, in that the villain has goals and a plan, while the nominal hero merely reacts. Richard Reynolds calls supervillains the "engines" of superhero narrative: "The villains are concerned with change and the heroes with the maintenance of the status quo" (51). As far back as the *Writer's Digest Yearbook* of 1942, advice for would-be writers of superhero comics stated this plainly. In every story, "the villain should attempt one major offensive, run across obstacles to this major offensive, and finally be frustrated by the hero," who functions primarily "to frustrate the villain's plan which is drawing to its culmination" (Sundell 36). In duopoly blockbusters, that plan most often involves pirating the hero's powers.

This melodrama supplements the pedagogical project of texts like "Piracy: It's a Crime" by incorporating the propaganda of industry lobbyists directly into the narrative. Villains in the comics sometimes copy the superhero's powers, but conglomerate Hollywood obsesses over this crime. Chuck Tryon argues that the financial success of DVDs in the 2000s pushed studios to think of films as gateways to other commodities and "to reconceptualize film narrative in ways that tie together the fictional world of a film with the economic goals of a studio" (30). The anticopying narratives of duopoly films align the seemingly altruistic superhero with the commercial and political goals of the copyright industries. We first see such a narrative in the VHS era, in *Superman IV: The Quest for Peace* (Sidney J. Furie, 1987), where Lex Luthor clones Superman, intending to use the evil duplicate to conquer the world. But the trope did not return to the screen until the DVD era, when the torrenting and bootlegging of DVDs became such worries for studios. In duopoly films, the studios present illicit copiers as fools and bunglers at best, and at worst, genocidal psychopaths.[8]

This pattern cuts across studio lines. For example, in the 2000s, two different studios produced films based on Marvel's Hulk, and each film's narrative revolves around competing factions of villains trying to copy the hero's powers. Universal Pictures produced *Hulk* (Ang Lee, 2003), where scientist Bruce Banner (Eric Bana) works on "nanomeds" that will regenerate living tissue. Banner tries to keep his research away from military scientist and biotechnology entrepreneur Talbot, who wants to field soldiers "embedded with technology that makes them instantly repairable on the battlefield, in our sole possession." A lab accident reveals Banner's Hulk powers, and halfway through the film, Banner gets captured by the army. Talbot attacks the captive Banner with a stun gun, trying to get him to transform into the Hulk so that Talbot can "carve off a piece," "analyze it, patent it, and make a fortune." Although Talbot revels in torturing Banner, this sadist plans to use the patent system to set up a lawful monopoly. Meanwhile, Banner's mad-scientist father (Nick Nolte) develops the ability to absorb the properties of objects he touches, and he soon realizes that he can thus absorb the powers of the Hulk. In contrast to the bullying Talbot, Banner's megalomaniac father uses persuasion:

> Son, I need your strength. I gave you life, now you must give it back to me— only a million times more radiant, more powerful. . . . Think of all those men out there in their uniforms, barking and swallowing orders, inflicting their petty rule over the entire globe. . . . We could make them and their flags and their anthems disappear in a flash.

Talbot just wants to get rich, but Banner's father proposes something like a one-man Armageddon. True to the melodrama's pattern, Bruce rejects both schemes, defeats his enemies, and escapes.

In 2006, the film rights to the Hulk reverted to Marvel, and Marvel Studios rebooted the franchise with *The Incredible Hulk* (Louis Leterrier, 2008). This film recasts all characters and gives Banner a radically different backstory, but it gives him essentially the same problem: two factions that want to copy his Hulk powers. In the opening act, the fugitive Banner hides from the US military, which wants, as Banner puts it, to "replicate" the Hulk, "to make it a weapon." From hiding in Brazil, Banner begins an encrypted correspondence with an American geneticist (Tim Blake Nelson), hoping to find a way to "cure" himself of the Hulk. When they finally meet, the geneticist reveals that he has secretly cultured Banner's cells, betraying Banner's trust. "This is potentially Olympian," says the geneticist, leading the horrified Banner through a gallery of cataloged blood cultures. "This gamma technology has limitless applications. We'll unlock hundreds of cures. We'll make humans impervious to disease! . . . This is Promethean fire!" But Banner refuses to entertain even medical applications of this research, demanding that the geneticist destroy all the samples. While the army takes Banner into custody, the geneticist injects a rogue Special Forces operative, Blonsky (Tim Roth), with a half-baked version of Hulk DNA. The geneticist warns that the result "could be an abomination." Readers of Hulk comics will recognize this as a reference to the Abomination, a perennial antagonist from *Incredible Hulk* comics, but anyone can recognize the abominability of the resultant knockoff.

Blonsky, now possessing the Hulk's power but lacking even the Hulk's limited conscience, rampages through Manhattan, wantonly killing soldiers and civilians. Unlike Banner, who wants to cure himself of his powers, Blonsky seeks them; unlike the Hulk, who only wants people to leave him alone, the Abomination craves violence. In the context of the film's anticopying melodrama, the Abomination's very name implies a judgment on the morality of unlicensed Hulks.

Unlike the Hulk, Prometheus lies in the public domain, so villains in both Marvel and DC franchises can invoke him without promoting their rivals. But duopoly films always side with Zeus, treating humanity as unworthy of godlike powers. In both the 1978 *Superman* (Richard Donner) and the 2006 *Superman Returns* (Bryan Singer), Lex Luthor threatens mass destruction, but with a key difference: the DVD-era Luthor uses technology that he has stolen from Superman's cache of records and tools from the lost planet Krypton. Both Luthors plan to create commercial empires by destroying swaths of North America, killing millions, but only the DVD-era Luthor steals uses Superman's own trade secrets against him—and against the world. Early in the film, we find Luthor (Kevin Spacey) in the library of his opulent yacht; the walls rise at obtuse angles, creating the illusion of canted framings like those often seen in the villains' hideouts on the *Batman* TV show. Luthor, donning a pair of reading glasses, compares himself to Prometheus, explaining the allusion for his moll, Kitty, as well as for the audience: "Do you know the story of Prometheus? No, of course you don't. Prometheus was a god who stole the power of fire from the other gods and gave control of it to mortals. In essence, he gave us technology." Here Luthor sounds reasonable if condescending, a caricature of a technology entrepreneur. When Kitty challenges him—"But you're not a god"—Luthor removes his eyeglasses and steps into a close-up just above an off-screen light source, illuminating his face from below. Never flattering, this lighting pushes Luthor into mad-scientist territory as he replies: "Gods are selfish beings in little red capes who fly around and don't share their power with mankind." Why does Luthor look hurt and angry? And why does he try to convince Kitty, when he looks down on her and his other accomplices as intellectual inferiors? Avi Santo, in his analysis of the legal struggles over the authorship and ownership of the Lone Ranger, observes that corporations expend considerable "discursive labor . . . in establishing cultural stewardship as central to their authorial rights" (185). Luthor performs a version of this here as he justifies seizing Superman's alien technology. Similar moments of wounded, self-righteous pride emerge in the letters of Jack Liebowitz, manager of National Periodical Publications, to Jerry

Siegel, in which Liebowitz defends the value of his managerial labor. In 1940, the *Cleveland Plain Dealer* ran an unauthorized interview with Siegel and Shuster, which incensed Liebowitz, who wrote to Siegel:

> You might have mentioned in your interview that the first ones who saw something in the Superman strip was Detective Comics, Inc., who bought all rights to it. You might have said that you have a very satisfactory arrangement with Detective Comics, Inc., as compensation for the transfer of all your rights, so hereafter *we forbid you* to grant any interviews relating to Superman and his development. (Liebowitz's emphasis; qtd. in Cotta Vaz 107)

Liebowitz's hurt seems real, as does Luthor's in the film. After his anger passes, Luthor relaxes, stepping back into ordinary lighting. Then he rejects mad-scientist goals in favor of tech-entrepreneur populism: "I don't want to be a god. I just want to bring fire to the people. And I want my cut." Luthor veers back toward rhetoric and motivations that would seem at home in Silicon Valley.

After Luthor steals technology from Superman's arctic fortress, we see more of his mad-scientist side. He seeds the floor of the Atlantic with crystals programmed to grow into a new continent, but while the towering and symmetrical crystals of Superman's fortress gleam white, the irregular crags of Luthor's new continent look more like coal, making visible the moral contrast between hero and villain. Although Superman possesses the complete archive of Kryptonian civilization, including surveys of the "twenty-eight known galaxies," he uses it to create a private Olympus where he can safeguard such knowledge from a species that he deems not yet ready. In contrast, Luthor plans to use the same knowledge to replace the old continents in a scheme that he gleefully acknowledges will kill "billions." As Toby Miller and coauthors point out, "copyright traditionally refuses to grant legitimacy to the pirated product as a form of social good" (220). Through figures like Luthor, duopoly films hold this ideological line, presenting any illicit use of the hero's IP as a moral and social evil. We see this even in cases when the copiers present their copying as a social good, as when the geneticist in *The Incredible Hulk* proposes eradicating all disease. Inside the diegesis of *Superman Returns*, only the villain suggests that Superman might have an obligation to share Kryptonian technology and archives with his human hosts. Outside the diegesis, we find two further motivations for its narrative of concentrated ownership and control. First, the norms of the Superman franchise require him to inhabit our recognizable world, not a science fiction wonderland. And second, Superman mirrors the unaccountable way corporations manage intellectual property, which includes locking it away from all eyes. Not even shareholders in Disney and Warner Bros. Discovery get to vote on how executives use intellectual property; they can only buy in or cash out.

Luthor's plan darkly mirrors Superman's proprietary relation to the Kryptonian archives, but it also mirrors Warner Bros. Discovery's proprietary relation to the Superman franchise. Although Luthor invokes Prometheus's radical sharing, he actually plans to create a monopoly, backed not by the state but by Kryptonian arms: "I'll have advanced alien weapons, thousands of years ahead of what anyone could throw at me. . . . The rest of the world will be begging me for a piece of high-tech beachfront property. In fact, they'll pay through the nose for it." Land, for both the 1978 and 2006 versions of Luthor, constitutes an absolute limit on wealth. The 2006 version recites something his father used to tell him: "You can print money, manufacture diamonds, and people are a dime a dozen, but they'll always need land. It's the one thing they're not making any more of." Unwilling to settle for the existing limits on the availability of land, Luthor seeks to create new limits by demolishing North America. As Miller and coauthors note, "Establishing scarcity through exclusivity is one of the enduring aims of copyright protection" (227), but here Luthor reveals another truth about the copyright industries: they prefer artificial scarcity to the social goods that might arise from circulation that they cannot use to extract rents or surplus value.

In a further dark mirroring of commercial firms, Luthor performs a homicidal version of conventional marketing. In his influential 1954 book *The Practice of Management*, Peter F. Drucker argued that the uniqueness of the commercial enterprise lay in marketing: "There is only one valid definition of business purpose: *to create a customer* [Drucker's emphasis]. Markets are not created by God, nature, or economic forces but by businessmen. . . . A business is set apart from all other human organizations by the fact that it markets a product or a service" (37). The provision of goods takes second place to the creation of demand: "There may have been no want at all until business action created it—by advertising, by salesmanship, or by inventing something new. In every case it is business action that creates the customer" (37). Elsewhere in the book, Drucker makes clear that by *inventing something new*, he primarily means inventing new techniques of management.[9] Lex Luthor, as if on Drucker's advice, seeks to create nothing except demand; by managing the works of now-anonymous Kryptonian scientists, he will manufacture not only land but, more importantly, demand for land, as his crystals destroy the familiar continents. Luthor understands this logic because DC Comics and Warner Bros. understand it. They understood it even before Jack Liebowitz told Jerry

Siegel that the *Superman* radio show would bring in licensing fees: the easiest money lies not in making things but in owning things to rent to others.

Luthor's 2006 speech about land sounds familiar because it repeats, verbatim, lines from the 1978 film. *Superman Returns* reuses much from the films that starred Christopher Reeve, from the mise-en-scène of giant crystals, to John Williams's "Superman March," and even to the footage of Marlon Brando as the computerized ghost of Jor-El, Superman's father. Meehan argued that investment in one film could help drive production of sequels for years, but *Superman Returns* shows that the resulting franchise can span twenty-eight years. Brando and Reeve both died in 2004, so we can also interpret the overdetermined nostalgia of *Superman Returns* as the reminder of another kind of scarcity: the scarcity of Superman movies themselves. But some dispute DC's claims to Superman, as well as Warner Bros.' ability to keep Superman films scarce. The estates of Jerry Siegel and Joe Shuster have continued to challenge DC and Warner into the twenty-first century, long after the creators' deaths, and in 2008, a federal judge ruled that if Warner did not begin production of a new Superman film by 2011, then the studio would face a potential lawsuit from the Siegel estate for damages, since nonproduction denied the heirs potential royalties (*Siegel v. Warner Bros. Entertainment Inc.*).[10] The court forced Warner Bros. to choose between either paying a larger share to Siegel's and Shuster's heirs or throwing DC's continuity capital into new production. Warner Bros. chose the latter.[11]

The resultant film, *Man of Steel* (Zack Snyder, 2013), takes the superhero as IP to baroque extremes. This Superman (Henry Cavill) faces the Kryptonian rogue General Zod (Michael Shannon), who arrives on Earth with a band of fellow Kryptonian survivors. Zod, once sworn to protect Krypton, now seeks to recover a Codex holding the genetic codes of the people of their lost planet, which Zod believes came to Earth with the baby Superman. With this science-fictional library of characters, Zod plans to reconstitute his dead race on Earth, incidentally exterminating humans. To overdetermine Zod's evil, the script also makes his plans explicitly racialist and genocidal even toward fellow Kryptonians: he declares that he plans not only to "save our race" but also to "sever the degenerate bloodlines that led us to this state." But Zod's forces cannot find the Codex until the icy Kryptonian scientist Jax-Ur (Mackenzie Gray) solves the mystery. Jax-Ur explains that before Jor-El launched his infant son to Earth, Jor-El "took the Codex, the DNA of a billion people, and he bonded it within his son's individual cells—all Krypton's heirs, living, hidden in one refugee's body." Thus the franchise's title character becomes, within the narrative, the source of more than a franchise's worth of supporting characters, continuity capital made flesh. In his seminal essay "The Myth of Superman," Umberto Eco writes about the mismatch between Superman's godlike powers and his preference for thwarting the likes of "mail truck robbers" (22). In Superman comics, "the only visible form that evil assumes is an attempt on private property. Outerspace evil is added spice; it is casual, and it always assumes unforeseeable and transitory forms" (22). But *Man of Steel* weaves these two elements together by making the "outerspace evil" into a high-end robbery and by making the hero himself into the mail truck—only this truck holds a delivery of continuity capital on a planetary scale.

But why does Jax-Ur, the Kryptonian scientist, have a German accent? Mackenzie Gray, the actor who plays Jax-Ur, hails from Canada and sounds it in interviews. But Jax-Ur's accent doesn't match the accents of the film's other Kryptonians, who sound nonspecifically North American. On the Vancouver television show *The Rush*, Gray explained that when he auditioned for the part, director Zack Snyder surprised Gray by asking him to do the audition "in a German accent." Snyder "loved it" and gave Gray the role "on the spot." Moreover, the filmmakers flew Gray to Chicago to rehearse with the German actress Antje Traue, who would play another evil Kryptonian. According to Gray, "They wanted us to be from the same place, and Antje's got a German accent, and they wanted me to adopt that" (Gray). But to my ear, Traue's character does not sound recognizably German, and General Zod, played by Michael Shannon (a Chicagoan) sounds as Midwestern American as does Superman, played Henry Cavill (a Jersey Islander). So what should we make of Gray's cod-German accent? Jax-Ur uses a metallic probe to perform painful, invasive medical tests on the bound Superman, a refugee he considers dangerous to a Kryptonian faction seeking to exterminate degenerate (*entartete*) bloodlines and to find living space (*Lebensraum*) for superior bloodlines. In this context, Jax-Ur, with his high-collared black-and-gray uniform and metallic torture probe, sounds not just German but unmistakably Third Reich, somewhere between central-casting SS and Dr. Szell from *Marathon Man* (John Schlesinger, 1976). And viewers recognized Jax-Ur as an evocation of the Third Reich. Joey Katz, a film-student blogger, remarks on the "out of place" "evil Kryptonian Nazi scientist" (Katz). A forum regular at the EyesSkyward Superman fan site begins his complaint about the film, "What was up with crazy Nazi Kryptonian guy? . . . He has a weird Nazi scientist vibe. He even has what sounds like a German accent" (Vadakin). But these writers do not look into Gray's nationality or Snyder's request for the accent, they do not discuss the rhetorical function of Nazis as shorthand, both in Hollywood and in discussion boards, for the Worst Bad Guys Evar, and they do not consider the court ruling that forced Time Warner into production. When the real-world heirs of a couple of Jews from Cleveland challenged Time Warner for larger shares of the franchise's profits, the resulting film quietly offered a comparison: those who would try to capture Superman and his library of supporting characters resemble the would-be enslavers of modern Europe.

The sequel, *Batman v. Superman: Dawn of Justice* (Zack Snyder, 2016), offers a different but equally apocalyptic warning, this time by showing what happens when mere humans copy Kryptonian DNA. This time, Lex Luthor (Jesse Eisenberg), rebooted as a mop-haired young tech billionaire, convinces the US government to give him access to Superman's Kryptonian ship and the corpse of General Zod. Luthor uses the ship's replication technology and Zod's DNA to create an ogreish monster that emits progressively larger blasts of destructive radiation, which even it cannot control. To the horrified Superman, Luthor identifies the monster as "your doomsday!" Comics readers will recognize it as the Doomsday of the infamous 1992 *Death of Superman* publishing gimmick, which killed Superman only to resurrect him in multiple versions over multiple new magazines. In the comics, Doomsday does not result from the copying of Kryptonian DNA but arrives on Earth already formed.[12] The comic book Doomsday merely stomps and rages like a spiny version of Marvel's Hulk, but the movie's Doomsday threatens the whole planet with its radiation. So while *Man of Steel*'s General Zod at least had a plan—and a prosocial one, if only from the perspective of his fellow space Nazis—the inarticulate Doomsday threatens human extinction without any corresponding rebirth.

"A FAIR, EFFICIENT, AND PREDICTABLE ENVIRONMENT"

Marvel's Iron Man films contain a paradox: Tony Stark invents technology that should radically alter human civilization, but each film begins in our familiar world, without clean fusion power and without people commuting to work by means of flying armor. This becomes most apparent in *Iron Man II* (Jon Favreau, 2010). Early in the film, in a set piece that shows director Favreau and his actors in top comedic form, Tony Stark testifies about the Iron Man armor to the US Senate Armed Services Committee. During the proceedings, Senator Stern (Gary Shandling) declares, "My priority is to get the Iron Man weapon turned over to the people of the United States of America." Yet the casting of Shandling as the senator telegraphs that we should not take seriously this *stern* and pompous man. When Stark mocks the proceedings and refuses to turn over his designs, Stern calls as an expert witness the defense contractor Justin Hammer (Sam Rockwell), CEO of Hammer Industries. Once again, casting supports the film's pedagogical aims. Rockwell, not unlike Robert Downey Jr., built his career on louche comic roles, and here he plays the smarmy, overdressed, and undercompetent Hammer as the farcical inverse of Stark. The hearing next calls Stark's friend and sidekick, Lieutenant Colonel James Rhodes (Don Cheadle), who reluctantly testifies that Iran and North Korea have developed their own versions of the Iron Man armor; Senator Stern presents satellite photos of the test sites, compelling Rhodes to narrate them. But Stark interrupts Rhodes by using a super-smartphone to hack the room's audiovisual system, and then he does one better than Stern: on the room's big-screen TV, Stark plays video taken on the ground by organizations trying to copy his armor. The North Korean armor malfunctions, spraying bullets among onlookers and seemingly killing the camera operator, and the Iranian suit crashes first into the ground and then into the camera. "No grave, immediate threat here," Stark declares. He then plays a video bearing the Hammer Industries logo, where Justin Hammer appears beside another knockoff suit as it malfunctions; the suit twists the operator's torso 180 degrees amid a burst of sparks and the operator's scream. In the Senate chamber, Hammer finally manages to cut off the video. Relative screen durations heighten the contrast between Stark's touch-screen wizardry and Hammer's analog bungling: while Stark needs only twenty-two seconds of running time to commandeer the video screens, and without leaving chair, Hammer spends twenty-four seconds on his feet, fumbling to unplug the TV. By hacking the monitors to show this highlight reel of failures, Stark demonstrates technological mastery not only compared to would-be imitators of his designs, but even compared to the government's intelligence services, whose spying he has surpassed. "You want my property? You can't have it!" cries Stark. "I have successfully privatized world peace!" Stark, already a billionaire, need not sell his technology, even to the state.

 While this sounds like a fantasy out of Ayn Rand, the rest of *Iron Man II*'s narrative actually presents the "private" element of privatization as a fragile ideal requiring defense. The film pits Stark against an alliance between copycat Hammer and Russian genius Ivan Vanko (Mickey Rourke). For Hammer Industries, Vanko develops not only a suit of powered armor but also a fleet of drone suits. In the film's climax, Stark confronts a swarm of hundreds of knockoff suits, all trying to kill him—the alienator of industrial labor now the victim of alienation—but Stark defeats the drones and Vanko, giving capital a happy ending. Labor doesn't get a happy ending or even screen time: in the interior shots of Justin Hammer's factories, workers rarely appear, and when they do, they appear far in the background, out of focus, and we never see anyone but Stark making official Iron Man armor. *Iron Man II* frames both the state and Hammer Industries as neither competent to duplicate the armor nor ethical enough to trust with it. Only the supervillain Vanko, motivated by a personal grudge rather than acquisitive aims, has the necessary ability, but his defeat in the film's climax ends his competition with Stark. The next two films that feature Iron Man, *The Avengers* (Joss Whedon, 2012) and *Iron Man III* (Shane Black, 2013), therefore take place in a world without competing brands of flying armor or miniature fusion reactors. Stark thus protects the world by protecting his intradiegetic monopoly, which allows him to refuse to sell his inventions.

Of all duopoly films, those of the Iron Man franchise show the most sustained interest in recent US military interventions overseas, and here too we see the logic of monopolies and trade secrets at play. The first film in the series rewrites the hero's place of origin from Vietnam to Afghanistan, into the context of Stark Industries' sale of weapons to US clients in the Islamic Republic of Afghanistan. The second film has Rhodes briefly surrender a suit of the Iron Man armor to the US Air Force, and the third film pits the hero against a terrorist organization, seemingly based in Muslim countries, that employs veterans of recent US wars and occupations. But neither the Iron Man films nor any other duopoly films send their heroes to Iraq, the most bloody and least popular US intervention since Vietnam; studio executives thus showed instrumental rationality in avoiding the appearance of taking a side that might provoke opposition from potential viewers. Yet if the US occupation of Iraq constitutes one subtext of Iron Man's adventures, then US attempts to rebuild Iraq along lines favorable to multinational corporations constitutes another. In 2004, the Coalition Provisional Authority, installed in Iraq by force, began to proclaim a series of legal and economic reforms known as the 100 Orders. Order 81, on "Patent, Industrial Design, Undisclosed Information, Integrated Circuits, and Plant Variety Law," granted to businesses operating in Iraq new protections on intellectual property, declaring that "companies, lenders and entrepreneurs require a fair, efficient, and predictable environment for protection of their intellectual property" (1). The language suggests neutrality, but the orders actually set the stage for the privatization of Iraqi industry and resources by foreign corporations.[13]

Like the Intellectual Property Office of Singapore, the Coalition Provisional Authority uses language that obscures the economic relations of exploitation and domination that it actually promotes. Order 81 frames its work in populist terms, "as necessary to improve the economic condition of the people of

Iraq" (1). In May 2003, Paul Bremer announced, "Iraq is open for business again" (qtd. in Tyler), but as many critics of the occupation pointed out, Bremer meant a particular kind of business: that of multinational corporations. Wendy Brown notes that Iraqi farmers had long obtained seed "from a national seed bank...in Abu Ghraib, where the entire bank vanished after the bombings and occupation" (144). Into this void stepped foreign agribusiness, which under Order 81 could apply for "plant variety protection" for genetically modified seeds under the protection of the Ministry of Agriculture (16). Nancy Scola argues that Bremer's announcement amounted to an invitation to agribusiness firms like Monsanto, reminding readers that hundreds of Indian farmers, bankrupted by their dependence on Monsanto seeds, committed suicide by drinking the company's Roundup herbicide (Scola). Scola also notes that genetically modified seeds contaminate the larger gene pools of related crops, such that "eventually much of the world's seeds could labor under patents controlled by one agribusiness or another." Lest we think Scola alarmist, or that Monsanto would not use such a scenario for acquisitive or monopolistic ends, the firm explicitly refused to pledge *not* to sue farmers who claim that Monsanto seeds have colonized their stocks. Monsanto instead declared, "A blanket covenant not to sue any present or future member of petitioners' organizations would enable virtually anyone to commit intentional infringement" (qtd. in "Monsanto Critics"). Like Luthor's growing crystals, Monsanto's patented seeds simply follow their programming.

Genetically modified plants figure in *Iron Man III*, which departs from its precursors' fixation on the copying of the Iron Man armor, even as its narrative focuses with greater clarity on the role of intellectual property law in the neoliberal advances of the 2000s. The film's first hint about the villain's plan comes when a genetically modified plant first regenerates, then explodes. The second hint appears in the spontaneous combustion of several returned US military veterans; hoping to recover limbs they lost in wars, these veterans have volunteered as test subjects for a mad-scientist-entrepreneur's experiments, and as a side effect, some explode. "I'll own the War on Terror," crows the villain. "I'll create supply and demand!" He plans to turn the cycle of US military intervention into a commercial monopoly: using his biotechnology, a bogus "terrorist" network will strike targets worldwide while he sells the same biotechnology to the US military to regenerate maimed soldiers. Like Luthor in *Superman Returns*, the villain of *Iron Man III* presents a version of what Naomi Klein has called "disaster capitalism," the use and even the engineering of large-scale destruction to create commercial opportunities (6). And like the neoliberals who tried to rebuild occupied Iraq for corporations, the villain of *Iron Man III* does not disdain state power; unlike an Objectivist or an "anarcho-capitalist," he requires the state's intervention even as he subverts the state's ostensibly public trust. While the occupation of Iraq represents an extreme example of the restructuring of a country's legal order for the benefit of corporations, it differs in tactics but not in strategic aims from legislation like the Copyright Term Extension Act. The CTEA privatized swaths of the public domain not by expanding by force and through space, as geopolitical empires do, but by politics and through time. Derek Khanna, making what he calls "the conservative case for taking on the copyright lobby," writes, "The recapture of works that would be in the public domain represents one of the biggest thefts of public property in history" (Khanna). The IP law scholar Chris Sprigman calls out the owners of DC and Marvel by name: "The only reason to extend the term is to give private benefits to companies like Disney or Time Warner" (qtd. in Lee). The villain of *Iron Man III*, like corporations at home and abroad, uses state power for private gain.

ANAMORPHOSIS AND THE BRAND AS HERO

Superhero blockbusters thus merge Wasko's explicit visions of the world with a normative model of conduct toward intellectual property. Yet if we dismiss these films for their propagandistic functions, we miss the sophistication that the studios demonstrate not only in deploying their continuity capital in new production, but also in curating that continuity capital in ways that groom audiences for long-term engagement with the brand. Marketing literature distinguishes between brand and commodity, but Scott Lash and Celia Lury develop this distinction further: "The commodity is produced. The brand is a source of production. The commodity is a single, discrete, fixed product. The brand instantiates itself in a range of products, is generated across a range of products" (6). Lash and Lury suggest framing the brand as I will here: as a nonmaterial element of the means of production. Since 1942, when Judge Leon Yankwich ruled in *Cain v. Universal Pictures*, US law has treated narrative genres and their conventional elements as public property, such that anyone can now make a generic or off-brand superhero movie. In this light, the ownership of trademarked characters with strong brand equity represents an important source of advantage, in that it enables a studio to market a film starring a character with decades of audience recognition while simultaneously preventing competitors from using characters too similar.

In *Building Strong Brands*, David A. Aaker argues that the quality of the commodities sold under the brand need only be perceived, not actual. He develops this point without apology: "Research in psychology has shown that recognition alone can result in more positive feelings toward nearly anything" (10). As an example, Aaker describes an experiment where subjects of a blind taste test report that a sample of peanut butter tastes better if the experimenters first identify the sample as a well-known brand. Crucially, the subjects report superior taste even when the experimenters actually give them a sample that scores worse in blind taste tests (11). Thus the trademark does not merely enable informed choice but can shape perception, such that imagined qualities drive real sales. Henry Jenkins calls brand loyalty "the holy grail of affective economics" because of its power to drive repeated sales over time (72). In Sir Thomas Malory's fifteenth-century telling, the Holy Grail lays out a miraculous feast, "and every knight had such meats and drinks as he best loved in this world"; Sir Gawain exclaims, "We have been served this day of what meats and drinks we thought on" (6). Compared to the Grail, which reads minds and then satisfies our wants, the commercial brand has a deceptive, satanic power: it can trick us into wanting whatever someone else has chosen to feed us.

For the duopoly, brand and character blur into each other such that narrative form and commercial function overlap. Aaker details a marketing strategy that he calls "brand-as-person": "Like a person, a brand can be perceived as being upscale, competent, impressive, trustworthy, fun, active, humorous, casual, formal, youthful, or intellectual" (83–84). For marketers, virtues of the brave, altruistic hero can thus become elements of corporate brand equity. We might invert Aaker's formula and read the superhero instead as a case of *person-as-brand*, the better to parse the affective appeals of duopoly films.

Take a scene from the film that arguably established the comic book superhero as the staple of twenty-first-century Hollywood: *Spider-Man* (Sam Raimi, 2002). J. Jonah Jameson (J. K. Simmons), editor of the tabloid *Daily Bugle*, sits behind his desk, opposite freelance photographer Peter Parker (Tobey Maguire). Jameson gives a name to the costumed villain who fought with Spider-Man in Times Square: "'Green Goblin,' you like that?" barks Jameson. "Made it up myself." With his feet on his desk, and between puffs on his cigar, Jameson tells his assistant, "Call the patent office! Copyright the name 'Green Goblin'—I want a quarter every time somebody says it!" Irony here works on two levels. On the dramatic level, the audience, but not Jameson, knows Parker's secret identity as Spider-Man. Yet on a second level the scene illustrates the logic of licensing proprietary characters while exaggerating that logic for comic effect. Simmons's boorish manner and rapid delivery steal the scene; the film reveals the commercial logic by which

Columbia Pictures uses its rights to Spider-Man and the Green Goblin, but only through the mouth of Jameson, whom the filmmakers want us to enjoy disliking. Shawna Kidman recounts the tortuous path of the film rights to Spider-Man, first acquired by "junk-bond-funded Cannon Films," then "debt-financed" 21st Century; MGM then scavenged both of those struggling firms, then faltered, only to get bought out by Sony, which ultimately developed the film at Columbia (207–8). In that film, Peter Parker learned, through his unwitting role in his uncle's murder, that he must never use his powers for gain, but the corporations behind this film cannot learn such lessons.

In duopoly films, the brand hides in the open, in the guise of the title character. In Edgar Allan Poe's tale "The Purloined Letter," the detective C. Auguste Dupin compares the methods of advertisers and the method of the blackmailer who has hidden the letter in the open. Dupin asks the narrator:

> Have you ever noticed which of the street signs, over the shop doors, are the most attractive of attention? . . . The over-largely lettered signs and placards of the street, escape observation by dint of being excessively obvious; and here the physical oversight is precisely analogous with the moral inapprehension by which the intellect suffers to pass unnoticed those considerations which are too obtrusively and too palpably self-evident. (345)

The superhero resembles these advertising slogans that we fail to recognize. We see the chevron on Superman's chest, or the spider icon on Spider-Man's back, but we see it as part of a costume, not as a trademark. David Bordwell, in homage to Poe's analysis, called classical Hollywood "an excessively obvious cinema" (11), but the duopoly blockbuster exceeds classical norms in this regard, in that the title character itself doubles as a trademark. In *Branded Entertainment*, Jean-Marc Lehu offers many criteria for effective product placement in films, but one he calls "the most important of all": "negotiating and controlling integration into the story" (118). He calls this integration "the necessary connection for passing from perception to persuasion" (118). When Spider-Man races to catch his uncle's murderer, he momentarily alights on a hurtling Carlsberg beer truck, and at this moment, we might notice that producers and advertisers address us through product placement. But we habitually forget that the duopoly addresses us through the trademarked heroes themselves. So where Raimi may fail to meet Lehu's standard of integration for Carlsberg, he succeeds with Spider-Man. The superhero's status as the mask of continuity capital hides before our eyes, such that we recognize one layer of commercial address (the beer truck) while misrecognizing the other (the superhero).

For visually iconic characters like Spider-Man, trademark law offers corporations potent means to assert monopoly rights, and active trademarks do not expire. Since the 1970s, courts have recognized trademark protection for characters when plaintiffs establish that a trademarked character has "acquired secondary meaning" beyond the story, such that the character stands for a commercial firm and its commodities in the minds of consumers ("Frederick Warne & Co. Inc. v. Book Sales Inc."). In 1986, Leslie Kurtz noted that courts "have found little difficulty protecting a cartoon character's appearance under the principles of trademark and unfair competition" (482–83). But this does not mean that deep-pocketed plaintiffs don't abuse these principles or even necessarily succeed against smaller competitors. In 2001, Sony Pictures Entertainment sued Fireworks Entertainment for developing a television series that Sony argued infringed its copyright to *The Mask of Zorro* (Martin Campbell, 1998) and its licensed trademark rights to Zorro, the character ("Sony Pictures v. Fireworks Entertainment"). Sony adduced "more than seventeen different aspects of Zorro" that, when combined, signified not only Zorro but therefore Sony's association with Zorro in the marketplace, such that the character stood for the company ("Sony Pictures v. Fireworks Entertainment"). The court rejected Sony's claims about substantial similarity and unfair competition, but even this failure highlights the key principle: if a firm can argue that a proprietary character represents that firm to the public, then even the inhuman longevity of corporate copyright becomes irrelevant, because unlike copyrights, active trademarks do not expire. As Stacey Lantagne has argued, not only has Disney registered many characters as trademarks, but many of its characters have begun to stand for Disney (163). In 2017, a company called Me and the Mouse Travel tried to register as its trademark a logo that showed a white-gloved cartoon hand holding a suitcase; the hand had three fingers and three dimples across its back. The examining attorney rejected the application because the combination of the word *mouse* with the gloved hand "falsely suggests a connection with Disney Enterprises, Inc." (*In Re Me and the Mouse Travel*). The applicant "amended the drawing to remove the wrinkles on the glove and add an additional finger," but the attorney refused again (Asbell and Weitzman). The Trademark Trial and Appeal Board then reviewed and granted the request, but as *World Trademark Review* reported, the Board's nonprecedential opinion "suggests that perhaps it would have upheld the refusal if the mark had shown a three-fingered glove" (Asbell and Weitzman), with or without wrinkles. Lantagne argues that this ruling indicates that the board "has already acknowledged that Mickey Mouse functions as a mark" (163). Attorneys representing the copyright industries will surely offer similar arguments.

To return to the 2002 *Spider-Man*, trademark law might not help Columbia Pictures, since audiences probably associate the character with Marvel Comics rather than with Columbia Pictures or Sony. But the scene with the beer truck illustrates a deeper pattern of corporate address in duopoly films: as the superhero's melodrama of altruism engrosses us, his status as brand becomes invisible. Here I draw on theories of the kind of misrecognition that Jacques Lacan called anamorphosis. In his analysis of product and brand placement in *I Am Legend* (Francis Lawrence, 2007), Kirk Boyle describes the advertisements that clutter the film's postapocalyptic Manhattan as "anamorphic advertising": a mise-en-scène laden with corporate signifiers that register from the corner of the eye (2). But duopoly films operate according to a bolder logic, more like that of Lacan's example, the 1533 portrait *The Ambassadors* by Hans Holbein the Younger. The smear across the lower third of the painting remains unintelligible from most viewing positions, but stand just so, and it becomes recognizable as a skull. Lacan proposes that if we accurately plot the anamorphic distortion, we have "the pleasure of obtaining not the restoration of the world that lies at its end, but the distortion, on another surface, of the image that I would have obtained on the first" (87). This distortion, once plotted, functions like a lens that we can move onto other images—as a theater projectionist swaps an anamorphic lens onto a projector to show films shot in wide-screen. Fredric Jameson argues that such a distorting lens can then let us read more clearly other texts produced under similar circumstances:

> Just as every idea is true at the point at which we are able to reckon its conceptual situation, its ideological distortion, back into it, so also every work is clear, provided we locate the angle from which the blur becomes so natural as to pass unnoticed—provided, in other words, we determine and repeat that conceptual operation, often of a very specialized and limited type, in which the style itself originates. ("Metacommentary" 9)

Duopoly films require the conceptual operation of misrecognizing the brand, the trademarked some*thing*, produced as a work for hire, as a character, as a some*one*. We see or half see the other trademarks and brand names in the mise-en-scène, and we might even groan at Hollywood's seemingly crass handling of a character that we remember fondly from texts far in our own pasts (far enough that we have forgotten their encrusting ads and product placements). But we fail to recognize the superhero as the anamorphic object, the mis-seen blot that holds the key to our understanding of the geometry of the whole. The moment we stand at the correct angle to recognize the blot in

The Ambassadors as a human skull, the painting becomes a memento mori that refigures ambassadors, artist, and viewer alike as food for the Worm; but with duopoly movies, such a standpoint requires not a physical repositioning but a deliberate opposition to the film's emotional appeals. Once we recognize the title character not as a striving and suffering fellow creature but as a trademarked site of production, a means of attracting investment and extracting surplus value, then the rest of the film becomes legible as an allegory of exploitation, licensing, and brand placement. The title character becomes recognizable as the most important brand, an advertisement among advertisements.

CONCLUSION

In *Four Futures*, Peter Frase imagines near-future dystopias that could result from the continuation and intensification of policy trends of the 2010s. In one, he imagines a future where automation reduces or eliminates the need for most labor, yet where intellectual property laws help intensify inequality through "the extraction of rents rather than the accumulation of capital through commodity production" (71). In *Spider-Man*, J. Jonah Jameson fantasizes about receiving licensing fees anytime someone uses the name he has registered for the Green Goblin, but in a world of search algorithms and invasive surveillance, a few revisions to a few laws would empower corporations to fine citizens for infringement without the intervention of the courts. Surely some would-be Edison or Jobs has already begun working late into the night developing an app that would allow Universal Music Group to bill people for nonlicensed performances when they sing in the shower.

Hollywood's lobbyists continue their side of the work. In 2019, the Motion Picture Association dropped the *America* from its title, but it continues to style itself as a defender of "the fundamental rights of creators." Creativity seems to obsess the MPA:

> U.S. public policy must support a robust copyright framework that protects the rights of creators . . . and appropriately addresses piracy and other violations of the law that cause creators harm. We must uphold America's existing copyright laws and resist efforts by those who seek to erode copyright to the detriment of the creative economy. Creators around the world deserve the same supportive policies to allow them to thrive. ("Safeguarding Creativity")

Nowhere does this text indicate what kind of entities it means by *creators*. As Miller and coauthors note, "Most infringement suits are brought by corporate owners of film copyright, since directors are considered 'workers for hire' under US law" (246). So when MPA goons praise *creators*, they mean corporations, not human beings.

To business audiences, the executives of the duopoly make their priorities almost clear. In 2008, David Maisel, chairman of Marvel Studios, spoke about the active role that Marvel had taken in working with licensee Sega on a game to tie in with the *Iron Man* movie: "We are in the Iron Man business. . . . So whether it be a major motion picture or a video game, we have somewhat of an obligation to our fans and the consumer to stay involved with the creative process" (qtd. in Ward). Somewhat of an obligation to fans and consumers, but total obligation to shareholders, whose hunger for return on investment remains just out of focus in the background of every shot. The duopoly's goals more closely resemble those of the bogus manager in *Action Comics* #6 than they resemble those of the altruistic Superman.

My proposal to read the superhero first as brand and second as character offers a materialist approach to these movies that acknowledges the pleasures they offer while also resisting the reification of corporate brands into myths, icons, or spontaneously occurring popular culture. Franchises based on trademarked heroes offer the pleasures of newness within familiar parameters, yet scholars and teachers should also attend to the more discontinuous pleasures of the off-brand and the subversively generic. Outside the duopoly, creator-owned superhero comics like *Astro City, Invincible,* and *Jupiter's Legacy* critique both the narrative conventions and political economy of the genre. Even brand-conscious duopoly productions like *Deadpool* (Tim Miller, 2016) show that these movies need not trudge through the routines of marketing-department "best practices" to succeed with audiences and critics. To its credit, the duopoly sometimes takes cinematic risks, revising familiar elements of the most valuable and time-tested characters in surprising ways.

CHAPTER TWO

NOLAN'S BATMAN
Criminogenic Capitalism and
the (Re)Birth of a Brand

After nearly a decade without Batman films, Time Warner threw DC's continuity capital back into wide circulation in the trilogy directed by Christopher Nolan: *Batman Begins* (2005), *The Dark Knight* (2008), and *The Dark Knight Rises* (2012). Unlike earlier Batman films, which introduce the vigilante already well established in Gotham City, Nolan's films tell the story of Bruce Wayne first synthesizing the Batman persona, then defending it against competitors and usurpers, and finally passing it to a successor. Many critics have read these films as allegories of the so-called war on terror, but I read them primarily as allegories of the synthesis and defense of corporate IP in a decade when the dividing line between American capitalism and organized crime became blurrier than usual.[1] In the 2000s, US invasions and occupations in western Asia offered new fields for corporate activity; at home, investment bankers and traders of mortgage-backed securities pocketed billions in a scheme that wrecked the economy, and for which only one person saw jail time. Time Warner crafted its Batman trilogy not to work through questions of imperial or domestic policy but to promote a range brand, thereby driving the sale of movie tickets, DVDs, computer games, and books from DC Comics. Despite the trilogy's psychological depth relative to most duopoly films, Nolan reimagines the vigilante less as an individual and more as a brand, such that the bat insignia functions within the trilogy as a trademark promising a certain standard of vigilantism. Each film shows the Batman defeat rival vigilantes who try to operate in Gotham, and each film styles the Batman's defense of his monopoly on vigilantism as a moral and social necessity.

Most versions of Batman style him as a genius inventor, but the Nolan films instead show Bruce Wayne first scavenging, then bespeaking high-tech gadgets from Wayne Enterprises, the company that bears his family's name. Wayne takes the works of other hands and minds and then synthesizes them into his brand, complete with a logo, creating the false appearance of a lone vigilante appearing from nowhere. Will Brooker notes that just as Batman functions as a "range brand" in our world, so also does the Batman insignia function in the Gotham City of Nolan's films, where the hero's every tool "carries this brand" (79). Yet if we focus on particular objects that carry the trademark—whether in the movies or in our world—we lose sight of the brand as a generative, abstract, and above all social power, made possible only by the labor of thousands. As Bruce Wayne stresses throughout the trilogy, he crafts the Batman as "a symbol," one that exceeds both himself and his branded gadgets, and his creation of the Batman inside the story therefore parallels the managerial work of DC Comics and Warner Bros. outside the story. Within Nolan's films, Batman repurposes the methods of other vigilantes, then uses misdirection and secrecy to hide his dependence on others, ranging from his butler, to his accomplice at Wayne Enterprises, to the never-seen Asian factory workers who make his tools. Paralleling Bruce Wayne's dissimulations in the fiction, Nolan and his screenwriters erased intertextual signs that would connect their version of Batman to the sources that inspired it, even as they repurposed and synthesized the work of earlier comics artists and filmmakers into new stories. Both processes, within and without the fiction, cloak the vigilante in an aura of spurious originality, inevitability, and wholeness, an aura that this chapter seeks to dispel.

At the same time, I also chart the ways that the trilogy frames the management of the superhero's intellectual property as necessary to avoid catastrophe. This thread runs through all three films, and it recurs, as we saw in chapter 1, in Batman's next appearance, *Batman v Superman*. Moreover, it recurs in an inverted form in *Joker* (Todd Phillips, 2019), the first duopoly film to surpass *The Dark Knight* in critical acclaim, winning Oscars for Best Actor and Best Original Score. Although *Joker* lies outside the time frame of this book, its reworking of the notion of branded character as a "symbol" shows the consistency of DC's message: heroes synthesize, then protect their intellectual property, whereas villains copy and freely share. Yet despite their seeming disapproval of open-source vigilantism, Nolan's Batman films have a surprisingly complex relationship to notions of originality and proprietary design, even within their narratives; Bruce Wayne conceals his debts to others in ways that parallel the filmmakers' concealment of their borrowing from other narratives and franchises. To help me parse these films' bivalent attitude toward copying, I will make comparisons to the Zorro film franchise, including disputes over the film rights to that other animal-themed, crime-fighting aristocrat.

NOLAN BEGINS: THE MARKS OF ZORRO

Nolan's films strategically align the Batman with Nolan's own style while distinguishing them from two earlier versions of the character: the Adam West Batman of the 1960s television show and the more recent Batman of Joel Schumacher's *Batman Forever* (1995) and *Batman and Robin* (1997). The latter film did poor business; critics and audiences, and especially comics fans, panned it for its camp tone, homoerotic humor, and focus on toylike gadgets. *Batman and Robin* became a costly misstep for the studio that critics had previously seen as the leader of conglomerate Hollywood's turn toward transmedia franchises.[2] Because Warner found success with the increasingly dark tones of its Matrix, Harry Potter, and Lord of the Rings franchises, the studio chose to try a darker, grimmer tone with its Batman reboot (Schatz 41). Nolan's Batman trilogy extends the neo-noir style of his *Following* (1998), *Memento* (2000), and *Insomnia* (2002) while offering an unsmiling and desexualized Batman. Unlike the sexually active Bruce Wayne of the 1989 film, Nolan's Batman remains celibate until the midpoint of *The Dark Knight Rises*, the film explicitly advertised as the conclusion of the series. Moreover, six minutes after Bruce Wayne's lone sexual encounter in the trilogy, the villain Bane breaks the Batman's spine, as if in punishment for violating the extradiegetic rules of his character. For writers at DC, the "Bat Bible" of editorial policies governing the character has long stipulated that he does not have romantic relationships (Brooker, *Batman Unmasked*, 277). Nolan's films also avoid the suggestion of homoeroticism by eliminating the Batman's youthful sidekick Robin; as Nick Winstead puts it, the Nolan films thereby "de-queered" Batman (Winstead 572), thus distancing them from the Schumacher films. Although a young orphan does come to regard Bruce Wayne as a mentor in *Rises*, the two share less than five minutes of screen time, and they seldom appear together in a single framing, so that the camera never lingers on an exchange of looks. And where *Batman and Robin* ends with Batman, Robin, and Batgirl looking to the future together, *The Dark Knight Rises* decisively ends Bruce Wayne's vigilante career: the Batman sacrifices himself to save Gotham City from a nuclear explosion.[3] The ending of *Rises* offers a hint of the kind ambiguity that Nolan used in the ending of *Inception* (2010), leaving us to wonder if Bruce Wayne might have survived the blast, but the ending's decisiveness about the end of Wayne's vigilantism gives trilogy a closure that further distinguishes it from the Schumacher films—and most other duopoly films, before and since.

Begins opens with a dream-flashback to Bruce Wayne's childhood. This traumatic memory signals that Nolan has brought to the franchise the seriousness and psychological realism that fans had accused the Schumacher Batman films of lacking. Rachel Dawes (Emma Lockheart), the daughter of one of the Wayne servants, plays with Bruce (Gus Lewis) in the garden of Wayne Manor. Rachel has found a flint arrowhead, which she does not want to show.

BRUCE: Let me see!
RACHEL: Finders, keepers. And I found it.
BRUCE: In *my* garden.

When Bruce invokes his family's property rights, Rachel opens her hand to let him see, but Bruce snatches the arrowhead and runs, exclaiming, "Finders, keepers!" This act defines Bruce Wayne's attitude for the whole the trilogy: he treats possession as the whole of the law. But as he runs with the stolen weapon—the first of many—Bruce falls into a cave full of bats, which terrify him. *Begins* uses subjective flashbacks extensively, interweaving Bruce's horror of the bats with happy memories of his parents as well as the traumatic memory of their murder. Nolan's earlier films had no well-developed child characters; the two teenagers in *Insomnia* play minor and disagreeable roles in a film that instead invites us to identify with Al Pacino's middle-aged detective. *Begins*, however, starts by suturing us into the optical and psychic of view of a young man remembering his childhood, and it sets the Bruce Wayne opposite what Kyle Killian describes as a "caravan of father figures" (81). From its opening scene, *Begins* thus synthesizes Nolan's thematic interests with the Bildungsroman common in action franchises, delivering the adolescent angst and Oedipal conflicts typical of the duopoly blockbuster, yet filtered through Nolan's uncomfortable subjective realism.

Nolan's Batman films also synthesize narrative material from sources outside the Batman franchise, but their scripts suppress obvious signs of these intertextual relationships, not only creating the illusion of greater originality but also avoiding potential legal challenges. *Begins* reimagines the Wayne family's fateful last evening out not as a trip to the movies but as a night at the opera, Arrigo Boito's *Mefistofele*. The opera goes unnamed until the end credits, but contrast this with two of the major comic book sources for *Begins*, Frank Miller's *Batman: The Dark Knight Returns* (1986) and *Batman: Year One* (1987). Each of these stories explicitly places the Waynes at a screening of

The Mark of Zorro just before the robbery. Miller's *Dark Knight Returns* shows young Bruce capering in the street after the screening, and it specifies the film as the 1940 version starring Tyrone Power (22); *Year One* shows the Waynes smiling in their seats, illuminated by the movie screen (22). In the comics' first telling of the murders from November 1939, a caption tells us only that the mugger catches the Waynes "walking home from a movie" (Fox, "The Batman Wars" 62). So Miller, like most writers who retell the origins of familiar characters, added his own details. Nolan's decision to shift from cinema to opera might seem like the adapter's prerogative, the same liberty Miller took, but Nolan's rationale offers a purpose for the change beyond mere license.

> We didn't have young Bruce going to see *Zorro* because a character in a movie watching a movie is very different than a character in a comic book watching a movie. A comic-book character reading a comic book is more analogous to a character in a movie watching a movie. It creates a deconstructionist thing that we were trying to avoid. (Nolan, *Christopher Nolan*)

Where Miller directs the reader's attention toward the intertextual relations between his 1986 Batman, the 1939 Batman, and the Zorro movies, Nolan does the opposite, obscuring these relations. And unless we know nineteenth-century French opera, we will not recognize *Mefistofele* or know that it adapts Goethe's *Faust*; furthermore, we will probably misrecognize the cowled, black devils on the stage as bats. As they swing upside down on ropes, these devils spark young Bruce's flashback to his fall into the cave, such that they now register for the viewer not as devils but as Batman prototypes. The script obscures other debts to other texts, which Nolan admits include "a lot of literary influences" (qtd. in Jordan and Gross 23). Nolan says he and Goyer kept the Batman characters isolated from the wider DC Universe for similar reasons, excluding other DC character brands to make Bruce Wayne seem more original: "We did take the position philosophically—that superheroes simply don't exist. If they did, if Bruce knew of Superman or even of comic books, then that's a completely different decision that he's making when he puts on a costume in an attempt to become a symbol" (Nolan, *Christopher Nolan Says*). As we will see, Bruce Wayne assembles that costume out of materials bearing the designs and even the trademarks of others, but like Nolan and Goyer, he hides the evidence of his borrowing.

Nolan had further reasons for eliminating references to *The Mark of Zorro*, chiefly the many elements that early Batman comics borrowed from Zorro stories by the pulp writer Johnston McCulley. From these stories, Kane and

Finger borrowed the aristocrat hero who feigns ineffectual weakness by day but steals forth at night, masked, under an animal-themed pseudonym—*zorro* meaning "fox" in Spanish—to perform feats of vigilante derring-do. Bob Kane, whom DC long treated as the sole creator of Batman, acknowledged these borrowings (Boichel 6); moreover, Frank Miller, by explicitly citing *The Mark of Zorro*, acknowledges this intertextual ancestry in his story.[4] In contrast, Nolan and Goyer deliberately excised Miller's Zorro references to "remove Zorro as a role model" because they "wanted nothing that would undermine the idea that Bruce came up with this crazy plan of putting on a mask all by himself" (Nolan, *Christopher Nolan Says*). Duopoly writers conventionally vary the details when retelling a character's origin story; here Nolan and Goyer exercise the screenwriters' prerogative to invest their Batman in an aura of creativity and originality, at least in their version of Gotham.

But while Nolan offers an artistic, even auteurist, explanation for avoiding references to Zorro, the history of litigation surrounding the rights to Zorro offers a different reason for this avoidance. Although 20th Century Fox owned the 1940 *Mark of Zorro*, TriStar Pictures had produced *The Mask of Zorro* (Martin Campbell, 1998), and in 1999, TriStar had sued Del Taco for using Zorro's likeness in advertisements ("TriStar Pictures Inc., et al."). Then, in 2001, TriStar's parent, Sony Pictures Entertainment, had sued a television production company for developing a series called *Queen of Swords*; Sony argued that the premise of a masked, aristocratic vigilante swordswoman in Spanish California infringed on both Sony's copyright to *The Mask of Zorro* and its trademarks to the character ("Sony Pictures Entertainment v. Fireworks"). Even though the court ruled against Sony's major claims in this case, the lawsuit must have given Warner reason to think twice. But most importantly, during the production of *Batman Begins*, Sony subsidiary Columbia Pictures had put into production *The Legend of Zorro* (Martin Campbell, 2005) ("Legend"). Studio executives don't read Frank Miller comics, but they do keep abreast of their rivals, and studio legal departments look for opportunities to demand rents and gain competitive advantage; Warner Bros. therefore had commercial grounds to eliminate references to Zorro, not only to avoid litigation but also to avoid providing free advertising for a competitor's adventure film, scheduled for release the same year. Nolan's removal of *The Mark of Zorro* therefore made commercial sense. The public-domain *Mefistofele* could stay because no rival studio had tried building a franchise around it, or around *Faust*.

Eliminating Zorro also helped Warner Bros. to avoid a more radical challenge: some might argue that because Batman's creators had copied so many elements from Zorro, the owners of Zorro therefore also had rights to Batman. For decades, Zorro Productions Incorporated (ZPI) has claimed "the worldwide trademarks and copyrights in the name, visual likeness and the character of Zorro" ("About Zorro Productions"). The company's founder, John Gertz, argues that he owns the Zorro trademark, presenting himself as an active steward of the brand:

> Since Gertz founded Zorro Productions in 1977, he has been responsible for four Zorro motion pictures including *Zorro, the Gay Blade* (1982), *The Mask of Zorro* (1998), and *The Legend of Zorro* (2005). . . . Also under his tenure, nine different Zorro TV series and made for TV movies have been produced, as well as some fifteen different Zorro stage productions. ("John Gertz")

John Gertz's father, Mitchell Gertz, had worked as literary agent for Johnston McCulley, author of the 1919 pulp serial where Zorro first appeared, and John Gertz had long maintained that McCulley assigned the rights to Zorro to Mitchell Gertz, who then transferred them to his heirs. But not everyone agrees about Gertz's degree of responsibility or control, or even that Gertz has the right to demand rents on Zorro. In 2001, ZPI joined Sony Pictures in suing Fireworks Productions for infringement, but the court's ruling brought up ZPI's proprietary claims only to dismiss them.

> When Mitchell Gertz died in 1961, he left his estate to his children who later formed ZPI and transferred to ZPI all the rights and goodwill in Zorro that they had inherited as part of their father's estate *and had created themselves* [my emphasis]. Plaintiffs argue that they have a common law trademark in the character Zorro because their licensees have used Zorro extensively for decades. . . . Plaintiffs' argument that they have a trademark in Zorro because they licensed others to use Zorro, however, is specious. It assumes that ZPI had the right to demand licenses to use Zorro at all. All of the essential character elements of Zorro expressed in "The Curse of Capistrano" and the silent picture, *The Mark of Zorro* moved into the public domain when the renewal terms of those copyrights expired. ("Sony Pictures Entertainment v. Fireworks")

Here we see a cleavage between authorship and ownership unlike the one that usually obtains in duopoly works, where a publisher expropriates an author. Here Gertz claims ownership of a character not even on the basis of having prompted or funded its creation, but simply on the basis of patrimony, a theme central to Nolan's Batman trilogy.

With Sony's lawsuit in the recent past, Nolan and Goyer's omission of Zorro showed commercial prudence, but that omission also helped them conceal their own heavy borrowings from the 1940 *Mark of Zorro*, still under copyright at Fox. The hero of that film, Don Diego Vega, has just returned from years overseas, where he, like Bruce Wayne, he has secretly trained in the martial arts. Like Bruce Wayne, Don Diego has a father who refuses to take violent, lawless action even against those who take such action against him; and like Bruce Wayne, Don Diego assumes a masked alter ego and leads police in elaborate chase sequences. At the end of *The Mark of Zorro*, Don Diego coerces the corrupt magistrate into resigning, thereby restoring his father, Don Vega, to this position, much as Bruce Wayne engineers both the ouster of the current CEO and the restoration of a Wayne—himself—to majority ownership of Wayne Enterprises. Elements from the 1920 *Mark of Zorro* constituted much of the template for Batman, from the animal code name and playboy cover to the secret passages beneath the ancestral manor. But *Batman Begins* derives not just mise-en-scène but also major plot elements and set pieces from the 1940 film. Moreover, the presence in *Batman Begins* of extensive swordplay, never a signature element of the Batman franchise, further suggests that Nolan and Goyer took inspiration from the 1940 swashbuckler. Drawing attention to Zorro in *Batman Begins* would have pointed the way for audiences to recognize not just DC Comics' borrowings from McCulley, but also Nolan's and Goyer's borrowings from 20th Century Fox.

BATMAN BEGINS: THE MARK OF KANE

Begins tells the story of Bruce Wayne's creation of his vigilante persona, followed by his use of that persona to save Gotham City from the vigilante cult that trained him. The film opens with Wayne imprisoned for taking part in a failed heist; the better to fight crime, the young heir has wandered the globe apprenticing to criminals. Leaving prison, he trains with the League of Shadows, led by the mysterious Ra's al Ghul (Ken Watanabe). As Wayne masters swordsmanship, unarmed combat, and the "ninja" tactics of "theatricality and deception" under mentor Henri Ducard (Liam Neeson), flashbacks reveal more of his traumatic past. When Wayne learns that the League of Shadows requires that he execute criminals, he defies them, destroys their mountain hideout, and returns to Gotham. There, at Wayne Enterprises, he gains access to the Applied Sciences division, a basement full of mothballed military prototypes. After airbrushing some these gadgets black, he begins a career of midnight vigilantism as the Batman, taking on a conspiracy of gangsters, a drug-dealing psychiatrist, and finally Ducard and the League of Shadows. Ducard reveals himself as the real Ra's al Ghul, who plans to destroy Gotham to save it from its "corruption." The Batman prevails, but only by destroying the city's elevated train system.

The film invents many of these elements but draws others from Batman comics, engaging in bricolage so that the film can both surprise comics readers and still flatter their own knowledge of the Batman canon, leading to new sales of comics. The film draws most from Miller's *Batman: The Dark Knight Returns* and *Batman: Year One*, graphic novels that appeared outside the regular continuity of monthly Batman comics, already repackaged as trade paperbacks long before 2005. Yet these two books otherwise make an unlikely pairing because of their settings at opposite ends of the Batman's career: *Year One* shows a young Bruce Wayne just beginning his vigilantism, while *Dark Knight Returns* shows an aging Wayne return to vigilantism after a decade's hiatus. Readers hold *The Dark Knight Returns* in particularly high esteem, such that it appears on many lists of best English-language comics and graphic novels.[5] And it sells well even without Batman films in theaters. In 2000, *The Dark Knight Returns* still held sixth place on comic distributor Diamond's list of best-selling collections (Wolk); in 2013, sales of the book jumped 161 percent after the announcement of *Batman v Superman: Dawn of Justice* (Langshaw). And corporate siblings Warner Bros. and DC Comics coordinate to see that *The Dark Knight Returns* and other Batman books continue to sell well. As Warner prepared to release *Begins*, DC arranged "to repackage existing titles that highlight the movie's main villains, the Scarecrow and Ra's al Ghul" (MacDonald). DC's publisher Paul Levitz said, "We have a handful of Batman titles that have proven themselves disproportionately over the years as catalogue titles that become natural promotional tools.... *Batman Begins*, for all the expectations, will still surprise people. It's an opportunity for the entire line" (qtd. in MacDonald). Yet despite *The Dark Knight Returns*' high sales and acclaim among fans, *Batman Begins* does not identify itself as an adaptation of any text, because to focus on one would foreclose on the "opportunity for the entire line." By giving the film a title not used by any prior Batman comic, Warner Bros. staked a claim to the film's relative originality even as DC used it to promote its wider Batman catalog.

In its most salient borrowing from Miller's work, *Begins* reimagines the Batman's car as a blocky military vehicle, a move that simultaneously reveals the film's debt to Miller and Nolan's determination not to treat the Batman as an object of lighthearted play. For decades, Batman has primarily driven a sleek roadster, known as the Batmobile both within the fiction and by fans, but Miller's *Dark Knight Returns* reimagined the vehicle with machine guns and caterpillar treads. Miller's Batman attributes the name *Batmobile* to his former sidekick, Robin, and calls it the "kind of a name a kid would come up with" (74), conveying the embarrassment that Miller, his book, and many Batman fans show regarding the more playful elements of the franchise. To please such fans and to distinguish *Begins* from the camp Schumacher films, Nolan went one better than Miller, eliminating the word *Batmobile* entirely from the trilogy. One Gotham cop, trying to give the color and model of the vehicle, describes it as a "black . . . tank." Much as Nolan exercises the freedom to borrow elements from stories like Miller's *Dark Knight Returns*, so Bruce Wayne exercises the freedom to borrow prototypes from the basement of his father's company—then drive them over police cars.

Wayne, like Nolan, synthesizes something new out of elements created by other parties and for other purposes. When Bruce Wayne returns to Gotham from abroad, he visits Wayne Enterprises, where demoted executive Lucius Fox (Morgan Freeman) gives him a tour of the Applied Sciences basement, showing off objects that the audience recognizes as precursors for familiar Batman gadgets: a "Kevlar utility harness," a "gas-powered magnetic grapple-gun," and a "Nomex survival suit for advanced infantry, [with] Kevlar bi-weave." DuPont holds the trademarks for aramid synthetics Nomex and Kevlar, so Fox's description of the suit doubles as product placement. When Wayne asks why the company never mass-produced the suit, Fox explains that the "bean counters didn't think a soldier's life was worth three hundred grand." Fox doesn't clarify the referent of *bean counters*, which could mean accountants at Wayne Enterprises or at the Defense Department, but his disapproval of such calculation secures audience sympathy while avoiding real-world geopolitics. The 2003 invasion of Iraq had prompted enormous protests, with even cool heads like United Nations secretary general Kofi Annan calling the invasion illegal, and in 2005, the United States had soldiers committed in two wars of occupation. But Lucius Fox takes no sides. His remark about the cost of the "survival suit"—a name that conveys protection, not violence—conveys a disinterested concern for human welfare. When Wayne asks to borrow the suit without the knowledge of the CEO, Fox replies, "Mister Wayne, the way I see it, all this stuff is yours anyway." As I have discussed elsewhere, few actors share Morgan Freeman's combination of gravitas and benevolence ("Ambiguous" 160–61). Throughout Nolan's trilogy, Freeman's star image does much to secure our approval of Nolan's version of the Batman, most obviously in *The Dark Knight*, when Fox objects to the Batman's surveillance of millions of Gothamites. In *Begins*, Fox not only enables Wayne to steal from the company but provides a moral justification; the avuncular Fox helps Wayne claim his patrimony while also aligning the Batman's vigilantism against the instrumental rationality of corporations and bureaucrats. The reassuring Freeman helps us forget that this version of Batman relies not on technical genius but on family connections and theft.

By sourcing the Batman's gear not to Wayne Manor but to the research and development wing of a multinational corporation, *Begins* seemingly offers a more realistic version of the character, yet this shift still obscures the relationship between that gear, its makers, and Bruce Wayne's wealth. Hollywood movies, especially blockbusters, usually conceal labor, but *Begins* performs a more complex dissimulation, for although we see only Bruce Wayne's amateur work of ordering and assembling gadgets, we do not see the alienated labor of those who manufacture the gadgets for their livelihood. We first see the survival suit not in a factory but in storage, and soon thereafter we see Wayne airbrushing it black; dressed in a T-shirt and wearing a respirator, the playboy resembles the industrial workers that create his wealth, but Wayne doesn't have to punch a time clock, live in an employee dormitory, or ask for permission to take restroom breaks.[6] In the same sequence, Wayne and his trusted butler Alfred (Michael Caine) hunch over factory catalogs and sketches for the Batman's cowl, for some exposition.

> ALFRED: We order the main part of this cowl from Singapore.
> BRUCE: Via a dummy corporation . . .
> ALFRED: And then, quite separately, we place an order to a Chinese company for these. [points to a sketch of the ears]
> BRUCE: Put it together ourselves . . .
> ALFRED: Precisely. They'll have to be large orders, to avoid suspicion.
> BRUCE: How large?
> ALFRED: Say, ten thousand.
> BRUCE: Well, at least we'll have spares.

Five minutes later, another scene opens with a close-up of the cowl's forehead getting shattered by a baseball bat. Alfred, satisfied with the demonstration but not with the product, removes a pair of safety glasses and declares, "Problem with the graphite, sir. The next ten thousand will be up to specifications." But Wayne Enterprises has not only provided a model for Bruce Wayne's outsourcing: its outsourcing seem to have contributed to the immiseration of Gotham. As Bruce Wayne uses shell companies and overseas factories to overproduce Batman gear by orders of magnitude, Wayne Enterprises outsources its manufacturing. When Chinese police arrest Bruce Wayne, they catch him and his accomplices with a shipment of goods prominently stamped "Wayne Enterprises" and "Made in China." The film presents this as a moment of dramatic irony, for the police do not realize the identity of the man that they have captured. Yet this moment also reminds us of the relationship between American outsourcing, deindustrialization, and the fall of wages since the 1970s, as well as the corresponding growth in wealth for the rich. In the postindustrial Gotham of *Begins*, we see no productive labor, but only caregiving work, law enforcement, corporate management, and homelessness.

While Wayne can outsource costume parts, he must make and sharpen by hand his bat-shaped throwing stars, as no quantity of these could avoid suspicion. As Bruce works at a bench-mounted grinding wheel, he wears safety glasses, work gloves, and a blue cotton shirt, as if acting in a recruitment film for a trade union. In this scene we first see Bruce's bat logo, and we see it not emblazoned on a weapon but purified into a spiky logo-as-weapon, ready to fly. Martin Fradley notes that Wayne's "neurotic branding of his crimefighting persona . . . all too clearly mirrors the American film industry's selfsame practices" (22), but I would go further. The exploitation of labor yields Wayne Enterprises' profits and the fortune that Bruce uses to pay for his new hobby, yet the film asks us to take the Batman as the creation of a heroic individual. This concealment of industrial or productive labor behind a screen of heroic executive labor—Bruce Wayne's factory-floor cosplay—actually continues and extends practices used by Batman's publisher since the 1930s.

Artists working on *Detective Comics* created the Batman of 1939 from elements of other characters, synthesizing a new character distinctive enough for Detective Comics Inc. to trademark.[7] Yet despite the character's composite origin, the publisher asserted singular authorship as well as singular ownership. Bob Kane and Bill Finger collaborated on the character, but Kane managed to negotiate sole credit and compensation he would never publicly discuss (Jones 150). Kane took this credit despite later using what he called "ghosts," subcontracted artists who supplied the illustrations to which DC would attach Kane's name (Boxer); Kane even kept his ghosts' identities secret from one another to limit their ability to negotiate (Jones 154). These practices made Kane less an independent artist than a middle manager. Kane's early art looks amateurish beside the work of contemporaries like Will Eisner, C. C. Beck, and even Joe Shuster, and not even the newness of the comic book medium explains the publisher's willingness to run art of such technical crudity. A better explanation lies in that publisher's haste to launch a new range brand to cash in on its success with Superman, a haste that did not allow time for more polished work. And Kane did not just draw mediocre comics: he copied and reused images from story to story. In 2005, to coincide with the release of *Begins*, DC released some of Kane's earliest stories as part of a series of trade paperbacks, *The Batman Chronicles*, which reprint the character's original appearances in chronological order, and this chronological order allows the reader to spot Kane's retreading drawings in stories like "Frenchy Blake's Jewel Gang" (Fox 12), "The Batman Meets Doctor Death" (23), and "The Return of Doctor Death" (36). DC calls the book as "an exciting new way to experience the rich history of the Dark Knight" ("The Batman Chronicles, Vol. 1"), wisely stressing the book's value as an archive. Not even fans read early Batman stories for the aesthetic quality.

DC continued to spread the fiction of Kane as sole creator of Batman long after Kane himself abandoned it, and long after comics fans had pieced together the truth. In 1965 the comics fanzine *CAPA-Alpha* publicly accused Kane of covering up Bill Finger's role in cocreating the Batman, but Kane continued to insist on his sole creative role. Gerard Jones writes that Kane

> would even go so far as to forge sketches that he supposedly drew in January 1934 [supposedly] inspired by Leonardo da Vinci's sketches of a winglike flying machine; so he tried to prove not only that Finger hadn't helped him but that the couldn't even have been inspired by [the Hawkmen] in *Flash Gordon*, which he'd already cited as an influence in interviews. (Jones 149)

Da Vinci, canonical and long dead, posed no legal challenge, but *Flash Gordon* did, because the powerful King Features Syndicate owned that comic strip, so Kane went to the public domain for a commercially expedient creation myth. Only in his 1989 autobiography did Kane finally acknowledge Finger's contributions (Andrae 391). The release of Kane's autobiography coincided with Tim Burton's *Batman*, for which Kane worked as a high-profile consultant; this timing suggests that pressure from Time Warner prompted Kane's admission. Both the 1989 *Batman* and the 2005 *Begins* use the same boilerplate language in their credits, "based upon characters appearing in magazines published by DC Comics." The credits in all three Nolan films nevertheless include the contractually mandated fiction: "Batman created by Bob Kane."

Nolan's trilogy lays great emphasis on the value of fictions that both assign and obscure authorship, yet in typical Nolan fashion, the trilogy also reveals the corrosive potential of such fictions as well as the contradictions that they hide. In Nolan's reimagining, Wayne Enterprises supplies the Batman with his gadgets, but the company also supplies his foes. In *Begins*, the vigilante-terrorist League of Shadows hijacks a ship carrying a Wayne Enterprises microwave emitter "designed for desert warfare," which "uses focused microwaves to vaporize the enemy's water supply." The league then brings the emitter to Gotham as the key to its plan to destroy the city. The military contracts of Wayne Industries evoke real-world companies like Halliburton, profiting from the American occupations of Afghanistan and Iraq through no-bid contracts, as does the script's reference to "desert warfare." The criminologist Nikos Passas, writing about US-occupied Iraq, calls the environment "inherently criminogenic," largely because the US "Defense Department led the government in outsourcing military tasks to private contractors" (5). Passas notes that $8.9 billion worth of matériel went missing "in just the first eighteen months" of the occupation (14); in 2006 and 2007, audits by the US special inspector general for Iraq found that "$36.4 million in weapons and equipment could not be accounted for" (19). Like the real-world weapons and logistics firms doing business in American war zones, Wayne Enterprises can't keep track of its hardware; if they could, Bruce Wayne wouldn't have his pick of it, and neither would the League of Shadows. Nolan posits fraud and military procurement theft as the necessary conditions for the Batman and the narratives of all three films.[8]

In another complication of the hero's originality, Bruce Wayne also performs the vigilante equivalent of industrial copying, incorporating into his arsenal both the techniques and the tools of the League of Shadows. Bruce Wayne's martial arts training includes the use of armored gauntlets with backward-raked metal blades, gauntlets that the league's fighters use for both offense and defense. Viewers will recognize them as militarized versions of the finned gloves that the Batman has worn since the 1940s. Neither Wayne nor anyone else ever mentions these gauntlets in the dialogue, relying on the audience to recognize the design. In his 1939 appearances in *Detective Comics*, the Batman wore plain gloves, but in spring 1940, the finned gloves appear on the cover of *Batman* #1; Nolan's inverts this historical order, putting the finned gloves before the rest of the Batman persona. When Bruce Wayne defects from the League of Shadows, fighting his way out, even his escape highlights his indebtedness to the league. As he and Ducard fall down an icy slope, Wayne uses the gauntlets to arrest their fall, such that what will become the Batman's costume saves his life. Recall from chapter 1 the 2017 case of Me and the Mouse Travel, and its focus on a drawing of a glove. The Trademark Trial and Appeal Board seemed to rule that if the typical citizen associates a glove of a particular design with a character that represents a particular firm, then even the unlicensed use of that glove may constitute trademark infringement.⁹ This ruling suggests that a character's fictional prop can function metonymically for the character's real-world owner. But a federal court has ruled that such props can also become "characters" in their own right. In 2015, the Ninth Circuit Court of Appeals ruled in favor of DC Comics against a mechanic who sold replicas of the Batmobile. The court not only argued that the car's design met the standard for trademark protection, owing to its association with DC Comics, but also argued that the car met the court's three-step test to establish the standard for copyright protection as a character. The ruling held that "even when a character lacks sentient attributes and does not speak (like a car), it can be a protectable character if it meets this standard" ("DC Comics v. Towle" 15). This suggests that the Batman's finned gloves could receive protection as trademarks *or* as characters. Like the 1930s comics artists who cobbled together the Batman from disparate elements, Nolan's Batman cobbles together his persona from the designs of others, then applies the "theatricality and deception" of branding, presenting his synthesis as a nonderivative work, and because he steals from fellow criminals, they cannot take him to court.

Yet despite their criminality, both Bruce Wayne and the League of Shadows remain attractive because they reject the venal, acquisitive order that surrounds them, an order seemingly without a notion of the public good. In Nolan's Gotham, only one sign remains of Thomas Wayne's philanthropic vision: the decaying elevated train. On this train, the League of Shadows mounts the stolen microwave emitter, which they plan to crash into Wayne Tower, thus turning even capitalist philanthropy against the city. The train does not reappear in Nolan's subsequent films, not as a hole in the ground, and not even as a construction project, confirming Justine Toh's reading of its destruction: "In saving the tower yet crashing the train, Bruce/Batman establishes a fresh covenant for the post-9/11 era" (133). In this new covenant, Gotham, unlike Manhattan, can move on without visible signs of trauma. Yet I would argue that the Nolan Batman thus establishes a covenant with a specifically neoliberal vision of social life, one that predates September 11, a vision where public goods only arise as the incidental side effects of the so-called free market and its necessary inequalities. By destroying the train to save the tower, the Batman protects the sign of capital at the expense of the public. The good vigilante saves Gotham from the bad vigilantes without altering the criminogenic environment that allows both factions to operate. As Toh points out, Batman, "far from solving Gotham's problems," "instead recreates the conditions for their reproduction" (136). In *Batman Begins*, the agents of an enfeebled public sector cannot protect Gotham from the dangers that Wayne

Enterprises creates, so the film ends with the Batman doing what the state cannot. As Michalowski and Kramer put it in the *International Handbook of White-Collar and Corporate Crime*, "Great power and great crimes are inseparable" (212). Wayne Enterprises makes possible the conflict between the opposed criminalities of the Batman and the League of Shadows, both endangering the city and making possible its salvation.

THE DARK KNIGHT: VIGILANTE JURISDICTION

The Dark Knight picks up at an unspecified time after *Begins*. A charismatic district attorney, Harvey Dent (Aaron Eckhart), has taken on organized crime, earning him the label "Gotham's White Knight." Gangsters feel pressure not just from Dent's office but also from the clown-faced Joker, who robs the traditional gangs. Meanwhile, the various mobs therefore pool their money for safekeeping by Mr. Lau (Chin Han), a Hong Kong financier, whose company tries to partner with Wayne Enterprises. As the Batman fights both the conventional mob and the Joker (Heath Ledger), the Joker engineers a series of increasingly daring and terroristic crimes; one of the bombings disfigures Harvey Dent, who becomes the homicidal Two-Face of the comics. As the Batman thwarts the Joker's most ambitious bombing, Dent tracks down and murders suborned police in a rampage that ultimately targets Commissioner Gordon's family. The Batman rescues them, incidentally killing Dent, but rather than reveal Dent as a cop killer, the Batman and Gordon conspire to blame the Batman for the murders, preserving Dent's good name. The film ends with Gordon's voice-over declaring the Batman the city's "dark knight."

The screenplay, by Christopher Nolan and brother Jonathan Nolan, once again draws elements from best-selling noncontinuity Batman stories available as trade paperbacks. According to *Publishers Weekly*, just the trailer of *The Dark Knight* boosted sales of DC's Batman-related catalog, including "Grant Morrison and Dave McKean's *Batman: Arkham Asylum*, Frank Miller and David Mazzucchelli's *Batman: Year One*, Miller's *The Dark Knight Returns*, and *The Long Halloween*" (Reid, "Graphic Novel Bestsellers" 18). The trailer also boosted sales of a new "hardcover edition of Alan Moore's *The Killing Joke*, which spent most of [2008] on this bestseller list" (16). Thus even Warner Bros.' advertising for *The Dark Knight* doubled as advertising for DC's books.

From Miller's *Dark Knight Returns* comes the subplot of copycat vigilantes who imitate the Batman's iconography but use firearms, attacking criminals with lethal force. Nolan repurposes this subplot for *The Dark Knight*, using it in a feint both typical of Nolan and also revelatory of the branding logic that animates the trilogy. Early in the film, two gangs meet in a parking garage, quarreling over the quality of some illegal drugs. The Chechen gang boss (Ritchie Coster) has brought rottweilers in case the Batman shows up, and when they begin to bark, an eyeline match from the Chechen boss shows a medium-long shot of a shadowed figure that we recognize as the Batman, silhouetted against the skyline—his first appearance in the film. But a series of rapid-fire cuts reveals our misrecognition. First, from behind a van, a different shadowy figure attacks one of the gunmen, even though the first Batman has not moved. Another eyeline match from the Chechen boss reveals a different Batman in medium shot, but standing well inside the garage, where the overhead lighting reveals him not as Bruce Wayne but a heavy-jowled impostor. Then a third Batman hurls another gangster over a railing of the parking-garage deck, and finally the first "Batman" racks a pump shotgun and fires. *Batman Begins* strongly emphasized Bruce Wayne's refusal to use guns, so any returning viewer will recognize these figures as impostors, and the Batman with the jowls looks not like a movie star but like a cosplayer.[10] In this windup to the film's first superhero action sequence, the framing, lighting, and editing conspire to create the kind of misunderstanding that trademark law aims to prevent: at first, both the characters and the audience think that the real Batman has arrived.

The rest of the sequence stages a compressed variation on the usual duopoly melodrama of IP defense as the Batman defends not his powers or gadgets but his likeness and brand identity. Jane Gaines has noted that since the 1950s, the copyright industries have increasingly relied on trademark law to police ownership of characters, and she argues that although trademark law originally sought to protect the public, it has undergone an "inversion," such that "the trademark comes to ensure not that the public is protected from merchant fraud but that the merchant-owner of the mark is protected against infringers" (211). The parking-garage sequence enacts a version of this, positing the copycats not as a danger to the public but as a danger to themselves and to the gangsters, and a waste of the Batman's energy. The copycats do succeed in disrupting the gangsters' parley, but then one copycat gets gassed in the face by the masked Scarecrow (Cillian Murphy) while another gets dragged down and mauled by the rottweilers. At this, the real Batman comes to the rescue by crashing the Batmobile through the wall, and even the Scarecrow declares, "That's more like it." In terms of injuries, the copycats resemble the "legitimate" Batman, who also got gassed by the Scarecrow in *Batman Begins*, and who, in the parking-garage fight, also gets bitten by a rottweiler. But the

Batman, more durable than the amateurs, keeps getting back up, even after getting shot though the panel of a van and slammed against a concrete piling. After the latter blow, a wider shot shows him stand up, bracing a hand on a knee, gasping in either pain or exertion. This action sequence, like so many in the trilogy, tries to have it both ways: on one hand, it presents Bruce Wayne as a more "realistic" Batman who cannot simply shrug off blows, but on the other, it presents him alone as having the prowess to merit the exclusive right to risk his safety beating up criminals. And despite his injuries, he prevails, leaving three copycats tied up with four gangsters in a tableau suggesting their similarity. As the Batman gets into his tank, one of the copycats angrily demands, "What gives you the right? What's the difference between you and me?" The Batman replies, "I'm not wearing hockey pads." The line gets a laugh through its schoolyard disdain: the copycats wear gear for a children's game, while the Batman wears a high-tech "survival suit." Yet the line also reminds us that both fake and "real" Batmen share a strategy of repurposing tools, and it suggests that the Batman's "right" comes not from moral authority but from the accident of his patrimony. Not every vigilante can help himself to three-hundred-thousand-dollar body armor from the basement of his daddy's company.

But we can also read the scene as a justification of the broader tendency of American trademark law toward protecting not the public but the holders of trademarks. As Rosemary Coombe argues, case law has extended a status like that of authorship even to manufacturers, such that trademarks, originally "the means by which the consumer's appreciation for business practices became transformed into monopolies over meaning in the public sphere" (59–60). And as Coombe notes, "Trademarks have never guaranteed a product's quality, ingredients, or uniformity, but the exclusive right to a trademark and the ability to build consumer goodwill were expected to provide incentives for producers to maintain markets by maintaining product consistency" (60). In this light, the scene where the "real" Batman defeats the "fake" Batmen reads as corporate wish fulfillment, a revenge fantasy where the real brand defeats a knockoff not as it would in court, on the basis of mere priority of filing with the US Patent and Trademark Office, but as it would in the marketplace of violence, where only quality decides. And by *The Dark Knight*, Wayne has quality firmly on his side; he no longer has to airbrush prototypes, because Lucius Fox and Applied Sciences now design new gear at his request. Each film in Nolan's trilogy pits the Batman against rival vigilantes, showing one or both factions copying the techniques or stealing the tools of its rivals, but each film in turn has the Batman triumph, suggesting that the strong should capture and use designs as they see fit. Nolan's non-Batman films from this period, *The Prestige* (2006) and *Inception* (2010), show ambivalence about industrial espionage and copying, but the Batman trilogy presents both as essentially just, at least when committed by the Batman.

Much as Bruce Wayne's wealth and brand management set him apart from small-time vigilantes, so the Joker's set him apart from other criminals, allowing him to create something like a new brand of crime. When the police arrest the Joker in the middle of the film, they cannot determine his real identity. "Clothing is custom," Commissioner Gordon tells the mayor. "No labels. Nothing in his pockets but knives and lint." Common criminals buy clothes off the rack, but gentleman freaks like the Joker and the Batman wear bespoke. The Joker thus appears simultaneously aristocratic *and* self-made, free from all particularities of biography or manufacture; part terrorist and part performance artist, he repeatedly voices his contempt for the goals of conventional gangsters. "All you care about is money," he says. "This town deserves a better class of criminal." I read this use of *class* in its structural sense, describing a relationship to the means of producing wealth: Gotham, the Joker asserts, deserves a criminal who makes his money not by stealing but by owning, a criminal capitalist. The Joker's robberies of the mob thus resemble what Marx calls primitive accumulation, the expropriation by force that establishes subsequent property relations (784). When the Joker offers to kill the Batman for the established gangs, he asks not for a fee but for a controlling interest, demanding simply, "Half." Such a share would resemble what Bruce Wayne owns in Wayne Enterprises. Dan Hassler-Forest notes that *The Dark Knight* depicts "the gangsters' financial resources, unlike those of Batman or the Joker . . . as cash," but not yet as capital (150). The ordinary gangsters "depend upon physical access to actual money, and are now forced to rely on Asian finance capitalists. . . . The Joker's grasp of the virtualization of money brings him conceptually closer to his nemesis Batman" (151). The Joker denies caring about money, but he makes many contradictory statements during the film (for example, telling incompatible stories about how he got his facial scars). We therefore have reason to take all his stories as entrepreneurial self-marketing. Like a capitalist, the Joker uses money to make money; his every stunt, even torching the gangsters' pile of cash, involves not only the labor of hired gunmen but tools ranging from guns and poison to trucks and explosives. Both the Joker and the Batman, like the rival magicians of *The Prestige*, treat wealth not as an end but as a means of seeking apparently principled ends.

The film presents Batman and the Joker as obverses of each other, a familiar trope from Batman comics, yet it innovates by offering not just a double for the Batman but a separate double for Bruce Wayne: the Hong Kong financier Mr. Lau. Like Wayne, Lau inherited a corporation bearing his family name, and like Wayne, Lau uses his company as a front for crime. Lucius Fox suspects irregularities, but the Wayne Enterprises accountants cannot find evidence of wrongdoing; Fox tells Bruce, "Lau's company has grown eight percent annually like clockwork. His revenue stream must be off the books, maybe even illegal." Lau's revenue streams include the crime syndicates of Gotham, whose money he launders. When Dent's investigation endangers the mob's money, Lau hides it, then flees to Hong Kong to avoid arrest, since, as he says, "the Chinese will not extradite one of their own." In a videoconference, Lau reassures the gangsters of the safety of their money, but the Joker dismisses this reassurance: "Batman has no jurisdiction. He'll find [Lau], and make him squeal." And so the Batman does, kidnapping Lau using a CIA-style skyhook (courtesy Lucius Fox), then delivering him to the Gotham police. Unlike Lau, the Joker understands that the Batman, like a brand, or like capital itself, does not stop for the borders of financial centers like Gotham or Hong Kong.

THE DARK KNIGHT RISES: BRAND SUCCESSION

Nolan's final Batman film opens by introducing villain Bane (Tom Hardy), a masked mercenary with fanatical henchmen. Eight years have passed since the events of *The Dark Knight*, with no sightings of the Batman in a city that now reveres Harvey Dent as a fallen hero. Bruce Wayne has become reclusive and has nearly bankrupted Wayne Enterprises by funding research into a fusion reactor with the help of investor Miranda Tate (Marion Cotillard); but after discovering the reactor's potential for conversion into a nuclear bomb, Wayne has halted the project. Meanwhile, a corporate raider named John Daggett (Ben Mendelsohn) plots to take over Wayne Enterprises and hires Bane and domino-masked burglar Selina Kyle (Anne Hathaway)—the Catwoman of the comics (never named so in the film). When the Batman comes out of retirement to stop them, Bane breaks the Batman's spine and casts him into a dungeon somewhere in Central Asia. Bane then reveals that he belongs to the League of Shadows and aims to fulfill the league's goal of destroying Gotham. To that end, Bane steals the experimental reactor and a fleet of armored vehicles from the Applied Sciences division of Wayne Enterprises, and Miranda Tate reveals her true identity as Talia al Ghul, daughter of the Batman's mentor, here to finish her father's work. But the Batman, with the help of Gotham police detective John Blake (Joseph Gordon-Levitt), defeats the League of Shadows and flies the bomb out to sea, sacrificing himself to save the city.

For *Rises*, the Nolan brothers once again wrote a script that cross-promotes books published by DC. The "Knightfall" story line from the Batman comics of 1993 and 1994 provides the villain Bane, the temporary crippling of Bruce Wayne, and Bruce's falling out with butler Alfred, but once again, much also comes from Miller's *Dark Knight Returns*. This material ranges from the Batman's return from retirement, to Bruce Wayne's use of high-tech braces to support a body worn down by years of brawling, to the funeral for Bruce Wayne, believed dead.[11] The film delays the Batman's first appearance until the forty-six-minute mark, in a scene adapted from *The Dark Knight Returns*: a veteran cop tells a rookie, "You are in for a show tonight, son!" The film even changes Bane's mask to resemble a character from *The Dark Knight Returns*. In the "Knightfall" story line, Bane's mask resembles the full-head covering of a Mexican *luchador*, but *Rises* substitutes a smaller respirator, exposing Bane's bald head while obscuring his mouth in a grille that suggests fangs. This makes Bane look like the leader of the Mutants gang from *The Dark Knight Returns*, who, like Bane, defeats Batman in hand-to-hand combat in the story's second act, only to fall to Batman in their next encounter. In 2010 and 2011, Miller's book had remained in *Publishers Weekly*'s top ten best-selling titles among backlist graphic novels (Reid, "Graphic Novel Bestsellers" 2010, 13; "Graphic Novel Bestsellers" 2011, 19), but it received a boost from advertising for *The Dark Knight Rises*. As *Publishers Weekly* reported on July 5, 2012:

> Though *The Dark Knight Rises* doesn't hit theaters until July 20, books starring the Caped Crusader are already making waves on Amazon's bestseller list. The most popular book as of July 5 was the upcoming graphic novel *Batman: Earth One* by Geoff Johns and Gary Frank. . . . Three other Batman books jumped in the past 24 hours: *The Dark Knight Manual: Tools, Weapons, Vehicles and Documents from the Batcave* by Brandon T. Snider (#781 to #315), Alan Moore's *Batman: The Killing Joke* (#329 to #195), and Frank Miller's *Batman: The Dark Knight Returns* (#378 to #278). ("Tracking Amazon: Batman Titles Rise")

By using the phrase *Dark Knight* in the title of the latter two films, Warner Bros. could evoke an acclaimed Batman title without styling the film as a one-to-one adaptation and thereby risking complaints about its fidelity to its source.[12] The strategy of borrowing from comics without singling out any one source had worked for DC on the two previous films, so Time Warner continued.

Rises continues and even intensifies the trilogy's fixation on branding, industrial secrecy, and the necessity of protecting superhero IP. During the Batman's retirement, Lucius Fox has kept Applied Sciences hidden from the rest of Wayne Enterprises, "consolidating all the different prototypes under one roof—my roof," he says, "to keep them from falling into the wrong hands." But while the Batman and his accomplices hide, the villains move into the open. Bane's first crime in Gotham targets the stock exchange, in broad daylight; his henchmen use guns to intimidate the brokers, but they use a laptop and a copy of Bruce Wayne's thumbprint to commit the real "theft." If *The Dark Knight* tells the story of the Joker becoming a predatory finance capitalist by trying to capture a controlling interest in the mob, then *Rises* shows Bane operating at this level of abstraction from the very start. Lucius Fox explains in the aftermath:

> FOX: It seems you made a series of large put options on the futures exchange, verified by thumbprint.... Long term we may be able to prove fraud, but for now, you're completely broke. And Wayne Enterprises is about to fall into the hands of John Daggett.
> WAYNE: The weapons. We can't let Daggett get his hands on Applied Sciences.
> FOX: Applied Sciences is all locked up and off the books. The energy project, however, is a different story.

Perhaps no cliché appears in duopoly movie dialogue more often than the need to keep the hero's superpowers out of "the wrong hands." The thumbprint's role in the stock exchange attack underscores Fox's and Wayne's talk of *hands*. A few minutes later, the Batman himself repeats the cliché. When Selina Kyle asks about a piece of legendary software called Blank Slate, which allows users to erase their criminal records, the Batman growls, "I acquired it to keep it out of the wrong hands." In an echo of the garden scene that opens *Batman Begins*, Bruce Wayne offers a sanctimonious reason why he won't share with a female peer. But in *Rises*, he speaks while framed in a medium close-up so that we cannot see his hands, because he wears the finned gauntlets that he copied—or, in the language of IP maximalists, stole—from the League of Shadows. Nolan's Batman, much like the Batman registered as a trademark by DC Comics, consists of a synthesis of elements presented as original within certain parameters. In our world, law defines those parameters; in the film, Batman defines them by duplicity and force. In *Begins*, the operatives from the League of Shadows all wore such gauntlets, but in *Rises*, only the Batman wears them, encouraging the audience to forget Bruce Wayne's appropriations.

The scene of the copycat Batmen in *The Dark Knight* presented the copying of the hero's methods as something like farce, as the amateur Batmen got gassed and mauled, but in *Rises*, copying returns as something closer to tragedy. Instead of schlubs doing a poor man's version of the rich man's hobby, *Rises* brings back the ur-vigilante League of Shadows, this time not to hijack a shipment of weapons but to break into Applied Sciences itself. "Your precious armory!" gloats Bane to the crippled Batman. "Gratefully accepted!" Wayne must then watch Gotham News Network broadcasts of the League of Shadows patrolling the city using the same model vehicle that he once used.[13] Gotham's police might have played a more effective role in thwarting the league's takeover if they had had better technology, but Bruce Wayne has never learned to share. After the attack on the stock exchange, faithful butler Alfred questions Wayne's paternalism.

> ALFRED: Are the police supposed to be investigating, then?
> WAYNE: They don't have the tools to analyze it.
> ALFRED: They would if you gave them to them.
> WAYNE: One man's tool is another man's weapon.

By hoarding these tools, Wayne and his conspirator Fox help generate Bane's threat to the city, not just by limiting the ability of the police to investigate but by assembling the arsenal that the league uses to hold the city hostage. Worse, the fusion reactor that investor Miranda Tate had called "free clean energy for an entire city" now threatens Gotham with destruction. In the film's eagerness to conclude the melodrama of Bruce Wayne's virtue and sacrifice, it fails to explain how Wayne's cancellation of the reactor project makes anyone safer in a country that already has a huge nuclear arsenal. Within the neoliberal political horizon of Nolan's Batman cycle, nobody even mentions the idea of trusting such power to an elected government, and the film offers a choice only between billionaire philanthropists and apocalyptic terrorists. More to the point for this book, Bruce Wayne's prerogative to vault the reactor mirrors a key value in the moral imaginary of media conglomerates: they see the creation of scarcity through the idleness of continuity capital as a moral good. Better that the world have no fusion reactors and no Batman films than someone other than Bruce Wayne or DC Comics make either.

The League of Shadows demonstrates that it understands the branding logic that the Batman follows, but it improves on his methods. In the film's opening scene, three men, all wearing black hoods, get renditioned by CIA agents. Because the three captives all wear hoods, the audience does not yet realize that Bane numbers among them; like the Joker in *The Dark Knight*, Bane has engineered his capture to stage an even more daring crime from within custody. The lead agent demands to know the still-hooded Bane's identity, to which Bane replies, "It doesn't matter who we are. What matters is our plan." At this, the agent removes Bane's hood, and Bane continues, "No one cared who I was until I put on the mask." Since *Batman Begins*, the League of Shadows has improved its brand strategy to a level beyond the Batman's. In *Begins*, members of the league wore recognizable ninja suits, but in *Rises*, they dress in either civilian clothing or generic fatigues, lacking a visual identity. Bane, with his mask, bizarre diction, and hulking frame, functions as a mascot of sorts for the new-look League of Shadows. For the first half of the film, this new look leads only to misrecognition of Bane and the league's motives. "Theatricality and deception," says Bane, taunting the Batman with Ra's al Ghul's line from *Begins*. "Powerful agents, to the uninitiated. But we are initiated, aren't we, Bruce?" In *Rises*, the league's major deception depends on emerging from the shadows, and the film makes this literal by setting its climactic action in daylight, in contrast to the noir nightscapes that predominate in *Begins* and *Dark Knight*. But the film also brings the League of Shadows into the daylight world of commerce when its true leader, Miranda Tate, takes over Wayne Enterprises. As camouflage-pattern Batmobiles patrol the streets, the ultimate horror of the film plays out in the boardroom: Talia al Ghul, the principled villain, captures not just the Batman's tools but the means of their production, establishing herself as CEO.[14]

The advertising for this apocalyptic film did something new for a duopoly franchise: it signaled the closure of the series. "The Legend Ends," declared the posters. Never before had the hero of a multifilm superhero cycle retired, let alone died, and neither had any cycle advertised a conclusion. Paradoxically, *Rises* deviates from these genre norms for the good of the brand. The previous Batman cycle had no formal conclusion; Warner Bros. gave each film an open ending, hopeful for a sequel. *Batman and Robin* (1997) ends with the silhouettes of Batman, Robin, and Batgirl running toward the viewer, promising further adventures. But by killing Bruce Wayne—or at least faking his death—*Rises* achieves a degree of narrative closure that we would not see in another superhero film franchise until the death of the title character of *Logan* (James Mangold, 2017). Yet while *Rises* brings Bruce Wayne's story to an end, it also begins the story of another vigilante to take Wayne's place: detective John Blake, the film's revision of Robin, the Boy Wonder.

Rises weaves Blake through its narrative, grooming him to take over where Wayne leaves off. Early in the film, Blake calls on Wayne at Wayne Manor, revealing that he has known of Wayne's identity as the Batman all along. Blake declares that he, too, grew up orphaned by gun crime, and Blake intimates that he witnessed his own father's murder. Furthermore, Blake declares that he intuited Wayne's double identity as the Batman years ago, during one of Wayne's charitable visits to the orphanage where Blake then lived. By "solving" the problem of the Batman's identity, supposedly while still a child, Blake demonstrates a less-than-plausible degree of talent as a detective, but he thereby establishes himself as a brand-plausible successor to the superdetective. In a later meeting with Wayne, Blake asks, "Why the mask?" "The idea was to be a symbol," replies Wayne. "Batman could be anybody. That was the point." This telegraphs the film's aim: to set up a successor. In Blake's next scene, he uses his police-issued handgun to defend himself against two of Bane's henchmen, killing both, but thereby rendering them unable to tell him of Bane's plan. Blake looks aghast at the gun, then hurls it away, much as Bruce Wayne hurled a revolver into the harbor in *Begins*. The film thus shows Blake moving toward his own "no guns" rule. But viewers don't have to work hard to make the connection, because the film bookends Blake's epiphany with scenes where the Batman and Selina Kyle disagree over the use of firearms, making sure that we understand the principle even if we have just arrived at the franchise. In her first action sequence alongside the Batman, Selina Kyle wrests a gun from one of Bane's lackeys, but before she can use it, the Batman knocks it from her hands, saying, "No guns." And at the film's end, she shoots Bane to death, saving the Batman, and remarks, "About the whole 'no guns' thing, I'm not sure I feel as strongly about it as you do." This comedic beat, one of the Nolan trilogy's few moments of levity, doubles as pedagogy in the norms of the Batman, norms that Blake will uphold.

The Dark Knight Rises does not merely show us that Blake merits taking up the Batman's cowl but actually has Wayne name Blake as his successor. When Blake quits the police force, he expresses regret to Commissioner Gordon that "no one's ever gonna know who saved the entire city." Gordon replies, "They know. It was the Batman," suggesting that Gordon also understands that the Batman has greatest value as a brand, and not when bound to any one person. After the reading of Wayne's will, Blake goes to claim an item left to him, but the estate clerk cannot find a John Blake on the list until he includes his full "legal name," Robin. At this moment, Blake suddenly becomes legible as the Nolans' revision of one of the oldest supporting characters from Batman stories. By keeping Blake and Wayne from working together in costume, and by keeping Blake heavily clothed throughout the film, *Rises* manages to include the famous sidekick without introducing the homoerotic possibilities that commentators have remarked on at least since Fredric Wertham's 1954 *Seduction of the Innocent*. Blake's inheritance from Wayne consists of a duffel bag containing climbing gear, a GPS handset, and a set of GPS coordinates, which Blake then uses to enter the cave beneath Wayne Manor. As he explores, a swarm of bats flies around him, and a cutaway shows us Commissioner Gordon lays a hand on the Bat-Signal, possibly in nostalgia, but possibly in preparation to switch it on. The next shot returns us to Blake, no longer fearful of the bats, making clear the implication: once again, the Batman begins. In the final shot of the film, as Blake wades across the stream that runs through the cave, beneath him suddenly rises the rectangular platform that Wayne once used as a landing pad for his helicopter. Within the frame, this black platform functions as a vertical wipe to black, and on the empty screen, the film's title suddenly appears, forcing the inference: Blake has risen, both physically and metaphorically, as the new Dark Knight. Should any copycat ask Blake what gives him the right, he could point not just to his expensive gear but to the last will and testament of the first Batman. Yet in this third and final film, we might say that the trilogy finally distills Bruce Wayne out of the Batman, fulfilling the series' rhetoric about Batman as a symbol. *Rises* converts the character into pure brand, a site of new vigilante productions nevertheless recognizable as Batman.

Successions have happened many times in the comics, but no duopoly film had portrayed the succession of its title character.[15] *Rises* thereby takes up the "problem" of three different actors—Michael Keaton, Val Kilmer, and George Clooney—playing the Batman in the four films of the Burton-Schumacher cycle, but it turns this into a strength for the brand. A new Dark Knight can rise, provided the brand remains continuous in terms of its salient tropes: bats, a cave under Wayne Manor, an orphan vigilante who eschews guns, and a friend at police headquarters, standing by with the Bat-Signal. Rather than simply producing open-ended films until one flopped, Warner Bros. produced a trilogy simultaneously self-contained and open-ended. By showing a different actor assuming the title role in the final moments of the film and of the trilogy, *The Dark Knight Rises* seeks to prepare audiences to expect or even to welcome different actors in the role.

CONCLUSION: PROPRIETARY HEROES AND OPEN-SOURCE VILLAINS

Nolan's Batman films repeatedly call their hero a symbol, but they do so in the service of a proprietary brand, policed inside the narrative by a billionaire armed with military weapons, and policed outside the narrative by a conglomerate armed with copyright and trademark law. Although the film *Joker* (Todd Phillips, 2019) lies outside the time frame of this project, it can help illustrate the duopoly's divide between proprietary heroism and open-source villainy. *Joker*'s protagonist, Arthur Fleck (Joaquin Phoenix), suffers from various mental illnesses and works as a party clown in a 1980s Gotham City that looks like the grungy Manhattan of *Taxi Driver* (Martin Scorsese, 1976) or *The Warriors* (Walter Hill, 1979), a dystopia ready to collapse into *Escape from New York* (John Carpenter, 1981). Cuts to public services have left garbage uncollected and Fleck without adequate mental health care. When a trio of drunken brokers from Wayne Investments attacks Fleck in a subway car, he shoots them to death, thereby becoming the reluctant symbol of Gothamite class resentment. The film labors to distinguish its Joker from that of *The Dark Knight*, partly by presenting Fleck as sick and sad, and partly by demystifying and deglamorizing him: he wears shabby clothes; he has a name, an address, and a day job; and he lacks the wherewithal to commit any but the most opportunistic crimes. Yet despite this restyling, the film explicitly continues the "symbol" talk of Nolan's trilogy. When Fleck appears, in his Joker persona, on a talk show, the host (Robert De Niro) asks, "You did this to start a movement? Become a symbol?" But Fleck disclaims this: "Come on ... do I look like the kind of clown that could start a movement?" Instead, he declares, "I don't believe in anything." But protesters now throng the streets wearing clown masks featuring the same green hair and diamond-shaped eye makeup that Fleck wore when he shot the brokers. In the film's most revealing sequence, Fleck uses these imitators to escape a pair of detectives. Fleck first leads the detectives through subway cars crowded with masked clowns and then snatches a mask from a clown, who begins a fistfight with another passenger. This fight both allows Fleck to escape and precipitates a larger brawl, in which the detectives shoot a different clown and then receive savage beatings from the others.

Unlike Nolan's Batman, Fleck makes no attempt to set limits on his imitators or to curb their violence; not only does Fleck not object, but he even uses his imitators to evade the law, prompting further violence. At the film's end, as police drive a captured Fleck through a city that has erupted in rioting, Fleck's clown followers rescue him by crashing an ambulance into the police cruiser. An uninvolved taxi also crashes into the pileup, underscoring the chaotic escalation that open-source villainy entails. A cutaway takes us to another street, where the Wayne family—father, mother, and young son—step out of a movie theater.[16] Seeing rioters, they duck into an alley, but an anonymous clown-masked thug follows them and murders the parents in front of their son, making Fleck an indirect cause of the murders. Back at the scene of the collision, the unconscious Fleck revives to the sight of his followers and then dances amid the smoke and flames of a Gotham in the midst of collapse. *Joker* shows what happens when people copy a duopoly character with no superhero around to put a stop to it.

We can usefully compare the open-source villainy of *Joker* with the seemingly open-source heroism depicted in another DC movie, *V for Vendetta* (James McTeigue, 2005). Based on the dystopian graphic novel by Alan Moore, *V for Vendetta* stars the terrorist-vigilante hero V, who wears a cloak, a hat, and a Guy Fawkes mask as he fights agents of the totalitarian Norsefire Party that rules Britain. V gained his superhuman powers when subjected to secret experiments in a concentration camp; a flashback shows his escape amid the explosions and flames that killed most of the scientists. One of those scientists has long lived under an assumed name, hiding from V, but before the film's halfway point, V finds and gently murders her. The midpoint of the film thus gives us the conclusion of the usual IP melodrama: by killing the last scientist, V ensures that the party-state cannot repeat the experiments that produced him.

With this danger past, V's endgame depends on sharing his likeness but *not* his powers. Late in the film, V ships hundreds of thousands of identical copies of his outfit to citizens, who begin to use the disguise to commit acts that precipitate an uprising against the ruling dictatorship. Ultimately, thousands of protesters, all wearing the identical disguise, take to the streets, but they do so only after V has died fighting the Party, and after his sidekick has destroyed his body in a huge explosion, and thus long past any possibility of the Party creating another V—or an army of V's.

Warner Bros., however, planned to profit from the fictional insurrectionist's sharing of his likeness. In 2001, the company registered a trademark for the name *Fawkes* ("Fawkes, Serial Number 78052947") and later began licensing official masks based on Alan Lloyd's design in the comics. In 2008, the hacker group Anonymous began using the masks, making them hugely popular, and by 2011, the *New York Times* reported that the design had become "the top-selling mask on Amazon" (Bilton). Warner Bros. uses trademark law to claim ownership of its version of Guy Fawkes, just as Marvel can with its version of Thor, and Disney with its version of Snow White. The Guy Fawkes mask's function as a "symbol" for the hacker group Anonymous does not prevent Warner Bros. from profiting from that symbol—unless Anonymous buys unlicensed knockoffs.

Joker and the Nolan Batman films all tell cautionary stories about copying and sharing, presenting them as virtuous when done by a hero grooming his sidekick-successor, but socially catastrophic when done by anyone else.

Nolan's films play like bedtime stories for brand managers, where the smartest, strongest, and richest guy in the room beats all rivals at their respective games, outpolicing the police and outcriming the criminals. Nolan's films model the construction, maintenance, and renewal of a brand in a world where the difference between criminal and hero depends less on obeying versus breaking the law and more on getting away with it.

In their emphasis on Batman as symbol, the Nolan films simultaneously reveal the productivity and the structuring hollowness of any expansive brand. The brand functions as a site to produce new Batmans as variations on the old, yet those variations also reveal the growing void at the heart of any brand that diversifies into a wide enough range of commodities. The Batman doesn't use guns in Nolan's trilogy, but in the 1989 *Batman* and the 2016 *Batman v Superman: Dawn of Justice*, he machine-guns foes by the dozen. Because the 1989 and 2016 films don't establish the Batman's opposition to firearms, those films could not execute the kind of feint that Nolan performs in the fake-Batmen scene in *The Dark Knight*. The Batman never uses guns, except when he does; he avoids romantic entanglements, except when he doesn't; and he has a youthful ward and sidekick, except when he doesn't. In the system of differences that constitutes Batman as a range brand, establishing or breaking such rules helps differentiate such new text from its predecessor; yet every such act of differentiation tends toward the emptiness of the system. A character brand posits only three necessities: recognition by the audience, continuation in time, and defense against any who would copy its proprietary elements. In the next chapter, I consider the ways that such brands function less as means to tell stories and more as means to advance a commercial firm's broader goals.

CHAPTER THREE

CAPTAIN AMERICA AND WONDER WOMAN
Instrumental Heroes

This chapter looks at two blockbusters with much in common, Marvel Studios' *Captain America: The First Avenger* (Joe Johnston, 2011) and Warner Bros.' *Wonder Woman* (Patty Jenkins, 2017). Each film revives character from World War II, and each film presents its title character as a virtuous outsider while nevertheless framing that outsider as integral to a larger cinematic franchise. The two films offer parallel case studies in how media production companies reuse old intellectual properties. The companies that own Captain America and Wonder Woman style these characters as enduring and beloved, transcending both their era and their medium of origin, yet my analysis of the history of their production and promotion reveals a different story, where publishers seek advantage not only over competitors but also over their own writers and artists. Moreover, the narratives of these two films reveal an awareness, not just on the part of the filmmakers or on the part of more savvy fans, but even on the part of the characters themselves, that Captain America and Wonder Woman began as instruments to serve other ends. Fans and promoters may claim iconic or mythic status for Captain America and Wonder Woman, but each character began as a marketing gimmick that borrowed elements from competitors. Against arguments that these characters "endure," I argue that these two films and their production histories show that Captain America and Wonder Woman returned to popular view in the 2010s because the conglomerates that own them considered them convenient means to manufacture demand for larger media franchises.

Moreover, I argue that the narratives of these two films celebrate the ways that their makers have taken old continuity capital and put it to new uses. Each outsider hero's story suggests a conglomerate's self-congratulation: *we knew we could do it, and you're welcome.* I read both of these films as allegories for the management of proprietary characters, but their allegories operate at different, and complementary, levels. Unusually for duopoly films, each presents its title character as a work, a thing created by a deliberate act and then used for purposes not its own; yet neither film presents the default plot of a villain who tries to copy the hero's powers. Instead, each film offers a narrative of its title character fulfilling the purpose of its creator and only thereafter becoming autonomous. Steve Rogers transforms from human test subject and war-bond fundraiser into Captain America, rule-breaking super-soldier, and Diana of Themyscira transforms from princess and living weapon into Wonder Woman, defender of humanity. I read both films as instances of the same underlying managerial fantasy: the fantasy of a trademarked character not only transcending its origins in comic books but also transcending the claims of the writers and artists who created it, claims that would endanger the duopoly's mode of producing superhero franchises. *Captain America: The First Avenger* and *Wonder Woman* both offer corporate daydreams of superhero creators who have the good grace to die, letting their creations become seemingly autonomous. My study of industrial, legal, and promotional discourses surrounding these films reveals an instrumental, opportunistic logic at play in the development of these seemingly altruistic characters, a logic that remains consistent from the 1940s to the 2010s. Understanding this logic lets us understand the ways that these two films imitate and innovate, recycling and revising tropes from competitors past and present.

THE TIMELY SUPER-SOLDIER

The cover of the first issue of *Captain America Comics*, dated March 1941, introduced its hero punching Adolf Hitler. While many now interpret this cover as a sign of America's eternal opposition to fascism, at the time the cover signified the comics industry's rush to cash in on anti-Nazi sentiment. Superman, the cause of the superhero craze, had stayed out of the war in Europe because National Periodical Publications did not want to risk losing its markets in Germany or its fascist allies (Jones 165). Jews dominated the American comics business; Jason Dittmer notes that many Jewish artists ended up drawing comics "because of exclusion from higher-end illustration jobs" (9). Often the children of immigrants, they filled both creative and managerial roles, but even some Jewish publishers, like National's Jack Liebowitz, saw fascist markets as markets first and kept their heroes out of the war in Europe. As Gerard Jones puts it, "Accountancy breeds complicity" (165). But where National saw an unacceptable risk of losing market access, competitors saw opportunity.

Captain America began as publisher Martin Goodman's plan to enter the suddenly growing field of patriotic heroes. At the end of 1939, MLJ Publications' *Pep Comics* #1 (dated January 1940) had featured on its cover the Shield, a superhero who wears on his chest an escutcheon-style shield emblazoned with the Stars and Stripes. This cover shows a smiling Shield punching one humanoid robot while two other robots fire guns at him; motion lines show bullets bouncing from his costume. Between the Shield's appearance at the end of 1939 and *Captain America Comics* #1 in early 1941, rival publishers rushed to field their own patriotic heroes, all dressed in "costumes that utilized the stars and stripes in their designs" (Goulart 36). These heroes included Captain Flag and Captain Freedom (36–38), two "captains" that predated Timely's. According to Stan Lee's hyperbolic 1947 telling, Martin Goodman felt he had to share "the truth about the Nazi menace!" (65) and therefore set "the nation's top writers and artists submitting ideas for a new patriotic type of character" (66). Timely already had both the Defender and Mr. Liberty, but artist Jack Kirby and writer Joe Simon delivered Captain America, a knockoff of the Shield (Jones 199–200). Kirby and Simon wrote Captain America as the result of an US military program to create a "super-soldier": injection of an experimental serum allows ordinary Steve Rogers to develop to the peak of human physical ability, but a Nazi spy kills the scientist responsible for the procedure, preventing replication of the process. Kirby and Simon's captain wore an escutcheon-style Stars and Stripes shield on his arm instead of on his chest, and where only two robots shot at the Shield on his debut cover, four Nazis shoot at Captain America on his. Simon and Kirby got word that John Goldwater, publisher MLJ of publications, considered Captain America too derivative of MLJ's Shield, and Simon declares that "to placate him, we changed Captain America's traditional shield to a round one" (Simon and Simon 53). In the early years of the American comics business, Will Wright notes, "imitation was not only a high form of flattery, it was company policy" (17–18). Nowhere do we see that more clearly than in the case of Captain America.

Timely did innovate, however, in its commercial handling of the character. In a field where most characters first appeared in anthology titles like *Whiz Comics*, *Adventure Comics*, and *More Fun Comics*, Timely launched Captain America in a dedicated magazine, and Timely offered Simon and Kirby what sounded like an extraordinary deal: the writer and artist would receive royalties as well as "salaried positions as Goodman's comics editor and art director," respectively (Jones 200). As Simon tells it, "Goodman offered 25 percent of the profits, 15 percent for me, 10 percent for the artists. We shook hands on the deal" (Simon and Simon 43). But according to both Kirby and Simon, Goodman reneged on the royalties (Jones 201). Simon declares that he learned from Goodman's accountant: "He confided to me that I was getting far less than the twenty-five percent that I had bargained for. 'They're piling salaries and most of the overhead for most of the operation on *Captain America*,' he said. 'You're getting the short end'" (Simon and Simon 53). Jones's history of the early comics industry stresses that publishers used various duplicitous accounting practices to hide profits from anyone who might seek a share (185–86). After just ten issues of *Captain America Comics*, Simon and Kirby left Timely for better pay at rival National (Simon and Simon 53). In the coming years, they would leave National, working for Crestwood Publications and starting Mainline Publications. In 1954 they created an imitation of their own imitation of the Shield, complete with a stars-and-stripes costume, as the anticommunist cash-in *Fighting American* (Stevens 73). Meanwhile Timely continued to publish and license Captain America stories and licensed the character to Republic Pictures for a fifteen-chapter serial in 1944. But the popularity of superheroes had already begun to wane, in the market Timely had helped to saturate.

Captain America then drifted in and out of publication on the basis of what Timely thought would either sell magazines or generate licensing revenue. After 1944, publishers had largely ceased introducing superhero characters (Wright 57), and by late 1946, sales of superhero titles had fallen by a third (Jones 234). Publishers scrambled to find the next big thing, experimenting with crime, romance, and western comics, often remixing successful characters into new genres; these experiments included Timely's decision to retitle *Captain America Comics* as *Captain America's Weird Tales*. But this two-issue attempt to cash in on the nascent horror genre failed, and in 1949 Timely halted all publication of Captain America stories (Stevens 40).

Most other publishers canceled their superhero titles by the end of the decade, but even as superhero comics declined, Superman achieved new popularity on television in *The Adventures of Superman* (Motion Pictures for Television, 1952–58). In the wake of the show's success, Martin Goodman sought to license a different Timely character, the Sub-Mariner, for television. But like Captain America, the Sub-Mariner had gone unpublished since 1949, so to demonstrate the commercial potential of Timely superheroes, Goodman actually had to put them in some comic books. Therefore, not only did the

December 1953 issue of the anthology series *Young Men* feature stories headlined by the Sub-Mariner, the Human Torch, and Captain America, but each story included "a brief origin and an explanation for the postwar absence" of its main character (Stevens 60). No television deal came to pass, but that same year, as Joseph McCarthy became chair of the Permanent Subcommittee on Investigations, Timely revived its super-soldier in *Captain America . . . Commie Smasher*.[1] Although the magazine appeared at the height of the second Red Scare, it sold so poorly that Timely canceled it after just three issues.

Captain America's third, lasting revival came only after deliberate market research. In the early 1960s, Jack Kirby had returned to work for Martin Goodman, seeking stable work after a failed attempt, with Joe Simon, to launch their own company (Hajdu 315). At the time, National's superhero team comic *Justice League of America* sold well, so Kirby and Stan Lee collaborated on a superhero team comic for Timely, *The Fantastic Four*. This new magazine not only sold well but led the company to invest in multiple superhero titles; in the next few years, Lee and Kirby would collaborate on many of the characters that would transform Timely—now operating under the name Marvel Comics—into a major player in American mass culture. In 1963, Lee invited readers to write in about the possibility of reviving Captain America, and enough responded positively that Marvel brought the character back for another team-up comic, *The Avengers* (Stevens 83). This time, the publishers wrote into the stories an explanation for Captain America's absence from publication: he had spent the missing years frozen in the Arctic. To make the character distinctive, the writers now turned to the very qualities that had made Captain America seem passé after World War II, so that he became a man out of time, longing for a past to which he could not return, and in some ways a figure for the constitutive nostalgia of comics fandom, which looks always fondly toward a receding and yellowing past. "Cap" became both a fan favorite and a mainstay of Marvel's wider continuity of overlapping titles, and the company again licensed the character for other media. In 1966 he appeared in a short-lived animated series, *Marvel Super Heroes* (Grantray-Lawrence Animation, 1966). Although comic book sales declined through the 1970s, Marvel licensed to Universal the live-action television rights to twelve characters for a mere $12,500 (Howe 195). This deal led to two TV movies, *Captain America* (Rod Holcomb, 1979) and *Captain America II: Death Too Soon* (Ivan Nagy, 1979). Meanwhile, Cannon Films obtained the film rights for its low-budget feature *Captain America* (Albert Pyun, 1990), but Captain America failed to achieve anything like the wide recognition or licensing revenues of a Batman or Superman.

In his authoritative history of the character, J. Richard Stevens traces the ways that writers and editors have tried to keep basic features of Captain America consistent while still updating him as audience tastes change, and Stevens thereby reveals the character's changing function within the corporate brand. The early years of Captain America stories presented the character as a super-soldier who "displays a moral certitude that allows him to take life without guilt or reservation" (42). During World War II, Cap and his boy sidekick Bucky kill enemy soldiers and spies, using guns, explosives, poison, and improvised weapons, and they kill in quantity, sometimes killing "dozens, hundreds, or even thousands of enemy soldiers" at a time, and once killing a million Japanese soldiers by flooding a tunnel (43). Cap and Bucky even torture enemies to extract information (43–44). But after Marvel revived Captain America in the 1960s, the stories presented him as less violent, and even stories that retold events from Cap's service in World War II rewrote him as a master tactician who seldom kills (87–88). Following the Watergate scandal, the company made a more radical change, when it had Steve Rogers briefly abandon his patriotic code name and adopt instead the persona of Nomad, "a wanderer without a country" (111). During the 1970s and 1980s, as the Comics Code eroded and readers' average age increased, Marvel experimented with violent antiheroes like Wolverine, who gladly killed enemies; such characters contrasted strongly with the reluctant and principled Marvel heroes of the 1960s, including the revived Captain America. In the 1980s, a further revision of Cap's origin reimagined Steve Rogers as a pacifist who "decided to join the war effort only when his brother perished in the attack on Pearl Harbor" (171). Stevens notes that Captain America's pacifism offered a contrast to Marvel's "increasingly dominant archetype of the violent hero, such as the Punisher" (171), a gun-toting, murderous vigilante. In *Captain America* #241 (dated January 1980), the Captain meets the Punisher, and they debate the ethics of their methods. Cap tells the Punisher, "I've never willingly taken a life" (qtd. in Stevens 171). Stevens reads this line as evidence of "just how far we Americans can stretch our myths when needed" (218), but I read it instead as evidence of a publisher strategically revising a character to differentiate range brands within its larger corporate brand. The exchange between Cap and the Punisher lets Marvel stage the differences between range brands as a part of the story, encouraging readers to follow both characters.

We need not resort to claims about supposedly shared myths to explain product differentiation. The owners of characters like Captain America prefer that we think of them as simultaneously timely and timeless, always relevant and yet always objects of nostalgia. Stevens's book appeared in 2015, a year before Captain America would have entered the public domain had not the CTEA lengthened the copyright on works of corporate authorship from 75 to a staggering 120 years. A corporation seeking to exploit a character over such a term will have to adjust that character, either in response to changing audience tastes or in the hope of shaping those tastes. Moreover, with such a duration comes the potential for bewildering contradictions: Cap fights Nazis when the United States allies with the Soviets, and he fights communists during the Cold War, but he abandons both his mission and his Captain America code name after Watergate. He carries a shield that some comics present as indestructible while other comics destroy it, repeatedly. The comics offer the Nazi-linked terrorist organization Hydra as Cap's perennial antagonist, yet they have also retroactively styled him as a Hydra sleeper agent, as revealed in *Captain America: Steve Rogers* #1, released on May 25, 2016. As Groucho Marx reputedly said, "Those are my principles, and if you don't like them, well . . . I have others." Captain America has principles, too, and if you don't like them, he has others. Amid this incoherence, I would argue that Captain America "stands" not for democracy, militarism or pacifism, antifascism or anticommunism, but for a commercial firm's revisions of a proprietary character as the political winds changed. The character's variations arise from Marvel's efforts to use its continuity to produce new texts and to acquire new licensing revenues. Whether owned privately by Martin Goodman and investors in the Timely era; whether owned by Cadence Industries in the 1960s, or MacAndrews and Forbes in the 1980s, or Disney in the 2010s; and whether traded on the New York Stock Exchange as Marvel Entertainment Group or as the Walt Disney Company, Captain America's status as a brand takes precedence over the fiction of this character's principles. For one thing above all else Cap stands: textual revision, managed for profit.

When the resurgent Marvel ventured into feature-film production in the 2000s, the company put Captain America to a new use: they put him up as collateral against a line of credit. On April 28, 2005, *Variety* reported the company's unprecedented deal with Merrill Lynch Wealth Management. The financial services firm would offer a credit line of $525 million to fund Marvel's production of films, and in exchange, Marvel would mortgage ten characters:

> Merrill Lynch said the unusual financing structure probably couldn't be replicated, considering the firepower of Marvel's characters. The characters themselves are the assets that Merrill Lynch will use to go to capital markets and raise money. Among those being put up for collateral, [Marvel Studios CEO Avi] Arad would

only reveal the identities of Captain America, the Avengers and Nick Fury. . . . To maximize possible audience, none of the films will be rated R. (McClintock)

Like a super-soldier formula or a radioactive spider bite, this line of credit seems unique in its power, and like heroes jealous of their powers, the executives keep secret many of the basic details of the transaction. In passing, *Variety* also notes that Marvel had reached a settlement with Stan Lee, former editor and writer, who sued the company for "withholding profit participation." This reminds us of the norms of exploitation that shaped even the work done by Lee, the public face of the company. For eight decades, the right to profit from Captain America has determined who would use the character and how, so we now turn to the struggles over those rights.

"I DIDN'T SAVE MY MONEY FOR A LAWYER"

After Martin Goodman failed to deliver the promised royalties, Kirby and Simon left Timely, and their experiences in the next decade illustrate the ways that the duopoly has always depended on the expropriation of artists. At Prize Comics, Kirby and Simon created *Young Romance* in 1947, which set the template for the genre of romance comics (Wright 127). Tired of having publishers claim ownership of their work, Simon and Kirby formed their own publishing company, launching Mainline Publications in 1954 (Hajdu 315), but they had the bad luck of starting in the year that nearly killed the American comics industry, the year of the US Senate Subcommittee on Juvenile Delinquency, which held televised hearings on the supposed malign influence of comic books on America's children. In Kirby's telling, the company folded both because the moral panic reduced demand and because Mainline lacked the capital of larger publishers (Groth 5). Those publishers that did survive—National, Timely, Charlton, MLJ—had deep pockets or heavily licensed characters or both.

Lack of collective bargaining and low pay in the comics industry kept artist expectations low. "Very few of us," recalls Simon, "were concerned with ownership of the characters" (38). Gary Groth questioned Kirby along these lines:

> GROTH: At the time you just assumed that the publisher owned it?
> KIRBY: Yes. I assumed that he took it, OK? [Laughter.] I assumed that he took it, and I didn't have the means to get it back. In other words, I didn't save my money for a lawyer. I was a very young man, and saved my money for having a good time. (5)

In 1947, the year of Jerry Siegel and Joe Shuster's failed lawsuit for the rights to Superman, Stan Lee wrote a nonfiction comic called *Secrets behind the Comics*, in which he sided firmly with his cousin by marriage, Martin Goodman, publisher of Timely Comics. In "Secret No. 12: How a Comic Strip Is Created!" Lee credited his cousin Goodman for Captain America. Over three pages, Lee repeats Goodman's name six times without ever mentioning Simon or Kirby (64–66). Lee gives a list of questions that a publisher must answer in creating a character, such as "What type of costume should he wear?" and, significantly, "Who should write and draw the strip?" (68). Lee writes Simon and Kirby out of this origin story and writes Captain America in: the sequence ends with Martin Goodman and Captain America shaking hands (68). Even in the 1940s, Stan Lee, the public face of Marvel Comics, presented the character as autonomous.[2]

In the 1960s, Simon began to challenge Marvel's control of Captain America. According to Simon, Marvel warned Kirby, who still worked there, of Simon's impending lawsuit, and management convinced Kirby to side with them (186). To secure Kirby's cooperation, Marvel even offered to pay Kirby a sum equal to any future settlement that Marvel reached with Simon, but on the condition that Kirby sign over "to Marvel Comics all rights to Captain America in perpetuity" (186). Simon sued Marvel in 1966, and in 1969 Marvel and Simon reached a settlement ("Marvel Characters Inc. v. Simon"). The terms of that settlement forbade Simon to disclose the dollar amount, but three years later, Kirby told Simon that Marvel had still not paid Kirby the fee the company had promised for siding with it against his former partner (Simon 186). Moreover, the terms of Simon's settlement required that he declare

> that his contribution to the Works "was done as an employee for hire of the Goodmans." . . . Pursuant to this Settlement Agreement, Simon assigned "any and all right, title and interest he may have or control or which he has had or controlled in [the works over which he sued] (without warranty that he has had or controlled any such right, title or interest)" to the Goodmans and their affiliates. ("Marvel Characters Inc. v. Simon")

That is, Marvel required Simon to disavow, retroactively, any claim to rights in works that he made for Marvel, works that under different industrial norms would have belonged to Simon and his cocreators by default. Marvel and other publishers use these declarations by artists the way that authoritarian governments use forced confessions: their truth matters less than their demonstration of the weakness of the human before the organization.

When Simon sued Marvel in the 1960s, he had sued under the provisions of the 1909 Copyright Act, but the Copyright Act of 1976 would offer new opportunities to artists and their descendants. Section 304(c) of the 1976 act gave creators a window during which they could terminate copyrights on their creations "notwithstanding any agreement to the contrary" (*Copyright Act of 1976*). The termination provisions seemed to mean that between 1996 and 2001, Simon could file papers to terminate Marvel's copyright on Captain America. Many commentators have remarked that Congress added these provisions to give artists a means to regain copyrights they had signed away in their need for paying work. The media industry watched closely, for studios like 20th Century Fox had already begun developing films based on Marvel characters. In 1993, during Marvel's hungry years, Fox had bought the film rights to the characters from *X-Men* and related titles, and in 1997, Tom Rothman, Fox president of production, spoke publicly of the studio's eagerness to develop them: "These properties cross several generations and have tremendous built-in awareness.... The underlying weighty themes set in a pop context makes these unique, and like gold" (qtd. in Fleming, "A Mania for Marvel"). But if creators could recapture the rights of such characters, what would become of the studios' plans?

In December 1999, the eighty-five-year-old Simon filed a termination notice on Marvel's copyright on copyright Captain America. He argued that because he and Kirby created the character and presented their work to Martin Goodman before taking jobs at Timely, *Captain America Comics* #1 did not constitute work for hire. The court ruled in favor of Marvel, but on appeal, the Second Circuit ruled in favor of Simon. In November 2002, Judge Joseph M. McLaughlin argued that Marvel's repeated demands that Simon and Kirby retroactively disclaim their copyrights to Captain America amounted to just the kind of coercive "agreement to the contrary" that the 1976 Copyright Act sought to address:

> If an agreement between an author and publisher that a work was created for hire were outside the purview of §304(c)(5), the termination provision would be rendered a nullity; litigation-savvy publishers would be able to utilize their superior bargaining position to compel authors to agree that a work was created for hire in order to get their works published. In effect, such an interpretation would likely ... provide a blueprint by which publishers could effectively eliminate an author's termination right. ("Marvel Characters Inc. v. Simon")

McLaughlin saw section 304 as balancing the interests of artists with those of publishers, in that it still allowed publishers some use of the property.

"Marvel," he wrote, "can continue to exploit every Captain America property created prior to the effective date of termination" ("Marvel Characters Inc. v. Simon"). But reprints of superhero comics do not bring in the kind of record-setting profits that Marvel had already seen Fox make on *X-Men* (Bryan Singer, 2000) and Columbia make on *Spider-Man* (Sam Raimi, 2002). Like a comic book artist who rued signing away his rights for a check to pay the rent, Marvel had learned a painful lesson in the importance of not ceding copyrights to others. The publisher therefore continued to deny Simon ownership.

In September 2003, Simon and Marvel reached a settlement, and Marvel paid Simon an undisclosed sum in exchange for his surrender of all claims to the copyright to Captain America. *Variety* noted that Marvel's stock price had risen because observers "expect the comicbook licenser and producer to generate total sales for the year of about $310 million" (Amdur). *Variety* also reported Marvel's declared plan "to build up the franchise through media including feature films, publishing, TV deals and the usual mix of merchandise licensing," because "Captain America ranks as one of the company's top 10 most recognizable characters." *Business Wire* reported that the settlement would allow Marvel

> to focus its attention on aggressively building the Captain America property across a variety of mediums. This will include feature film and television deals, licensing/merchandising, promotional programs and exciting new publishing initiatives. "Captain America ranks as one of the most recognizable Super Heroes in the world, who can stand quite firmly alongside Marvel's biggest name—Spider-Man," stated Allen Lipson, Marvel Enterprises CEO. "Now, with the legal issue behind us, we can fully explore the deep value that this property brings to the Marvel Universe." ("Marvel Enterprises Settles")

Lipson understands characters primarily as brands, sources of textual production valuable to shareholders in proportion to audiences' familiarity with them. His comparison to Spider-Man thus registers regret for parting with the Spider-Man film rights and hope for the Captain America rights, which Simon agreed to abandon. *Business Wire*, reporting on the settlement, echoed Lipson's understanding of both character and company, calling Marvel not a publisher but "a leading global character-based entertainment licensing company that has developed and owns a library of over 4,700 characters" ("Marvel Enterprises Settles"). *Business Wire* sees Marvel primarily as an enterprise that exploits and curates copyrighted material, and only secondarily as an enterprise that generates copyrighted material.

Jack Kirby died in 1994, too early to file termination notices against Marvel's copyrights on his work. But when Disney bought Marvel in 2009, Kirby's children filed copyright termination notices against forty-five characters that Kirby had created or cocreated for Marvel between 1958 and 1963 (Young). Following Simon's example, Kirby's heirs argued that their father's work for Marvel did not constitute work for hire, but they argued on different grounds. By the 1950s, Kirby worked not in an artists' bullpen but in a studio in his basement in Mineola, New York, making him an "independent contractor" who therefore "owned the original copyrights under section 26 of the 1909 Act" (*Kirby v. Marvel Characters*). Countering this, Marvel said, as always, that it only published work for hire by Kirby, and that neither he nor his heirs could therefore terminate their copyright; furthermore, Marvel said that it accepted and paid for Kirby's work only at the company's discretion, such that whatever of his Marvel chose to publish became work for hire. The court ruled in favor of Marvel, and the Second Circuit Court of Appeals affirmed the decision (House 933). So the Kirbys petitioned the Supreme Court of the United States. Marc Toberoff, the Kirbys' attorney, offered a counterargument both legal and ontological:

> Authorship cannot be based on contingent post-creation events like Marvel's discretionary payment for that material it wished to publish—authorship is fixed at creation. If Marvel was not legally obligated to pay Kirby for conforming services, and did not own Kirby's material until it chose to pay for it, how could it have authored and owned such material at inception? . . . Marvel's revisionist "work-for-hire" defense . . . leads to absurd contradictions. It means that Marvel authored those Kirby works it chose after completion to buy, and Kirby authored those works Marvel ultimately rejected. This stands fundamental principles of authorship and "work for hire" on their head. (*Kirby v. Marvel Characters*)

The stakes ran high. The Directors Guild of America, the Writers Guild of America, the Screen Actors Guild–American Federation of Television and Radio Artists (SAG-AFTRA) filed a joint amicus brief arguing against Marvel's attempt to define Kirby's work as work for hire. The brief argued that Marvel's definition of work for hire creates "an onerous, nearly insurmountable presumption that copyright ownership vests in a commissioning party as a work made for hire, rather than in the work's creator" and thereby "jeopardizes the statutory termination rights that many Guild members may possess in works they created" (*Brief of Screen Actors Guild*). Media conglomerates want a barrier that jeopardizes the statutory termination rights of workers, and the more onerous, the better. The *Hollywood Reporter* reported, "The guilds argue that works made for hire are the product of traditional employment relationships, and that to extend the interpretation broadly to commissioned works as well would be a consequential power shift in the entertainment industry" (Gardner, "Hollywood Guilds"). A ruling in favor of the Kirbys could set a precedent whereby only the works of traditional salaried employees would count as work for hire; works by many freelancers would suddenly become subject to copyright termination by many artists previously excluded from the privilege. As an attorney for SAG-AFTRA put it, after such a ruling, "Kirby's heirs could license several current Marvel properties, valued in the billions of dollars, to other entities. Even if the Kirbys licensed those properties back to Marvel, its plans to commercialize those properties through films, comics, and elsewhere may be profoundly altered" (Young). Apocalypse loomed.

Then, with guilds and corporations waiting nervously, the Kirbys and Marvel abruptly settled, avoiding the scrutiny of Supreme Court decision. Comics writer Kurt Busiek noted that the Kirbys accepted a settlement "on the last possible business day before the Supreme Court started discussing whether to take the case" (Busiek, "Marvel"). *Deadline Hollywood* speculated:

> If there had been a hearing and if then the High Court had found for the Kirbys, the results would have thrown Marvel/Disney into turmoil as they would have to negotiate for millions and millions with the family.... As well a wide variety of copyrights across the industry, including those at Warner Bros and DC Comics, would suddenly be in play as the work of writers, composers and others designated under a freelancer or the work for hire status could suddenly gain a piece of what they created. (Patten)

By paying the Kirbys to settle, Marvel staved off a tremendous danger to the way that the duopoly produces texts and generates licensing fees, as well as a danger to the way that their parent conglomerates operate. Like the protagonist of a duopoly blockbuster, Marvel succeeded just in time, preserving the status quo and aborting the apocalyptic redistribution sought by the company's enemies. I hope that the Kirbys extracted a high price, but rich Kirbys do not change the structural conditions that confront other media workers. For that, workers have to organize, change laws, and restructure industries for their own ends, rather than the ends of managers and investors.

I WAS A MALE WAR BOND

In promoting the 2011 film *Captain America: The First Avenger*, Marvel Studios focused on the relationship between the character and the filmmakers' craft, without mentioning the character's origin. Producer and studio president Kevin Feige, interviewed for the film's digital press kit, talked up the studio's adaptation, which he says

> brings a whole other level to what [Captain America]'s been doing in the comics all these years.... And we've got the best artists working on it.... It's the same artists, the same team that's working with us now on not only Captain America, but the Red Skull, but the iconic shield, the motorcycle. Everything that you want to see in a Captain America movie we're bringing to life in a way that I think is going to be absolutely a nod to the comics, but inspired in how believable it is for the time period and hit that box of feeling like it stepped out of the comics, but feeling like it's always existed in our real world. (*Captain America: First Avenger [2011]: Kevin Feige Sound Bite*)

Feige stresses the film's continuity with "comics," yet he does not say which comics or which artists, and wisely so, for two reasons. First, he understands that he speaks not to comic book fans but to film critics, distributors, and promoters. For this audience, he performs a tourist-friendly version of comics fandom, modeling the enthusiasm that fans will supposedly have at seeing their beloved hero brought to life, yet he omits the minutiae that fans would demand from a sales pitch, such as which comics artists' or writers' work the film draws on. But Feige names no comics artists for another reason: doing so would embolden those who would challenge Marvel's claims to authorship of the character.

The film itself contains elements of the intellectual-property melodrama so common in superhero blockbusters, but not in their classical form, where the hero must prevent the copying or distribution of his powers. Most of the film consists of a flashback that tells the story of scrawny, earnest Steve Rogers, who hopes to join the army to fight the Axis but finds himself the subject of a secret military program to create a super-soldier. Rogers meets a German scientist who fled the Nazis and chooses Rogers as his first American test subject. But after this test, a spy murders the scientist and tries to steal the formula. Meanwhile, the Nazis have one super-soldier of their own, the Red Skull, who heads their secret and cultlike Hydra division. Curiously, the film does not have the Red Skull try again to steal or duplicate the formula; instead, the Red Skull builds ray guns and other machines of war evocative of pulp science fiction magazines, powering them with a mysterious cube left on Earth by aliens. The Red Skull's machines, and not the duplication of the hero's signature powers, constitute the primary threat in the film; these ray guns allow the film to offer a bloodless vision of war in Europe, as targets disappear in PG-13 puffs of vapor. Rogers falls in love with a British agent, but in the climactic sequence, he separates from her, undertaking an apparently suicidal mission to stop the Red Skull's superbomber from destroying the Eastern Seaboard of the United States. Rogers succeeds but ends up frozen in the Arctic; the film's ending shows him revived in 2011. The film borrows much from Captain America comics, especially from Marvel's 2002 *Ultimates* reboot of the Avengers. Stevens notes that in the *Ultimates* series, most villains exist because of attempts to duplicate the 1940s super-soldier process (235–37). Atypically, the film inverts this, and with it, the superhero film genre's usual moral logic of copying: in *The First Avenger*, the Nazis developed the process, creating the film's villain first, and Steve Rogers gains his powers only through an unauthorized duplication.

Although the film does not center on a melodrama of thwarting duplication of the hero's powers, it nevertheless offers another allegory of the duopoly's mode of production. After the murder of the scientist, the army decides to keep Rogers out of combat so that scientists can reverse engineer him. The colonel in charge of the project laments, "I asked for a army, and all I got was you. You are not enough." But a visiting senator sees an opportunity. He shows a photo of Rogers on the front page of *New York Examiner*, taken during Rogers's extemporaneous capture of the Hydra assassin:

> SENATOR: [pointing to the photo] You don't take a soldier—a symbol—like that and hide him in a lab. Son, do you want to serve your country on the most important battlefield of the war?
> ROGERS: Sir, that's all I want.
> SENATOR: Then congratulations. You just got promoted.

The next scene reveals that the "promotion" has turned Steve Rogers into "Captain America," the costumed lead in a traveling musical stage show to promote the sale of war bonds. The super-soldier becomes a fundraising tool, a means to secure investment, in a fictional arc that recapitulates the role of Captain America in the history of Timely Comics, Marvel Comics, and Marvel Studios. In the film, Rogers initially appears to have only limited strategic value, until the senator sees the opportunity to use Rogers to attract investment. Similarly, Captain America, created to sell comics magazines, seemed of limited value to Timely Comics, so limited that the company ceased publishing his stories not once but twice. Eventually, however, the publisher realized the value of the character to attract investment, and in the 2000s, Marvel used the character as collateral to bankroll its own movies. The film presents this instrumental use of Steve Rogers not as a scheme to benefit investors in Marvel or Disney but as a just and prosocial mission to save the world from a post-Nazi cult. The film thus reads as a triumphant allegory of Timely/Marvel/Disney "discovering" the value of Captain America as a brand, which they defrosted first in the 1950s and again in the 1960s, before eventually using him as a means to fund not just Captain America movies but a whole cinematic franchise. By analogy, the film offers Marvel, the corporate brand, as the underdog hero, physically (financially) weak at first but morally (creatively) strong, persevering until it achieves greatness.

The film's bravura sequence comes not in a superhero fight but in a musical number, a montage sequence narrating Captain America's tour as part of a stage show soliciting investment in war bonds. The sequence begins with Rogers performing clumsily, in an ill-fitting costume; as chorines march in place behind him, Rogers reads his lines from cards taped to the back of his shield: "Series E Defense Bonds. Each one you buy is a bullet in the barrel of your best guy's gun." Sepia tones predominate, except for the vivid reds, whites, and blues of the performers' costumes. As the sequence continues, it foregrounds both the theatricality of the stage show and the sequence's own evocation of 1940s Hollywood. The chorines' song follows on the soundtrack as cuts begin to traverse space, as, for instance, when we see Rogers on a treadmill before a rear-projection screen, beside other soldier-actors. A subsequent close-up of Rogers, anonymous in a movie house, shows his shy amusement at the propaganda short he has just made. While the early part of the sequence uses plain cuts, as the hero's self-confidence grows, the sequence begins to use irises and complex horizontal wipes that evoke the stripes on the American flag. Meanwhile the cinematography begins to resemble that of a Freed Unit musical number, a dance between chorines and gliding boom-mounted cameras. In the intradiegetic show, Captain America stage-punches an actor dressed as Hitler, provoking applause from children. The punch-out scene then repeats as cursive titles identify the cities where the punches land: Buffalo, Milwaukee, Philadelphia, and Chicago, manufacturing cities that prospered due to wartime production. A cut takes us to a newsstand selling stacks of Timely Comics' *Captain America Comics* #1, here presented implicitly as a tie-in to the war bond campaign. The sequence thus gives priority to Captain America the fundraiser, and making Captain America the comic book character into the spin-off. Clean young boys wearing overdetermined 1940s attire read the comic on the streets of a New York with that idealized, Disneyland look. Well-dressed people smile, and only late-model cars gleam on the street; no battered Model Ts or horse-drawn carts recall the decades before this simulacrum of 1941. Moreover, unlike actual newsstands from the era, this one displays not hundreds of different comics, pulps, slicks, and newspapers, but only *Captain America Comics*.

The film's wittiest and most technically striking sequence celebrates the power of a superhero to raise money in a simulated and idealized America.[3] Yet that sequence also positions Rogers as a make-believe soldier, feminized by performing in a stage show while other men fight on the front lines. When the show tours Allied bases in Europe to boost troop morale, Rogers learns that his friend Bucky's division has fallen captive to Hydra behind enemy lines. Rogers asks Colonel Phillips (Tommy Lee Jones) if the army plans a rescue mission, but Phillips dismisses the possibility as too dangerous. Earlier, Phillips had dismissed Rogers, too, as an "experiment," and now he dismisses Rogers as a "chorus girl" unable to understand the strategic risks of such a raid. This prompts Rogers to don some fatigues, a chorus girl's army helmet, and the shield from his stage show; then steal a motorcycle; and finally mount an unauthorized commando raid. Rogers not only finds Bucky but also liberates a prison full of Allied POWs, who help him destroy a Hydra base. Only by defying Colonel Phillips and transcending his status as a fundraising tool does the stage character "Captain America" become the superhero that the film's audience paid to see. The stage costume, with its saturated colors that resemble those of the early comics, appears no more in the film. After this illicit rescue, Rogers gets a new costume in dark colors that code him as serious, as if the studio were rebooting the character with a more gritty and stereotypically masculine look only halfway through the film. The stage-play and comic book soldier becomes real not only by transcending his source media but also by transcending his original purpose. As we will see, the plot of *Wonder Woman* also hinges on its title character's gendered acts of defiance of and transcendence.

"SUPREMA, THE WONDER WOMAN"

Wonder Woman began as a publisher's attempt to respond not to an opportunity but to a crisis. More than six months before Captain America would punch Hitler, on May 8, 1940, the *Chicago Daily News* ran an opinion piece by the children's book writer Sterling North, titled "A National Disgrace (and a Challenge to American Parents)." North attacked comic books as "sex-horror serials" that "depend for their appeal upon mayhem, murder, torture, and abduction—often with a child as the victim" (North). He named no magazines or stories, instead depending on the audience's ignorance and preconceptions about comics. Over the coming year, dozens of American newspapers reprinted the screed to widespread approval (Hajdu 44). Though not the first to attack comics as a medium and an industry, North helped revive public debates about the methods and merits of censoring comics. He called on "parents and teachers throughout America" to "band together to break the 'comic' magazine" (North), and the response gave the industry cause for alarm.

Several larger publishers organized advisory boards of experts to certify the wholesomeness of their comics magazines. Fawcett Comics created an advisory board, as did the relatively prestigious *Parents Magazine*, which had just launched a spin-off comics magazine, *True Comics* (Lepore 186). National Periodical Publications organized its own board, but as David Hajdu notes, the board had little to no involvement in editorial decisions (Hajdu 46). In *More Fun Comics* #72, cover-dated October 1941, National announced its "Editorial Advisory Board," which included professors of education and literature, psychologists, and Gene Tunney, former heavyweight boxing champion and member of the Board of Directors of the Catholic Youth Organization ("A Message to Our Readers"). National would also add William Moulton Marston, a member of the American Psychological Association (Mitchell 42). Marston had a PhD in psychology and a professorship at Tufts University, at least until a scandal over his polyamorous relationship with a graduate student ended his academic career. Marston, however, would soon depart National's board not due to scandal but due to a conflict of interest, for National hired Marston as a writer (Lepore 186). Marston had pitched to M. C. Gaines an idea for a female superhero, a character that promised to expand National's range of characters while also shielding the publisher from the nascent moral panic.

Marston wrote a story called "Suprema, the Wonder Woman," whose lead character combined feminism, a censor-friendly unwillingness to kill, and Marston's obsession with bondage and domination. Accounts differ on the genesis of the character, with a minority of historians asserting, anecdotally, that Marston's wife, Elizabeth Holloway Marston, proposed the idea (Lepore 186–87). Editor Sheldon Mayer nixed the *Suprema* handle but otherwise approved of the character design and story (189), and Marston's renamed Wonder Woman first appeared in *All-Star Comics* #8, cover-dated December 1941. Batman's early history of gunplay had left editor Gaines shy about parental backlash, so Gaines ruled that new characters would not use guns (Lepore 183, 186). Marston's Wonder Woman therefore rejected firearms, which distinguished her from Batman and similar "mystery men" who combined elements of masked-detective pulp fiction with the new superhero genre.[4] Although Superman had never used guns, in his early appearances he had routinely terrorized enemies, dangling them from skyscrapers or throwing them around like rag dolls; Superman bullied the bullies, offering readers a vicarious experience of righteous cruelty that stopped short of grievous bodily harm. In contrast, Wonder Woman subdued opponents without terrorizing them, using her bracelets to deflect bullets, and swinging a magic lasso to capture and interrogate foes. As Lepore argues, Wonder Woman answered critics' objections by eliminating the narrative elements most worrisome to potential censors (200). Marston's Wonder Woman stories offered a fantasy of submission not to superior force but to feminine "love," stories nevertheless filled with bloodless violence and with bondage and domination. As Lepore notes, when Marston wrote the stories, "*Every* woman in the *Wonder Woman* comic books is bound" (233; Lepore's emphasis). Perhaps even more strikingly, Marston broke with industry norms in his shrewd negotiations with National. The Harvard-educated self-promoter negotiated "royalties on sales in perpetuity" and a reversion clause that would transfer all rights to him or his estate if National ceased publishing Wonder Woman stories (Jones 208). I have written elsewhere about Marston's work between academia and comics, as a paid consultant for companies like Gillette ("Folklore" 981); the combination of his prior consulting experience and his role on National's advisory board gave him leverage to negotiate with National, leverage that most writers lacked.

Like Captain America, Wonder Woman presented a combination of elements that other publishers had already tested. Female adventurers in skimpy costumes, like Amazona the Mighty Woman and Sheena, Queen of the Jungle, had already appeared in comics published by Fiction House (Lepore 139, 178). Wonder Woman's flag-themed costume combined red, white, and blue with a golden eagle on her bustier and white stars on her blue skirt, making her legible as part of the wave of patriotic heroes that swept the industry between the Nazi invasion of Poland and the Japanese attack on Pearl Harbor. But Wonder Woman appeared after other patriotic female adventurers, like the Spirit of Old Glory, who first appeared in *Feature Comics* #42, cover-dated March 1941, and Miss Victory, who first appeared in *Captain Fearless* #1, cover-dated August 1941 (Goulart 38). Despite borrowing elements already seen in other comics, Marston's creation proved more successful, likely because of the established dominance of his publisher. Although Wonder Woman books never sold better than National's flagship titles featuring Batman and Superman, they nevertheless sold well enough over the next few months that the publisher gave the character its own magazine.[5] In the summer of 1942, *Wonder Woman* became the first comic book headlined by a female superhero (Lepore 220). That summer National also revealed Marston's identity as the magazine's author in a press release: "'Wonder Woman' was conceived by Dr. Marston to set up a standard among children and young people of strong, free, courageous womanhood; and to combat the idea that women are inferior to men, and to inspire girls to self-confidence and achievement in athletics, occupations and professions monopolized by men" (qtd. in Lepore 220). The new magazine included a feature called "Wonder Women of History," a "four-page centerfold" of biographical comics about famous historical women (220–21). Even so, as Jones notes, a reader survey from the era indicates an audience "90 percent male" (211). And as Lepore points out, the publishers received grateful and admiring letters from men with sexual tastes in bondage and domination (239, 241). Marston died in 1947, and in the years that followed, Wonder Woman comics largely abandoned both his feminist aims and his obsession with women tied up, though not his obsession with the exposed female body. On that readers could rely.

"SOMETIMES SHE LANGUISHES"

To maintain ownership of the character, National/DC continued printing Wonder Woman comics for the next seven decades, and for this reason, the character remained intermittently visible on the margins of American mass culture. Wonder Woman fandom, though small, spans multiple generations and includes prominent female comics artists. The artist Trina Robbins points out that the majority of the letters pages from Wonder Woman comics through the 1960s come from girls (Robbins). But as Ramzi Fawaz notes, the duopoly used letters sections as a marketing tool, using the letters they published to curate the image of the publisher, the magazine, and the title (101–2). The letters section of Wonder Woman comics therefore indicates that National at least wished to convey the impression that girls read the magazine in large numbers. No doubt many girls and women did, for in the early 1970s, nostalgic American feminists began appropriating Wonder Woman's likeness for their own uses, as in 1970, when the Women's Liberation Basement Press in Berkeley put the character on cover of the underground comic *It Aint Me Babe*, alongside Sheena, Olive Oyl, Mary Marvel, Little Lulu, and Elsie the Cow (Lepore 286–87), all unlicensed. In the most famous case of feminist adoption of Wonder Woman as a mascot, *Ms.* magazine arranged with DC Comics to license the image of the superhero for the cover of its first issue and to reprint the first Wonder Woman story inside the magazine (284–86). *Ms.* also arranged to release *Wonder Woman: A "Ms." Book*, which reprinted a collection of Wonder Woman stories that Warner Communications, DC's corporate parent, distributed (286). In 1967, William Dozier, producer of ABC's *Batman* television show (1966–68) had tried but failed to develop a Wonder Woman show, but as Lepore notes, *Ms.* magazine's revival of the character "made ABC take another look" (290). This led ABC to develop a *Wonder Woman* TV series that ran from 1975 to 1979, with Lynda Carter, 1972 Miss World USA, in the title role. Both in the United States and in foreign markets for American television, the *Wonder Woman* TV series increased the character's exposure far beyond the shrinking audience for comic books. The lyrics to the show's theme song address Wonder Woman directly, singing, "Now the world is ready for you," a teleological and aspirational claim directed toward licensors and licensees. *Ms.* magazine convinced ABC of the potential audience for an action-adventure TV show starring a beauty queen in a skimpy outfit, and the theme song told the world that her time had come.

But for most of the next three decades, DC and its parent conglomerates made only halfhearted and mercenary uses of the character. As Wonder Woman's fortieth anniversary neared, DC tried once again to link its property to real-life women. In October 1981, Warner Communications set up the Wonder Woman Foundation, which would offer awards to women over the age of forty "and outstanding women who had exhibited some of the qualities of Wonder Woman" (Klemesrud). DC's publisher, Jenette Kahn, said, "Most women don't begin their work lives until forty because they've been busy raising children" (qtd. in Klemesrud). *Ms.* magazine's enthusiasm for Wonder Woman seems to have suggested to executives at Warner Communications that linking the character to professional women could once again boost the brand's profile. Moreover, the foundation allowed Warner Communications to advertise that brand through an ostensible nonprofit organization that would simultaneously attract donors and function as a tax write-off. The foundation's board included a range of men and women united in wealth and prestige, including William Sarnoff, chairman of Warner Publishing Inc. (Klemesrud).

Yet the foundation's decision to focus on women over forty seems at best half-baked, because of the demographics of comics readers. Throughout the seventies and eighties, the duopoly had focused its marketing energy on retaining a core audience of male readers in their teens and twenties (Lopes

73, 112–13). Furthermore, in 1981, Warner Communications had no mass-market Wonder Woman commodities to cross-promote except for children's animated cartoons like *Super Friends* (ABC, 1973–86). The foundation continued only until 1986 ("76 Years of Wonder Woman"), the same year that saw DC publish only four issues of Wonder Woman comics, a miniseries called *The Legend of Wonder Woman*. Trina Robbins, the first woman to draw the character for an official DC series, worked with writer Kurt Busiek, but as Busiek notes, DC published the series only to keep copyright:

> DC's deal with the Marston Estate was that if DC didn't publish at least four issues of a series headlining Wonder Woman a year (and by "headlining," that meant as the lead character, not in a team book), the rights would revert. When it became clear that the [1987] *Wonder Woman* revival wasn't going to be ready to launch as quickly as DC would like, they needed to publish *something* headlining Wonder Woman to maintain the rights. ("Through the Mail Slot")

This fit with Kahn's policy as president of DC Comics, as discussed in the introduction. Because DC focused not on selling comic books but on licensing copyrighted characters, it should surprise nobody that DC sometimes published only the minimum number of comics necessary to prevent reversion to Marston's heirs. A narrowly identitarian reading of Robbins's work on *The Legend of Wonder Woman* sees it as a historic "first" for the duopoly (though not for independent and underground comics). But a materialist reading instead sees DC's assignment of Trina Robbins to *The Legend of Wonder Woman* as a low-risk staffing decision, made to retain the rights to a character. Robbins, like others at DC, worked for hire, so this first female penciller of Wonder Woman got to experience the same terms of expropriation long enjoyed by male pencillers.

We can most usefully think of DC's expense in publishing *The Legend of Wonder Woman* less as the production of new continuity capital—new stories—and more as the maintenance of continuity capital. As Marx notes:

> Fixed capital entails special maintenance costs. A part of this maintenance is provided by the labour-process itself; fixed capital spoils, if it is not employed in the labour-process [and it] requires also a positive expenditure of labour for its maintenance in good repair. The machinery must be cleaned from time to time. It is a question here of additional labour without which the machinery becomes useless, of merely warding off the noxious influences of the elements. (176)

DC doesn't have to worry about the elements damaging its continuity capital, because even if its roof leaks, the company still holds the copyright on Wonder Woman. But if DC doesn't put this portion of its continuity capital into circulation by publishing comics, then the reversion clause will do worse than let in the rain. Reversion of ownership to another legal person, whether to an heir or to a trust, would mean the catastrophic loss of the "creative rights" that Kahn sought to control. In 2012 Robbins expressed hope that DC would cease publishing Wonder Woman comics, so that "the rights would revert back to the Marston family, where they belong" (Robbins). But to do so would go against decades of company strategy, instituted in the 1940s, then intensified by Jenette Kahn.

Although DC Comics and its licensees have largely determined the path of Wonder Woman in and out of public awareness, other groups have made their own uses of the character. Some feminists explicitly challenged *Ms.* magazine's use of Wonder Woman. In 1975 the Redstockings, a radical leftist feminist group, published a critique of *Ms.* in the *Berkeley Barb*, which took the magazine to task for its use of the superhero, among other things. Gabrielle Schang noted that although *Ms.* refuses "blatantly sexist ads" and "ads for cosmetic and fashion products," the magazine has "no moral problem accepting public relations and job recruitment ads for large corporations" (9). The liberal-feminist *Ms.* "owes its existence to the highest ranks of corporate America" (9). So, obviously, does the surge in Wonder Woman's popularity in 2016 and 2017. Despite the appropriation of the character by self-styled feminists in the 2010s—like the thousands of women who changed their Facebook profile images to images of Wonder Woman surrounding the release of the film—we would do well to remember an observation Eileen Meehan made, occasioned by the 1989 *Batman* film: "For much of American culture, corporate imperatives operate as the primary constraints shaping the narratives and iconography of the text as well as the manufacture and licensing of the intertextual materials necessary for a 'mania' to sweep the country" (71). Time Warner had good long-term success with its Superman and Batman movie franchises, but *Catwoman* (Pitof, 2004) and *Green Lantern* (Martin Campbell, 2011), also based on DC characters from the 1940s, had flopped. So before DC and Warner Bros. took a chance on letting Wonder Woman headline a film, they first merged their proven Superman and Batman film franchises into a larger, shared franchise in *Batman v Superman: Dawn of Justice* (Zack Snyder, 2016) and then introduced Wonder Woman in the final third of that film. Only then did the companies invest in building a mania for a stand-alone Wonder Woman film.

By the time *Wonder Woman* appeared in 2017, the film had spent more than two decades in what Hollywood producers call development hell. As early as 1996, Time Warner subsidiary *Entertainment Weekly* reported that Warner Bros. had Ivan Reitman lined up to "produce and possibly direct" a Wonder Woman feature (Burr), but this led nowhere. In 1999, *Variety* reported the attachment of a screenwriter to the project (Fleming, "Hoffman"), but in January 2001, *Variety* reported the attachment of a different screenwriter (Lyons). In April 2001, the *Washington Post* ran a profile on Phil Jimenez, one of the few gay artists at the duopoly, who drew Wonder Woman for DC, and this profile repeats Hollywood "gossip" about castings in a supposed Wonder Woman film: Mariah Carey, Sandra Bullock, and Catherine Zeta-Jones (Stuever). But because the article focused on Jimenez rather than on Wonder Woman, and because it appeared in a venue not owned by Time Warner, it minced no words about the character's marginality:

> Most of the world has forgotten about Wonder Woman. Sixty years ago, she stirred imaginations and helped vanquish Hitler. In a trade magazine called *Wizard*, on a list of the 100 top-selling comic books, Wonder Woman ranks 86th this month. Still, we'd know her if we saw her. This is what happens to spent icons. They become easily recognizable Halloween costumes with no context, aging reference points to outdated ideas that may have once been a metaphor for something—which was what, in her case? Feminism? Love? Sacrifice? (Stuever)

The author of the profile interviews Jenette Kahn, who offers a mixture of corporate self-critique and corporate self-congratulation, and straight promotion: "[Wonder Woman] has transcended 40 years of bad scripts, after all. . . . She's the first feminist in popular fiction. She's had a lot of high-profile artists and writers working on her over the years, and she has defied many of their abilities. Sometimes she languishes" (qtd. in Stuever). Kahn reifies the character, treating it as a person that has an existence that transcends the texts in which it appears. Kahn also continues DC's practice of focusing strategically on the character rather than on artists or particular texts. Stuever notes Kahn's interested position here as holder of this "important trademark," as well as the contract that obliges DC to publish Wonder Woman comics on pain of the character rights reverting to Marston's estate. But Kahn refuses to discuss the contract and rejects any instrumental reading of the company's relationship to the character: "That's certainly not how we think of it, as a legal obligation. . . . I feel it's an honor" (qtd. in Stuever). DC's history, both before and during

Kahn's tenure, suggests we should remain skeptical about any of Kahn's statements about how the Warner subsidiary "thinks" or "feels" about a character; her strategy of treating DC as a license farm contradicts her sentimental account. Because Kahn only ran DC and not the deeper-pocketed divisions of the conglomerate, she could not green-light a new TV series or a Wonder Woman movie, so despite DC's supposed "honor" at holding the rights to the character, it did not appear on screens for almost forty years.

But once Time Warner committed to introducing the character to its DC cinematic franchise, then the conglomerate's subsidiaries got to work building both a Wonder Woman film and a mania to see it. In January 2014, *Variety* announced that the Israeli actress Gal Gadot had signed a three-film contract to play the character (Kroll, "Wonder Woman"). Yet in this age of interconnected franchise films, *Variety* read even this three-film deal as a sign of caution on the studio's part, "since the studio still doesn't know how [audiences] will react to Wonder Woman in the untitled Batman-Superman movie" (Kroll, "Wonder Woman"). Both official promotion and journalistic reporting on the film routinely noted both Gadot's win of the 2004 Miss Israel beauty pageant as well as her service in the Israeli Defense Force (IDF), stressing the actor's supposedly ideal combination of beauty and martial strength. Some, however, saw these as points of dubious merit, if not demerit, for not only did the casting of a second consecutive beauty queen reinforce normative Western standards regarding female bodies, but Gadot's two-year service in the Israeli military made her complicit in that state's occupation and ongoing colonization of Palestine. During the 2014 Israel-Gaza War, Gadot had posted a message on both Twitter and Facebook: "I am sending my love and prayers to my fellow Israeli citizens. Especially to all the boys and girls who are risking their lives protecting my country against the horrific acts conducted by Hamas, who are hiding like cowards behind women and children" (qtd. in Ziv). In the fighting, Hamas and other Gazan combatants killed seventy-two Israelis, sixty-six of them soldiers, while the IDF killed over two thousand Gazans, the majority civilians. Gadot's concern therefore seems at best lopsided. Gadot had served in the IDF during Israel's 2006 invasion of Lebanon, and Lebanon banned *Wonder Woman* over her starring role (Moore, "'Wonder Woman' Faces a Ban"). Jordan could not legally ban the film, but Salam Al-Mahadin writes that Jordanians understood Gadot "as an enthusiastic soldier in an occupation army, a positionality that transcended the supposed feminism of her superheroine character, rendering it almost impossible to separate the actor from the film" (248). Others responded to Gadot's endorsement of the IDF by redoubling their commitment to the State of Israel, to Wonder Woman, or both. A cinema in Israel changed its name to Gal Cinema to honor the veteran (Moore, "'Wonder Woman' Star Gal Gadot"). Each set of responses to Gadot's speech made news, giving free publicity to Time Warner's revived brand.

"THE 'SHE' BECAME 'WE'"

In 2016 Time Warner arranged for a powerful partner to help engineer a mania for Wonder Woman: the United Nations. DC Entertainment first contacted the UN's Department of Public Information to develop a project that would celebrate the character's seventy-fifth anniversary (Ross), and then in the spring of 2015, they began planning the promotion (Aizenman). In October 2016, a few months after the release of *Batman v Superman: Dawn of Justice*, DC and the United Nations announced that Wonder Woman would serve as Honorary Ambassador for the Empowerment of Women and Girls. DC and Warner Bros. also announced a special Wonder Woman comic tied to the campaign, to appear in all six official languages of the United Nations. The UN uses only fictional characters as honorary ambassadors (Kennedy). Few trademarked characters had received such a seeming honor. The red Angry Bird had served as the "Ambassador of Green" ("UN Secretary-General Appoints Red"), as had Disney's version of Tinkerbell, and Disney's version of Winnie the Pooh had served as "Ambassador of Friendship" (*Reconsider*). But as in licensing revenues, so in UN cross-promotion: Time Warner imitated Disney's methods, but with less success.

On October 21, the New York headquarters of the UN hosted a public appearance by representatives of the brand. This promotional detachment included Gal Gadot and Lynda Carter; Patty Jenkins, director of *Wonder Woman*; and Diane Nelson, executive vice president of global brand management for Warner Bros. Entertainment. Time Warner personnel gave out Wonder Woman T-shirts to the audience (Puglise), and in a ceremony in the Economic and Social Council chamber, Nelson addressed an audience of both UN staff and Time Warner employees, speaking of events planned for the promotional collaboration "over the course of the next year" (Ross). Carter also addressed the crowd:

> In some magical and mystical way, there lies within each of us Wonder Woman. . . . She is real. She lives and she breathes. I know this because she lives in me, and she lives in the stories that these women tell me, day in and day out. . . . This miracle of an idea that came from a forty-eight-year-old woman named Elizabeth started to have an influence in some girls' and women's lives. That was when Wonder Woman became flesh. This idea became a reality, and the "she" became "we." (qtd. in Coggan)

Through explicitly magical thinking, Carter tries to conjure a brand into the illusion of life. She attributes the creation of Wonder Woman not to William Moulton Marston or even to a collaboration between Marston and his wife, Elizabeth Holloway Marston, but to Elizabeth alone, which fits the theme of the event but not the historical record. After her address, Carter and Gadot posed before backdrops emblazoned with images of Wonder Woman and DC's "Wonder Woman 75" logo, and a new "modestly garbed version" of the character specially designed for the Honorary Ambassador role (Aizenman). This medium-shot portrait shows Wonder Woman in an outfit that shows no cleavage, with a cloak that that covers her shoulders; she holds a shield that covers still more of her. This costume had another UN-friendly feature: it eliminates American iconography like the eagle on her chest and the white stars on the blue field of her skirt or shorts.

During the ceremony, some fifty UN staff rose and silently turned their backs toward the stage in protest, while others carried placards rejecting the promotional campaign. Their online petition noted that Wonder Woman belongs to DC Comics, "a for-profit entertainment corporation" (*Reconsider*). Moreover, despite the makeover of the heroine's costume, decades of pinup-style images of the character led the petitioners to reject "a large breasted, white woman of impossible proportions, scantily clad in a shimmery, thigh-baring body suit with an American flag motif and knee high boots" as symbol for the struggle for female emancipation and equality (*Reconsider*). Former UN staffer Shazia Z. Rafi complained that the organization's choice of a "muscled version of a Barbie" as its means of "saying 'This is what represents gender equality' . . . [is] culturally insensitive. It's insulting" (qtd. in Kennedy). Other commentators noted that the announcement of the ambassadorship followed close on the news of the UN's choice of António Guterres as its ninth secretary-general, despite a yearlong campaign by activists to install a female secretary-general and the rejection of seven female candidates for the position, which no woman has yet held (Sengupta). New York University professor of global affairs Anne Marie Goetz called the timing of the Wonder Woman announcement "an insult": "It's frivolous, it's fatuous, and it reduces an extremely serious human rights problem experienced by half of the world to a cartoon" (qtd. in Aizenman). The petition and protests worked: on December 13, 2016, less than two months into the ambassadorship, the UN announced the end of Wonder Woman's role (Ross). A DC spokeswoman optimistically told the *New York Times*, "Wonder Woman stands for peace, justice and equality, and for seventy-five years she has been a motivating force for many and will continue to be long after the conclusion of her

U.N. honorary ambassadorship" (qtd. in McCann). Even in defeat, DC's public relations stressed the longevity of the character the company had long made a low priority, and the feminist value of a character it had long sexualized for a core audience of teenage boys and young men.

Just three days after the United Nations prematurely terminated Wonder Woman's ambassadorship, *Time* magazine published online an essay titled "Wonder Woman Breaks Through," in which Eliana Dockterman offers a teleological argument for "why we need Wonder Woman now" (100).[6] The piece offers a textbook example of the power of a media conglomerate to cross-promote its own brands via ostensible news outlets. Dockterman styles the film as a major development in the history of cinema, if not world culture. She notes that Paul Feig, George Miller, and Joss Whedon "all failed to bring the Amazonian princess to the big screen," but where men failed, "a woman," Patty Jenkins, has "finally" made the movie (101), as if Jenkins had crowdfunded the film rather than taking a job. Jenkins ended up attached to the project after Marvel Studios dismissed her from the sequel to *Thor*, and after Warner Bros. dismissed Michelle MacLaren, the first female director that the studio had attached to direct the Wonder Woman movie (Sperling 42). Dockterman proposes that *Wonder Woman* "could change the kinds of role models we find at the movies" (101). This statement holds vaguely true of any film, but in this case, it suggests that nobody had ever made an action melodrama with a female protagonist. This reasoning only works if we forget DC's earlier *Supergirl* (Jeannot Szwarc, 1984) and *Catwoman* (Pitof, 2004), as well as other comic book superheroine movies like *Tank Girl* (Rachel Talalay, 1995), *Barb Wire* (David Hogan, 1996), and *Elektra* (Rob Bowman, 2005). Furthermore, we have to forget about films as varied as *The Red Detachment of Women* (Xie Jin, 1961), *Come Drink with Me* (King Hu, 1966), *Coffy* (Jack Hill, 1973), *Lady Snowblood* (Toshiya Fujita, 1973), *Aliens* (James Cameron, 1986), and *Heroic Trio* (Johnny To, 1993), as well as franchises like Resident Evil (2002–16), Tomb Raider (2001–18), and the Hunger Games (2012–15).[7] Dockterman also reifies the film's title character: "In 1972, Wonder Woman experienced a resurgence when Gloria Steinem put her on the first cover of the feminist magazine *Ms*. . . . A few years later, she got a TV series starring Lynda Carter" (101). Fannish syntax frames the character as the grammatical subject of both sentences, erasing the agency of commercial actors entering into licensor-licensee transactions. Dockterman makes no mention of the web of ownership that connected *Time*, DC Comics, and Warner Bros. under the corporate umbrella of Time Warner, or the interest that all three share in ginning up a mania like that for *Batman* in 1989. But such an omission will surprise no one familiar with this conglomerate's history of using news subsidiaries to cross-promote its franchises.

In preparation for the film's release, DC Comics issued a press release inaugurating an ersatz holiday, "Wonder Woman Day," to coincide with the film's opening on June 3 ("Holy Hera!").[8] Here again, Time Warner imitates its rival's successful model. Fans of the *Star Wars* films and franchise have for years called the fourth of May "May the Fourth," hailing each other, "May the Fourth be with you," in loving parody of the franchise's catchphrase, "May the Force be with you."[9] For "Wonder Woman Day," Time Warner organized

> an array of retail partners including, Barnes & Noble, Books-A-Million, Walmart, Costco and Amazon for exclusive in-store and digital promotions to create the ultimate "Wonder Woman Day" experience. Cross-divisional activations will also include Warner Bros. Interactive Entertainment and Warner Bros. Consumer Products, alongside key partners including Six Flags Theme Parks, to further spotlight the groundbreaking DC Super Hero. . . . Fans can download the official "Wonder Woman Day" activity kit, including comic book activity sheets, coloring pages, trivia, and games. . . . Fans can journey through Wonder Woman's illustrious history and share their favorite Super Hero moments, social media activations on Snapchat, Facebook and Instagram. ("DC Celebrates Wonder Woman Day")

Commercial media producers have long recruited fans as unpaid workers on behalf of their trademarked properties, and here DC invites them to download, journey, share, and most of all, buy. Wonder Woman, brand as person, becomes an occasion for an immersive "experience" of purchasing as promotion, a *Gesamtbrandwerk*.

Time Warner subsidiary *Entertainment Weekly* also played a part in promoting *Wonder Woman*, releasing a special stand-alone magazine, *The Ultimate Guide to Wonder Woman*. In the summer of 2017, you could find this publication at every airport shop from Shanghai to Louisville. The guide bore no advertisements, because its ninety-six pages already served as advertising for Time Warner properties. Its cover bears a large image of Gal Gadot and a smaller inset of Lynda Carter, both in costume, reaching for potential fans across generations. Throughout, its contributors plug Warner Bros.' *Justice League* (Zack Snyder, 2017), which was scheduled for release in November and would unite Wonder Woman, Batman, and Superman with DC's Aquaman, Cyborg, and the Flash. The guide opens with an essay called "The One & Only Wonder Woman," a primer on the character's powers and media history. Although the essay's title emphasizes singleness, and although it calls the character "the *singular* icon for half the population" (Breznican 4; my emphasis), the art in this two-page spread shows not one but four different renderings of the character, from four different media: television (Lynda Carter as *Wonder Woman*), animation (*Super Friends*), comics (a painting by Alex Ross), and film (Gal Gadot astride a horse) (4–5). Here we see the logic of character as brand, where singularity exists only through multiplicity. The essay emphasizes the way this brand functions as a site of production of multiple texts and multiple commodities, across decades.

> No matter what the medium—the early dynamic drawings by artist H. G. Peter, the sunny fearlessness of Lynda Carter on the 1970s TV series, or the quiet determination of Gal Gadot, the strong, stunning actress who stars in director Patty Jenkins's new movie—Wonder Woman's power can't be denied. It leaps off the page, radiates from the screen, and offers much-needed hope to us all. (5)

Despite the *Ultimate Guide's* obvious goal of promoting the new film, its writers continually stress the dizzying variety of products bearing Wonder Woman's likeness: bobbleheads, handbags, wristwatches, computer games, coloring books, roller-coasters, and so on. A spread of Wonder Woman merchandise includes both prices and the names of vendors (88–89). The guide's latter third devotes itself to nostalgia for the 1970s *Wonder Woman* TV show and DC Comics, presenting a staggeringly detailed seven-page timeline that tracks the character across various media. In an entry for 1986, the timeline even reminds us how Time Warner, and not some other studio, managed to deliver the 2017 *Wonder Woman* film: "Artist Trina Robbins and writer Kurt Busiek whip up *The Legend of Wonder Woman*, a four-issue tribute to the Marston-Peter era—and a contractual stopgap so that DC can keep its rights to the character" (Breznican 80). In its mania to include all things Wonder Woman, the guide blurts the truth about the exploitative logic that underlies more than seven decades of the supposed icon.

"SHE MUST NEVER KNOW THE TRUTH ABOUT WHAT SHE IS"

Like the imitative comics of the early 1940s, the 2017 *Wonder Woman* film borrows readily from its successful rival's earlier work, *Captain America: The First Avenger*, and also from another film in the DC film franchise, *Man of Steel* (Zack Snyder, 2013). Like *Captain America: The First Avenger*, *Wonder Woman* consists of a present-day frame story surrounding a feature-length flashback to a world war. Also like *Captain America*, the title character develops a romance with an ordinary human military officer of the opposite sex, but a suicidal mission to stop a bomber separates them, giving the title character occasion for grief and nostalgia. Both films have German villains who execute underlings at any excuse, and both films feature climactic battles to prevent experimental, retrofuturist aircraft from delivering weapons of mass destruction to Allied cities, followed by victory scenes set in London. But *Wonder Woman*, like a bad paraphrase, also substitutes important elements so as to avoid easy accusations of copying. Although both characters had their origins in World War II, *Wonder Woman* revises its setting to World War I. Although both characters have long incorporated elements of the American flag in their costumes, *Wonder Woman* eliminates them; the heroine's blue skirt bears no stars that movie viewers might take as poaching on Marvel Studios' three successful Captain America films. Even the casting call worked to distinguish the Warner Bros. film, asking for women "tall, brunette, athletic and exotic" (Kroll, "New Actresses Test"). The word *exotic* literally means foreign, not American, but when used to describe women, it hints at Orientalism or a one-drop touch of the nonwhite, which contrasts strongly with the blond, WASPish (and paradoxically "Aryan"-looking) Chris Evans who plays Captain America.

Wonder Woman imagines World War I as the work of Ares, the Greek god, and positions Diana, the Wonder Woman of the title, as the nemesis who must defeat Ares to save the world. Early scenes show us Diana as a child, determined to learn to fight despite the opposition of her mother, Hippolyta, queen of the Amazons. Little Diana aspires to her mother's kind of martial glory, but the queen offers her only a cautionary bedtime story about Diana's mysterious origin after Ares's massacre of the other gods. The queen anxiously tells one of her lieutenants, "[Diana] must never know the truth about what she is, or how she came to be." But as Diana grows, she begins to train secretly in the arts of war. When an American aviator, Steve Trevor, crashes on the supernaturally hidden island of Themyscira, the Imperial German Navy pursues him ashore. Only then does the isolated, all-female society allow Diana abroad to participate in the war engulfing Europe. In its early scenes, the film offers only ambiguous hints about Diana's powers; not until the film's midpoint do we begin to see the extent of her superhuman speed, strength, and invulnerability. When she leaves Themyscira, she takes with her a shield, a magic lasso that compels those bound to tell the truth, and a legendary sword known as the "God-Killer," which she believes will enable her to slay Ares. Fish-out-of-water comedy and sanitized, PG-13 trench warfare ensue.

From *The First Avenger*, the film borrows the technique of delaying its main character's entry into combat, then staging that entry as a humanitarian mutiny. Moreover, *Wonder Woman* stages this mutiny at roughly the same point in its running time. Halfway through the film, Diana learns of civilians trapped and suffering on the far side of the disputed territory between Allied and German trenches, and amid the whine and thump of artillery fire, she demands that her commando team intervene. Steve Trevor (Chris Pine), the team's nominal leader, says that they have neither the time nor the power. "This is no-man's land," declares Trevor. "It means no *man* can cross it." Script and acting make sure we grasp the feminist subtext of the scene. Diana then defies Trevor, sheds her cloak, and goes over the top; swelling symphonic music and a series of close-ups of Diana's shield and bracelets heighten the scene's effect. Soon the rest of the soldiers follow. In the battle sequence that follows, the daylit setting, speed ramping, counterfactual tracer bullets, and virtual dirt splattered on the camera lens distract us from the scene's structural similarity to the homologous mutiny halfway through *The First Avenger*, where Steve Rogers shows a different set of Germans what a chorus girl can do.

In the third act, Diana defeats and kills the German officer that both she and the audience have come suspect as the disguised Ares. After some brawling, she captures him in her lasso; while he lies helpless, she declares, "I hereby complete the mission of the Amazons, by ridding this world of you," then runs him through with her sword. The scene breaks with the norms of PG-13 superhero movies by having its title character deliberately kill a helpless foe, and it renders hollow DC's assertions that Wonder Woman "stands for peace." And, to Diana's surprise, the war does not end. Instead British minister Sir Patrick (David Thewlis) suddenly appears, revealing himself as the disguised Ares. He tells Diana the secret of her origin: Zeus fathered her on Hippolyta, making Ares and Diana siblings. With his open palm, Ares effortlessly destroys Diana's sword.

DIANA: The God-Killer!
SIR PATRICK: My dear child, that is not the God-Killer. You are. Only a god can kill another god. Zeus left the child he had with the queen of the Amazons as a weapon to use against me.
DIANA: No. You liar! [Here Diana ropes him with her magic lasso of truth.] I compel you to tell me the truth!
SIR PATRICK: I am.... I am not the god of war, Diana, I am the god of truth.

Diana, like the audience, has mistaken the sword for its namesake. Yet after Steve Trevor sacrifices himself to destroy a bomber filled with poison gas destined for Allied cities, Diana accepts her instrumental destiny just long enough to defeat Ares. Once again, she kills deliberately, and even signals her intention: "Goodbye, brother." Diana's willingness to kill not one but two of her opponents distinguishes the big-screen version of Wonder Woman, making the character significantly more violent than the version that Marston wrote or that audiences might remember from the 1970s *Wonder Woman* TV show. As Warner Bros. did with its gangster films of the 1930s and 1940s, the studio now does with its superhero films: they tell relatively dark and grim stories to distinguish themselves from those of the competing studio.

Diana's confrontations with Ares actually retread scenes from a precursor in the DC film franchise, *Man of Steel*. At the end of that film, Superman deliberately kills General Zod, in a violation of audience expectation that the hero does not kill. But *Wonder Woman* also stages an inversion of Superman's first significant interaction with General Zod. As discussed in chapter 1, Zod holds Superman captive. While Superman lies bound and sedated, Zod appears in something like a dream sequence, a high-tech interrogation that projects both Zod and Superman into a simulacrum of Smallville. In that simulacrum, Zod reveals his plan to reverse terraform the Earth, converting it into another Krypton, thereby exterminating humanity. Blast waves rake the land, and Superman finds himself sucked down into a morass of human skulls. In *Wonder Woman*, when Diana first meets Ares, she lassos him, reversing the positions of captor and captive. From Ares's hand crackles wizardly lightning, and as he grasps the lasso, Diana begins to have visions. Ares then narrates a montage of his fall from Olympus and his engineering of the Great War. He reveals that he seeks to cause humans to exterminate themselves:

> Mankind stole this world from us. They ruined it day by day, and I, the only one wise to see it, was left too weak to stop them.... When you first arrived, I was going to crush you, but I knew if only you could see what the other gods could not, then you would join me, and with our powers combined, we could finally end all the pain, all the suffering, the destruction they bring, and we could return this world to the paradise it was before them. Forever.

Although Ares's monologue reads as a boilerplate "We are not so different" recruitment pitch from Hollywood villain to hero, the images that play over this monologue recapitulate and invert the analogous scene from *Man of Steel*. There, General Zod seeks Superman's cooperation in the genocide of humanity; with the help of the genetic Codex stored in Superman's cells, Zod seeks the resurrection of the Kryptonian race on Earth. In that montage,

Zod shows Superman images of an idyllic Kansas present laid waste by Kryptonian machines. In *Wonder Woman*, by contrast, the Great War present already looks apocalyptic, a muddy landscape of craters and trees denuded by constant shelling, but as Ares narrates, the trees return to bloom, and the birds begin to sing. Could this inversion mean anything, apart from signifying Warner Bros.' willingness to recycle scenes that worked well enough the last time it launched a franchise?

I read this scene as an allegory of Time Warner's self-congratulation at reviving Wonder Woman as a brand for mass audiences. Between the 1970s and the late 2010s, Wonder Woman lay in a no-man's land between, on the one hand, the conglomerate's heavy investments in its live-action Superman and Batman franchises, and, on the other, the apocalyptic possibility of Wonder Woman's reversion to the Marston estate. In the film, Queen Hippolyta's unwillingness to let Diana learn to fight, coupled with the film's teasing hints of Diana's power, suggests a deliberate withholding, like a conglomerate sitting on a potentially huge opportunity, unwilling to risk investing it or to rope in partners like the United Nations to help with the promotion. Ares shows Diana blackened earth, skeletal trees, and muddy trenches; world-historical destruction has already come to pass because Diana did not fight sooner, because Warner Bros. did not make a Wonder Woman film sooner. Therefore the narrative of *Wonder Woman* does not hinge on the classical defense of the proprietary character, as in *Man of Steel*. Nobody tries to copy or decode Wonder Woman's powers because the Marston estate never sued Warner Bros. Instead, as Jenette Kahn would put it, Wonder Woman had *languished*, hidden on an island, known only to comic book nerds and nostalgic fans of 1970s TV. But once Diana leaves for the wider world—that is, once Time Warner develops a blockbuster, investing Wonder Woman with the aegis of its many subsidiaries—only then do we see the extent of her potential, both fictional and financial. The character not only fulfills its destiny but exceeds it, destroying a god empty-handed, and earning box office receipts to challenge, though not to kill, the Walt Disney Company.

DIVERSIFYING THE PORTFOLIO

These two films, like the histories of the characters that headline them, parallel each other in ways that reveal the underlying industrial logic that they share. Much as Timely Comics published Captain America to cash in on rising anti-Nazi sentiment, National published Wonder Woman as a means to differentiate its product line, placate censors, and cash in on the popularity of patriotic heroes like the Shield and Captain America. In their blockbuster films, both Captain America and Wonder Woman fulfill their missions, yet those films also fulfill their commercial missions within their respective franchises. *The First Avenger* introduced a central character to Marvel's *Avengers* franchise and spawned two *Captain America* sequels, each grossing more than the last, and each further integrating Cap into the Marvel Cinematic Universe. *Wonder Woman* proved a "megahit," grossing over $800 million worldwide, leading to a sequel. Like Captain America, the protagonist of *Wonder Woman* shows her ability to transcend her instrumental function even as she fulfills it. To compete with Disney, Time Warner fielded its own shield-carrying super-soldier, then integrated that super-soldier into its larger cinematic franchise. Had DC Comics allowed the rights to revert to the Marston estate, that cinematic franchise would look very different. But had the Kirbys' suit against Disney gone to the Supreme Court, this whole branch of the American media industry might look different, for the basis of its mode of production might have changed.

That mode of production has proved immensely profitable to investors. Marvel's use of Captain America as collateral enabled it to launch the independent film production that made the company's name famous worldwide; on the streets of Shanghai, I used to pass adults and children, men and women—all citizens of a nominally communist state—wearing shirts bearing the Marvel logo and characters codesigned or drawn by Jack Kirby. Marvel's former CEO Ike Perlmutter, who wrested the company from the control of investors Carl Icahn and Ron Perelman, owned 37 percent of Marvel's stock when Disney purchased the company in 2009, and in that transaction, Perlmutter alone received "about $880 million in cash and $590 million in Disney stock" (Bond). Steven Mnuchin, second-generation Goldman Sachs executive and United States secretary of the treasury under the Trump administration, made an undisclosed amount from serving as executive producer of *Wonder Woman*. Some commentators noted the irony of a Trump nominee producing an ostensibly feminist film, but we can safely assume that Mnuchin invests in movies not to make superhero stories or feminist propaganda but to make more money. Mnuchin's résumé includes service on the board of a bank purchased and reorganized in 2008 as a "foreclosure machine,":

> It was unusual for unregulated private investors to buy it instead of a bank holding company . . . and only possible because the federal government had eased regulations on such transactions. The buyers renamed the bank OneWest

and worked out a loss-share agreement with the FDIC so the agency would partially reimburse the bank for handling foreclosures. (Kutner)

The investors behind OneWest then profited from foreclosures caused by the speculative housing bubble that the financial class had created. In 2015 they sold the bank for an estimated $1.5 billion (Ydstie). Wherever capital can find ways to expand, we find people like Mnuchin, arranging new ways to skim wealth from people unlucky enough to have to work for it. As a film producer, Mnuchin arranged for Bill Gates and the Koch brothers to invest in the production company RatPac-Dune Entertainment, which funded both *Wonder Woman* and other films on the Warner production slate (Siegel).

The cartoonish, far-right Koch brothers—sons of an oil baron who helped found the John Birch Society—seem like villains in a left-liberal superhero movie. The *Hollywood Reporter*'s source for the story on RatPac-Dune even reassured readers that the Kochs had only invested in the company "to make money" (Siegel). But as investors, they share a common purpose with the centrist, liberal philanthropist Gates: to extract surplus value from workers who must sell their labor. To capital, it matters not whether those workers design software or draw comics, whether they sew Wonder Woman backpacks in Dhaka or gaff sets for Marvel Studios in Atlanta. Although the details of their personal or political styles seem to distinguish them, Gates, the Kochs, Perlmutter, and Mnuchin all occupy a class position that unites them as owners of the means of production. Thanks to timely court settlements and ash-can editions of comic books, that means of production still includes comic book characters created as works made for hire more than eighty years ago.

CHAPTER FOUR

THE ADULT TURN
Reproduction of the Brand

In 2016 and 2017, studios began to diversify duopoly film offerings by making movies that addressed themselves more to adults, featuring protagonists with grown-up personal problems rarely seen in the duopoly films of the 2000s. These adult-facing films still warn of the evils of copying a hero's superpowers, rehearsing the familiar managerial obsession, but these films also tell stories of protagonists who have to find work, deal with chronic illness, care for elders, and, most importantly, care for children. Furthermore, they foreground elements designed to trigger nostalgia in audiences, thereby creating multigenerational modes of address hitherto unseen in duopoly films. In this chapter, I therefore look less at the production histories of specific films and more at the position of those films within their larger franchises, explaining their adult turn in light of marketing literature on the commercial rhetoric and managerial uses of nostalgia.

If we think in terms of maturation, 2008 arguably marked the year when the duopoly blockbuster came of age. A decade had passed since *Blade* legitimized Marvel characters to movie producers. In 2008, Warner Bros. released *The Dark Knight* (Christopher Nolan) to unprecedented acclaim and equally unprecedented box office success, while Marvel Studios began producing and releasing its own films, with *Iron Man* (Jon Favreau) marking the beginning of Marvel's rise to Hollywood dominance. But if 2008 marks the year of the duopoly film's maturation, then 2016 marks the year of its saturation, the point at which a new version of the form begins to precipitate: a duopoly blockbuster still connected to and serving the larger cinematic brand, but aimed at adults. We can read these films as theatrical analogues of adult-oriented duopoly TV shows like *Arrow* (The CW, 2012–20), *Gotham* (Fox, 2014–19), *Daredevil*

(Netflix, 2015–18), and *Jessica Jones* (Netflix, 2015–19), which extended DC and Marvel range brands in new ways.

This chapter looks at three films: Marvel Studios' PG-13 *Ant-Man* (Peyton Reed, 2015), Warner Bros.' PG-13 *Suicide Squad* (David Ayer, 2016), and 20th Century Fox's R-rated *Logan* (James Mangold, 2017). All three present melodramas centered on plots to capture and abuse proprietary superpowers, but all three extend these melodramas into new territory, both narrative and demographic, as they suture the viewer into the position not of an angst-ridden youth but of a troubled and nostalgic adult.

Since at least 2012's *Dark Knight Rises*, duopoly films have increasingly addressed the problems of aging and the intergenerational transfer of knowledge, power, and virtue. In 2015, teenagers who had queued up for the first *X-Men* film in the summer of 2000 found themselves well into adulthood, and we began to see superhero films with heroes written increasingly for middle-aged (though still implicitly white and male) viewers nostalgic for their own youth at the multiplex or in front of the DVD player. With the Marvel Cinematic Universe, Marvel Studios held the largest share of the theatrical market, but both the studio and its parent Disney depend on their family-friendly brand identity, so it comes as little surprise that competitor Fox should try to establish itself in the adult market niche with the R-rated *Deadpool* (Tim Miller, 2016). Marvel Studios' dominant position no doubt prompted Fox, then not yet a Disney subsidiary, to take a chance. *Deadpool* cost only $58 million, a tiny budget for this genre, but it took in a staggering $783 million in its worldwide theatrical run and did so despite Beijing's refusal of distribution in the world's second theatrical largest. *Deadpool* actively subverted and mocked the norms of its own mode of production, yet at the box office, it proved the most profitable superhero movie anyone had ever made. The success of *Deadpool* shaped Fox's *Logan* (James Mangold, 2017) the following year. Yet despite their novel concern for the social and biological realities of adulthood, *Logan*, *Ant-Man*, and *Suicide Squad* all continue the duopoly film's larger pedagogical project of linking copying with the arrival of dystopias and apocalypses.

ANT-MAN: REPAIRING THE FAMILY

Despite starring a largely forgotten Marvel Comics character, *Ant-Man* distinguished itself from the run of duopoly films through its sense of humor and by making its protagonist a father. Where many superhero films force young heroes to choose between various father figures, *Ant-Man* instead forces Scott Lang (Paul Rudd) to transform himself into a good father, and the film thus expands both the storytelling range and the demographic appeal of the Marvel Cinematic Universe. We meet Lang in San Quentin State Prison on the last day of his three-year sentence for grand larceny; this principled technical wizard hacked into the security system of his dishonest employers to return money that they had bilked from customers. Yet despite his background in electrical engineering, Lang finds that his criminal record prevents him from finding a job in the Bay Area's tech sector, and because Lang cannot pay child support, his ex forbids him to visit their daughter. When Lang loses a hard-won fast-food job for lying about his criminal record, he resorts to burglary, only to find himself recruited by a rich and aging inventor, Dr. Hank Pym (Michael Douglas). Decades ago, Pym invented a suit that allows its wearer to shrink, but he kept the invention secret; now Pym wants Lang to use the suit to sabotage the plans of an unscrupulous executive at Pym Technologies, who has duplicated the suit to sell as a weapon. *Ant-Man* folds two family dramas into one film about safeguarding superhero IP, casting its protagonist in dual positions as both literal father and metaphorical son-in-law. As Lang helps Pym protect his invention, Lang also helps Pym mend relations with Pym's adult daughter, Hope van Dyne (Evangeline Lily). At the film's end, Lang and Van Dyne form a new couple, and Lang's work protecting Pym's invention enables him to pay the child support that lets him return to his daughter's life.

Yet while the film's focus on two interconnected family dramas distinguishes it from other duopoly films, its stridency about the defense of monopolies on superhero trade secrets sees and raises the genre's usual bets. The film cold-opens with a flashback to 1989, where we find a younger Pym working for SHIELD, Marvel's fictional national security agency. Pym confronts his superiors over their secret attempts to duplicate the shrinking technology that he has used in covert operations on SHIELD's behalf. Less than a minute into the film, Michael Douglas, his face digitally smoothed almost thirty years, accuses SHIELD of making a "poor attempt to replicate my work" and trying "to steal my research." Pym resigns, vowing, "As long as I'm alive, nobody will ever get that formula!" When we next see Pym, he has suffered a series of defeats, forced out of the directorship of the company that he founded, and now reduced to doing new research in his own basement. Yet he continues to safeguard both his suit and the "Pym Particle" that fuels it. "It was too dangerous," he tells Lang, "so I hid it from the world." Meanwhile, Pym's former protégé, Dr. Darren Cross (Corey Stoll), has used the company's facilities to try to replicate Pym's legendary technology.

For a group of potential military buyers, Cross screens a promotional video for his proprietary Yellowjacket suit, "an all-purpose weapon of war" that will allow users to infiltrate enemy targets. The video shows computer animations of the suit in action while a stentorian voice-over promises "surveillance, industrial sabotage, and the elimination of obstacles on the road to peace." Yet at the word *surveillance*, we see the suit lasering a microchip beneath reactor cooling towers and the legend "CRITICAL: OVERLAOD IMMINENT." At *industrial sabotage*, a cut takes us into what looks like a reactor-monitoring room, from which men in radiation suits scream and flee. The actions of the Yellowjacket's fictional operator look less like what most observers would call *war* and more like what they would call *terrorism*. At the phrase *obstacles on the road to peace*, the Yellowjacket enters a limousine beside the legend "DIPLOMATIC TARGET." The windows flash white, and the limousine swerves, suggesting an assassination. In case we missed the point, the next animation shows an executive open a briefcase, only to be lasered through the head and chest by the miniaturized assassin inside. Despite the 2015 setting of the film, the animation of Cross's video looks as if made in the early 2000s, clumsy and dated enough to embarrass but not enough for retro cool. Thus Cross's self-promotion makes him seem not just typically evil by duopoly standards, but also blind to the weaknesses in his own presentation, like Justin Hammer in *Iron Man 2* (Favreau, 2010). After the demonstration video, one of the guests expresses concern: "Imagine what our enemies could do with this tech." Cross later surprises this guest in a men's room to declare, "The laws of nature transcend the laws of man, and I've transcended the laws of nature." Cross then calmly uses a miniaturization gun to murder the skeptic, reducing his victim to a gobbet of reddish phlegm. A man who would copy a superhero's powers also kills without passion or remorse.

Unlike *Iron Man* and many other films in the genre, which map evil onto a father figure, *Ant-Man* reverses this, inviting us instead to sympathize with fathers while mapping evil onto Cross, the wicked but materially successful son.[1] Pym says of Cross, "I thought I saw something in him, the son I never had, perhaps. He was brilliant, but as we became close, he began to suspect that I wasn't telling him everything. . . . He became obsessed with recreating my formula, but I wouldn't help him, so he conspired against me, and he voted me out of my own company." Not only has Cross duplicated Pym's technology, but he now prepares to sell that technology to the arms dealer Mitchell. Pym describes Mitchell as "presently in the business of toppling governments." Mitchell's purchase thus constitutes a public and international threat, which Pym articulates for Lang and the audience: "Now, unless we break in and steal the Yellowjacket and destroy all the data, Darren Cross is going to unleash chaos upon the world." Yet Cross, for his homicidal evil, still seeks Pym's approval. When he shows up at Pym's house to gloat about the impending sale, he reveals a deep sense of grievance, asking Pym, "All those years ago . . . why did you push me away?" Later, when Cross prepares to complete the sale, he again confronts Pym:

> CROSS: What do you call the only man who can arm the most powerful weapon in the world?
> PYM: The most powerful man in the world.
> CROSS: You proud of me yet?
> PYM: You can stop this, Darren. It's not too late.
> CROSS: [angrily] It's been too late for a long time now.

Cross feels bitter because he cannot retroactively make Pym take him into confidence; he cannot make up for lost time. At the end of this exchange, Cross prepares to murder Pym, but Ant-Man saves the day. With the help of some ex-con friends, Lang destroys the copied data, defeats Cross, and even gets to kiss Pym's daughter at the film's end. Pym declares, "You can't destroy power. All you can do is make sure it's in the right hands." The patriarch declares the monopoly restored.

Like the Nolan Batman films and *Iron Man 2*, *Ant-Man* treats the vigilante protection of superhero technology as a matter of both world security and family honor. Pym recruits Lang because Pym's advancing age and years of exposure to the Pym Particle make the suit too dangerous for the old man. Pym will not allow Van Dyne to use it, and this refusal causes much friction between Van Dyne, Pym, and Lang. Eventually, Pym reveals to Lang and Van Dyne the truth, that Pym forbids his daughter to use the suit because of what happened to her mother. Van Dyne's mother, code named the Wasp, had a shrink-suit of her own, and in a 1987 covert mission she helped stop a stolen ICBM from striking the United States. She sacrificed her life, shrinking beyond safety into "the quantum realm" to disrupt the missile's guidance. Lang's mission thus not only becomes instrumental to mending the relationship between Pym and Van Dyne but even recapitulates the sacrifice that killed Van Dyne's mother. To defeat Cross, Lang too must shrink beyond safe limits, and afterward he finds himself falling into a psychedelic microcosm. In the quantum realm, Lang hears Pym's voice in echoing voice-off, repeating warnings, and he hears the voice of his daughter crying for him to return. In this moment of geometric abstraction, Lang bridges three generations, but only by defying Pym's warning, "Do not mess with your regulator," does Lang manage to return to the macroscopic world. As in *Superman: The Movie* (Richard Donner, 1978), the hero faces a moment of crisis when, to succeed, he must defy limits placed on him by an adoptive father. Through this defiance, Lang destroys the bad son, vindicates the lost mother's quantum sacrifice, and becomes a good father himself, rectifying the relationships across the three generations and the two families that intersect in him.

Yet while the film restores Lang so that he can appear in subsequent Marvel films, it also continually reminds us of the irreversible passage of time, activating nostalgia through flashbacks to its diegetic past and allusions to the past of the audience's world. Psychologists have long investigated nostalgia for therapeutic reasons, but since the late 1980s, marketing researchers have studied this affect as a means of advancing their clients' ends. A recent essay summarizes work in this area:

> Firms such as General Mills, McDonald's, GE, Coca-Cola, Target, Volkswagen, and Unilever, to name a few, have used nostalgic appeals with the hope of strengthening consumers' attitudes toward their brands and enhancing the likelihood of product purchase.... Although often conceptualized as "bittersweet," nostalgic reflections have been hypothesized and found to be predominantly positive.... Unlike autobiographical memories ... nostalgic memories tend to be skewed toward the positive. (Muehling et al. 73–74)

Marketers therefore trade less in the *algia* and more in the *nostos*—Odysseus's longing for Ithaca—crafting appeals to convince audiences that certain brands or commodities will allow the return to lost times or feelings. As the authors point out, social media platforms have grasped the utility of nostalgia, citing BuzzFeed's "Time Machine" and Twitter's "Throwback Thursdays," "where images and memories of the past are incorporated in company websites and posted on personal web pages with the intent to evoke nostalgic thoughts and feelings" (Muehling et al. 73). On these free platforms, users provide the data that the host companies then monetize, as the data lets the companies fine-tune advertising as well as nostalgic appeals to keep users coming back.

Critical approaches to nostalgia recognize the potential of nostalgia to shape the future. Svetlana Boym theorizes nostalgia's "prospective" function, noting that "fantasies of the past determined by needs of the present have a direct impact on realities of the future" (xvi). But when the needs of media conglomerates determine the nostalgic address of films, our dispositions toward the past become raw material for commercial and discursive systems designed to shape the future by manipulating us. Marketing-induced nostalgia can even lead audiences to believe false stories about their own pasts. Braun, Ellis, and Loftus explore this phenomenon in a study inspired by Disney's "Remember the Magic" advertising campaign:

> Disney celebrated the 25th anniversary of Disney World in Orlando with an advertising campaign entitled "Remember the Magic." The ads resembled vintage home movies and featured scenes of people swimming, meeting Mickey Mouse, and enjoying themselves on the theme park's exciting rides. The campaign's aim may have been to remind consumers of their own past happy childhood memories of the park in order to get them to revisit.... But what if such referencing could change what consumers remember about their childhood memories of visiting the park? . . . What if Disney's "Remember the Magic" campaign implanted memories into consumers of things that never happened? The possibility that marketing stimuli can direct, guide, or change consumers' autobiographical memories has gone largely untested. (7)

So the authors tested their theory, using a nonautobiographical control ad that makes no assertions about the subject's past, and an autobiographical experimental ad that prompts subjects to "recall the day your parents finally brought you to their 'home' at Walt Disney World® resort.... Mickey, the character you've idolized on TV, is only several feet away. Your heart stops but that doesn't stop your hands from sweating" (6). The investigators discovered that by priming subjects with false information, they "could make consumers more confident that they had experienced an advertised-suggested event as a child" (12). Though the authors mention "ethical ramifications" (2) and "ethical considerations" (20), they do not discuss either in depth. They shrewdly note, "The power of memory alteration is that consumers are not aware they have been influenced" (18). Nostalgic messaging can thus create false memories that build brand loyalty. Many scholars and critics already hold Disney resorts as the paradigm of nostalgic simulation, yet this experiment shows that some marketers seek not merely to accelerate the precession of simulacra about which Baudrillard warned, but to convert it into a technique of deceptive manipulation.[2] The work of Braun, Ellis, and Loftus suggests that the audience doesn't even need to encounter the simulacrum: if marketers craft the right message, then some of the audience will falsely remember it, and they will long to "return."

Ant-Man first activates nostalgia in its opening scene by alluding to its most prestigious star's past. As noted earlier, the film begins with a flashback labeled "1989," in a scene that presents Michael Douglas made digitally young. Marvel and parent Disney have improved on this technique that other studios developed. *Terminator Salvation* (McG, 2009) gave us a Terminator in the computer-generated likeness of a 1984 Arnold Schwarzenegger, and *Terminator Genisys* (Alan Taylor, 2015) went one better, reconstructing the opening sequence of the original *Terminator* (James Cameron, 1984), complete with a nude CG Schwarzenegger. *Ant-Man* has no analogous archive to draw from, but Michael Douglas's star image from three decades ago will do. The film gives 1987 as the year of the special operation in which Pym's wife died, the year of Douglas's career-defining turn as Gordon Gekko, which won him Best Actor for *Wall Street* (Oliver Stone). The next film in which Ant-Man would appear, *Captain America: Civil War* (Anthony Russo and Joe Russo, 2016), features a boyish Tony Stark, played by Robert Downey Jr. digitally de-aged so that he looks as he did in his breakout roles in *Less than Zero* (Marek Kanievska, 1987) and *The Pick-Up Artist* (James Toback, 1987). For viewers old enough to remember 1987, scenes like these bring a complex pang like that brought by a forgotten or unfamiliar photo of a loved one from years past. As we recognize our habituation to the aged face that our mind remembers from more recent encounters, we feel the passage of years, in the temporal equivalent of a *Vertigo*-style dolly zoom. Provided we can get over the uncanny quality of the computer-generated faces, we can now see our screen elders look younger than ourselves.[3]

Ant-Man also dramatizes Lang's nostalgia, inflecting it as a desire for social belonging. Early in the film, Lang arrives late and uninvited to his daughter's birthday party, where his ex's fiancé, a cop, confronts him: "What are you doing here, Lang? You haven't paid a dime of child support. You know, right now, if I wanted to, I could arrest you?" Lang calls his ex "the first love of my life" despite her ejecting him from her home. Lang bluntly tells his ex and us that he wants to reconnect with his daughter: "I love her so much. I missed so much time, and I want to be a part of her life. What do I do?" In *Ant-Man*, Rudd looks boyish for his forty-six years (at time of release), but we get no flashbacks to a younger version; instead Lang tells us of the past he seeks to recover. He also models a social exclusion that marketers have studied experimentally:

> Individuals who are socially excluded show an increased preference for nostalgic, as compared with contemporary, products in a variety of product categories ranging from hedonic foods (cookies and candy) to shower gel and automobiles.... The need to belong mediates the relationship between social exclusion and a preference for nostalgic products. (Loveland et al. 399)

Over the past four decades, monthly comic books retreated into a direct market of specialty retailers, and comic book stores and fans became cultural shorthand for social exclusion. As its company logo, Marvel Studios long used an animation of superhero comics pages, which signifies the brand's nostalgic address, as if asking, "Remember when 'Marvel' meant 'comic books'? Remember before *Blade*?" Among comics fans, everyone always feels like a latecomer; no matter when you started reading or collecting, some old-timer read So-and-So's run on *Series X* when it first appeared and has a copy bagged and boarded. Lang's bluntly stated desire to reconnect with his family probably activates our sympathy for him, but if it doesn't, his context in a nostalgic film activates our sympathy for ourselves. We, too, have missed so much time.

Both the film's gambit with the de-aged Douglas and its endgame among a child's toys activate such feelings. Although Lang and his accomplices succeed in destroying Cross's research, Cross himself escapes with a Yellowjacket suit and takes hostage Lang's daughter, Cassie. Ant-Man shows up with an army of ant reinforcements, and he and the Yellowjacket shrink to fight in Cassie's room, so that the climactic set piece takes place in a wonderland of colossal toys. This reverses the usual effect of returning to childhood places, which now look small to our adult selves; instead the cars of Cassie's toy train appear full-size, and the ants loom as big as Clydesdales. The suited combatants have, relative to their surroundings, the strength of giants. In slow motion, they hurl train cars at each other as the Yellowjacket lasers obstacles and ants into fireballs. But while the cinematography makes these spectacles look awe-inspiring when we occupy the optical scale of Ant-Man and the Yellowjacket, the sequence also generates laughs by cutting away to human-scaled wide shots of the same views, and at normal image speed. When finally the train derails in a soft clatter of plastic, it harms nothing. The alternation between the two registers evokes the imaginative play of children with their toys, which to observers may appear quiet and trivial but to a player may resemble a war among gods. The Yellowjacket really does intend to kill Lang, and Cassie watches from her closet door in real fear, yet the sequence's comedic moments undercut this fear, moving the sequence away from *The Incredible Shrinking Man* (Jack Arnold, 1957) and closer to Disney's *Honey, I Shrunk the Kids* (Joe Johnston, 1989). The sequence's modulation between two registers encourages us to enjoy the scene alternately from the perspectives of deadly serious children, immersed in the struggle, and from that of adults, delighted by this play-battle.

Curiously, among the toys, only one branded character stands out: Thomas the Tank Engine. Look at the toy-stocked bedrooms of most well-off girls, whether in San Francisco or Shanghai, and you will find many trademarked characters, but other than Thomas, Cassie seems to have only generic toys like train cars, wooden blocks, and plastic cows, and—most improbably—not one Disney princess. By using a mise-en-scène of mostly generic and gender-neutral toys of classic designs, the sequence can activate nostalgia across a variety of demographics and viewing positions without unduly distracting from the main action with cameo after cameo of iconic, trademarked characters towering over the film's trademarked but still far from iconic protagonist. Instead, the generic toys allow viewers of any age to enter this nostalgic wonderland, which, despite its notable lack of Disney characters, nevertheless resembles a theme park. In a genre not famed for subtlety, and in a film otherwise not shy about cross-promotion, the climactic battle of *Ant-Man* opts for a mise-en-scène that generates nostalgic wonder for the play of children without displacing its branded protagonist from the center the audience's attention.

The trade press noted that *Ant-Man* did solid but not impressive business for a Marvel film, but as Brent Lang of *Variety* reported, "It's doubtful that many other companies could have made a movie about a man with the powers of a household pest and enjoyed stronger results":

> The film, which is noticeably lighter in tone, was intended to bring in younger audiences, Disney distribution chief Dave Hollis argued. "We were able to successfully launch a new character and to do so in a way that expands the audience of who is coming to see our movies," he said. "In the long run, that's of overwhelming value." (Lang, "Ant-Man Shows")

Herein lies the paradox of *Ant-Man*: If Disney really wanted to attract younger viewers, why would the studio make a film that uses an ex-con dad as a protagonist? Does this render void my argument that the film participates in some kind of adult turn? Not if we consider the complementarity of audience segments, especially the role of parents in taking their children to see PG-13 movies during summer theatrical releases. Despite the film's relatively light tone, this film labors to appeal to those parents, making parenting not peripheral but central to the story. *Ant-Man* widens the superhero film genre's range by giving us a protagonist who must reconcile himself to demands placed on him not only by a fatherly mentor but also by his own dependent and his former spouse. Despite the prevalence of boy sidekicks in the comics of the 1930s and 1940s, the superhero film since 1998 has largely eliminated this trope, especially after the failure of *Batman and Robin* (Joel Schumacher, 1997).[4] In contrast, *Ant-Man* shows Lang assuming responsibility for his daughter in interpersonal, economic, and legal senses. This film thereby appeals to parents numbed by franchise films that adapt young-adult novels or tell superhero coming-of-age stories. What little psychological depth *Ant-Man* has comes from its protagonist's responsibility not to fight crime or save the world but to care for his daughter.

Despite the restraint that the climactic battle shows in terms of cross-promotion, neither this film nor the Avengers franchise that comprises it avoids cross-promotion on principle. When Pym's team infiltrates Cross's laboratories during their raid, Lang's former cellmate, Luis, whistles "It's a Small World (After All)." The song has a triple function: as a reminder of the film's preoccupation with tiny creatures and objects; as corporate brand placement for Marvel parent, Disney; and as advertising for Disney theme parks, each of which, around the world, has a ride of this title that also plays the song. Disney has used the song since the 1960s, so it functions here as a multigenerational appeal, what the marketing researchers Kusumi, Matsuda, and Sugimori call "a nostalgic trigger" in their research on appeals in marketing (150). They find that "aging facilitates a predisposition toward nostalgia," and "nostalgic triggers facilitate the retrieval of past events and memorization of advertisements that evoke familiarity and positive attitudes, which, in turn, facilitates the intention to purchase" (150). Moreover, among their experimental subjects, "music to which they were frequently exposed in the past" triggered nostalgia most effectively (156). All the most salient songs in *Ant-Man* hail from 1989 or earlier, suggesting that despite Disney's story about seeking a younger audience, the company cared less about the responses of children or teenagers than about the responses of parents.

For viewers who knew these songs well already, they may trigger nostalgia, but their wider appeal lies in their ability to suggest the past by connoting it, and lending the film a pop-cultural authenticity on the basis of a well-curated playlist. After the film's opening flashback to 1989, where Pym and three other white people in business suits discuss the copying of proprietary technology, the screen goes black, and "Borombon," a Latin song from the 1970s by the Afro-Panamanian Camilo Azuquita, begins to play as the Marvel company credits fade in. This song then functions as a sound bridge to film's first present-day scene, Lang's last day in San Quentin. A Black inmate gives Lang a ritual going-away beating, while outside, former cellmate Luis (Michael Peña) picks him up in a van whose horn plays "La Cucaracha." "Borombon" functions as a floating signifier of nonwhiteness and "fun," as if to cleanse the palate after the SHIELD flashback, but the song also recalls music of bygone decades.[5] When Luis tells Lang a comically overcomplicated story about how Luis lined up their new heist, the urgent funk of "Escape" by Roy Ayers begins to play nondiegetically. "Escape" appeared in American International Pictures' first Pam Grier vehicle, *Coffy* (Jack Hill, 1973); moreover, Quentin Tarantino used the song in his 1997 homage to Blaxploitation, *Jackie Brown*, which starred Grier. "Escape" thus imbues Luis's story with multiple layers of dated cool. So does Luis's van, a 1970s Ford Econoline, with primer on its lower body and bubble windows at the back that recall the West Coast's van-customization scene of the late 1970s. The opening styles Lang as the disreputable but cool uncle of its hypothetical thirtyish viewer.

Later in the film, when Ant-Man battles the Yellowjacket, they end up inside Cross's briefcase. As the pair battles amid gigantic keys, phone chargers, and a roll of Life Savers candy, the Yellowjacket vows to "disintegrate" Ant-Man, but this activates Siri on Cross's iPhone, who says, "Playing *Disintegration* by the Cure." "Plainsong," the synth-heavy opener of the British goth-rock album, then begins to play over the fight. *Disintegration*, the Cure's most commercially successful album, appeared in 1989, the year around which the film's nostalgia seems to orbit. Cross looks about forty, old enough to have not just appreciation but firsthand memories of the album from junior high. Although even viewers who have never heard of the Cure can get the joke about the well-meaning stupidity of the phone's AI, for those who recognize the allusion—or, better yet, remember "Plainsong" from their own youth—even the villain's playlist can activate nostalgia.

But *Ant-Man*'s nostalgic use of music instantiates a wider pattern in both the films and even the trailers of the Marvel Cinematic Universe: the cross-promotion of Disney properties. The first full-length trailer for *Avengers: Age of Ultron* (Joss Whedon, 2015) presents scenes of urban destruction and superhero action. A humanoid robot shambles toward the Avengers as a sinister male voice-off narrator intones, "You're all puppets, tangled in strings." More exterior shots show destruction as a crowd of matching robots takes flight; on the soundtrack drifts a slow, minor-key, and nondiegetic arrangement of "I've Got No Strings" from *Pinocchio* (Hamilton Luske and Ben Sharpsteen, 1940), sung by a child. The trailer ends by revealing the speaker of the voice-over as the murderous robot Ultron, villain from *Avengers* comics, who steps into close-up and declares, "There are no strings on me," the song's refrain. *Doctor Strange* (Scott Derrickson, 2016) does something similar.[6] While performing surgery, physician Stephen Strange plays a music-trivia game that both establishes his encyclopedic memory and cues audience nostalgia. We hear Earth, Wind & Fire's 1975 "Shining Star," which begins with the lyric "When you wish upon a star," itself the title and opening lyric of another song from the *Pinocchio* soundtrack. Strange gets the question right, but he disputes the result of the next, modeling the historical minutiae that comic book fans enjoy:

> STRANGE: "Feels So Good," Chuck Mangione, nineteen seventy-seven. Honestly, Billy, you said this one would be hard.
> BILLY: Ha! It's nineteen seventy-*eight*.
> STRANGE: No, Billy, while "Feels So Good" may have *charted* in nineteen seventy-eight, the album was released in December of nineteen seventy-seven.

Mangione's hit may trigger little nostalgia in the audience, but the scene does establish, early in the film, a curiously double sense of temporal proximity and temporal distance: distance from the late 1970s, but proximity to Disney's eternal present of reused copyrights and simulations of the past. Disney's adaptation of *Pinocchio* would already have become public domain if not for the CTEA. Hollywood's copyright dilation depends on political favors bought in Washington, DC, and paid for with the profits of nostalgia.

Ant-Man's next appearance on the big screen would further elaborate Disney's intergenerational cross-promotion of its own franchises. In *Captain America: Civil War*, the Avengers fight among themselves, and in the film's major action set piece, Ant-Man reveals a new power: he can also transform into a giant. Amid this battle, the teenage Spider-Man (on temporary loan from Sony) suddenly waxes nostalgic.

> SPIDER-MAN: Hey, guys, you ever see that really old movie, *Empire Strikes Back*?
> WAR MACHINE: Jesus, Tony, how old is this guy?
> IRON MAN: I don't know. I didn't carbon-date him. He's on the young side.
> SPIDER-MAN: You know that part, where they're on the snow planet, with the walking-thingies? [Spider-Man begins to swing webs around the giant's legs, tangling them.]
> IRON MAN: Maybe the kid's onto something.
> WAR MACHINE: High, now, Tony, go high! [In unison, they punch the giant's face, toppling him.]

Despite War Machine's shock at Spider-Man's youth, Spider-Man shows that he has the mass-cultural literacy necessary to fit in with the Avengers: he may not remember the name of the giant machines in *The Empire Strikes Back* (Irvin Kershner, 1980), but he remembers the scene well enough to convey his plan to the other Avengers. He could, of course, simply say, "I'll tangle his legs, and you two knock him off balance," but that would neither convey his intergenerational awkwardness nor would it cross-promote Star Wars. The gawky Spider-Man achieves social belonging with the older, cool-uncle Avengers while modeling for the audience the value of mass-cultural allusion as a means to overcome real or perceived social exclusion.[7] I saw this movie at a noon screening on June 6, 2016, at the AMC Esquire 7 theater in Saint Louis, and before the movie, the management had screened a trailer for *Rogue One: A Star Wars Story* (Gareth Edwards, 2016). That trailer included a shot of Imperial Walkers in battle for the first time since *Empire*. Then, an hour and forty-two minutes into *Civil War*, a Marvel Cinematic Universe character reminded me not only of *The Empire Strikes Back* but of the *Rogue One* trailer that earlier had played on the same screen. When Iron Man and War Machine strike the giant in unison, they strike as Marvel and Lucasfilm struck me at the Esquire that day, right in the face.

Whether or not viewers remember *Empire* matters little, because marketing researchers have found that audiences can learn to feel nostalgia for the experiences of others. Personal nostalgia and vicarious, "historical nostalgia" can complement each other. Darrel Muehling writes:

> Historical nostalgia thoughts are believed to be comprised of an "imagined" past—a more abstract representation of a past activity/event. Goulding (2002) suggests that this type of nostalgia is for a period "outside of the individual's living memory." As such, vicariously experienced "historical" nostalgia is not "lived" nostalgia per se, but instead is nostalgia that is either experienced through others (e.g., a young individual hearing tales of the past by an elder) or experienced through other means (e.g., a movie or book featuring/referencing a period in time before one's birth). (101)

In *Civil War*, the gawky Spider-Man tells the "tales of the past" for audience members too young to remember *Empire*; the son becomes the father, at least to the kids in the audience. *Civil War*, like *Ant-Man* before it, uses tactical allusions to, and quotations from, four decades of mass culture as part of Disney's larger strategy for building franchises that appeal to multiple generations. Derek Johnson writes of Hasbro's work building the Transformers into a franchise that crossed from Hasbro toys, to Marvel Comics, to Paramount Pictures. Hasbro used

> new twenty-first century marketing appeals attuned to the specific generation and social reproduction patterns of contemporary American culture, focusing on relationships between parents and children as a nexus of affective exchange

and franchising nostalgia. . . . Hasbro and its partners thought generationally, working through parental nostalgia to create waves of fan offspring who might sustain interest in Transformers products for another quarter century. (Johnson, *Media Franchising* 189–90)

Disney has done this for decades and has extended these techniques into the Marvel Cinematic Universe, such that *Ant-Man* models the reproduction of human families and the reproduction of mass-media fandom from one generation to the next, in ways that duopoly films had not used before. Human reproduction and the family become, for the marketer, means to reproduce brand loyalty.

SUICIDE SQUAD: THE BAD GUY AS GOOD FATHER

In 1960, DC had pioneered the use of a team of superheroes, assembled from their solo titles, to headline a new series, *Justice League*; and in 1963 Marvel had followed suit with *The Avengers*. But in the intervening decades, fortunes had reversed, and now DC found its former imitator in the dominant position, with Marvel Studios' *The Avengers* (Joss Whedon, 2012) breaking global box office records while Warner Bros. floundered. In *Batman v Superman: Dawn of Justice* (Zack Snyder, 2016), DC had failed to equal either the commercial or critical success of *The Avengers*; nine days after *Batman v Superman* opened, the Manchester *Guardian* ran an article titled "'A Stink Bucket of Disappointment': The Most Savage *Batman v Superman* Reviews." In *Suicide Squad* (David Ayer, 2016), Warner Bros. wisely tried something else, something that no studio had done yet with comic book characters: headlining a movie with an ensemble of villains.[8] Despite a solidly negative reaction from critics, *Suicide Squad* nevertheless broke box office records for its August opening weekend and came in eighth place overall in total US box office in 2016 (Lang and Rainey 21). The film borrows the premise of *The Dirty Dozen* (Robert Aldrich, 1967), assembling a team of imprisoned supervillains for a mission regarded as too dangerous for normal government operatives, and it focuses on three characters: Rick Flag (Joel Kinnaman), the Special Forces officer assigned to lead the team; Harley Quinn (Margot Robbie), girlfriend of the Joker; and Deadshot (Will Smith), a hitman with preternatural firearm skills. Each has adult romantic relationships, but Deadshot, like Ant-Man, has a daughter. My analysis will therefore focus on Deadshot's story in the context of the film's other appeals to adult viewers. All the film's villains characters want, in some sense, to go home (*nostos*), but the three focal characters' desires center on relationships, which the film develops through flashbacks. Harley Quinn misses the Joker; Rick Flag, his archaeologist girlfriend possessed by an immortal witch, the Enchantress; and Deadshot, his daughter Zoe. The government agent who assembles the team, Amanda Waller (Viola Davis), calls Deadshot's daughter his "weakness" and exploits that weakness to encourage his cooperation. Like *Ant-Man*, *Suicide Squad* has a PG-13 rating and invites audiences to identify not with an adolescent protagonist trying to grow up but with an incarcerated father trying to do right by his child.

Suicide Squad puts an unusual spin on the usual duopoly melodrama of the dangers of copying superpowers. At the start of the film, Waller has the Enchantress's "heart," a dusty talisman, and uses it to command the witch, sending her on dangerous government errands. But the Enchantress soon tricks her captors and runs amok, transforming normal people into nigh-indestructible asphaltic blob-soldiers as she prepares to exterminate humanity. When Waller sends in the Suicide Squad, she sends them not in the hope of destroying the Enchantress but in the hope of recapturing her for military use. The Enchantress, says Waller, "takes an average person—a yoga mom, an elderly retiree—and she turns them into a soldier who can take a head-shot and still fight? That's an instant army." If this did not convince the audience of Waller's evil, less than a minute later, Waller coldly executes four of her own agents, including one wearing an FBI jacket, because "they weren't cleared for any of this." This all-villain film reworks the standard duopoly IP plot by targeting someone other than the protagonists, then making those protagonists unwitting pawns in that plan. But the Suicide Squad does not deliver the Enchantress or the instant army; instead they defeat the witch, rescue Flag's possessed girlfriend, and save the world.

Waller wants an instant army because DC had experience buying them. When the comics market contracted in 1955, larger comics publishers like National and Charlton bought up the copyrights of their failing rivals, "amassing vast catalogs of defunct companies that they could exploit in the near or distant future" (Kidman 31). The founder of Charlton had learned about the power of copyright the hard way: in the early 1930s, John Santangelo spent over a year in the New Haven County Jail for selling unauthorized reproductions of popular song lyrics. After regaining his freedom, Santangelo began publishing popular-music and song-lyric magazines like *Hit Parade* and *Song Hits* ("Charlton Comics"). Over the next fifteen years, Santangelo and his business partners integrated vertically, establishing subsidiaries dedicated to advertising, engraving, printing, and distribution (Du Bois 9). During the collapse of the 1950s, Charlton bought titles from Fawcett and five other publishers that had either failed or shuttered their comics divisions (Benton 99). Until the early 1960s, Charlton published mostly horror and war comics, but when Marvel's successes led to a revival of the superhero genre, Charlton launched their "Action Heroes" line of characters like Captain Atom, Judomaster, Mercury Man, the Peacemaker, the Question, and Thunderbolt (Lopes 66, 204). These characters never gained the popularity of their duopoly competitors, and Charlton gradually reduced its comics offerings until 1984, when it sold the entire "Action Heroes" line to DC ("Charlton Comics"). Never known for high quality, Charlton died as it lived, a scavenger scavenged. But DC later revived many of the Charlton characters, and Alan Moore used some as the inspiration for his *Watchmen* graphic novel, one of the best-selling comics of all time, which Time Warner later spun into a feature film, home video franchise, and TV series. Like the witch in *Suicide Squad*, DC knows how transform less-than-promising characters, and so does Warner Bros., which used a half-dozen second- and third-tier villains to make one of the top-grossing films of the year.

In its opening act, *Suicide Squad* batters viewers with nostalgic FM radio staples from the 1960s and 1970s. Before the adult turn of the mid-2010s, duopoly films seldom made extensive use of popular music from decades past; Christopher Nolan's Batman films eschew popular music, and it seldom appears in the X-Men franchise before *Deadpool*. But *Suicide Squad* seems to borrow a move from *Guardians of the Galaxy* (James Gunn, 2014): if your ensemble film features a bunch of characters unknown to a mass audience, throw in a bunch of songs that the mass audience does know. In *Suicide Squad*, the Animals' 1964 "House of the Rising Sun" introduces Deadshot, while Lesley Gore's 1963 "You Don't Own Me" introduces Harley Quinn. Elsewhere in the film, we hear the Rolling Stones' "Sympathy for the Devil," Creedence Clearwater Revival's "Fortunate Son," Black Sabbath's "Paranoid," AC/DC's "Dirty Deeds Done Dirt Cheap," and Queen's "Bohemian Rhapsody," each song a contender for Most Played to Death by its respective artist. Such songs all qualify as the "oldies music" that Kusumi, Matsuda, and Sugimori consider most effective for triggering nostalgia (156). As the film progresses, the soundtrack increasingly adds more recent hip-hop songs, but the first thirty minutes suggest a film trying to ingratiate itself to baby boomers and to Gen Xers nostalgic for music they associate with their parents.

The film also activates nostalgia through its use of characters from the DC Comics continuity. Flashbacks give the Batman (Ben Affleck) a minor but key role in capturing several of the criminals who end up constituting the Suicide Squad, while the Joker (Jared Leto) plays a more salient if revisionist role as

Quinn's love. This film reimagines the Joker through a filter of hip-hop fashion, with chrome grills over his teeth and tattoos on his cheeks and forehead; he often appears shirtless or with his collar open to his waist to display tattoos beneath gold necklaces. We can read these as part of Time Warner's larger strategy of differentiating the Joker as a brand and product line, making Leto's version appear novel against those played by Caesar Romero (makeup over the mustache), Jack Nicholson (face cut into a smile), Heath Ledger (makeup over scars), or Joaquin Phoenix (professional clown turned killer). Will Brooker has argued that we should think of Batman not as a single character but as a multitude of complementary, sometimes competing versions (25–29), and *Suicide Squad* clearly expects us to apply this principle to the Joker. Derek Johnson argues that such modulations "extend the appeal of franchised product across generations" (165). According to Flint Dille, a writer for the Transformers franchise (in various media), a good franchise reuses material, and even missteps—"horrible manifestations" of established characters—can extend the brand's overall appeal (qtd. in Johnson 165). Even a "horrible" reinterpretation of beloved character can arguably strengthen a brand, inasmuch as it prompts audiences to recall or declare their affection for a favorite version. The more we dislike Leto's Joker, the more fondly we might remember another.

The film's standout sequence depends on our knowledge of the Batman franchise, in particular the traumatic origin of its hero, but the sequence's brilliance lies in its use of that origin story to develop not Batman but Deadshot. A mere seven minutes into the film, a flashback takes us to Deadshot and his daughter Zoe, Christmas shopping on crowded street in downtown Gotham City. Snow flurries fall amid Christmas lights and elaborate window displays, nostalgic anachronisms in an era when most Americans shop online or at big-box stores. Father and daughter talk about Zoe's life with her mother.

> DEADSHOT: She still going out at night?
> ZOE: Dad, it's okay. I can take care of her. I know how to make pancakes now.
> DEADSHOT: Hey, babe . . . she's supposed to be taking care of you, you know? . . . I want you to come live with me. Aright? I came into some resources. Imma get us a spot. It's gonna be nice. Aright?
> ZOE: Mama says I can't live with you because you kill people.
> DEADSHOT: That's not true. That's a lie! She's lying to you!
> ZOE: Daddy, I know you do bad things. Don't worry. I still love you.

They take a shortcut through an alley, where the Batman suddenly swoops down to confront Deadshot. "I don't want to do this in front of your daughter," growls Batman. But Deadshot resists, and as he levels a gun at Batman, Zoe steps between them.

> ZOE: [tearfully] Daddy, please!
> DEADSHOT: Zoe, move!
> ZOE: Please, Daddy, don't do it.

At this, Deadshot lowers his pistol, allowing Batman to capture him. The scene inverts Batman's formative trauma, the shooting of Bruce Wayne's parents by a robber, then rewrites it as the source of Deadshot's motivation. In *Batman v Superman* (Zack Snyder, 2016), Affleck's Batman indulged in sadistic violence, branding criminals' skin with his bat insignia, but here he shows restraint. So does Deadshot; when Deadshot lowers his pistol, he does so not as a ruse but as a genuine surrender, as if overwhelmed by Zoe's conviction or chastened by the opportunity to atone for earlier misdeeds, which now include lying to his daughter about his work. Near the end of the film, when the witch antagonist offers the main characters visions of what they most desire, Deadshot sees a new version of the encounter with Batman, in which Deadshot guns down his would-be captor. The revision of the earlier scene, and the repetition of it near the film's end, underscores its role in forming Deadshot's character. *Suicide Squad* repurposes the Batman franchise's most familiar traumatic story about parents and children, turning it into the motivation for a father.

As in *Ant-Man*, the coda of *Suicide Squad* shows the sympathetic felon resuming his responsibilities as a father. When his captors recruited him for the mission, Deadshot set as a condition not money but the right to visit his daughter, and at the film's end, we see Zoe not in a flashback or hallucination but in the present, at a kitchen table, where Deadshot helps her with her geometry homework. Zoe struggles to understand how to solve for a hypotenuse, but she spontaneously proposes an example of the long side of a right triangle: "So if you're up here, like in a building, and you shoot a man down here on the street, that's how far the bullet actually goes?" Rick Flag, Deadshot's minder, quietly interrupts to tell Deadshot that they have run out of time, and SWAT officers file in with shackles. Despite the corruption and violence of the justice system in this version (and most versions) of Gotham City, *Suicide Squad* ends with the state honoring its promises. Zoe's front door has a double bar, and it opens onto a cinder-block corridor spray-painted with graffiti tags. Although Zoe appears to live in a high-rise housing project, the scene does not otherwise indulge in clichés about urban or Black poverty. In a film that otherwise merits little praise for its realism or subtlety (or anything else), this scene stands out for both. Zoe does not reveal math-based superpowers, and Deadshot does not break free and take Zoe on as his sidekick. Instead, Deadshot acts like a loving and dutiful father making the best of constrained circumstances.[9]

We can attribute part of the film's financial success to such flickers of social and psychological realism embedded in a film otherwise given to fantasies of power, freedom, and abjection, unsubtle even by duopoly standards. The media analytics firm ComScore reported that despite poor early reviews, the film did well with minority audiences through word of mouth on social media: "The combination of African American and Hispanic moviegoers made up a huge 41% of the audience with both audiences giving the film a whopping 81% positive score" (qtd. in McNary). In contrast to previous DC and Marvel Studios films, *Suicide Squad* gave audiences a Black character with both a family and an interior life. *Captain America: Civil War*, another ensemble film, offered Black Panther, but to that point, other Marvel Studios films used one-dimensional Black sidekicks who have neither interior lives nor relationships with other Black people. To play Deadshot, Warner Bros. cast Will Smith, the most white-audience-friendly Black actor this side of Morgan Freeman, but Deadshot still amounts to more than just a marketing tool to expand the film's appeal.[10] He has the most poignant and psychologically realistic relationship in the film.

Nevertheless, one well-drawn relationship given less than five minutes of screen time does not make a good movie, and in this case, it did not even make a good second weekend: *Suicide Squad* "followed the lead of *Batman v. Superman* (−69%), tumbling 67.3% in its sophomore session" (Flinn). So while *Suicide Squad* did not break *Batman v Superman*'s record for steepest second-week drop of a film to open with over $100 million, it came close. Despite this crash, *Suicide Squad* helped confirm that audiences would pay to see Black characters with interior lives, and they would pay to see superhero—or supervillain—fathers who help their daughters with their homework. The Oedipal drama of the youthful hero who comes of age by defeating an evil father now has a competing narrative template: the troubled and nostalgic father who learns to do good. Although the Suicide Squad's mission revolves around a villain's failed attempt to capture the means of superhero production, audiences forget this as they focus on the relationship melodramas of Flag, Quinn, and most of all, Deadshot.

LOGAN: MUTANT ELEGY

Fifty-four weeks after *Deadpool*'s record opening for an R-rated movie, Fox released *Logan* (James Mangold, 2017), which also featured a relatively low budget, R rating, and a narrative addressed toward adults. Both films pit their heroes against evil corporations who manufacture mutant super-soldiers to sell as slaves and as weapons. But where *Deadpool* traded in comedy, *Logan* trades in nostalgia and grief for the passing of youth, ranging from the youth of the characters, to the youth of the X-Men franchise, and finally to the youth of the implied viewer. Most X-Men films have centered on the potential danger of a character's powers getting captured and misused by an enemy, as in *X-Men* (Bryan Singer, 2000), *X2: X-Men United* (Singer, 2003), *X-Men Origins: Wolverine* (Gavin Hood, 2009), *X-Men: Apocalypse* (Singer, 2016), and director James Mangold's earlier turn for the franchise, *The Wolverine* (2013). Other films in the franchise, *X-Men: The Last Stand* (Brett Ratner, 2006) and *X-Men: Days of Future Past* (Singer, 2014), hinged on the duplication and mass production of a superhero's powers. All warned of nightmarish, dystopian results if the heroes did not thwart the piracy of superheroes' powers. We can read this film franchise as an allegory of Fox's bad conscience: having acquired the X-Men film rights from a floundering Marvel, Fox used those rights to make a fortune, but in the process, the studio could only imagine narratives of the acquisition of the X-Men by someone else.

Logan takes place in the dystopia that arrives after villains crack the code to the powers of multiple heroes and begin manufacturing living weapons. Moreover, *Logan* shows us a near-future America seemingly devoid of young mutants. "There hasn't been a new one born in twenty-five years," says Logan, making this film the superhero analogue to *Children of Men* (Alfonso Cuarón, 2006), with which *Logan* shares both its grieving tone and its quest narrative. Why make an X-Men film without teenage mutants, the sine qua non of a franchise traditionally centered on Professor Xavier's School for Gifted Youngsters? Fox developed *Logan* during the years when Marvel's comics division not only reduced its output of X-Men titles but deliberately ceased creating new characters in its current X-Men titles so that Fox would not automatically acquire the film rights (as discussed in chapter 1). We can therefore read *Logan*'s narrative of sterility as an allegory of the drought of new characters that Marvel enforced on its competitor. The film tells the story of Logan helping a runaway child mutant, who flees the genetic engineers who manufactured her; this narrative suggests Fox's own position relative to Marvel: a movie studio using characters originated by the publisher, but coveted by that publisher. We can read this narrative of a running custody fight as an allegory of the fight between Fox and Marvel over film rights. Back in the 1990s, Fox had bought a bundle of film rights from Marvel, not only to the X-Men but also to the Fantastic Four, using the latter to make *Fantastic Four* (Tim Story,

2005) and *Fantastic Four: Rise of the Silver Surfer* (Story, 2007). After Disney acquired Marvel in 2009, Marvel Studios executives had tried to negotiate the return of these rights, to no avail; rumors held that the negotiations went badly. In 2014, as Fox produced a reboot film, *The Fantastic Four* (Josh Trank, 2015), Marvel announced that it would suspend work on comics starring the Fantastic Four. As Rich Johnston wrote in *Bleeding Cool*, disconnected pieces of evidence all pointed to a policy by Marvel to starve Fox of any potential cross-promotion for their Fantastic Four movie, even if that meant canceling the series that put Marvel on the map.

> *Comic Book Reporter* independently confirmed that it was intended for the *Fantastic Four* to be cancelled. Then the letter about sketch card artists being forbidden to use *Fantastic Four* characters was made public, Mondo talked about being forbidden to use *Fantastic Four* characters and today, we were already planning to run another story about Diamond Select Toys confirming that they are unable to make any *Fantastic Four* toys. . . . Expect the announcement of the cancellation of *The Fantastic Four* at NYCC [New York Comic Con]. And expect a story-based reason for the cancellation—that they have a great final story for the team and want to give it impact. (Johnston)

The bigger news came when Marvel announced in January 2016 that it would not only cancel its *Fantastic Four* titles but disband the superhero team itself. Marvel would end the story of its "first family," the superheroes with everyday problems who set the template for the company's revival in the 1960s—and for characters like Spider-Man, Iron Man, and the Hulk—and cease publishing the monthly title that for over six hundred issues had served as the "primary idea lab for the Marvel Universe" (Carmody). If Marvel Studios couldn't have the Fantastic Four, nobody could.

This helps us understand why Fox took such a self-consciously adult turn first with *Deadpool* and then with *Logan*. The first line of *Logan* makes sure that audiences will not mistake it for kid-friendly MCU fare. "Ah, fuck," moans Logan (Hugh Jackman), waking beside a whiskey bottle on the back seat of the limo he now drives for a living.[11] Makeup adds scars and ten years to Jackman's face, clues that the regenerative powers of the mutant known as the Wolverine have dimmed. Logan stumbles from the car to find thieves stealing the wheels, and when he tries to talk them out of it, they shoot him. Logan not only falls to the ground, but he rises only after a long interval, reinforcing the diminution of his healing powers. In the ensuing fight, one of the robbers shoots at Logan but hits the limo instead, and Logan becomes frantic. "Not the car!" he cries. Few action heroes take care to keep their cars from sustaining damage, but Logan actually leaps between the shooter and the limo, taking a bullet rather than allowing his livelihood to suffer further. For the first time in a X-Men movie, the franchise's breakout character has to worry about making a living. Unlike the nomad of *X-Men* (Bryan Singer, 2000), who shows no regard for his truck camper when an enemy destroys it, or the tortured bad boy of *X2* (Singer, 2003), who hotwires his teammate's sports car, this Logan shows not just an adult's responsibility but a precarious, gig-economy worker's fear of losing the means of his livelihood. We soon learn that Logan works to buy medicine for the aging and ailing Professor Charles Xavier (Patrick Stewart), and to save up for a boat so that he, Xavier, and fellow mutant Caliban (Stephen Merchant) can flee North America. When Logan returns to their postindustrial hideout with pills for Xavier, Caliban says, "This is not enough, you know. Won't see us through the week." Logan, former loner, has become the struggling breadwinner of a mutant family.

On the poster for the movie, Logan wears neither the yellow-and-black leotard of the comics nor the black leather flight-suit uniforms of the X-Men films of the 2000s, but a matched business suit without a necktie, with only his extended claws and the film's title to denote his superhero identity.[12] During *Deadpool*'s record-breaking opening weekend in February 2016, Fox announced at the New York Toy Fair that "they would be targeting an R-rating for Hugh Jackman's final run as Wolverine next year" (Davis). *Logan*, the third and final Wolverine film spun from the X-Men franchise, had a budget of only $97 million, a step down from the $150 million of *X-Men Origins: Wolverine* and even from the $120 million of *The Wolverine*, but the latter two films had PG-13 ratings that ensured wider distribution and lower risk. A month before *Logan* opened, *Variety* noted that while the Wolverine spin-offs had done respectable business, "the movies in which Wolverine is featured alongside the X-Men team average nearly $100 million higher" (158). But then *Logan* took a worldwide gross of $616 million, far more than its predecessor spin-offs, recouping over six times its cost in its theatrical run alone, a franchise record second only to *Deadpool*.[13] Just after *Logan*'s release on March 3, 2017, *Variety* reported:

> Like *Deadpool* before it, the blockbuster differentiated itself from the flood of films about costumed heroes by embracing a hard-R rating.... [Fox] seems intent on carving out a niche for itself by making grittier, tougher comic-book fare that's in stark contrast to Disney's sunnier *Avengers* series.... "Fox needs to be bold and continue to blaze this trail," said Jeff Bock, an analyst with Exhibitor Relations. "I think the world is now ready for an R-rated X-Men film." ("Next Up" 10)

The same issue of *Variety* reported *Logan* in the number one box office spot, noting, "Rave reviews helped drive interest in the R-rated comic-book movie" ("Film Box Office Grosses"). Not the R rating but the focused and poignant story drove audiences to the film.

Logan's drama of a surrogate family, spanning three generations, most distinguishes the film from others in the genre. Logan takes in Laura (Dafne Keen), a silent preteen girl on the run from Mexico City, pursued by paramilitary security from the Transigen Corporation. The American company has taken advantage of lax Mexican laws to do biomedical research, creating artificial mutants in laboratories, hoping to market them as weapons. Transigen has used Logan's DNA to create a "daughter" who also heals with preternatural speed, whose wrists hide metal claws, and who fights with bestial ferocity, slicing Transigen's security men to pieces. After Transigen captures Caliban, Logan takes both Laura and the aging Xavier on the run. Through the film's middle section, what begins as a metaphor becomes a masquerade as the three actively pose as a family on a cross-country trip. Logan calls Xavier "Pop." Laura, feral and silent after years of abuse at Transigen, has little knowledge of the outside world, and she responds to perceived threats with violence, so Logan must not only keep her out of her pursuers' reach but also keep her from hurting others. Xavier, in his nineties and using a wheelchair, requires Logan's help using the restroom and resists taking the medicine that controls his seizures. Xavier's natural telepathy broadcasts his seizures to everyone nearby, and the film hints that one of his seizures destroyed the X-Men as well as Xavier's school for mutants. A radio broadcast refers to "the Westchester incident," an allusion to the upstate New York school where Xavier trained his team. This incident "left over six hundred injured and took the lives of seven mutants, including several of the X—" but at this moment, Logan switches off the radio. Where *Ant-Man* and *Suicide Squad* present visitation rights as the goal of their father-protagonists, *Logan* gives us a protagonist whose main duty, through most of the film, lies in caring for both a child and an elder.

No superhero film has yet dwelt so on the pain and debility of aging. The film's opening establishes Logan's present weakness relative to his inhuman vitality in the earlier films; his wounds no longer close as we watch, one of his claws no longer extends fully, and he needs reading glasses to distinguish medicine bottles. *The Dark Knight Rises* (Christopher Nolan, 2012) had opened with a Bruce Wayne retired from fighting crime, walking with a cane. Most characters in duopoly films get thrown around without any lasting injuries, but the Bruce Wayne of *Rises* suffered long-term consequences. Just after his decision to come out of retirement, he consults a physician.

> Physician: I have seen worse cartilage in knees.
> Wayne: That's good!
> Physician: No, that's because there *is* no cartilage in your knee, and not much of any use in your elbows or your shoulders. Between that and the scar tissue on your kidneys, the residual concussive damage to your brain tissue, and the general scarred-over quality of your body, I cannot recommend that you go heli-skiing, Mister Wayne.

Rises used the tagline "The Legend Ends," and the scene between Bruce Wayne and his doctor seemed to ground the film in the realities of the mortal body. Yet it quickly abandoned them. Despite bad knees and a literally broken back, the Batman put on a leg brace, did some push-ups, and then pummeled his way to victory. Not so in *Logan*. Although the film still revels in Logan's combat prowess—here with R-rated blood spurts and severed limbs—now his foes continually get the better of him. When Pierce (Boyd Holbrook), leader of the paramilitaries who pursue Laura, first shows up at Logan's compound, Pierce's goons wrestle Logan to the ground while suffering only one casualty. Pierce has described himself as "a fan" of Wolverine, even reporting that he read the *X-Men* comics that exist within the film's setting, and when Pierce sees Logan wrestled down by the paramilitaries, he exclaims, "Jesus . . . seeing you like this just breaks my damn heart." The film wants to break our hearts, too, by putting this object of fandom through a series of escalating injuries, humiliations, and sorrows, culminating in something unprecedented in the superhero film genre: the death of the headlining character, defeated hand to hand by his foe, and without promise of resurrection.

Logan offers not simply nostalgia and grief, but nostalgia and grief for the X-Men franchise's own past, as it narrates the passing of the movie franchise's old guard of actors. Just past the film's halfway point, the weary mutant family gets a break from the hardships of flight, when the Munsons, a Black family of farmers, takes them in. The Munsons do this in payment after Logan helps them secure some runaway horses, one of the film's many gestures to that always-nostalgic film genre, the western. But during this respite, we learn that Transigen's cloning program has produced a creature they call the X-24, a mute and bestial clone of Wolverine, all metal claws and no conscience. Hugh Jackman also plays this younger version, and with the help of makeup and digital de-aging, he looks like a buzz-cut version of himself from the X-Men films of the early 2000s. We first see the X-24 in dim light, when it enters Xavier's bedroom; Xavier misrecognizes it as Logan and tells it that he has finally "remembered what happened in Westchester," when Xavier hurt or killed fellow X-Men during a seizure. "You wouldn't tell me," says Xavier, turning in bed to face the backlit figure looming over him. "I think I finally understand you. Logan—" But at this, the X-24 stabs the gentle old teacher through the chest. Xavier does not die immediately, but he has no more lines in the film, leaving the audience with the horrifying suspicion that Xavier dies believing that Logan has stabbed him. When Logan finds his dying mentor, he tries to stanch the bleeding, whispering reassurance: "It wasn't me . . . it wasn't me." Yet this reassurance only confirms our fear, and Xavier dies without ever confirming that he understands who hurt him.[14]

Xavier's sudden recollection, just before his murder, becomes more poignant in light of Wolverine's own struggle to recover lost memories, which runs throughout the franchise. The X-24 therefore kills Xavier at a moment of climactic drama not just for this film but for the series: the X-24's murder happens just as the old man has begun to remember and regret his own actions, yet Logan's absence from the scene denies Logan this moment of closure with this mentor. Back in *X-Men* (Bryan Singer, 2000), Xavier used his telepathic powers to read Logan's mind, learning of his amnesia. "It's been almost fifteen years, hasn't it?" says Xavier. "Living from day to day, moving from place to place with no memory of who or what you are? . . . I may be able to help you find some answers." *X2: X-Men United* (Brian Singer, 2003) continues to trade on Wolverine's lost memory, with the mysterious Colonel William Stryker (Brian Cox), recognizing Logan, and teasing him with knowledge of his past:

> STRYKER: How long has it been? Fifteen years? You haven't changed one bit! Me, on the other hand . . . [he gestures toward graying temples] Nature. . . .
> I didn't realize Xavier was taking in animals, even animals as unique as you.
> LOGAN: Who are you?
> STRYKER: [smiling] Don't you remember?

Answers about Logan's past come in the prequel *X-Men Origins: Wolverine*, which tells how he gained his metal skeleton and lost his memory, but while these may satisfy the audience, they cannot satisfy the character, who doesn't get to watch prequels. With its grieving hero denied even memory of his past, *Logan* resembles Jameson's description of J. G. Ballard's work on memory: "From this nostalgic and regressive perspective . . . what is mourned is the memory of deep memory; what is enacted is a nostalgia for nostalgia, for the grand older extinct questions of origin and telos" (Jameson, *Postmodernism* 156). In most of the X-Men films, Wolverine suffers *algia* without a *nostos* to match, since he cannot remember his past before his escape from the Weapon X program. *Logan* intensifies the pastness of this past by making Logan, Xavier, and the audience grieve not just for lost memory but also for Xavier's lost School for Gifted Youngsters, and not just for the characters but also for the sunnier X-Men films set there. In showing us the last days of its amnesiac hero, *Logan* sorrows over the character's multilayered history of feeling unable to go home.

Logan uses allusions to and quotations from mass-cultural texts not to generate a pleasant nostalgia but to generate something between grief and the chill of a memento mori. The film draws most on the unlikely juxtaposition of Hollywood westerns and *X-Men* comic books. Not quite an hour into the film, we find Xavier and Laura watching *Shane* (George Stevens, 1953) on the big flat-screen TV in their Oklahoma City hotel room. The scene then cuts between three views. Shots of the TV present scenes from the latter half of *Shane*. Reaction shots show Laura and Xavier watching together, as Xavier falls into (great-)grandfatherly reminiscence: "This is a very famous picture, Laura. It's almost a hundred years old. . . . I first saw this picture at the Essoldo Cinema in my hometown, when I was your age." Cutaways take us to Logan, first coughing into a towel, like a consumptive in a frontier narrative, then looking through the documents that Laura's rescuer packed for her.

Logan thus stumbles upon Laura's cache of several battered but vintage *X-Men* comics. Earlier in the film, Logan had dismissed these comics as sensationalized retellings of his friends' real struggles. Now, he takes off his reading glasses, and with a look as disapproving as that of a 1950s father discovering *Vault of Horror* or *Shock SuspensStories* under his child's bed, he interrupts Laura and Xavier during the climactic shootout of *Shane*, "Charles, we got ourselves an X-Men fan. [brandishing the comics] You do know they're all bullshit, right? Maybe a quarter of it happened, but not like this. In the real world, people die, and no self-promoting asshole in a fucking leotard can stop it. This is ice cream for bed-wetters . . . grade-A bullshit."

The poster for *Logan* had already signified maturation relative to the X-Men films of the 2000s by dressing the title character in a business suit rather than even a subdued superhero costume. Logan's outburst about the childishness of X-Men comics confirms the film's aim to transform not just its title character but the wider X-Men franchise into something more realistic, self-consciously adult, and even didactic about the compromises, sacrifices, and failures of adult life. Xavier interrupts Logan's rant to exclaim, "I don't think Laura needs reminding of life's impermanence." Stewart, aged seventy-six, plays a self-described "nonagenarian," giving this comment a doubled hint of self-consciousness. After Logan storms out, Mangold's camera returns to Shane's farewell to Joey, which we hear in its entirety.

A man has to be what he is, Joey. Can't break the mold. I tried, and it didn't work for me. . . . Joey, there's no living with—with a killing. There's no going back from one. Right or wrong, it's a brand. A brand sticks. . . . Now you run on home to your mother, and tell her . . . tell her everything's all right. And there aren't any more guns in the valley.

But as Alan Ladd speaks on the soundtrack, our view pushes in not on the intradiegetic TV screen but on Laura's face, in rapt close-up. Then begins a striking shot–reverse-shot pattern, cutting between Laura and the TV screen. The TV, also framed with a slow push-in, shows the shot–reverse shot in Stevens's film, as the framings get tighter on Shane and Joey. Our view now lingers first on Joey's face, streaked with tears, then on Laura's, intent but inscrutable. As the camera continues to push in on Laura, we hear Shane, now effectively in voice-off, telling Joey to go home to his mother. Yet as anyone who has seen the film knows, Shane suffered a wound in the climactic gunfight, and he will now depart, despite Joey's demands that he stay. This sequence thus closes with a *mise en abyme* that invites us to identify with two children, each in a moment of growing into new awareness about the relationship between violence, irrevocability, and family. The scene telegraphs one of the aims of *Logan*: it wants to leave our faces, like Joey's, streaked with tears, and asking in vain for Logan to come back.

Despite Logan's rant about comics, the film as a whole does not share his contempt for mass-culture texts and instead presents them as objects for nostalgic but critical attention, like the attention that Laura—already an experienced killer—bestows on *Shane*. *Logan* invites us to recall a time when we believed in simpler stories about heroism, while simultaneously inviting us to consider the shortcomings of those stories, which omit most of the real suffering of human life. Age-based disavowals of mass media usually contain a whiff of shame, a new or remembered sense that we have grown too old or too sophisticated for the funnybooks or horse operas we once enjoyed without self-consciousness. Mark Fisher, discussing the self-consciously "adult" superhero comics of Frank Miller, calls this a "male adolescent desire to both have comics and to feel superior to them" (par. 3). Within the film's narrative, Logan's anger about the comic books arises from their reminder of his personal suffering and loss, but he also articulates the common pain of witnessing our tastes change as we grow older, and the concomitant loss of textual pleasures no longer accessible. Moreover, Logan articulates that medium-specific shame that many readers of comic books, superhero and otherwise, have experienced, whether because their tastes change or because others ridicule their choice of reading. Despite Logan's dismissal, Laura believes that the vintage *X-Men* comics provide clues to the location of a real hideout for fugitive mutants on the Canadian border. Logan tries in vain to shake her faith, but having no better option, he finally agrees to take her there. Despite the film's gritty insistence on the inevitability of age and death, and its unwillingness to give characters the resolutions they want, here the script thinks magically: the sanctuary that these vintage comics call Eden proves real, proving Logan wrong. This revelation justifies Laura's seemingly childish faith, and it justifies the love that it presumes the audience has for comic books. *Logan* lets both its characters and its audience not only have their comics, but also feel superior to comics.

Yet the film has not finished with *Shane*. Like the gunfighter, Logan carries a brand, his scarred and metal-laced body, but in our world, he also carries the X-Men brand licensed to Fox. Logan has not the luxury of simply riding on, because he has already assumed too many responsibilities, familial, narrative, and commercial. His transformation from loner to father therefore implicitly refutes Shane's line about breaking the mold. Still, *Shane*'s emphasis on irrevocability parallels *Logan*'s focus on mortality, which departs from the norms of the superhero genre in general and the X-Men films in particular. Unlike X-Men comics or earlier X-Men films, which kill and resurrect central characters like Professor Xavier and Jean Grey, *Logan* offers no returns from death. Instead it shows characters trying to live through loss and trauma. Late in the film, father and daughter discuss their nightmares:

> LAURA: People hurt me.
> LOGAN: Mine are different. I hurt people....
> LAURA: I've hurt people, too.
> LOGAN: You're gonna have to learn how to live with that.
> LAURA: They were bad people.
> LOGAN: All the same.

Here Logan inverts Shane's speech to Joey, as if understanding that *Shane* offers a fictional solution not available to him or his daughter. As living weapons crafted for war within the fiction, they get treated as instruments to capture and exploit; but as works made for hire in our world, by an industry that focuses on character rather than narrative closure, they also get treated as instruments to capture and exploit. The comics industry's focus on developing licensable characters has led to a greater emphasis on open-ended seriality in superhero stories compared to westerns, where villains, at least, usually die in the last reel while heroes usually ride on. Writing about *The Dark Knight* (Christopher Nolan, 2008), Todd McGowan discusses *Shane* and violence:

> In order for the social order that his violence founds to function as a legal entity, Shane must leave at the end of the film. His violence has a purely exceptional status, and his departure confirms that the exception can disappear after the new social order comes into existence. There is no such recourse for exceptionality in the superhero film. This type of film confronts not the necessity of lawmaking violence but that of a certain necessary violence that exists outside the law. (1)

The superhero narrative traditionally offers a temporally open but spatially restricted series of violent contests, as heroes repeatedly save the city, whereas the western usually offers temporal restriction and spatial openness, forcing the gunfighter to depart after delivering foundational violence. *Logan* takes a third path: the death of the hero to make possible a future for the next generation. Mangold has trodden this path before, in his *3:10 to Yuma* (2007). Mangold remakes the 1957 Delmer Daves western by making it more bloody and making protagonist Dan Evans suffer more throughout. Not only does Mangold's version of Evans begin the film with only one leg, lost to war, but Mangold's revision also kills Evans in the final reel, in the process of accomplishing his mission of delivering the outlaw to the train. Mangold takes Logan on a similar path, not just to put a new spin on a familiar story but to serve the needs of a movie franchise in its seventeenth year. Hugh Jackman's advancing age means that he can no longer credibly play a character whose regenerative superpowers keep him from aging. Fox merges the duopoly's anxieties about copying with the western's model of foundational violence, using this mixture to tell a distinctive story while also handling a casting problem that has begun to impinge on the franchise's realism.

The film's use of the *X-Men* comics within its narrative reminds us that realism consists not of reality but of artistic techniques, conditioned by history, that audiences take for representations of reality. For Laura's stash of *X-Men* comics, the filmmakers did not use real back issues; instead, with help from Marvel Comics editor and executive Joe Quesada, they created fictional props for the film (Leadbeater). Although the magazines look like well-read *X-Men* floppies from the 1970s and 1980s, the legend across the top of each cover reads "X-Men Comics Group," not "Marvel Comics Group." As production designer François Audouy explained, "The comic was designed specifically for the location and the camera angles that we were going to be using" (qtd. in Zakarin). These prop comics, simulacra of continuity capital, fooled my eye, and their worn covers and their distinctive graphic design activated my nostalgia for remembered back-issue bins. In the director's commentary, Mangold cites as inspiration the western *Unforgiven* (Clint Eastwood, 1992). A subplot in that film deals with the failures of a writer of western dime novels to understand the reality of frontier violence as embodied in protagonist William Munny (Clint Eastwood). The prop comics in *Logan* remind viewers of their earlier selves as more naive readers, whether or not they personally encountered monthly comics, and whether or not they recognize the covers.

Unlike *Ant-Man* and *Suicide Squad*, *Logan* uses popular music only sparingly, but uses it to powerful effect, starting in the film's first trailer. As a mournful acoustic guitar plays, Logan and Xavier exchange words in voice-over. "Charles, the world is not the same as it was," says Logan. "Mutants: they're gone now." At this, Johnny Cash begins to sing, and we recognize the song as his 2002 cover version of Nine Inch Nails' "Hurt." Cash's voice, gravelly and tremulous, declares, "I hurt myself today, to see if I still feel." On the screen, we see Logan's bloody knuckles in close-up; then Logan, his hands shaking, pulls a shirt over his heavily scarred back.[15] Even audiences who do not know Cash can recognize his voice as that of an old man; Cash, seventy years old at the time of the recording, sounds much older due to the Shy-Drager syndrome from which he suffered in his final years. The images in the trailer signal the decline of Logan's previously superhuman health, and a shot of Xavier staring upward in a hospital bed strengthens the aura of decrepitude and looming death. The trailer thus evokes losses both past and imminent; past, in the use a late-career recording by a famous American singer, and imminent, in the presentation of formerly superheroic characters suffering physical decline analogous to what we hear in Cash's voice and in Trent Reznor's lyrics. At the trailer's end, Xavier rasps, "Logan, you still have time," over a shot of Logan, bloodied but not healing, an image that undercuts the optimism of Xavier's words. Johnny Cash's star image of authenticity and outlaw masculinity roughly matches Logan's character, as Mangold knows well, having directed the acclaimed 2005 Cash biopic *Walk the Line*. Cash's own death 2003 also helps foreshadow Logan's at the film's end. The end credits of *Logan* use another song by Cash, "The Man Comes Around," from the final album Cash released during his lifetime. The song's apocalyptic lyrics draw imagery from the book of Revelation, imagining the returned Jesus in terms of both redemption and wrath:

> The hairs on your arm will stand up
> At the terror in each sip and in each sup

Will you partake of that last offered cup?
Or disappear into the potter's ground
When the man comes around?

Logan, with its finality, represents the last offered cup of this fan-favorite character, in Jackman's ninth turn in the role. Other characters in the franchise have seen actors come and go, but only Jackman played Logan, the Wolverine.[16]

As in *Ant-Man*, so too in *Logan* the anticopying melodrama becomes a melodrama of parental responsibility. Logan learns of Transigen's creation of mutants through a smuggled video, which shows abuse in a setting combining features of a mental hospital and a factory farm. Transigen artificially inseminates host mothers, who then disappear. Both the whistleblower's video and the mercenary Pierce's business card give the name of Transigen's parent company, Alkali, a callback to the Alkali Lake facility that housed the Weapon X program in *X2: X-Men United* (Bryan Singer, 2003). This program gave Logan his metal skeleton and took his memories; it must also have provided the DNA of Logan and other mutants to Transigen. In the whistleblower's video, Transigen caregivers make the mistake of treating the mutant children like human children, and executive-scientist Dr. Rice (Richard E. Grant) instructs them to the contrary: "Do not think of them as children. Think of them as things, with patents and copyrights. *Comprende*?" Copyright law does not cover industrial processes or genetically modified organisms, but it does govern the world of superhero publishing and the licensing deals that produced *Logan*, and it shows that this mad scientist sees intellectual property laws as means to his monopolistic ends. As in most of these films, the villains at Transigen want to manufacture weapons, and in the smuggled footage we see vat-grown limbs of what will become the murderous X-24. When Rice sends the X-24 into the home of Logan's hosts to murder Xavier and the Munson family, Rice watches over a video feed. "He's fantastic," declares Rice in awe, as the X-24 slaughters the teenage son. As the child of Rice's mad science destroys the biological child of the film's only nuclear family, *Logan* suggests that such horrors occur when villains copy superheroes without license.

Surprisingly, in light of such pro-copyright moralizing, *Logan* also embeds in its narrative an implicit critique of conglomerates. The night that Logan's party stays with the Munsons, the water pressure at their house suddenly falls. Will Munson (Eriq La Salle) hints at a pattern of harassment by neighbors, which one might attribute to his neighbors' racism against this Black family, especially considering the X-Men franchise's history of using mutants as metaphors for human identity politics. But Munson soon reveals that his harassers, white only by coincidence, act on behalf of Canewood Beverage.[17] Earlier, as Logan perused *X-Men* comics in a bar, a Canewood ad boasted "the most nutritious and best-tasting corn ever produced." But Munson disagrees:

> MUNSON: Canewood Beverage bought up everything out here except for us. When we wouldn't sell, they tried eminent domain, then screwing with our water. Couple of months ago somebody poisoned our dogs. [He points to the company's huge robot harvesters.] Look at them . . . shucking their cloned-up super-corn. You know it tastes like shit, too.
> LOGAN: Why to people eat it?
> MUNSON: They don't. They drink it. Corn syrup. It's in those drinks that everyone's having, you know, to stay awake, cheer up, feel strong, sexy, whatever. Used to be a time when a bad day was just a bad day.
> LOGAN: Mine still are.

Logan goes with Munson to break into Canewood's pump station, first helping Munson fix the pipe, then helping Munson fend off the Canewood goons who show up to bully him. Without mentioning *Shane*, the script of *Logan* here returns to its well. In both films, a drifter, expert in violence, helps a family of farmers resist unscrupulous and deep-pocketed competitors willing to use extralegal violence to monopolize land. When Marvel cut off the flow of mutants to Fox, Fox had no such help.

The film implies that Canewood and Transigen share the same goals, if not the same ownership. In the film's climax, Rice addresses Logan as "Mister Howlett," the birth name Logan cannot remember. "I believe you knew my father on the Weapon X program," says Rice, hinting at how Transigen got Logan's DNA and how Rice got his job. But now comes the revelation that Rice has not just copied mutants but also stands behind the cessation of mutant births:

> RICE: The goal was not to end mutantkind but to control it. I realized we needn't stop perfecting what we eat and drink, that we could use those products to perfect ourselves, to distribute gene therapy discreetly through everything from sweet drinks to breakfast cereals. And it worked. Random mutancy went the way of polio. We embarked on our next endeavor—
> LOGAN: Growing mutants of your own.
> RICE: Precisely.

Canewood distributes Transigen's covert gene therapy, thus decreasing the "supply" of natural mutants, to increase "demand" for Transigen's tailor-made mutants. The film's narrative of mutant sterility now becomes legible as an allegory of Disney-Marvel's decision to stop creating new mutant characters for which Fox would own film rights. Rice uses prosocial rhetoric to pursue his corporation's acquisitive ends while treating both mutants and normal humans like tools.

True to its elegiac tone and R rating, *Logan* offers no time-traveling do-overs. Logan and Laura defeat most of their pursuers, but Logan dies fighting the X-24, and neither the heroes nor the law ever threaten Transigen. Laura and her fugitive friends build for Logan a cairn with a wooden cross, opposite a grove of aspens and beneath a mountain, an iconically western version of Cash's potter's ground. As Laura departs the cairn, she turns the cross on its side to form an X, shifting the film's register back from the generic to the proprietary, searing the X-Men brand onto the film's last shot; and as Shane would put it, "A brand sticks." Even in death, *Logan* belongs to Fox. But we know from duopoly history that death has no power over characters with brand equity and licensing potential. The duopoly, like something out of the book of Revelation, will raise the dead, provided those dead bear the mark of the Beast: ©. How Disney's acquisition of Fox will shape the future of the X-Men franchise, none can say. Marvel may once have cut the flow of mutants to Fox, much as the Canewood goons cut the water to the Munsons' farm, but through *Logan*, Fox played the poor farmer standing up to big rancher, with the Wolverine fighting at its side.

CONCLUSION

This chapter has shown how studios have retuned superhero films to address, in both obvious and subtle ways, viewers older than the blockbuster's traditional target audience of viewers under twenty-five. *Ant-Man* represents Marvel's approach, informed by the strategy of corporate parent Disney, which includes nostalgic appeals to adults while keeping the film light in tone. *Ant-Man* replaces the coming-of-age narrative, de rigueur in opening solo films for new characters, with a different kind of family drama, where the hero must prove himself a good father while protecting his surrogate father's monopoly on shrinking powers. The film contains plenty of action, but only four deaths, and only one premeditated murder, all bloodless; the film's hero, although an ex-con, wants to go straight, and he assumes responsibility in a socially normative role. Warner Bros.' *Suicide Squad*, through its subplot about Deadshot's longing to provide a better life for his daughter, offers flashes of something like social realism. But in contrast to *Ant-Man*, and despite its

PG-13 rating, *Suicide Squad* revels in the antisocial criminality of its villain protagonists. *Logan* offers a nostalgic farewell to the X-Men franchise's most popular character and the most consistent actor in any duopoly franchise. Logan becomes a father for just long enough to find new ways to suffer, then die heroically in a film that confirmed Fox's ability to make R-rated X-Men films with better box office profit margins, if not better licensing opportunities, than their PG-13 fare.

Fox's successes with *Deadpool* and *Logan* show the potential for hit R-rated films based on properties originally aimed at children and adolescents. Furthermore, these hits challenged the consensus, growing through the 2010s, that blockbusters must court distribution in mainland China. *Ant-Man*'s light tone and family-man protagonist made the film friendly to Communist Party censors, who disapprove of gore, sexuality, and the glorification of criminals almost as strongly as they disapprove of critiques of party policy. In contrast to *Ant-Man*, *Suicide Squad*, with its ensemble of unrepentant felons, did not receive distribution in the mainland; *Business Insider* called this a "huge blow" to the film's overseas commercial prospects (Guerrasio). Yet a year after *Deadpool*, the party allowed *Logan* distribution after cutting fourteen minutes of footage, and the film took top box office spot in the otherwise slow month of March, showing that MPAA rating alone need not exclude a superhero film. Furthermore, *Logan* became the first film distributed in mainland China to carry something like a rating: under a new law apparently timed for the film's release, *Logan* carried a warning that "elementary school students and preschool children must be accompanied by parents" (Yang).[18] Marvel filmmakers have shown themselves willing to self-censor for Beijing with films like *Doctor Strange*, whose screenwriter told of revising a Tibetan character into a white woman to secure party approval.[19] Rather than showing Fox's willingness to court Beijing, the R-rated X-Men films suggest instead a readiness to diversify the company's product line by placing smaller bets on R-rated films based on a well-known franchise. And the mainland Chinese distribution even of a censored *Logan* suggests the willingness of bureaucrats in State Administration of Press, Publication, Radio, Film and Television (SAPPRFT) to adapt to such changes. Although Xi Jinping's presidency has brought an ever-deepening chill to Beijing's line on most matters of speech, art, and ideology, *Logan* seems to have engineered a minor thaw.

How the successes of these adult-facing superhero films will shape the hegemonic franchises at Columbia Pictures, Warner Bros., and Disney—now owner of both Marvel and Fox—remains an open question. That these studios have begun to address films explicitly to older audiences and to vary their production formulas suggest a film genre forced, by the duration of its own success, to adapt and diversify. In 2033 the first appearance of Superman will enter the public domain, as will Marvel's Captain America in 2036, unless, of course, media conglomerates can again induce Congress to extend copyright durations. If duopoly films continue to occupy a prominent place in studio production over the next decade, then we can expect major changes to this mode of production unless Hollywood makes its own changes to the law.

CHAPTER FIVE

BLADE *AND* BLACK PANTHER
Strategic Blackness and the Rights of Kings

In this chapter, I examine the two chronological bookends to this project, *Blade* (Stephen Norrington, 1998) and *Black Panther* (Ryan Coogler, 2018). Both films use Black actors and signifiers of Black culture strategically to reach audiences eager to see such elements in superhero films, yet both films avoid engaging deeply with racial politics or historical racism while staging melodramas of the defense of proprietary superpowers. Comparing the two helps us see what screen adaptations of Black duopoly characters have in common, whether produced by independent studios as with *Blade* or by conglomerated majors as with *Black Panther*. Such a comparison also lets us see how blockbusters avoid substantively discussing racism even as they use Blackness to stand out in the marketplace.

The wave of superhero films that came to dominate the blockbuster market began with *Blade*, a Wesley Snipes vehicle based on a third-tier Marvel Comics character. New Line Cinema used an established Black star to make an unexpected hit out of an R-rated, self-consciously grim, vampire-superhero martial arts movie, leading to two sequels.[1] While the film contains many signifiers of an oppositional Black masculinity, it presents a critique of vampire racism rather than a critique human racism. Partly through its genre-blending brio and partly through its strategic avoidance of adopting any clear positions regarding real-world politics, the film took in enough money to prove to other studios the viability of Marvel characters. Although the R-rated Blade films look like outliers in a genre dominated by PG-13 Bildungsroman stories about young white heroes, these films actually set the precedent of placing at the center of each film's narrative the struggle to protect a superhero's powers from would-be pirates and copiers. In the first two Blade films, the hero must solve potentially global problems caused by enemies who capture or try to duplicate his powers. The third film, unusually, reverses this conflict, as its heroes seek to capture the villain's DNA, and their success at the film's end only underscores the dangers of inadequate security and copy protection.

Where *Blade* strove for an "urban" feel—hip-hop soundtrack, trash swirling beneath graffiti-tagged walls—*Black Panther* aims for something like an ad for an Afrofuturist theme park, where gorgeous Black people in African-inspired couture walk streets lined with boutiques and food courts. In the fictional kingdom of Wakanda, a deposit of an alien super-metal has allowed the people not only to develop futuristic technology but also to hide their power and prosperity from the rest of the world. Despite gestures of concern with past and present racism, the film avoids substantive discussion of social reality and instead centers its narrative on a dispute over succession to the Wakandan throne, which forces the superpowered king, the Black Panther of the title, to defend his monopoly on the kingdom's mineral wealth and advanced technology. In the end, the king decides to begin charitable missions to less futuristic parts of the world, like the United States. *Black Panther* arrived after duopoly films had dominated the American box office for more than a decade, and film after film had worked through anticopying melodramas; the film reveals the imperatives of the companies that produced and distributed it, from the defense of their copyrights to the expansion into new theatrical markets. These markets include the Kingdom of Saudi Arabia, where *Black Panther* had the dubious honor of becoming the first film to receive a public screening in more than three decades; the film's defense of kingly prerogative takes on a different cast in light of its producers' goal to receive distribution in a country repressive even by the standards of the few surviving absolute monarchies. Though characters in *Black Panther* sometimes discuss matters of state policy, none question the wisdom of monarchy or of hereditary monopolies of power and wealth. Adilifu Nama praises the T'Challa of the comics of the 1960s as "an idealized composite of third-world Black revolutionaries and the anticolonialist movement" (*Super Black* 43), but the T'Challa of the *Black Panther* film offers only a defense of the status quo. We cannot even call the film reactionary, for although some challenge the king, none challenge the institution of kingship.

BLADE: "UNTAPPED WEALTH"

The Blade trilogy began as a collaboration between film producers Michael De Luca and Peter Frankfurt. In 1992, Frankfurt had helped produce the crime drama *Juice* (Ernest R. Dickerson, 1992), starring Tupac Shakur. This film, shot in six weeks on a budget of only $5 million ("The Making"), quadrupled its money ("Juice"). During the film's production, some of its above-the-line hands spoke of the film in terms we will hear again.

> "Studios finally realize the dollar potential of making Black films," says [coproducer David] Heyman. . . . "They cost so little to make, and they don't have to bring in $150 million to be considered a hit." "It's a good thing, too," says the 40-year-old [director Ernest] Dickerson, "because there's an untapped wealth of Black stories, and now some of them will finally get told." ("The Making")

Frankfurt approached Marvel asking for Black characters to license. And as he recounted, "They responded with, 'Yeah, we've got Blade. It's kind of a midlevel character. He had a couple of comics that he was on the cover, but mostly he's a secondary character'" (qtd. in Clark). The Black vampire hunter had first appeared in print in 1973, as part of a spate of new Marvel characters inspired by 1970s Black-directed and Blaxploitation cinema (Nama, *Super Black* 139); Marvel tried to cash in on these films by offering superhero thrills mixed with attempts at social realism. Frankfurt licensed Blade during the wave of Black-themed and largely Black-directed films that S. Craig Watkins has called the "ghetto action film cycle" (236). After the success of *New Jack City* (Mario Van Peebles, 1991), which cost $8 million but grossed $47 million ("New Jack City"), other producers and studios invested in low-budget, social-realist, Black-directed crime films, which included *Boyz n the Hood* (John Singleton, 1991), *Menace II Society* (Albert Hughes and Allen Hughes, 1993), *Dead Presidents* (Albert Hughes and Allen Hughes, 1995), and *Set It Off* (F. Gary Gray, 1996). Watkins notes that the parody *Don't Be a Menace to South Central While Drinking Your Juice in the Hood* (Paris Barclay, 1996) indicated the cycle's peak and the beginning of its creative decline (236).

Even before *Blade*, this wave had produced four movies about Black superheroes. The superhero comedies *The Meteor Man* (Robert Townsend, 1993) and *Blankman* (Mike Binder, 1994) featured Black heroes not adapted from comics but written for the screen; they parodied superhero tropes while still addressing Black cultural, political, and economic concerns. Both, as Jeffrey Brown notes, featured "inept superheroes," and both films "failed miserably" (126). *Spawn* (Mark A. Z. Dippé, 1997) adapted the title character of the Image Comics series. This Black Special Forces operative returns from the dead with supernatural powers. But *Spawn*'s narrative deals with concerns remote from Black life, and for most of its running time, it keeps its star, Michael Jai White, under either heavy burn-scar prosthetics or a mask, rendering the actor and the character a racial blank. Yet *Spawn* did good business, and just sixteen days after the film opened, *Steel* (Kenneth Johnson, 1997) followed. Where *Spawn* made good money despite bad reviews, *Steel* made bad everything, taking in just over 10 percent of its production budget ("Steel"). Yet on paper, *Steel* must have looked promising. Unexpectedly, we can best understand *Blade* by beginning with *Steel*, *Blade*'s nearest precursor in time and the only other duopoly peer among the Black action films of that era.

Steel came about through a partnership between music producer Quincy Jones and movie producer David Salzman. The title character, John Henry Irons, invents an armored suit that gives him superpowers; he had first appeared just four years earlier, during the infamous "Death of Superman" crossover in DC Comics. Jones and Salzman's QDE Entertainment acquired the rights to Steel and then arranged for the basketball player Shaquille O'Neal to star in the kid-friendly picture. Meanwhile, Jones assembled a soundtrack album featuring major hip-hop and R&B artists; no doubt he understood the role of hit singles by Black musicians like Prince and Seal in promoting *Batman* (Tim Burton, 1989) and *Batman and Robin* (Joel Schumacher, 1994). QDE hired writer-director Kenneth Johnson, creator of the successful *Incredible Hulk* (CBS, 1978–82) TV series, to helm the production. Yet even in the 1970s, Johnson had taken a dim view of superheroes, in part because of his insider position in the media industry. In 1977, Frank Price, head of Universal Television, had paid for the TV rights to twelve Marvel characters, and Price had asked Johnson to look through the portfolio and direct a live-action TV series based on whichever character Johnson liked. According to Johnson,

> I ran screaming from the room and said "none of them!" But I was reading *Les Miserables* so I had Jan Val Jean and Javert . . . in my head. I thought, "well, maybe there's a way to take a little Victor Hugo, a little Robert Louis Stevenson, and this ridiculous premise called *The Incredible Hulk* and turn it into something, if they allow me to do it as a psychological drama with real adult appeal." (qtd. in Rathwell)

So when QDE Entertainment approached Johnson asking him to helm *Steel*, the situation must have looked familiar: optimistic producers have licensed a character on the cheap, and they need a director. Warner Bros. would only distribute *Steel*, not produce it, so the studio stood to lose little, and it did correspondingly little to promote the film. Not that promotion would have helped much: *Steel* looks and sounds like a second-rate telefilm, even down to its superficial, sentimentalized, and PG-rated depiction of Black poverty and gang violence in Los Angeles. It tells a familiar story of a genius engineer who invents super-weapons for the US Army, but when a rogue officer copies them for sale to terrorists and gangsters, the engineer creates the alter ego Steel to thwart the scheme. This essentially parallels Steel's origin in the print stories, a rare case of a superhero film adapting its anticopying melodrama directly from the comics. But because the producers did not acquire the rights to other characters, Johnson's script removes Steel from the Superman franchise and from the DC universe, creating new supporting characters and villains. Steel's earnest and thankless crusade to protect the world mirrors the task of writer-director Johnson, who did the job to QDE's specifications, penning an eager but inept script, thick with allusions not only to the *Batman* TV show (ABC, 1966–68) but also to Black media ranging from *Shaft* (Gordon Parks, 1971) to *Sanford and Son* (NBC, 1972–77), and from MC Hammer to the Wu-Tang Clan.

Steel bombed, but the duopoly had bigger problems. *Batman and Robin* (Joel Schumacher, 1997) demonstrated that even Time Warner could manufacture an event film unpopular enough to kill the conglomerate's only active superhero movie franchise. Marvel, still the underdog, fared worse: bankruptcy, corporate takeovers, and the mid-1990s collapse of the US comics market all seemed to threaten the end of the publisher. Amid these flops and failures, the success of New Line Cinema's *Blade* seemed like the kind of last-minute rescue one would only believe in a superhero movie.

FEAR OF A VAMPIRE PLANET

Like its half-vampire protagonist, *Blade* occupies a liminal position both in terms of its crossover success and in terms of its mixture of tropes from marginal and cult film genres. The filmmakers licensed from Marvel a Black vampire hunter with a penchant for leather, but they took significant liberties in embellishing that character, not only by making Blade a superpowered hybrid, but also by hybridizing Marvel's proprietary elements with nonproprietary elements from genre films, tropes for which they did not have to pay licensing fees. Many films of the ghetto action cycle paid homage to the Black and Blacksploitation crime films of the 1970s, but *Blade* went further in its recombinations. From the vampire films of Hammer Studios, *Blade* borrowed its liberality with gore and its vampires that combust in sunlight, and from *The Lost Boys* (Joel Schumacher, 1987) it borrowed vampires as hypersexual nightclub kids. But it also borrowed from the martial arts cinema of Hong

Kong, and here the casting of Wesley Snipes in the title role becomes pivotal. Snipes made his name in race-conscious dramas like *Jungle Fever* (Spike Lee, 1991) and the gangster hit *New Jack City*, but he brought to *Blade* more than acting chops and star power: he brought martial arts skills that allowed him to do most of his own fight scenes, thereby lending the film's action sequences speed and the visual authenticity of relatively long takes, rare outside Hong Kong films but absent from the CG-heavy duopoly films that would follow, more eager to protect their costly, clumsy stars than to stage a good fight.[2] Wirework enables Blade and his vampire combatants to make superhuman leaps like those seen in *wuxia* films.[3] When Blade hunts vampires, he brings a sword and multiple firearms, but the series contrives again and again to separate him from his guns, making every disarmament an occasion for Blade to fight hand to hand. In the manner of Bruce Lee, Snipes often begins a set piece empty-handed, facing multiple armed foes, but he then either reveals previously hidden weapons or seizes his attackers' weapons to use against them. *Blade* thus channels Hong Kong cinema as well as Black American martial arts films like *Black Belt Jones* (Robert Clouse, 1974) and *The Last Dragon* (Michael Schultz, 1985). Blade's name denotes part of a weapon, recalling Blaxploitation heroes like *Hammer* (Bruce Clark, 1972) and *Black Gunn* (Robert Hartford-Davis, 1972). Even Blade's muscle car recalls 1970s cult cinema: the matte black Dodge Charger fastback would look at home in *Vanishing Point* (Richard C. Sarafian, 1971), *Dirty Mary, Crazy Larry* (John Hough, 1974), or *Mad Max* (George Miller, 1979). But a score of techno and hip-hop accompanies Blade's pursuits of vampires and escapes from the police, mixing nineties beats with seventies nostalgia.

Adilifu Nama has called Blaxploitation film "a bloody referendum on white authority" (19), and *Blade* offers plenty of blood from white authority figures, both human and vampire. For example, Blade's first encounter with the police goes badly. As Blade tries to stop a wounded vampire's rampage through a hospital, two white police officers enter the frame, behind Blade, and yell, "Freeze!" When Blade turns in response, they unload their revolvers not at the nude, skinless gore-monster but at the Black guy. Unhurt, Blade merely says, "Motherfucker, are you out of your damn mind?" The opening-reel defiance and R-rated language recall *Sweet Sweetback's Baadasssss Song* (Melvin Van Peebles, 1971), whose protagonist takes on the police and becomes a folk hero. Like the antihero of *Super Fly* (Gordon Parks Jr., 1972), Blade also uses an underground economy to fund his resistance, but rather than sell cocaine, Blade robs "familiars," the human stooges of vampires, selling their jewelry to a Black occultist fence. The fence greets Blade with an elaborate dap handshake, just out of frame, which suggests an ambiguous solidarity: humans against vampires, or Blacks against a white establishment, or maybe both. And like the protagonist of *Blacula* (William Crain, 1972), Blade uses his vampire strength to fight police, both singly and in groups. One white cop, a familiar of the vampires, receives from Blade a humiliating beating not once but in two different scenes, underscoring the point.

On a budget of $45 million, *Blade* took in $70 million domestically and $131 million worldwide ("Blade"). This success not only brought Marvel new attention from movie studios but also spurred those studios that had already bought live-action film rights from Marvel but had not yet exploited them. Licensing helped Marvel recover from its mid-1990s bankruptcy. As Derek Johnson writes:

> While Marvel sold the rights to make the first *X-Men* film to 20th Century Fox for only a few hundred thousand dollars . . . Sony Pictures subsequently paid Marvel $10 million for the rights to make the first *Spider-Man* film in addition to agreeing to a first-dollar participation deal. Marvel received a percentage of each ticket sold to the licensed film—regardless of how much the studio needed to recoup to turn a profit. (*Media Franchising* 96)

Fox's *X-Men* (Bryan Singer, 2000) took $54.5 million in its opening weekend, setting a record for a nonsequel film's opening weekend (B. Gray, "Weekend Box Office"). But less than two years later, Columbia's *Spider-Man* left Hollywood "slack-jawed" with its "record-shattering $115 million opening weekend" (Lyman), not only setting an opening-day record of $39.4 million but also becoming the first movie to take more than $100 million in its opening weekend (Gray, "*Spider-Man*"). Fox and Sony both set to work making sequels, while Marvel began work toward producing its own films. As Johnson notes, "By 2005, these successes encouraged a stabilized Marvel to finance production on its own and recapture creative control and box-office profit from its studio partners" ("Cinematic Destiny" 1). The R-rated *Blade* franchise never matched the box office or licensing successes of the PG-13 *X-Men* or *Spider-Man* films, but without the vampire-killing crossover hit, Marvel might never have risen from the grave.

Despite its kinship with the Black-themed action films of its era and the past, *Blade* uses vampires as an allegory of American racial categories, and here *Blade* diverges most from its 1970s inspirations. Despite the film's urban-coded setting and hip-hop soundtrack, its script, by David S. Goyer, does not address racialized poverty, police brutality, or Black politics, and it avoids even the word *black*. Instead it substitutes the racial politics of the vampires. This allegory begins in the opening scene, a washed-out flashback to 1967: paramedics rush a young Black woman, pregnant and bleeding from the neck, into an operating theater. They deliver her baby just before the sound of a flatlined electrocardiogram informs us of her death. The baby, young Eric Brooks, will grow up with a vampire's strength and near immortality, but without any of a vampire's vulnerabilities to silver, garlic, and sunlight. Taken in and raised by a human vampire hunter, Brooks will become Blade, known to the vampires he hunts as the "Daywalker." Blade generally protects humans but treats vampire familiars with hostility and scorn, remarking on the "cattle brand" that each wears, identifying that familiar as the "property" of a vampire. Although Blade does not consider himself a vampire, he nevertheless must inject a serum to suppress his urge to drink blood. And he rejects the vampires' racial categories, killing both "pure bloods" (those born of vampire parents) and those "turned" by a vampire's bite.

The film tells the story of Blade's conflict with Deacon Frost (Stephen Dorff), a vampire who seeks to overthrow the pure bloods' monopoly on power. Early in the film, Frost challenges the vampires' ruling assembly, which maintains a policy of careful hiding among the humans. The assembly meets at a conference table in a shadowed, cavernous room; members wear dark business attire, most of the men in three-piece suits with neckties and subdued pocket squares. The assembly's head, Dragonetti (Udo Kier), sits at the table's far end. At Dragonetti's elbow sits a Black vampire, conspicuous for his shoulder-length braids, three-piece suit, paisley-medallion tie, and elaborate tie bar. This Black vampire's physical position beside Dragonetti makes him salient in framing after framing, yet he says nothing in the scene. He doesn't have to, because his mere presence works to signify that this vampire assembly does not go in for American-style color lines or racial divisions of labor. When Frost arrives, a white vampire doorman ushers Frost in, reinforcing the impression that while vampires care deeply about the fiction of race, they don't care about the same races that Americans care about. In contrast to the waistcoated and necktied vampire elders, Frost wears a leather jacket over a white dress shirt open to its third button, showing his chest hair. He swaggers in, smoking a cigarette to highlight his contempt of the assembly, and the assembly reciprocates. Dragonetti dismisses Frost for lacking the "pure blood" that the rest of them share, gently sneering at those like Frost, "merely turned." The assembly's conservative dress fits with their policy of caution; Dragonetti insists on "discretion" in dealing with humans. But Frost rejects this approach: "We should be ruling the humans. . . . For fuck's sake, these people are our food, not our allies.... The world belongs to us, not to humans." Property and blood, as well as the properties *of* blood, here emerge as the central thematic concerns of the Blade trilogy.

For the first hour of the film, Blade pursues Frost while Frost in turn pursues Blade, seemingly intent on killing the elusive Daywalker. Blade rescues hematologist Karen Jensen (N'Bushe Wright) from a vampire and takes her to the hideout he shares with Whistler (Kris Kristofferson), the vampire hunter who rescued him. Using Whistler's laboratory, Dr. Jensen begins working on a cure not only for her own nascent vampirism but for vampirism at large.[4] In a raid on a vampire archive, Blade captures ancient vampire documents and an encrypted computer disk, and after this raid, Frost's attitude seems to change. Frost still scoffs at Blade's sympathy for humans, but he proposes an alliance: "Spare me the Uncle Tom routine.... You think the humans'll ever accept a half-breed like you? They can't. They're afraid of you. And they should be.... I'm offering you a truce. I want you with us." In Frost's speech, the film alludes to American forms of racism as Frost offers Blade something like solidarity. But soon we learn that Frost has other plans for Blade, or at least plans for his blood. Whistler decrypts the vampire disk and tells Blade of Frost's plan to cause a "vampire apocalypse": "You're the key. He needs your blood. The blood of the Daywalker.... You can't go after him. If Frost gets his hands on you, it's all over. There'll be armies of the motherfuckers." A few minutes later, we hear as much from Frost himself as he boasts to Dr. Jensen: "The Blood God's coming, and after tonight, you people are fucking history.... Anyone caught in his path will instantly be turned. Everyone you've ever known, everyone you've ever fucking loved. It won't matter who's pure blood and who's not. How you going to cure the whole fucking world?" Through most of Frost's rant, sinister orchestral music swells on the soundtrack, but when he says, "It won't matter who's pure blood and who's not," the music falls silent for a beat, letting us consider the implications. The laws of vampire hypodescent relegate Frost and those like him to inferior status compared to pure bloods, so Frost will use supernatural means to "turn" the whole world vampire, overwhelming the pure bloods by numbers, in a pulp-horror version of the demographic threat imagined by white nationalists. (Whose blood the vampires will drink, Frost doesn't say.) Late in the film, Frost captures Blade long enough to get the blood he needs for his ritual, but with Dr. Jensen's timely help, Blade kills Frost's minions and the Blood God, preventing the apocalypse.

Frost's reference to *Uncle Tom's Cabin* at least alludes to America's history of racism, but the next two films in the series export their allusions to Europe while continuing the first film's preoccupation with blood, in multiple senses of the word. In *Blade II* (Guillermo del Toro, 2002), also scripted by Goyer, a new "Reaper Strain" of meta-vampires arises. These Nosferatu-like creatures not only prey on vampires but also lack vampires' weaknesses for silver, garlic, and stakes through the heart. The Reapers' predation drives the vampires to recruit Blade to help them hunt Reapers in Europe. When Blade arrives in Prague, he meets the team of paramilitaries that he will assist, led by a burly vampire skinhead named Reinhardt (Ron Perlman). When Reinhardt steps forward to meet Blade, a military snare drum plays momentarily on the soundtrack; the vampire's name recalls Operation Reinhardt, the Nazis' name for their plan to open extermination camps in occupied Poland. If Reinhardt's name, look, and military theme did not already signify undisguised racism—especially in Prague, a city from which the Nazis deported Jews—then Reinhardt's dialogue forces the point. He leans close to Blade and says, in an American accent, "Me and the gang were wondering... can you blush?" Two of the other white vampires laugh and fist-bump over the taunt, seemingly a jab at Blade's dark skin.⁵ But this allusion refers not to Nazism but to the Christian Identity movement, which gained prominence in the United States during the 1980s and 1990s, after its followers committed a spate of murders and bombings. This white supremacist doctrine holds that only the true descendants of Adam have souls, and only skin pale enough to blush signifies this ancestry. As one Christian Identity website puts it, "The Hebrew word for man is Adam itself and actually means to show blood in the face; to be fair; rosy cheeked; to be ruddy; and to be able to blush or flush. One must admit that the other races do not fit this description and therefore, cannot descend through Adam" (Downey). Reinhardt thus signifies not vampire racism but an overdetermined and incoherent human racism, and of a kind that Blade did not have to deal with in the first film, set in some unspecified American city.

Fittingly, this film that uses "blood in the face" as shorthand for human racism also presents heredity as the central concern of its vampires. As the final act of *Blade II* begins, we learn that the Reapers arose because of the mad science of a vampire eugenicist. In a cathedral-like laboratory, the ancient vampire Damaskinos stands beside a rack of vampire clone fetuses and declares the truth: "For years I've struggled to rid our kind of any hereditary weaknesses, so recombining DNA was simply the next logical step.... In time, there will be a new, pure race, begun from my own flesh, immune to silver—soon, even sunlight!" Unsurprisingly, Blade's own body once again contains the secret ingredient that the villains need. A human familiar details the vampires' plan: "We are going to harvest your blood, every drop of it. Then bone marrow, organs, everything. We'll find the missing key to creating

Daywalkers." But Blade escapes, kills the last of the Reapers, and thereby prevents the vampires from mass-producing Daywalkers.

Blade: Trinity (David S. Goyer, 2004), this time both scripted and directed by Goyer, repeats these central tropes while inverting them and taking them to new pulp extremes. Because the vampires' scheme to use Blade's blood has now failed twice, they go back to the original Daywalker. The vampires unearth and awaken "Drake," the ancient Sumerian ur-vampire that the wider world knew as Count Dracula. Drake himself notes that "Stoker's fable" got right his ability to live in sunlight. But Stoker also got right Drake's ability to change shape; this and his ability to walk in daylight make him, like Blade, a superhero even among fellow monsters. The vampires behind the scheme speak to Drake in religious awe: "Your blood, your sacrament, can set us free now." Yet while the vampires want to use Drake's blood to become Daywalkers, Blade falls in with a group of human vampire hunters who have developed a biological weapon called Daystar, "an artificial virus targeted specifically at vampires." Because vampires have genetically drifted, Daystar lacks the potency to create an apocalyptic pandemic. As one of the hunters puts it, "We need a better strain of DNA to work with. We need Dracula's blood." This line recalls both the super-science of comic books and Hammer films like *Taste the Blood of Dracula* (Peter Sasdy, 1970), but in this scheme lies the film's most distinctive twist: its inversion of the typical duopoly melodrama. Blade has spent two movies fighting to prevent vampires from stealing his blood, but he now joins a scheme to steal the blood of a monster from the public domain.

Blade: Trinity lends both temporal and moral urgency to this explicitly genocidal plan by framing it as a last-ditch effort to stop the enslavement of humans. As one of the vampire hunters puts it, vampires have decided that "hunting humans on a piecemeal basis was too inefficient," so the vampires have built "processing centers" to hold comatose humans and harvest their blood. One of the humans calls this the "vampire Final Solution," and when Blade enters one of the blood-farming warehouses, lined with bagged and comatose humans, Blade repeats the line. Like *Blade II*, *Blade: Trinity* makes only one allusion to real-world racism, but *Trinity* also uses Nazi Germany as its example, exporting racism in space and time, rather than using a more recent American example like redlining or de jure segregation.[6] Goyer's scripts all locate racism somewhere other than the implied white American audience for his movies, a common trope in white discourses on racism. As Teun van Dijk argues, attributing racism to others enables the denial of racism among the attributor's "ingroup of moderate white citizens" (Van Dijk 96). Blade inhabits a fictional world where racism lives among vampire senators and vampire skinheads, or in abolitionist novels by Harriet Beecher Stowe, but not the films' implied American audience. The franchise's "crossover" success no doubt depended on its ability to appeal to Blacks while avoiding any implication that American whites or their living elders might have done anything racist. But the vampires' Final Solution does not come to pass. In the climactic battle, while Blade's comrades fight with lesser vampires, Blade fights Drake hand to hand, finally stabbing him with the vial of Daystar virus. The ur-vampire exhales a cloud of CG blood cells, which immediately cause all the nearby vampires to shrivel and die. The film does not show us the wider results of this pandemic, this Final Solution of the Vampire Question; a montage of vampires unable to save their dying vampire children might align the audience too closely with historical perpetrators of genocide. Yet the film shows the necessity of protecting superhero (or supervillain) DNA. Drake's failure brings about not only his own death but the destruction of his people, the kind of apocalypse that duopoly superheroes always thwart.

BLACK PANTHER: BRANDING, MINING, AND THEFT

In the two decades after *Blade* opened, Marvel's fortunes changed beyond recognition. Marvel Studios launched multiple, parallel film series based on Thor, Iron Man, and Captain America, weaving them into the larger Avengers franchise, and the company continued to develop new films based on lesser-known characters like Ant-Man, Doctor Strange, and the Guardians of the Galaxy. In August 2014, Marvel Studios president Kevin Feige declared that fans had clamored for a Black Panther movie, in "a groundswell" of demand (qtd. in Cornet). But we have reason to doubt this. Janet Wasko warns us that contrary to the myth of a "democratic" Hollywood that produces content "determined by audience demand," the conglomerated studios instead manufacture demand for the kinds of products that they and exhibitors find most profitable based on their current business models ("Critiquing Hollywood" 17). For the duopoly, this means making films using characters already tested with mass audiences, and Marvel had not yet tested the Black Panther.

On social media, we can find some evidence of popular demand for Black Panther movies, but that demand seemed confined to a tiny number of fans. In October 2014, the Facebook group "Black Panther Movie Now" began promoting their demand for "diversity in superhero movies," yet in the next two years, the group gained fewer than three thousand followers ("Black Panther Movie Now"). In 2014 and 2015, three campaigns on the crowdfunding website Kickstarter sought money for Black Panther fan films, and all three failed, not because Kickstarter shut them down on orders from Marvel lawyers, but because they failed to meet their fundraising goals. *DeadPool / Black Panther: The Gauntlet* raised just $10 out of its goal of $10,000 ("DeadPool / Black Panther"), and *DeadPool / Black Panther Back in Red & Black* raised $66 out of $10,000 ("DeadPool / Black Panther Back in Red & Black"). *Reign of Wakanda: Return of the Black Panther* surpassed these in both ambition and takings, raising $106 out of $20,000 ("Reign of Wakanda"). As of early 2024, all three campaigns remain visible on Kickstarter, where their aggregate haul of just $182 suggests only niche interest. Feige's announcement of a "groundswell" therefore seems like corporate aspiration informed by an opportunistic response to the Black Lives Matter movement. Less than two weeks before Feige's interview, the Ferguson police had killed Michael Brown, and protests continued to shake American cities.

Yet if independent studios like New Line can produce hits based on lesser-known characters like Blade, then so can the conglomerated majors. Thirteen months after Feige's claim of a groundswell, Marvel Comics began raising the profile of the Black Panther and priming audiences for a mania. In September 2015, Marvel Comics hired longtime comics fan Ta-Nehisi Coates to write a new series of Black Panther comics. Coates had no experience writing comics, but he had credibility as one of the most prominent Black critics of American culture, specifically American racism. Furthermore, Coates was famous for winning the National Book Award for Nonfiction in 2015 for his best-selling memoir *Between the World and Me*. Marvel's recruitment of Coates made national news, with the *New York Times* noting that "it may seem odd for Mr. Coates to write a mainstream superhero comic," but "diversity—in characters and creators—is a drumbeat to which the comic book industry is increasingly trying to march" (Gustines). The *Times* raised no challenging questions like, Why this year? Did Marvel try to recruit any Black writers already working in comics? What other National Book Award winners has Marvel tried to recruit? But the celebratory coverage by the *Times* informed millions of readers who follow neither comic books nor staffing decisions in the comics industry. For the price of a celebrity writer, Marvel thus secured free advertising in America's newspaper of record. Coates's first issue of *Black Panther* appeared in April, and by May, it had sold "a record-breaking 300,000 copies," 50 percent more than a typical top-selling issue (Dockterman).[7]

Meanwhile, Marvel Studios used its own methods to boost the profile of the character. Marvel gave the Black Panther (Chadwick Boseman) a key supporting role in the third Captain America film, *Captain America: Civil War* (Anthony Russo and Joe Russo, 2016). In the first official trailer for *Civil War*, released in November 2015, the Black Panther appears in costume, but only in several wide shots of action (Marvel Entertainment, *The Civil War Begins*). Then, in the second trailer, released in March 2016, the Black Panther first appears unmasked and in close-up, then costumed in three different clips from action sequences (Marvel Entertainment, *Marvel's Captain America: Civil War*). Between these full-length trailers, a thirty-second ad for the film aired during the 2016 Super Bowl. This ad ended with a pair of tracking shots, each revealing a line of Avengers squaring off before battle, and the second of these tracking shots—the trailer's final image—ends on the costumed Black Panther. Of the eleven Avengers revealed in these two shots, only the Black Panther appears in close-up, and the trailer's suspenseful music reaches its crescendo just as he comes into frame. The image then cuts to black with the film's title and billing block (*Captain America: Civil War Official Super Bowl TV Spot*, 2016). Without mentioning the Black Panther or giving him any dialogue, the ad presented him as *Civil War*'s most mysterious and compelling new character. If Coates's work on the *Black Panther* comic didn't start people talking, this ad would, and at untold thousands of Super Bowl parties.

Black Panther (Ryan Coogler, 2018) opens with exposition, and even here the film's mode of production leaves fingerprints on the narrative. The opening shot shows a night sky. "*Baba*," says an unseen boy, "tell me a story." The unseen father gives the boy and the audience a primer on the history of the fictional African nation of Wakanda, rendered in dreamlike CGI. By presenting this exposition as an act of interpersonal storytelling, the film treads paths worn by the *Lord of the Rings* films and the recent success of *Wonder Woman*, but it also recalls the West African tradition of the *griot*, reciter of oral history and adviser to royalty. This exposition begins with an accident: "Millions of years ago, a meteorite made of vibranium, the strongest substance in the universe, struck the continent of Africa." Five tribes wage war over the place of this windfall until a "warrior-shaman" unifies them by force. This first Black Panther gains superhuman powers by consuming an herb transformed by the meteorite, and he uses these powers to establish himself as superhero-king of Wakanda. Using their super-metal, the Wakandans develop the world's most sophisticated technology but deliberately hide from the outside world— "to keep vibranium safe," intones the *griot*. The notion of a technologically advanced civilization hidden in a tropical forest has antecedents in "lost race" fictions of writers like H. Rider Haggard and Abraham Merritt, popular during the waning years of Europe's colonial expansions in Africa and Asia. But where most lost-race novels posit a European or Asian civilization hidden in some unexpected land, Jack Kirby's Black Panther stories posited an indigenous civilization hidden in central Africa. The Black Panther franchise therefore offers a revision of the lost-race template, an Afrofuturist fantasy of a nation that never suffered colonization or "underdevelopment" at the hands of European powers but instead exceeded the technological achievements of those powers.[8] But the film adds a preoccupation specific to duopoly films: the hero must struggle and suffer to maintain custody over powers or technologies too dangerous for the world at large.[9]

Viewers who know superhero comics will note another kind of revision. The *griot* calls vibranium the strongest metal "in the universe," but in what the publisher has long called the "Marvel Universe" of interconnected comic books, vibranium comes in second to a metal called adamantium. When Marvel sold the film rights to the X-Men comics to 20th Century Fox in 1994, Marvel sold the rights to adamantium, which laces Wolverine's bones and makes his claws so sharp. So in *Black Panther*, Marvel Studios promotes vibranium from second to first place. By reassigning the title of strongest metal, Marvel unintentionally reminds viewers of the real-world property relations that determine fictional metallurgy.

The villains of *Black Panther*, unsurprisingly, seek to disrupt the status quo of Wakanda's custody of vibranium, and these schemes not only intertwine with but actually motivate the film's main narrative of dynastic succession. After the opening exposition, the film proper opens with another kind of flashback, this time to 1992. Ulysses Klaue, a white South African, has stolen a "quarter ton" of vibranium and bombed a border station to escape Wakanda. The then-current Black Panther, King T'Chaka, learns that his brother Prince N'Jobu gave Klaue information to commit the robbery, so the king travels to Oakland, California, where Prince N'Jobu works as a spy. N'Jobu, while undercover, has become a Black militant, and we first see him leaning over street maps and AR-15–style rifles as he describes his plan for a raid or robbery. Later shots reveal two posters of the hip-hop act Public Enemy, including an image of Chuck D and Flavor Flav behind prison bars, from the cover of their magnum opus *It Takes a Nation of Millions to Hold Us Back*. King T'Chaka enters, and with these posters behind him, he confronts Prince N'Jobu and seemingly takes the prince back to Wakanda. Yet this first version of the flashback only tells part of the story, and halfway through the film, we get a fuller version, where Prince N'Jobu offers principled reasons for his betrayal of Wakandan sovereignty over vibranium. He says that he has seen too much Black suffering during his undercover work: "Their leaders have been assassinated, communities flooded with drugs and weapons. They are overly policed and incarcerated. All over the planet our people suffer because they don't have the tools to fight back. With vibranium weapons they could overthrow every country, and Wakanda could rule them all the right way." When N'Jobu makes this speech, the audience realizes that *Black Panther* will not talk around racism the way most superhero films have. Yet the script keeps critiques of systemic racism short and shallow, putting them in the mouths of its villains, and it couples these critiques with plans to use vibranium to establish a Wakandan empire. King T'Chaka, like most of the film's Wakandan characters, rejects N'Jobu's call to imperialism, as well as N'Jobu's attempt to collapse Wakandans and other persons of African descent into a single imagined community. Instead the king seeks to protect strictly Wakandan interests: "You will return home at once, where you will face the Council and inform them of your crimes." At this, N'Jobu draws a gun to kill the counterspy who informed on him. But T'Chaka, with his preternatural speed and strength, deflects the gun, then sinks vibranium claws into his brother's heart. This royal fratricide sets up the film's main drama, as the sons of Prince N'Jobu and King T'Challa fight for the throne and its prerogative to distribute or withhold super-metal and super-technology from the world.

Noble even in death, N'Jobu dies on his feet, and the dignity of this death helps us focus on the dynastic melodrama rather than on the more fundamental melodrama of Wakandan resource management. Coogler frames N'Jobu's final moment as a close-up two-shot, an echo of the framing Coogler used earlier in the scene, when the brothers embraced in greeting. Once again, T'Chaka faces the camera over his brother's shoulder, but now his eyes shut in a scowl of grief as N'Jobu's knees begin to buckle. Despite the careful framing of this and other quiet moments in the film, the scene as a whole does not make clear the reason that the king slew the prince, and this lack of clarity begins on the visual level in their brief fight. The fight happens not just quickly but too quickly for the eye to follow. Like most non-CG fight scenes in Marvel Studios films, rapid cutting between extremely brief shots here creates what David Bordwell has called Hollywood's signature action style, an "overwhelming but loose and sketchy *impression* of physical activity" (74; his emphasis). If we slow down the video, we see that T'Chaka has his back on N'Jobu when N'Jobu pulls a gun from the waistband of his jeans. The next shot shows N'Jobu level the gun, and the following shows T'Chaka not in the act of whirling but already turned toward N'Jobu and stationary, except for the flick of his wrists that extends the claws of his vibranium battle suit. In the next shot, T'Chaka first uses his right hand to deflect N'Jobu's gun and then closes for a lethal strike with the same hand. But why strike the heart? If this armored superhuman has the speed to turn around, stop, and then extend his claws all in the time it takes the shooter to draw and aim, then why can't the armored superhuman just snatch the gun that he has already deflected? Rapid cutting and extremely short takes try to hide the egregious fight choreography, but the scene's lack of credible spatial economy matches its lack of narrative motivation. The film otherwise presents King T'Chaka as disciplined and self-possessed, so his blow seems gratuitously lethal. Superheroes have the necessary power and precision to save whoever screenwriters decide need saving, but here the film needs to set up a fratricide to haunt a royal family. T'Chaka therefore uses excessive force, and N'Jobu dies "overpoliced" by his superpowered sovereign. The king tells the spy, the only witness to the killing, "Speak nothing of this," thereby beginning a cover-up not only of the murder but also of the dead prince's collusion with foreign vibranium thieves. Yet T'Chaka's "speak nothing of this" also seems addressed to us, as if instructing viewers not to question a scene that reveals inconsistent superhero mechanics, bad fight choreography, and a lawless violence at the heart of the Wakandan state.

The Marvel Cinematic Universe had actually introduced Wakanda's problem with vibranium loss before it introduced Wakanda or even Wakandan characters. Ulysses Klaue (Andy Serkis) appeared in *Avengers: Age of Ultron* (Joss Whedon, 2015), and although he had only five minutes of screen time, he made a memorable impression as a grubby, chatty gunrunner, his neck branded with the Wakandan word for "thief." But Klaue suffers worse than a brand when the robot Ultron, buying stolen vibranium, (bloodlessly) severs Klaue's left arm during a moment of pique; this second mutilation sets up Klaue's use of a prosthetic mechanical hand. In *Black Panther*, T'Challa and CIA operatives capture Klaue and seize the mechanical hand, which doubles as a sonic ray gun. When CIA Agent Ross (Martin Freeman) asks Klaue about the ray gun's origin, Klaue dismisses it as "an old mining tool that I made some adjustments to." Agent Ross only knows Wakanda as an undeveloped and isolationist backwater, but Klaue tells Ross otherwise:

> KLAUE: It's all a front. Explorers searched for it for centuries. El Dorado, the Golden City. They thought they could find it in South America, but it was in Africa the whole time, a technological marvel. All because it was built on a mound of the most valuable metal known to man. *Isipho*, they called it, "the gift." Vibranium.
>
> ROSS: Vibranium. [skeptical] Yeah. Strongest metal on Earth.
>
> KLAUE: . . . They've been mining it for thousands of years, and they still haven't scratched the surface. I'm the only outsider who's seen it and got out of there alive.

Klaue steals a tool used for mining vibranium, a tool that also incorporates vibranium for its wondrous powers. In Marxian terms, we can read this tool as the result of labor applied to raw materials to make a new means of production, and in such a light, the mining tool becomes analogous to a character brand within Marvel's portfolio of copyrights, simultaneously the product of human narrative labor and a means of producing new narratives, first made by one group of workers and then later modified by another.[10] The literal brand on Klaue's neck reminds us of the violent, corporeal origin of a now-banal commercial term: the searing of a proprietor's *brand* onto goods, livestock, or human chattel.

We can therefore read Klaue's crimes allegorically, as the piecemeal captures of Marvel's "mountain" of film rights by other firms. In our world, Marvel sold the film rights to characters that the company thought it wouldn't miss, but characters like Blade (also named for a tool) would prove surprisingly valuable to other firms, and therefore bitterly troubling to Marvel. When Wakandan intelligence learns of Klaue and Killmonger's theft of an ancient vibranium hammer, the general Okoye reports to the court, "A misidentified Wakandan artifact was stolen yesterday from a British museum. We have learned Ulysses Klaue plans to sell the vibranium to an American buyer in South Korea tomorrow night." She makes no mention of the three museum guards shot and the curator poisoned; despite the film's overarching fixation on saving the world from Wakandan technology, this briefing scene does not even acknowledge the deaths of non-Wakandans. Yet the same scene encourages us to grieve for Wakandan characters who don't appear in the movie. During the briefing on Klaue's robbery, the nobleman W'Kabi reminisces about Klaue's long-ago raid: "My parents were killed when he attacked. Not a day goes by when I do not think about what Klaue took from us. From me." We learn nothing else about W'Kabi's family; he grieves for characters who are absent from the movie, or to put it in terms that Marvel would use, characters missing from the continuity.[11] After Okoye briefs the court on the robbery, the newly created King T'Challa tells them, "Klaue has escaped our pursuits for almost thirty years. Not capturing him is perhaps my father's greatest regret." Just as Marvel Studios executives rued the decisions of an earlier generation of executives who licensed film rights to Cannon, New Line, and Fox, so T'Challa rues Klaue's unpunished thefts. When the Black Panther and a team of Wakandan operatives capture Klaue, the Black Panther (bloodlessly) rips the prosthetic from Klaue's arm, a symbolic amputation for this sticky-fingered vibranium thief. Through the figure of Klaue, both *Civil War* and *Black Panther* perform a fantasy of revenge on the firms that "stole" from

Marvel's hoard, first branding, then dismembering, then arresting, then killing him, and finally allowing Killmonger to present the corpse as a gift to the people of Wakanda.

Lest readers think I have stretched this reading too far, consider the commonplace use of mining as a metaphor for the way that the duopoly, its licensees, and its parent companies treat superheroes as intellectual property. Duopoly writers use it, as when Jeph Loeb noted that Frank Miller "approved of our mining his stunning *Batman: Year One*" for Loeb's *Batman: The Long Halloween* (6). In 2008, the year Marvel Studios released its self-produced *Iron Man* (Jon Favreau, 2008), *Sight and Sound* ran an article titled "The Perils of Strip Mining," in which Roger Sabin wrote about the duopoly's functional transformation into sources of IP for "event" movies "marketed in systematic fashion by multi-national conglomerates" (Sabin 24). The following year, when Disney bought Marvel, *The Guardian* reported Disney CEO Bob Iger using the same metaphor when he said, "Marvel had a 'treasure trove' of intellectual property that 'transcends gender, age, culture and geographical barriers.' 'There are so many opportunities to mine both characters that are known and characters that are not widely known'" (A. Clark). The Motley Fool had an instrumental take on the acquisition, arguing that Disney had brought a "character library" to "mine for theme park content" while helping Disney fill its "young, male void," attracting teen boys not fascinated Pixar and princesses (Munarriz). In *Slate*, Sean Howe described Marvel's rise to summer box office dominance as the result of Hollywood's recognition of the publisher "as a gold mine" (Howe, "Avengers"). *Deadline* published a retrospective on former Marvel executive Avi Arad with the subtitle "From *Blade* to *Morbius*, Three Decades of Mining Marvel," which noted that the company's fortunes had reversed since their 1990s bankruptcy: "Today, Marvel represents Hollywood's gold standard for source material" (Boucher). In the metaphors of these writers, Marvel constitutes a *library* without authors, a *mine* without miners, a *treasure trove* and a *gold standard*, in all cases a fetishized collection of valuable objects rather than the result of past and present human activity. Scholars use the same metaphor. Liam Burke notes that despite Marvel's origin as a publisher of comic books, Marvel Entertainment and Disney "continue to mine the transmedia potential of these characters" (66). Jeffrey A. Brown notes that the "fictional universes of Marvel and DC Comics provide a wealth of characters and stories that can be mined for decades" (23). Even scholars who primarily concern themselves with the industrial and legal systems of production, expropriation, and licensing that structure the duopoly also turn to this metaphor, as when Shawna Kidman describes studios revisiting their film rights as "digging into their vaults to mine old characters for new adaptations" (186). These comparisons to mining obscure the very processes that my project seeks to reveal.[12] This metaphor obscures the results of human labor by treating those results as a natural resource, produced by geological forces, awaiting discovery or extraction; the metaphor thus conceals not only the work of the earlier creators but also the legal arrangements that made possible their expropriation.[13] *Deadline*'s talk of a *gold standard* suggests a better metaphor, and one more relevant to *Black Panther*'s melodrama of precious metal. The duopoly's continuity capital resembles not ore in the ground but a hoard of precious metal refined into coins and kept in a vault when "idle," as Marx would put it (*Capital*, vol. 2, 86–87). The owners of this hoard throw parts of it back into circulation, making new movies, TV shows, and theme park attractions, making occasions to exploit new waves of creative labor.

BLOOD AND SAVAGES

The plan of the film's villain, Eric Killmonger, ostensibly seeks to redress anti-Black racism, but in typical duopoly blockbuster fashion, his plan will result in mass death through the sharing of proprietary technology. The villain's scheme thus leads to a curious reversal: in a film seemingly calculated to please Western liberal-progressive sensibilities, a monarchist hero must thwart a nationalist villain. Although the film's opening *griot* exposition does show Africans led in chains to slave ships, we learn nothing about the motives of the Africans who sold such captives to foreigners, or the motives of the foreigners who bought and employed them. As Barbara Fields has noted, "A majority of American historians think of slavery in the United States as primarily a system of race relations—as though the chief business of slavery were the production of white supremacy rather than the production of cotton, sugar, rice and tobacco" (99). When Prince N'Jobu rails against drugs and police violence affecting African Americans, he speaks in the passive voice, naming no agents or interests, and he says nothing about inequalities of wealth. Throughout the film, the script thus engages in what Adolph Reed calls the "disconnection from political economy [typical] of postwar liberalism's construction of racial inequality as prejudice or intolerance" (53). Coogler made his debut with *Fruitvale Station* (2013), a dramatization of the final hours of Oscar Grant, an unarmed Black man shot dead by a white Bay Area Rapid Transit police officer, but *Black Panther* does not interrupt its PG-13 running time with anything so harrowing. The film's villains kill only nameless bit players, who die bloodlessly or off-camera, never mentioned again. No Oakland police harass the youthful Killmonger, and no bank manager denies Killmonger's mother a loan. Instead the film concentrates its trace amounts of contemporary racism in the white villain Ulysses Klaue.[14]

Black Panther uses subtle, plausibly deniable racism to increase the evil of this character who would challenge the hero's custody of his superpowers. Here the film seeks the kind of political ambiguity typical of blockbusters, sounding dog whistles to those listening; by coupling only a vague antiracism with an overdetermined Blackness, the film offers a master class in how a blockbuster can appear to take a bold and controversial position while actually avoiding taking clear positions on anything (except the virtue of monarchy). And paradoxically, in the ambiguous racism of Klaue, we hear something like this film's whisper of conscience. Although *Age of Ultron* showed Klaue commanding a predominantly Black crew of henchmen, the film did nothing to depict Klaue as racist, but *Black Panther* wastes little time in changing this. We first meet Klaue during the London museum robbery with Killmonger. After the robbers kill the guards and secure the loot, Klaue exults to Killmonger, "You're gonna be rich, boy!" The graying Klaue does look a generation older than Killmonger, and he did work with Killmonger's father, but the word *boy* has a history of racist use by whites that makes Klaue's use here suspect. The word can play as pally or avuncular only if one ignores its racist connotations. Later, Klaue uses the word again, after Killmonger has rescued Klaue from CIA custody.

> KLAUE: When I get back to Joburg [gesturing at Killmonger and his moll], I'll make sure both you guys get paid.
> KILLMONGER: Oh, I ain't worried about the money, bro. I know you're good for it. On our way back, just drop us off in Wakanda.
> KLAUE: You don't wanna go *there*, boy!
> KILLMONGER: Yeah, I do—

At this, Killmonger draws his pistol and shoots dead an unnamed white member of their crew (never given dialogue) and then turns his gun on Klaue. Has Killmonger planned, all along, to betray Klaue so that he can use Klaue's corpse to gain an audience in the Wakandan court? In that case, Killmonger could have murdered Klaue and captured Wakanda without bothering to rob the museum. Or has Killmonger finally snapped, tired of having Klaue call him *boy*? The cool that Killmonger displays in the scene suggests otherwise. Neither interpretation makes much sense, but although the film denies us a satisfying motivation for the attack, it still leaves us to decide.

But the film has given us a nudge by having Klaue twice call Wakandans *savages*. Surely this noun from the heyday of imperialism, here used against a people who make ray guns and flying cars, marks Klaue as a racist, because it suggests that Klaue considers the Wakandans fundamentally crude, wild, or lesser no matter what they achieve. Cedric J. Robinson discusses the economic and political utility of the figure of the savage:

> English colonialism had had available to it the savagery of the Irish to draw upon.... When the need was for labor, the Irish, the poor of the metropole's cities, the African and the native American were comfortably herded together under the notion of savagery. When the issue had been the expropriation of the lands of the natives, there was little cause to respect the claims of savages or to comprehend their resistance as anything more than savagery. (186–87)

Klaue, like a European colonizer, seeks wealth controlled by people he dismisses as *savages*, which suggests racism as a pretext for his thefts and robberies. Yet the anachronism of the word also makes it ring false. Even in the light of nineteenth-century anthropology, which grouped cultures into hierarchies of savagery, barbarism, and civilization according to developmental schemata, Klaue seems to misuse the word.[15] I therefore call Klaue's racism ambiguous, for this and three further reasons.

First, the Wakandans, like nineteenth-century racialist anthropologists, evaluate other cultures according to an ethnocentric and developmentalist hierarchy that treats technology as the moral measure of a people. During the set piece where the Wakandans fight Klaue's mostly white gang in Seoul, the gang uses automatic weapons. But the Wakandans have high-tech bulletproof cars and clothing; General Okoye, in the passenger seat of a pursuing sedan, reclines, languid as bullets bounce harmlessly from the hood and windshield. "Guns," she sighs. "So primitive." This moment shows the Wakandans' seemingly effortless technological superiority over their foes and inverts the trope of the Western male action hero who uses a gun to defeat the superior skill of a non-Western foe armed with simpler technology. A classic example of this trope appears in *Raiders of the Lost Ark* (Steven Spielberg, 1981), where Indiana Jones shoots dead an Arab swordsman, in moment that Li Siu Leung calls "an arrogant and Orientalist travesty" (536). *Black Panther* contains many moments of similar arrogance, when Wakandans, and especially Okoye, display casual contempt for the primitiveness of other nations, especially America. Such moments play for laughs by inverting the ethnocentric hierarchy, but without subverting that hierarchy. Less than three minutes after

Okoye's remark, the Black Panther captures Klaue, then tears the prosthetic arm from Klaue's stump. "Where did you get this weapon?" the king demands. Klaue all but spits his reply: "You savages didn't deserve it." At this, the Black Panther grabs Klaue by the throat and, with his free hand, extends vibranium claws as if to kill. Suddenly Klaue's tone changes, and he whimpers, "Mercy, King! Mercy!" while his eyes roll in what looks like terror. In a murderous undertone, the Black Panther grates, "Every breath you take is mercy from me," and he draws back his clawed hand as if to strike. Just then, Okoye interrupts, and when the king turns, an eyeline match reveals the object of Klaue's gaze and Okoye's concern: a crowd of onlookers stands with smartphones, recording the king's actions. As in America, the mere recording of state violence does not stop that violence, but Okoye, by bringing the videographers to the Black Panther's attention, saves both Klaue and the Wakandan king's public image. Does Klaue call Wakandans *savages* here because he finally decides to give voice to suppressed anti-Black animus? If so, then English and Afrikaans both have racial slurs that would do the job with greater force and fewer syllables, but such talk would push the film toward more uncomfortable realism, and possibly out of its PG-13 rating.

A second basis for reading Klaue's racism as ambiguous emerges from a close look at, and listen to, his interactions with Killmonger. Early in the film, Klaue treats Killmonger, his Black accomplice, not just with respect but with apparent solidarity, as when Klaue notes the Wakandans' attitude toward non-Wakandans who steal vibranium. "They're savages," Klaue says, and he points to the brand on his neck: "This is what they do to people like us. . . . To them, you'll just be an outsider." Klaue's *people like us* groups him and Killmonger together; furthermore, Klaue's insider-outsider distinction lacks the developmentalist connotations of a word like *savage* or *primitive*. This recalls the moment in *Blade* when Frost appeals to Blade for vampire solidarity against the humans. And much as Blade remains committed to humans, Killmonger reveals his commitment to Wakanda, by pulling down his lower lip to show the secret tattoo that marks him as Wakandan royalty. Nowhere in the film does Klaue mention racial categories or express any anti-Black affect. Even at the point of death, Klaue laughs, ruing his mistake in misrecognizing his Wakandan murderer as "some crazy American," Klaue's dying words. Klaue's warning that the Wakandans will reject Killmonger implies that Klaue understands the historical contingency of national and racial categories; Wakanda's do not match those of the United States any more than those of the United States match those of Klaue's South Africa.[16] When Killmonger presents himself—and Klaue's corpse—to the Wakandan court, the scene only confirms the accuracy of Klaue's understanding of national and racial categories as social constructions that vary in both time and space.

The scene where Killmonger presents himself at court warrants particular scrutiny, not only because it validates Klaue's understanding of Wakandan culture, but also because it entwines the defense of vibranium with the most retrograde forms of statecraft and identity politics. When Killmonger enters the throne room, handcuffed, he boasts, "I'm standing in your house, serving justice to [Klaue] who stole your vibranium and murdered your people—justice your king couldn't deliver." Since we have seen Killmonger casually commit murder, we can dismiss his talk about justice as anything but a taunt directed at the king. But the taunt works, and the king rises in anger as his guards sweep forward, spears in hand. King T'Challa steps close to Killmonger and whispers, "Only reason I don't kill you where you stand is because I know who you are." The close-up that frames T'Challa and Killmonger ear-to-ear recalls the two earlier framings of their fathers, much as the new king's threat recalls the old king's fratricide. The new king's threat, coupled with the mobilization of his guards, implies that in Wakanda, lèse-majesté constitutes grounds for the king to slay critics. But King T'Challa still does not admit his knowledge of Killmonger's identity. Only when Killmonger declares himself son of N'Jobu and reveals his father's signet ring does the court, horrified, treat him as one of its own. "I'm exercising my blood-right," cries Killmonger, "the challenge for the mantles of king *and* Black Panther!" The family melodrama conceals the implication that Killmonger has escaped death by virtue of aristocratic Wakandan birth. Killmonger convinces the court that although he may lack the correct manners, he does have the correct blood.

To return to Klaue, the third and final reason I call his racism ambiguous appears when we look at the behavior of the Wakandan state, particularly its uses of violence. This futuristic kingdom does not reform or rehabilitate Klaue by means of superior psychology, psychiatry, or technology but instead brands his flesh. When King T'Chaka slays his own brother, no journalist breaks the story in Wakandan news outlets; instead T'Chaka easily covers up the incident, such that even his successor, T'Challa, learns of the murder only after assuming the throne. And the film devotes not one but two lengthy sequences to the Wakandan method of crowning kings. On a sun-drenched Wakandan river, a dozen barges drift, their decks filled with revelers. The Wakandan royal family and aristocrats dance, dressed in ritual finery. Soldiers activate machines that redirect the river's flow, turning a great waterfall into a trickle, revealing a shelf below the river's level, which functions as an arena for ritual combat. The sequence thus looks less like a state event and more like an advertisement for a theme park, part cod Africana, part gee-whiz stagecraft. In the broad, shallow pool now exposed near the top of the waterfall, T'Challa, the heir to the throne, stands before representatives of the Five Tribes. A minister gives T'Challa a drug that neutralizes his Black Panther powers, and then declares that "any member of a royal blood" may now challenge the heir to ritual combat for the throne. The film features two such contests. In the first, the leader of the Jabari Tribe, wearing a stylized ape mask, challenges T'Challa but yields; in the second, Killmonger challenges T'Challa and wins, throwing the unconscious T'Challa over the waterfall to certain death. In each scene, the combatants begin with weapons like swords, spears, and clubs, but to maintain its PG-13 rating and to work around the actors' limited martial arts skills, each scene contrives for the combatants to disarm each other, so that they end up grappling in the water.

Both in its method of determining royal succession and in the mise-en-scène of these contests, the film blends reverential, theme-park Afrofuturism with the most lurid colonial- and pulp-era fantasies about sub-Saharan Africa.[17] Writing about Black Panther comics stories of the 1960s, Nama notes that the futuristic Wakanda of the 1960s comics offers a "stark contrast to the historical and symbolic constructions of Africans as simple tribal people" and Africa as "primitive" or "backward" (42). Yet the 2018 film's succession by combat seems nothing but primitive and backward, appropriate for one of the more barbarous peoples in a sword-and-sorcery film. One does not have to have anti-Black sentiments to consider hand-to-hand combat a *savage* way to choose leaders. To a viewer opposed to monarchy, the waterfall battles in *Black Panther* recall *Monty Python and the Holy Grail* (Terry Gilliam and Terry Jones, 1975):

> KING ARTHUR: I am your king.
> OLD WOMAN: Well, I didn't vote for you!
> KING ARTHUR: You don't vote for kings.
> WOMAN: Well, how do you become king, then?
> ARTHUR: [in reverie] The Lady of the Lake, her arm clad in the purest shimmering samite [choir rises on the soundtrack], held aloft Excalibur from the bosom of the water, signifying by divine providence that I, Arthur, was to carry Excalibur. [choir stops] That is why I am your king!
> DENNIS: Listen, strange women lying in ponds distributing swords is no basis for a system of government. Supreme executive power derives from a mandate from the masses, not from some farcical aquatic ceremony.

To viewers who regard torture and absolute monarchy as institutions fit for the dustbin of history, the Wakandans, with their branding, homicidal kings, and succession by combat, do indeed appear *savage*, in that word's senses of violence and chronological atavism. Furthermore, the Wakandans' practices also seem *savage* in the manner of twentieth-century fascists, for the Wakandan state combines ethnonationalism and autocracy, reverence for tradition and a self-conscious technological futurism. This monarchy legitimates itself through evocations of an imagined past where the strongest strongman ruled.

Thus Klaue's characterization of the Wakandans as *savage* does smell of racism, but nevertheless Klaue raises the lone note of opposition and contempt in a film that otherwise asks us to cheer for odious political forms. Rather than make Klaue unambiguously racist, the film carefully constructs him to read in different ways to different viewers. To audiences who take Blackness as a natural and real category, and who then perform white-glove tests for signs of insensitivity or racial animus, Klaue seems guilty of racism. To viewers who acknowledge that Wakandans might have their own identity categories shaped by their own history, Klaue brings a hint of a critical, even anthropological, spirit to the film. Human populations differ physically and culturally, but humans invent "races" through discourse and politics. Nama wisely calls race "the ultimate science fiction" (*Black Space* 42). Klaue seems to understand that the Wakandans have their own racial categories that will lead them to reject a Black American as at least foreign, if not also racially Other. Thus to viewers who reject absolute monarchy as a crime not yet punished by its victims, Klaue's assessment of the Wakandans as *savages* marks him as the lone skeptic in a film otherwise bent on making Wakanda's resource-rich monarchy seem like a gift to the viewer.

Lest we excuse the defense of absolute monarchy, corporal punishment, and the extrajudicial violence of kings as falling within the artistic license of an adventure film, we should recall that *Black Panther* holds a dubious honor as the first movie to screen commercially in the Kingdom of Saudi Arabia after a thirty-five-year ban on cinemas. Adam Aron, CEO of AMC Entertainment Holdings, assured investors that the major studios "long ago dealt with the sensitivities of the Middle East and have adjusted film product accordingly" (qtd. in "Saudi Arabia to End 35-Year Cinema Ban"). Aron even joked about the film's parallels with the House of Saud: "This is a story about a young [royal] who transforms a nation. That might sound familiar to some of you" (qtd. in "Saudi Arabia's First Cinema"; brackets in original). Compared to Saudi stoning, amputation, and crucifixion, Wakanda's branding seems not *savage* but positively genteel. The elder king's killing of a state enemy overseas recalls the cat-themed agent of Saudi state power, the Rapid Intervention Force, nicknamed the Tiger Squad, that went to Istanbul to murder and dismember *Washington Post* contributor Jamal Kashoggi a few months after *Black Panther*'s debut.[18] Despite the film's willingness to name and at least briefly critique American racism, *Black Panther* just as carefully avoids critiquing monarchy, thus appealing to the "sensitivities" of the most authoritarian gatekeepers of foreign markets. AMC Entertainment Holdings, from experience, understands the necessity of working with authoritarian gatekeepers. In 2012, the Dalian Wanda Group, a mainland Chinese conglomerate, purchased the Missouri-born theater chain, thereby making Wanda the world's largest exhibitor (Voigt). Disney, like the villain of *Black Panther*, seeks to acquire the creations of others and then use them to "conquer" new territories. In the real world, Marvel's continuity capital becomes analogous to vibranium, enabling feats of market penetration previously thought impossible. Disney's expansion simultaneously entails the conquest of new markets and capitulation to the demands of princelings and one-party dictatorships, but media empire pays. *Black Panther* took in over $1.3 billion worldwide ("Black Panther").[19]

OF COPYRIGHTS AND KINGS

Killmonger, like the movie *Black Panther*, seems driven by ethical concerns only if we ignore his methods and the property relations behind those methods. We first meet Killmonger and his team of armed robbers during their London museum robbery, and at the beginning of the heist, Killmonger taunts a curator over the museum's West African collection. "How do you think your ancestors got these?" demands Killmonger. "You think they paid a fair price? Or did they take it, like they took everything else?" This suggests that Killmonger works from a sense of grievance over the injustices of colonialism, but during the robbery, Killmonger poisons the museum curator and raises no objection to his accomplices' gratuitous killing of the museum's unarmed guards. He has no objection to stealing or murder, provided they further his goals. Furthermore, this operation to reclaim long-lost Wakandan property recalls Marvel's own struggles to recover film rights that it sold to other companies during Marvel's hungry years. When *Black Panther* appeared in theaters, Disney had placed a bid of $52.4 million to buy 20th Century Fox (Castillo). Fox had long exploited the film rights to the X-Men but had not managed nearly as well with Marvel's Fantastic Four. The 2015 *Fantastic Four* reboot featured Michael B. Jordan as Johnny Storm, the Human Torch; the reboot flopped, but it helped establish Jordan as a draw for duopoly films. Jordan's more memorable performance in *Black Panther* oscillates from reserved to sullen to wrathful, reminding us of Killmonger's grief over his father's death, always ready to erupt as violence. But Killmonger's desire to take what he considers his birthright suggests the desire of Marvel-Disney on the verge of acquiring 20th Century Fox, which would return the majority of the properties that Marvel sold to equally unscrupulous firms. When Killmonger challenges T'Challa in single combat, T'Challa loses, and Killmonger lawfully assumes the Wakandan throne; and although the other aristocrats stand aghast, they do not dispute the legality of the succession. Meanwhile, in the real world, the US Department of Justice required Fox to divest itself of sports networks before approving the purchase by Disney; antitrust regulators argued that competition between sports networks would preserve a vibrant-enough media marketplace to offset the Big Six studios consolidating into the Big Five (Littleton). Now Marvel Studios can have a film version of the Black Panther marry Storm from the X-Men, and Johnny Storm of the Fantastic Four can attend the wedding.

Killmonger's arc from orphan to king does give him a note of pathos, but his murders and self-pitying cruelty squander much audience goodwill; he does explain his schemes in terms of social goods, but in typical duopoly-movie fashion, his schemes will lead to mass destruction. He offers what sounds like a principled critique of Wakanda's policy of noninterference on behalf of the Black diaspora: "There's about two billion people all over the world that looks like us, but their lives are a lot harder. Wakanda has the tools to liberate them all." But T'Challa rejects Killmonger's racialist demand: "It is not our way to be judge, jury, and executioner to people who are not our own." Admire the subtlety of this line, which works whether we treat the plural possessive *our* as standing for Wakanda or as standing for the king using the royal *we*. This absolute monarch wraps nationalism around the duopoly's pro-monopoly clichés: "It is my responsibility to make sure that our people are safe, and that vibranium does not fall into the hands of a person like you." When Killmonger assumes the throne, the former royal family worries less about Killmonger's capture of state power or extermination of political rivals than about the prospect of Killmonger sharing vibranium and the technologies based on it. T'Challa's sister, Princess Shuri (Letitia Wright), serves as something like Wakanda's version of Q from the James Bond franchise, inventing new technologies for T'Challa to use in his covert foreign operations (which, like Bond's, become spectacularly overt). When Shuri realizes that Killmonger has captured the state, she expresses concern not for Wakanda's citizens but for "our vibranium." In quiet horror, she elaborates:

"All of my designs.... If he gets control of our technology, nowhere will be safe." Technology and territory, not persons, matter most. Disney's first Black superhero princess fights to protect the means of superhero production from a villain who would distribute it.

Disputes about the proper use of vibranium become occasions to work through the standard duopoly narrative of defending a monopoly, but these disputes also double as justifications of the ways of monarchs. Shortly after T'Challa's coronation, he walks with his former lover, the spy Nakia (Lupita Nyong'o), who argues that Wakanda should "share what we have. We could provide aid, and access to technology, and refuge to those who need it. Other countries do it—we could do better.... Wakanda is strong enough to help others and protect ourselves at the same time." The vagueness of Nakia's proposal makes it anodyne; unlike the villains' proposals, it omits vibranium and weapons. Yet the inexperienced king still dismisses her proposal, because he can. *Black Panther* never mentions any legal limits on the power of Wakanda's kings. They seem to rule by conscience alone, recalling Seneca's observation that "a tyrant differs from a king in his behavior, not his title" (158). When Killmonger assumes the throne, no conscience restrains his wrath, and he explicitly proposes imperialism.

> We got spies embedded in every nation on earth, already in place. We know how colonizers think, so we gonna use they own strategy against them. We're gonna send vibranium weapons out to our [spies]. They'll arm oppressed people all over the world, so they can finally rise up and kill those in power, and their children, and anyone else who takes their side.... The world is gonna start over, and we're gonna be on top. The sun will never set on the Wakandan empire.

We have already seen Killmonger murder each of his three accomplices as they became inconvenient, so we have no basis to expect that such a man, given unlimited power, will make anything but a tyrant. Even so, the crudity of this apocalyptic revenge fantasy makes Killmonger's evil legible even to the film's least sophisticated viewers. Like Bane in *The Dark Knight Rises* (Christopher Nolan, 2012), Killmonger offers a pulp caricature of actual revolutionary political programs, and like Bane, Killmonger seizes control of the hero's institution—the source of the hero's powers—according to the very rules of that institution.

Unlike Bane, however, Killmonger has no secret agenda, and in the film's last act, he proceeds with his plan as described. Killmonger's metaphor of the sun never setting on a Wakandan empire reminds us not only of the British Empire but also of Killmonger's self-righteous cruelty during his robbery of the museum in London, promising greater cruelties to come. No Wakandan speaks openly against Killmonger's plan, and the film thus implies that the Wakandans have no lawful means to oppose their king. Later, as his servants execute his plan, one of them confirms Wakandan agents "in New York, London, and Hong Kong standing by."[20] But by a deus ex machina implausible even by the standards of duopoly movies, T'Challa has escaped death, and he returns, leading rebels against Killmonger. When T'Challa reappears, he does not challenge the legitimacy of the system that installed Killmonger on the throne, but instead contests the procedure: "I never yielded, and as you can see, I am not dead." The ensuing CG battle takes duopoly bloodlessness to absurd heights. Jeffrey Brown notes that according to the PG-13 visual norms of superhero films, "bodies can be shot, stabbed, and beaten to a pulp with very little actual blood being spilled" (154), but the climactic battle of *Black Panther* spills not little but none, despite all the spears, swords, and a charge by rhinoceros cavalry. When Killmonger kills a hostage by cutting her throat, no blood or even a wound appears as her body falls in slow motion. T'Challa ends the battle for the throne by stabbing Killmonger with a spear, its blade as wide as a human hand, but even then we see no blood. T'Challa's allies stop the departing airships, restoring control over vibranium to the restored monarch. By finishing the trial by combat, T'Challa demonstrates the resiliency of Wakanda's system for choosing leaders.

The film stages this decisive battle on the mountain containing Wakanda's vibranium, bringing the narrative back to its root obsession. The battle unfolds in two stages, first among the airships taking vibranium weapons abroad, and second in the depths of the mine itself. For no reason either within the narrative or from historical precedent, the military airship hangar sits directly above the pit leading down into the mine, such that when T'Challa grapples with Killmonger, they plummet into their source of power, still fighting as they dodge maglev trains laden with vibranium ore. After T'Challa lands his killing blow, the scene turns quiet, strangely intimate for a battle to determine not just the leadership of one nation but the fate of the world. Nobody looks in on the two would-be kings, and nobody sees T'Challa stab Killmonger, so the king has no witness to swear to silence and nobody to vouch for the fairness of the contest. Killmonger rejects T'Challa's offer of medical care: "So you can lock me up? Nah. Just bury me in the ocean, with my ancestors that jumped from the ships. Cause they knew that death was better than bondage." This final, defiant speech snaps our attention back to the transatlantic slave trade, shown but not named in the film's expository flashbacks. Yet despite the bookending position of these references to the slave trade, the film otherwise doesn't handle the topic. We never learn if Wakandan kings agonized over the triangular trade or instead sold their criminals and prisoners of war to Portuguese slavers. In the 2010s, Wakanda brands the flesh of criminals, even though most cultures regard such a punishment as *savage* in all senses of the word, so why would we expect that the Wakandans of the 1500s and 1600s rejected slavery on ethical grounds, especially when the surrounding trade networks depended on it? In Killmonger's dying reference to "the ships," historical allusion becomes historical illusion, a feint toward substance, even as *Black Panther* subsumes all into a fight over dynastic succession and a fictional metal.

Both the film's intergenerational struggle for ownership and the last-minute end of that struggle recall the legal fight between Marvel and the heirs of Jack Kirby, cocreator of the Black Panther. The Kirbys' escalation of the case to the threshold of the Supreme Court constituted a crisis not just for the duopoly but for Hollywood's conglomerated studios, since their ability to profit from media franchises depends on their ability to exclude artists from ownership of the works they create. Killmonger's arrival in Wakanda represents a similar crisis, but in fictional guise. The child who has never set foot in Wakanda (never worked for Marvel) appears after King T'Challa's joyous ascension to the throne (Disney's purchase of Marvel), demanding control of the state and its vibranium (copyrighted characters), thereby endangering the world (the duopoly's business model). Marvel's last-minute settlement averted catastrophe, but as Asher Elbein noted in *The Atlantic*, "while Kirby's family may have finally gotten some measure of compensation, they are very much the exception." The weirdly quiet ending of *Black Panther*, where cousin slays cousin out of public view, now resembles the Kirby family's secret negotiation for undisclosed sums. As King T'Chaka would say, "Speak nothing of this." Secrecy, in both the fictional and real struggles, protects entrenched interests.

Marvel likes to call Jack Kirby the "King of Comics," but we shouldn't believe them. The year before *Black Panther* appeared, Marvel announced the centenary of Kirby's birth, asking readers to celebrate "100 Years of Jack 'King' Kirby" ("Creator Spotlight"). But Marvel has a history of treating such language as dangerous. During the 1980s, when independent publishers began to lure artists away from the duopoly with promises of greater profit sharing, name billing on the cover, or even the copyrights to their work, the duopoly scrambled to improve its terms. But as Sean Howe notes, Marvel took particular care to avoid the word *royalty*: as internal communication between its lawyers stated, "most definitions of that word contain language which indicated that it is a payment to an 'owner' or 'author' of use of *his* work. Indeed, the derivation of the word is that of royal status or the privilege of a monarch or sovereign." Thus, in future company correspondence, such monies were always referred to as "incentives." (246; emphases in original)

Internally, Marvel strove to eliminate language that gave workers even a metaphorical basis to challenge the legal fiction of corporate authorship. Work for hire depends on this fiction, but if Marvel Comics could have lifted a pencil, it would have, and because it could not, it hired writers, pencillers, inkers, letterers, and editors. After Jack Kirby's death, and now that Marvel has bought off Kirby's heirs, Marvel speaks of "King" Kirby out of meretricious reverence, offering the artist as another kind of character to brand and sell. But as C. L. R. James put it, "Nothing, however profitable, goes on forever" (26). Settlement with the Kirbys delayed a ruling that may still disrupt this system.

Not only did the next Marvel Studios film feature the Black Panther as well as Wakanda as a major setting, but its narrative also doubled as an allegory of the crisis that the Kirby heirs precipitated. *Avengers: Infinity War* (Anthony Russo and Joe Russo, 2018) tells the story of the alien conqueror Thanos, who fights the Avengers for possession of the magic stones necessary to power the Infinity Gauntlet, which will allow him to exterminate half of all living things in the universe. The Avengers struggle to separate one of the Infinity Stones from the body of their android teammate, Vision, but when the task proves beyond the technical skill of Tony Stark, they take their comrade to Wakanda. There, Princess Shuri proves capable, but too slow; Thanos battles the Avengers and the Wakandans and narrowly succeeds in assembling his magic glove. A snap of his fingers then causes half of the characters to dissolve into something like ashes. The film enacts the nightmare scenario of a corporate holder of copyrights facing a case like the one the Supreme Court nearly heard: with the blow of a gavel, the corporation could lose vast swaths of its continuity capital. But Marvel's subsequent film, *Avengers: Endgame* (Anthony Russo and Joe Russo, 2019), offers a simple fantasy solution, sending the Avengers back in time to save the day. The missing characters return, with the Wakandans literally leading the charge. Like a copyright-term extension act or a last-minute private settlement, *Endgame* grants media conglomerates the happy ending they believe they deserve.

CONCLUSION

Before he starred in *Blade*, Wesley Snipes wanted to play the Black Panther. At the height of Snipes's stardom, Marvel approached Snipes and his manager about a Black Panther film project, and they even managed to interest Columbia Pictures. Snipes envisioned a film that would evoke both the "fantastic, glorious periods of African empires and African royalty" from real-world history and the advanced technology of comic books. But when Snipes discussed the project with prospective director John Singleton, he found their visions diverging:

> John was like, "Nah! . . . See, he's got the spirit of the Black Panther, but he is trying to get his son to join the [Black Panther Party]. And he and his son have a problem, and they have some strife because he is trying to be politically correct and his son wants to be a knucklehead. . . . John wanted to take the character and put him in the civil rights movement. And I'm like, "Dude! Where's the toys?! They are highly technically advanced, and it will be fantastic to see Africa in this light opposed to how Africa is typically portrayed." I wanted to see the glory and the beautiful Africa. The jewel Africa. (qtd. in Parker and Couch)

As with most other films based on characters licensed from Marvel in the 1990s, this project stalled, but Snipes moved on to play the lead in the first hit film based on a Marvel character. *Blade* and its sequels, through their obsession with the need to protect a superhero's unique properties from others who would exploit or copy them, revealed the underlying mode of production of such films, a mode that depends first on the expropriation of artists and second on the control of film rights. In 2012, the film rights to Blade reverted from New Line back to Marvel (Kit), and Marvel plans to reboot the character as part of its wider transmedia franchise (Liptak).

By the time Marvel Studios produced *Black Panther*, it did so as part of a larger and commercially dominant Avengers franchise. The resultant film flirts with Black politics but ultimately presents bowdlerized pictures of American racism and Pan-Africanism, focusing instead on what Snipes calls "the glory" of an idealized Africa and "the toys" of its superhero-king. *Black Panther* brings to the Marvel Cinematic Universe "diversity" of the kind demanded by many fans and critics, but the film also brings diversification of Marvel's corporate product line, through a film tailored to the media gatekeepers of the most repressive nation-states. But this film's kind of diversity has no need for equality or democracy, ideas that might impede distribution in key markets; the film's

"Afrofuturism" looks admiringly to monarchy and the rule of tribal strongmen, doing neither Africa nor the future any favors. As Dikeledi A. Mokoena notes, "The movie responded to a gap in the 'woke' community and capitalized on that growing consciousness among Black people through commodification of that consciousness" (13). Mokoena points out that taking her family to see *Black Panther* (with popcorn and snacks) cost R421 for one evening, just shy of the South African government's Food Poverty Line of R441, the sum that the poorest families live on for a month. As she notes, "The monetary dividends of the movie will not be benefitting the Black community" (13). Such material realities do not stop the film from engaging in a fantasy of charity. The final scene shows T'Challa bringing Shuri to the run-down and seemingly all-Black neighborhood in Oakland where their cousin Killmonger grew up. Princess Shuri complains, "When you said you would take me to California for the first time, I thought you meant Coachella or Disneyland." But T'Challa reminds Shuri of the neighborhood's connection to the royal family's history: "This is where our father killed our uncle." He also tells her of his purchase of the nearby buildings as part of his plan to open Wakandan International Outreach Centers, where he will put Shuri in charge of "the Science and Information Exchange." True to its duopoly bloodline, *Black Panther* only countenances sharing of the hero's powers on the hero's terms, here the terms of a philanthropist and real-estate investor. As George Faithful writes:

> For an action/adventure blockbuster, such a display of humanitarian largesse verges on unprecedented sophistication. In realistic terms, it is also a gesture of profound futility. T'Challa seems to be in danger of developing an Afro-centric version of the "white savior complex," in which an outsider lacking first-hand local knowledge but flush with cash arrives hoping to make a difference, but ends up either accomplishing nothing or doing damage. (10)

The script's moral faith in a wealthy superhero follows the precedent of the Batman and Iron Man films. King T'Challa's charity scheme also recalls not only the missionary activities of westerners in Africa—the direction now inverted—but also the "racial uplift" projects of the Black bourgeoisie in the nineteenth century and the early twentieth. Cedric Robinson characterizes that bourgeoisie as "mystically chauvinist, authoritarian, and paternalistic" (191), a description that applies equally well to *Black Panther*, which asks viewers celebrate, with its hero-monarch, "Wakanda forever."

Yet nothing, however profitable, goes on forever, as the sudden death of Chadwick Boseman at forty-three reminds us. This first death of a star actor in the Marvel Cinematic Universe highlights the contingencies that shake even the most dominant firms and franchises. Although Ryan Coogler had already begun preproduction work on the sequel *Black Panther: Wakanda Forever* (2022), even Coogler had not known of Boseman's cancer: "After [Boseman's] family released their statement, I realized that he was living with his illness the entire time I knew him. . . . He shielded his collaborators from his suffering. . . . I spent the last year preparing, imagining and writing words for him to say, that we weren't destined to see" (qtd. in Rubin). The star's death may leave Marvel Studios unable to use Wakanda in the ways the firm had planned, but Disney will find ways to exploit the property. A few days after Boseman's death, Whoopi Goldberg called for Disney to create a Wakanda attraction, noting "we don't really need another Frozen land" (qtd. in Owoseje). With due respect to the grief of Goldberg and other fans, nobody needs another Disney theme park attraction of any kind, whether dedicated to a white ice-princess, or to a Black panther-king, or to that panther-king's science-princess sister—the one who, in her final scene, explicitly declares her eagerness to visit Disney theme parks, which Disney clearly hopes *Black Panther* will help instill in audiences. The Walt Disney Company raids and encloses the public domain for stories like Hans Christian Andersen's "Snow Queen," the basis for *Frozen* (Chris Buck and Jennifer Lee, 2013), and it defends these enclosures as vigorously as it busts unions and expropriates the work of animators, writers, and comics artists. The world can and should remember Boseman, but without involving Disney's acquisitive, exploitative, and monopolistic hand.

CODA
DREAMING LIKE A SUPERVILLAIN

Americans live in a time of dystopian concentrations of wealth and power. The media conglomerates that control Hollywood's Big Five studios exemplify these concentrations and the attendant cultural pathologies. High among those pathologies we must rank the inability of most Americans even to imagine human beings transforming their working conditions for the better. Anyone who can suspend disbelief for stories of superhuman crime fighters has the capacity to imagine a unionization drive, or universal health care, or the expropriation of the shareholding classes—as well as the reactions that would follow. But imaginative capacity does not mean imaginative practice, and the duopoly has offered movie audiences much more practice in imagining the last-minute rescue of the status quo as corporations wish to see it preserved.

In his seminal 1972 essay on "The Myth of Superman," Umberto Eco remarked on the juxtaposition of Superman's godlike power and his unwillingness to improve the world:

> From a man who could produce work and wealth in astronomic dimensions in a few seconds, one could expect the most bewildering political, economic, and technological upheavals in the world. . . . Superman could exercise good on a cosmic level, or a galactic level, and furnish us in the meantime with a definition that through fantastic amplification could clarify precise ethical lines everywhere. Instead, Superman carries on his activity on the level of the small community where he lives. (22)

Twenty years later, Richard Reynolds would elaborate on Eco's analyses, noting a similar structural peculiarity not just in Superman stories but in narratives across the genre:

> Heroes are generally obliged to defeat at least one supervillain per issue, but the events which lead up to the confrontation are normally initiated by the supervillain. The hero is in this sense passive: he is not called upon to act unless the status quo is threatened by the villain's plans.... The common outcome, as far as the structure of the plot is concerned, is that the villains are concerned with change and the heroes with the maintenance of the status quo. (50–51)

Reynolds identifies the villain as the "protagonist" in superhero narratives (51), but he stops short of stating the corollary: that the superhero therefore functions as the antagonist, the one who blocks or thwarts. This seems to reverse the usual polarities of narrative agency, especially in stories aimed at children and adolescents.

Northrop Frye's analyses of comedy and romance suggest a useful description of this reversal. Frye calls comedy "the mythos of spring," a system for telling stories about social change: "At the beginning of the play the obstructing characters are in charge of the play's society, and the audience recognizes that they are usurpers" (131). But the hero and heroine overcome the opposition of these elders, thereby causing "a new society to crystallize around the hero" (131). Frye calls romance "the mythos of summer," where one adventure follows another without overall progress, "an endless form in which a central character who never develops or ages goes through one adventure after another until the author himself collapses. We see this form in comic strips, where the central characters persist for years in a state of refrigerated deathlessness" (186). We could read the duopoly's anticopying melodramas as a straightforward instance of romantic repetition, but this interpretation ignores the business model that drives the repetition. We might better read these melodramas as *perversions* of the mythos of spring. In Frye's model, the youthful protagonist of the comedy serves as an agent of transformation, while the antagonist, an elder male, serves as an agent of stasis; but superhero stories, especially in their duopoly blockbuster versions, turn this relationship upside down. Even when the villain proposes explicitly utopian ends, the hero always at least implicitly proposes to defend whatever harms and exploitations exist in the present order, because the duopoly and its licensees depend on that order. In our world, the usurpers bankroll the movies, so the usurpers give us the endings they want us to see.

Most organizations have a caste of managers who wield power inversely proportional to its usefulness to other people, but the duopoly reveals this with special clarity. Investors, publishing executives, and vulture capitalists can't draw storyboards or write good scripts or direct even third-rate movies, so they hire people who can. The commercial firm gets to enjoy collective ownership of the resultant continuity—socialism for the shareholders—while excluding from ownership the people who actually produce the continuity. Yet even within the current norms of American commerce, some publishers, like Image Comics, offer an alternative to the duopoly's expropriative model, allowing creators to hold the copyright to their works. Imagine a duopoly where human creators held the biggest stake in their work.

But why stop within the actually existing norms of American commerce? As Eames puts it in *Inception* (Christopher Nolan, 2010), "You mustn't be afraid to dream a little bigger, darling."

Think of the aggregate brainpower expended daily in debates about which version of which superhero would win in a fight, or which obscure comic book character "needs" blockbuster treatment, and then imagine half of that energy spent imagining ways to counteract corporate rent seeking or the enclosure of the commons or the decline of organized labor. Most of the resultant ideas would suck—but most ideas suck. Just a few would have promise, and a few of those, if put into collective action, would work.

DC and Marvel have long used their characters in hypothetical stories, framed as happening outside the official continuity: what if Superman married Lois Lane, what if the radioactive spider bit Aunt May instead of Peter Parker, and so on. DC and Marvel both have catalogs of numbered, alternate versions of Earth ranging from the goofy to the nightmarish, where supervillains rule as kings or where anthropomorphic animals replace starring characters. So imagine some alternate Earths of a different kind.

Earth-39: In 1939, comics artists and writers inspired by Spanish anarchists begin setting up their own worker-owned shops in Manhattan. Competition with these independent, "black" shops leads the traditional publishers to form a self-regulating body modeled on the Hays Office. Over the next six years, the Comics Code Administration uses its seal of approval to woo distributors and retailers, driving most "black" shops out of business. Nevertheless, a staunchly anti-Stalinist council communism becomes established as a credible position in American political and trade-union culture.

Earth-40: In the 1930s, a wave of unionization sweeps the comics business. Collective bargaining leads to contracts that require publishers to pay royalties into pension and health funds for workers. In 1940, the United Pencil Workers sends delegates to Los Angeles to help the Screen Cartoonists Guild organize at Disney, MGM, and Warner Bros. The writers and artists in Siegel and Shuster's shop organize under the UPW Local #47 and negotiate for shares of licensing fees from Superman.

Earth-67: In 1967, Kinney National Service acquires both National Comics Publications (DC) and Marvel Comics, merging their fictional universes. Warner Communications Inc. later sells both publishers to Viacom. Over the next twenty years, Viacom uses superheroes to become the dominant producer of children's entertainment, eclipsing Disney.

Earth-68: In 1968, radical workers at Marvel take over their workplace in an armed occupation. The Great Four-Color Siege lasts over a week, after which Governor Rockefeller authorizes the use of SWAT teams to recapture the building. The duopoly hires new workforces to replace the blacklisted, the imprisoned, and the dead. Quality and output drop, but a story where the Justice League breaks up a Cuban-orchestrated strike leads the *National Review* to declare Superman "Man of the Year."

Earth-69: In 1969, workers at DC and Marvel take over their respective workplaces in armed occupations, prompting a general strike that precipitates first a civil war, then war with the Soviet Union. After the nuclear winter, the Goldwater Amendment authorizes the federal government to use the military against "any conspiracy to impede the operation of a lawful commercial enterprise," thus criminalizing trade unions.

Earth-84: In 1984, Cannon Films acquires Charlton Comics and begins producing a series of cheap but highly profitable films based on Charlton's "Action Hero" line of characters. Over the next decade, franchises based on Nightshade, Thunderbolt, and Captain Atom break box office and home video records, while Charlton first revives its publishing operation and then comes to rival the sales of DC and Marvel. In 1996, Cannon acquires the bankrupt Marvel, and the triopoly becomes a duopoly once more.

Earth-86: In 1986, the Supreme Court's majority of hard-line constitutional originalists declare the Copyright Acts of 1976, 1909, 1870, and 1831 unconstitutional, thereby reducing the duration of copyright back to the fourteen years stipulated by the Copyright Act of 1790. DC and Marvel lose their senior creative staffs to independent publishers that offer copyright to creators. Dozens of publishers launch their own versions of Batman, Wonder Woman, and Spider-Man.

Earth-98: In 1998, the Copyright Term Extension Act extends copyright duration to the author's life plus fifty thousand years, and for works of corporate authorship, to fifty million years. Mary Bono (R-CA), tells Congress that her late husband

> was active on intellectual property issues because he truly understood the goals of the framers of the Constitution: that by maximizing the incentives for

original creation, we help expand the public store-house of art, films, music, books, and now also software. . . . Actually, Sonny wanted the term of copyright protection to last forever. I am informed by staff that such a change would violate the Constitution. I invite all of you to work with me to strengthen our copyright laws in all of the ways available to us. As you know there is also Jack Valenti's proposal for [the] term to last forever less one day. Perhaps the Committee may look to that next Congress. ("H9952")

Improbably, Bono's testimony in the Earth-98 timeline differs not one word from her testimony in ours.

We humans make our social world and the cultures we inhabit, from our laws and our workplaces to our magazines and our TV shows. We can cede this work to the fictive persons we call corporations, or we can take it on ourselves, seeking more egalitarian and democratic ways to make a living on this planet. Humans have done so before, and they can do as much, and more, again.

Dream like a supervillain.

ACKNOWLEDGMENTS

This book refines arguments that I developed during my time at the University of Illinois, Urbana-Champaign, so my gratitude goes to Jim Hansen, Lilya Kaganovsky, Robert A. Rushing, and especially José B. Capino. Frank Grady, at the distant University of Missouri, Saint Louis, has my special commendation.

I learned much from the faculty at Illinois, notably Anustup Basu, Sandy Camargo, Ramona Curry, David Desser, Catherine E. Gray, Gordon Hutner, and Anthony Pollock. But I also learned from peers like John Claborn, Megan Condis, Patrick Fadely, Erin McQuiston, John Lee Moore, Reshmi Mukherjee, Donghee Om, Matthew Schroyer, Gautam Basu Thakur, Billy Vermillion, Aida Sefic Williams, and Kyle Williams. And I learned most from Shawn Gilmore, who taught me more about comics than anyone before or since.

Julia Lesage and the departed Chuck Kleinhans, the architects and editors of *Jump Cut: A Review of Contemporary Media*, helped me refine the article that became "The Hollywood Superhero as Brand Manager: An Allegory of Intellectual Property," in volume 57 of that journal. Lesage, Kleinhans, and the journal's anonymous reviewers identified gaps in my knowledge while also leading me toward greater concision.

In 2016, I presented some of the arguments in this book at the conference "Literary Form and Reform" at Fudan University, organized by Miles Link, who would become a dear friend. In 2017, I presented part of the chapter on Wonder Woman at the conference of the English Language and Literature Association of Korea (ELLAK) in Seoul.

At NYU Shanghai, I benefited from the fellowship, writing expertise, and research skill of colleagues like Mark Branter, Alice Chu-Jiun Chuang, Marcel Daniels, Lin Chen, Noriaki Hoshino, Emily Murphy, Joshua M. Paiz, Arina Rotaru, Jennifer Tomscha, Daniel Joseph Woody, and Rodrigo Zeidan. At every turn, I received help from NYU Shanghai's librarians: Edward Junhao Lim, Lin Zhiren, Caitlin MacKenzie Mannion, Jennifer Stubbs, Xu

Qinghua, and Zu Xiaojing. For five years, the students in my Perspectives on the Humanities course "American Superheroes" continually challenged my preconceptions, my inferences, and my conclusions, thereby proving Robert A. Heinlein's adage: "When one teaches, two learn." Liu Zhijing, Peter Wang, and Zhang Ruike have my special gratitude.

I finished drafting *Copyright Vigilantes* while under house arrest during Shanghai's "zero COVID" lockdowns in the spring of 2022. On the morning of Sunday, March 27, my wife flew to the United States to visit her family, and a few hours later our *ayi*—domestic helper—came for her weekly visit to help with laundry and other cleaning. An hour into her shift, police clad in white personal protective equipment sealed our building with "do not cross" tape, trapping us. Yáng Yàn (杨艳, a.k.a. Naya) had worked for us for six years, but she had a full-time job during the week and no urge to stay with her part-time employer for "seven plus seven" days. Soon the citywide lockdown began, and the two weeks became three, with no end in sight, while everyone's supplies ran down. We could not go out to buy groceries or medicine or drinking water; across the city, people died because they could not get to the doors of hospitals or past the guards blocking those doors. From March 27 to April 19, Naya helped me stay fed, informed, and sane; on the first afternoon of our captivity, she helped me spirit our dogs to a kennel where they could have a semblance of normal life; she helped me negotiate with the neighborhood committee for a transit letter allowing me to escape (on condition I would not try to return); she packed food for my nights of sleeping on the floor of Pudong International Airport, trying to get a flight out of mainland China; and she helped me and my wife by packing our belongings during the seven weeks she remained trapped at our apartment after I left. No blood auntie ever took better care of her kin. 感谢, Naya.

In the Shaw neighborhood, thanks to Elsa Hart for her encouragement, her novels, and her lemon cake—the next best thing to yak-butter tea for getting over that last hill. In Tower Grove South, thanks to Scott Weiss for introducing me to the Arkadin Cinema and for showing me, through his example, how to finish a monograph.

This book would not have appeared without the help of Emily Bandy, Michael Martella, and others at the University Press of Mississippi, as well as copy editor Bill Henry and the two anonymous readers who reviewed the manuscript and suggested ways to make it stronger.

Most of all, I thank my wife, Sara T. Holt, for her patience, faith, and love, through this project and through everything else.

NOTES

INTRODUCTION

1. The United States Constitution, article I, section 8, clause 8, grants Congress the power to enact copyright laws "to promote the Progress of Science and useful Arts, by securing for limited Times to Authors and Inventors the exclusive Right to their respective Writings and Discoveries." The Copyright Act of 1790 set the duration of copyright at fourteen years, renewable once, but the Copyright Act of 1831 extended this to twenty-eight years, again renewable once. Thus American copyright terms originally tracked human life spans, but by the 1970s, corporations like Disney, named for the founder it had outlived, had begun to lobby for dilations.

2. The serial publication of comic book characters means that early stories featuring a character may enter the public domain while later stories, with their supporting characters or different iterations of a character, still remain under copyright.

3. For example, see respective works by Allen, Anders, J. Brown, Feblowitz, Mendelson, and Pollard.

4. In the comedy *My Super Ex-Girlfriend* (Ivan Reitman, 2006), the villain enlists the protagonist in a farcical scheme to neutralize the title heroine's superpowers. Bungling ensues, and both the protagonist's ex-girlfriend and his current girlfriend end up with superpowers.

5. Wheeler-Nicholson speaks of "an idea," but US copyright law does not protect ideas, only their expression in words, lines, pigments, and narrative sequences. Patent law protects underlying ideas but requires their public explanation.

6. National Allied Publications later merged with Detective Comics, becoming National Comics Publications, and renaming itself in 1961 as National Periodical Publications. In the 1970s, it changed its name to the redundant DC Comics. I will generally use the name National to refer to the publisher before its 1967 acquisition by Kinney National Service Inc. and use DC to refer to the publisher after the acquisition.

7. See, e.g., Cotta Vaz 118–19.

8. For a lucid analysis of the different kinds of intertextual relation covered by the fan term *continuity*, see Reynolds 38–52.

9. Frank Herbert's observation about governments applies here: "Power attracts pathological personalities. It is not that power corrupts but that it is magnetic to the corruptible" (59).

10. For an example, see my discussion of *Time* magazine's role in boosting the profile of *Watchmen* after Warner Bros. (re)acquired the film rights to this DC Comics graphic novel: "From Off-Brand to Franchise: *Watchmen* as Advertisement," *Jump Cut* 58 (Spring 2018).

11. The student forwarded me these email threads. I have omitted the names of the Marvel executive, the student, and the Disney agent.

12. From 2016 to 2019, the street-sweeping machines in Xuhui District played "It's a Small World" from loudspeakers as they made their rounds, helping to advertise the Shanghai Disney Resort, which opened in June 2016.

CHAPTER 1: COPYRIGHT VIGILANTES

1. In 2019, the Motion Picture Association of America dropped the last two words of its name.

2. In later reprints, DC Comics titles this story "Superman's Phony Manager."

3. Siegel and Shuster's records of trying to sell their strip to newspaper syndicates, as well as National's requirement that they reformat the strip for *Action Comics*, led judges to rule in the 1940s and the 2000s that the strip did not count as a work for hire but was a work produced at Siegel and Shuster's own initiative. Yet these rulings did not prevent other judges from ruling that the pair had nevertheless signed away their rights to DC. See Gordon 111–13; Cotta Vaz, 286–88.

4. Some of the recurring characters in the Superman franchise had their origins in other media, created by other writers. Newspaper editor Perry White and cub reporter Jimmy Olsen, for example, first appeared in the *Superman* radio series.

5. For an account of how dominant publishers used the Kefauver hearings on juvenile delinquency as an occasion to create the self-regulating Comics Code Authority and force competitors out of the industry, see Kidman.

6. The *Oxford English Dictionary* reports this extended sense of *piracy*, referring to unauthorized copying and sale of another's work, as early as Edward Ward's 1700 poem *A Journey to Hell, or A Visit Paid to the Devil*: "Piracy, Piracy, they cry'd aloud, What made you print my Copy, Sir" ("Piracy, n.").

7. Valenti's nodding at his son's elision of commercials reads another way: the former adman can't blame anyone for wanting to skip commercials, because he knows that admen make the world worse. Nobody loves the work of a goon.

8. In superhero stories, the villain functions as the story's true and secret protagonist, in that the villain has goals and a plan, whereas the nominal hero merely reacts. Richard Reynolds calls supervillains the "engines" of superhero narrative: "The villains are concerned with change and the heroes with the maintenance of the status quo" (51). As far back as the *Writer's Digest Yearbook* of 1942, advice for would-be comics writers stated this plainly. In every story, "the villain should attempt one major offensive, run across obstacles to this major offensive, and finally be frustrated by the hero," who functions primarily "to frustrate the villain's plan which is drawing to its culmination" (Sundell 36).

9. Although Drucker obtained his degree at the University of Frankfurt am Main and then settled in the United States, his work largely reads as the antithesis of the Frankfurt school, seeking and cultivating the totalitarian impulses latent in liberal capitalism. Drucker argues that a commercial firm "must demand something much bigger than a fair day's labor. It must demand, over and above fairness, willing dedication. It cannot aim at acquiescence. It must aim at building aggressive *esprit de corps*" (267).

10. As Judge Larson wrote in his ruling, "It is only the *possibility* that filming could begin on a Superman sequel in 2011 that has stayed the Court from making a finding on the reasonable certainty of harm having occurred. Given that the *potential* for said commencement of filming exists at the *present time*, plaintiffs have not shown that the Superman film agreement, sans a reversion clause, is below the reasonable range for what a willing buyer would pay for the property from a willing seller. If, however, by 2011, no filming has commenced on a Superman sequel, plaintiffs could bring an accounting action at that time to recoup the damages then realized for the Superman film agreement's failure to contain a reversion clause" (*Siegel v. Warner Bros. Entertainment Inc.*; emphasis in original).

11. Even among writers who take the side of comics writers and artists against publishers, I have never seen anyone mention the interests of the ghostwriters and ghost artists who helped Siegel and Shuster deliver stories to National. Somehow, in our eagerness to tell the romantic story of Siegel and Shuster standing up to National, we forget that Siegel and Shuster engaged in the same form of expropriation, just on a smaller scale. Similarly, we forget about the work-for-hire labor of the radio scriptwriters who invented Perry White, Jimmy Olsen, and kryptonite, key elements in the larger Superman franchise.

12. The comics' Doomsday results not from illicit copying but from a Kryptonian mad scientist's attempt to create an unkillable super-being. See Dan Jurgens and Brett Breeding, *Superman/Doomsday: Hunter/Prey*, vols. 2–3, DC Comics, 1994.

13. Like the Supreme Court's 2010 ruling in *Citizens United v. Federal Election Commission*, Order 81 says nothing about structural inequalities of power or wealth. *Citizens United* frames corporations as mere "associations of citizens," so laws that restrict corporate spending therefore discriminate against a category of those associations (4).

CHAPTER 2: NOLAN'S BATMAN: CRIMINOGENIC CAPITALISM AND THE (RE)BIRTH OF A BRAND

1. For examples, see the respective works by Adlakha, Donini, Fradley, Ip, Kerstein, Klavan, and McGowan.

2. Thomas Schatz calls the 1989 *Batman*, directed by Tim Burton, "a true industry watershed—a tipping point that sent both conglomeration and blockbuster filmmaking into another register" (40).

3. Despite Nolan's three-film effort to construct his Batman as serious, the scene where Batman flies the bomb out to sea strongly evokes a scene in *Batman: The Movie* (Leslie Martinson, 1966). Adam West tries to dispose of a stagey-looking bomb by throwing it over a pier into the sea, only to stop when he sees a family of ducks below. West intones, "Some days you just can't get rid of a bomb."

4. *The Bat Whispers* (Ronald West, 1930), which mixed crime melodrama and haunted-house Gothicism, provided another inspiration to Kane and Finger. The protagonists pursue the Bat, a criminal who wears a mask and cape modeled on bat wings, through secret passages in a mansion. The Bat taunts police via pirate radio and even leaves a calling card, suggesting that the character also inspired Batman's perennial foe, the Joker.

5. For example, *The Dark Knight Returns* took second place in a 2014 poll by the Sequart Organization (Carpenter).

6. Tim Burton's *Batman* (1989) briefly shows industrial production in American factories, where the Joker manufactures poisoned cosmetics, but the postindustrial *Begins* hides them off-screen and overseas.

7. In 1939, the pulp magazine *Black Book Detective* began publishing stories featuring a detective code named the Black Bat, whose costume bears a strong resemblance to the one worn by the Bat-Man in *Detective Comics*. DC quickly reached an agreement with Better Publications, publishers of *Black Book Detective*: "Black Bat would stay out of comic books; Batman would steer clear of the pulps" (Cotta Vaz 60–61).

8. *Begins* marks a shift in the thematic preoccupations of Nolan's wider body of work, a shift toward narratives about industrial espionage and the theft of trade secrets, the subject matter of both *The Prestige* (2006) and *Inception* (2010). If we can call Nolan's films from 2000 to 2003 neo-noir, then we might call his work from 2005 to 2012 industrial noir. Time Warner's preoccupations with branding and intellectual property seem to have influenced Nolan even in his non-Batman work.

9. The Trademark Trial and Appeal Board notes that Mickey Mouse had no gloves in early appearances but gained them only in 1935 *(In Re Me and the Mouse Travel* 5). As with Batman's yellow insignia, which first appeared in the 1950s, Mickey Mouse's most iconic props came later, refinements to a character that had already become popular.

10. In some stories from 1939 and 1940, the Batman uses guns to threaten or to shoot foes, as does the Batman of Miller's *The Dark Knight Returns*. But in the main continuity of Batman stories since 1941, he rejects the use of guns. The no-guns rule emerged as part of the publisher's efforts to refute assertions that comic book violence corrupted children, efforts that included the October 1941 announcement of their "Editorial Advisory Board" of child-development experts. See my essay "Folklore, Fakelore, Scholars, and Shills: Superheroes as 'Myth'" (979–80).

11. Only here, at the end of the last film in the trilogy, does the cycle explicitly quote an earlier print text, when Gordon reads Sydney Carton's last words from *A Tale of Two Cities* in his eulogy for Bruce Wayne.

12. Critics complained of excessive fidelity in the case of *Watchmen* (Zack Snyder, 2009). See my essay "From Off-Brand to Franchise: *Watchmen* as Advertisement."

13. Throughout Nolan's Batman trilogy, the Gotham News Network's "GNN" logo doubles as a subtle brand placement for Warner Bros.' conglomerate sibling CNN. No competing news outlets appear.

14. *The Dark Knight* showed one diligent accountant at Wayne Enterprises uncover the conspiracy between Fox and Wayne to equip the Batman, but in *Rises*, nobody even remarks on the identity of the Batman's car with the vehicles that Bane's men use to patrol the city. Surely millions would recognize the vehicle from footage of the Batman evading police, but if the script acknowledged this, it would complicate Nolan's efforts to make Bruce Wayne into a heroic innovator. So in this third film, the Batman uses a motorcycle and a stealth helicopter, and nobody mentions that he once had a car.

15. Sam Raimi's Spider-Man films showed the succession of the Green Goblin villain.

16. Unlike the Nolan Batman films, *Joker* includes a reference to Zorro, updating it for the 1980s setting: the Wayne family walks out of a movie house showing *Zorro: The Gay Blade* (Peter Medak, 1981). By the mid-2010s, Zorro Productions Inc. found its claims to Zorro denied by courts, first in 2015 when the European Union's Office for Harmonization in the Internal Market declared Zorro invalid as a trademark (Gardner, "Zorro Trademark"), and again in 2018 when a judge ruled that ZPI held no copyright on Zorro (*Cabell v. Zorro Productions Inc., et al.*). Between this reversal of ZPI's fortunes and the absence of any new Zorro films since 2005, *Joker* had little reason to suppress such a reference.

CHAPTER 3: CAPTAIN AMERICA AND WONDER WOMAN: INSTRUMENTAL HEROES

1. This magazine appeared under the imprint of Atlas Comics. Over the years, Martin Goodman exploited tax loopholes by publishing under "at least eighty different company names . . . usually several simultaneously" (Jones 198).

2. Lee self-published *Secrets behind the Comics*, but Danny Fingeroth argues that Lee's erasure of Kirby and Simon from the origin of Captain America suggests that Lee either "rewr[ote] history at Goodman's request" or hoped to curry favor with Goodman (38).

3. The montage also plays as an advertisement for an America not still hobbling after the Great Depression, and, perhaps more importantly, not an America with an armed forces still segregated until 1948. Indeed, the film labors to dilute the whiteness of its lead cast by placing Black extras into scenes otherwise dominated by white extras. For example, in the newsreel shoot, a Black serviceman marches at Cap's elbow, suggesting that Black soldiers fought as

commandos, rather than serving in noncombat support roles, handling logistics, cooking meals, and the like. As Henry Louis Gates Jr. puts it, the US military in World War II "was as segregated as the Deep South" (Gates). But one would never know from *The First Avenger*, which instead invites viewers to feel good not just about the past but also about the present, in which they get to watch superhero movies that celebrate American history as they might prefer to imagine it.

4. These include, in chronological order to suggest their derivations from one another, the Sandman, *Adventure Comics* #40 (National, July 1939); the Flame, *Wonderworld Comics* #3 (Fox Comics, July 1939); the Blue Beetle, *Mystery Men Comics* (Fox Comics, August 1939); the Green Mask, *Mystery Men Comics* (Fox Comics, August 1939); the Fiery Mask, *Daring Mystery Comics* (Timely Comics, January 1940); the Blue Bolt, *Blue Bolt Comics* #1 (Novelty Press, June 1940); and the Green Hornet, *Green Hornet Comics* (Helnit Comics, December 1940).

5. Many writers on the early comic book industry lament the lack of exact sales figures for comics. Even publishers had little idea what sold well until months after titles hit newsstands.

6. A print version then appeared in the issues for December 26, 2016, to January 2, 2017, from which I have taken the page numbers used in these citations.

7. This sampling of female-led action melodramas ignores what Scott Higgins called Hollywood's "trend" (111) of female-led action serials in the 1930s and 1940s, which included *The Perils of Pauline* (Ray Taylor, 1933), *Jungle Girl* (William Witney and John English, 1941), *Perils of Nyoka* (William Witney, 1942), *The Tiger Woman* (Spencer Bennet and Wallace Grissel, 1944), *Brenda Starr, Reporter* (Wallace Fox, 1945), *Jungle Queen* (Lewis D. Collins and Ray Taylor, 1945), *Daughter of Don Q* (Spencer Gordon Bennet and Fred C. Brannon, 1946), and *Panther Girl of the Kongo* (Franklin Adreon, 1955).

8. The website Women You Should Know reproduced the press release and featured with it an Amazon.com ad inviting visitors to "shop related products," where eight of nine bore Wonder Woman's logo ("Holy Hera!").

9. In 2011, the Toronto Underground Cinema hosted a "Star Wars Day" event for fans (Annett). After Disney's purchase of Lucasfilm in 2012, the conglomerate appropriated the name and began to astroturf their own official Star Wars Day events. In 2013, Walt Disney World offered "a one-of-a-kind Star Wars–themed celebration for both parents and kids alike," which would include "meeting classic characters" and "collecting limited-edition merchandise," though Disney shrewdly warned that "entertainment and character experiences are subject to change" ("Star Wars: May the 4th Be with You"). The following year, Disney announced not a single event but a series of "Star Wars Weekends" beginning on the fourth of May, which included events like "Star Wars Dine-In Galactic Breakfast" and a buffet dinner called "Jedi Mickey's Star Wars Dine at Hollywood & Vine," at which, "wearing his very own Jedi robe, Mickey joins a host of characters at guests' tables for an intergalactic celebration of the saga" for $33.99 per child and $55.99 per adult (Slater).

CHAPTER 4: THE ADULT TURN: REPRODUCTION OF THE BRAND

1. In this, *Ant-Man* follows the model of *Thor* (Kenneth Branagh, 2011), where the adopted son, Loki, proves irredeemably evil.

2. See, e.g., Budd and Kirsch, or Fjellman.

3. Disney subsidiary Lucasfilm goes further in *Rogue One*, which digitally resurrects Peter Cushing and Carrie Fisher to serve the franchise from beyond the grave.

4. *Superman Returns* (Bryan Singer, 2006) presented Superman's son with Lois Lane, but Superman takes no part in raising the boy, leaving that to the boy's adoptive human father.

5. Azuquita's original vinyl single bore no date, so Discogs and other online sources lack a year for the song. One can find it, however, on the audio CD compilation *Panama! 2: Latin Sounds, Cumbia Tropical & Calypso Funk on the Isthmus, 1967–77* (Soundway, 2009).

6. The story of *Doctor Strange*, unsurprisingly, hinges on a version of the de rigueur narrative of a villain who makes illicit use of superhero IP, when a sorcerer steals a spell from the forbidden library of Dr. Strange's teachers, thereby threatening the destruction of Earth. The film's anxiety about forbidden knowledge owes less to literary precursors like the forbidden tomes of H. P. Lovecraft and more to the duopoly's managerial obsessions, since Dr. Strange proves more than capable of handling the forbidden material and defeating both the sorcerer and the demon that the sorcerer calls to Earth.

7. *The Force Awakens* (J. J. Abrams, 2015) performs similar intergenerational modeling: when Rey and Finn meet Han Solo, they appear impressed like teens meeting a star their parents admired, but whose work they don't directly know. They recite various rumors about him, getting wrong important details, but getting right the attitude of breathless excitement that Disney wants to instill in newcomers.

8. The duopoly had used supervillain teams for decades, even using them to headline comics like Marvel's *Supervillain Team-Up* (1975–80) and DC's various *Suicide Squad* series, comprising a roster of second- and third-tier villains since 1987.

9. *Salon*'s Matthew Rozsa wrote about the film's "daring political subtext," its implicit critique of the prison-industrial complex. Rozsa stops short of proposing that this subtext accounts for the film's opening-weekend popularity.

10. See my essay "Ambiguous Mr. Fox: Black Actors and Interest Convergence in the Superhero Film."

11. Like a teenager trying to sound grown-up, *Logan* overcompensates: Charles Xavier uses the word *fuck* four times in his first scene.

12. The main poster for the film presented the movie as serious, abandoning the visual rhetoric of superhero franchise ads. A plain, white sans serif font announces the film's title with no tagline. Logan stands alone, not crowded among the secondary characters typical of franchise movie posters. Behind him, the sun sets over a desert, evoking the westerns from which the film borrows while also suggesting the end of the series.

13. Compare this to the performance of *X-Men*, the franchise's best return on investment until 2016, which on a budget of $75 million took $296 million worldwide, not quite four times its official cost. *X-Men: Apocalypse* (Bryan Singer, 2016) made only $543 million on a budget of $178 million, a mere tripling of investment.

14. The X-24 also massacres the Munson family. The father survives long enough to try to kill both the X-24 and Logan, as if in suspicion that Logan had betrayed him. But Munson, like Xavier, dies before Logan can clear his name.

15. The image and the lyrics to "Hurt" recall scenes from Wolverine's first live-action appearance, in *X-Men*. After Logan first uses his claws, we see him rubbing his knuckles. Rogue, another mutant, asks him, "When they come out, does it hurt?" The camera pans to Logan in a choker close-up as he answers, "Every time."

16. In *X-Men Origins: Wolverine*, child actor Troye Sivan plays the young James Howlett, who will later take the nom de guerre Logan.

17. Here, as throughout the X-Men movie franchise, the script does not blame American whites for racism but locates this evil elsewhere. My essay "Storm and the Angels of History: Blackness and Star Image in the *X-Men* Films" addresses this pattern at length.

18. Previously, mainland China allowed distribution only of films that SAPPRFT approved for general audiences, with no additional ratings for content.

19. Marvel, owner of Captain America, eager to style itself as a defender of freedom, denied the screenwriter's explanation. See my "Ambiguous Mr. Fox."

CHAPTER 5: *BLADE* AND *BLACK PANTHER*: STRATEGIC BLACKNESS AND THE RIGHTS OF KINGS

1. New Line began as an independent distributor. Its successes in the 1980s and 1990s led Warner Bros. to acquire New Line in 1996.

2. As early as *Blade II*, we see the series resort too readily to CGI, as when Blade duels with the messengers from the vampire government. Human actors perform most of the swordfight in medium and medium-wide shots, but the film intercuts wide shots of rubbery CG stand-ins performing impossible movements.

3. In the climactic duel between Blade and the villain, a stunt double fills in for Snipes in the wider shots.

4. While *Blade* borrows and recombines many tropes from action and adventure films, it borrows a particular combination that *Steel* used the year before: a Black hero with a monosyllabic code name, an elderly mentor and technical helper, and a physically damaged woman scientist in a chaste relationship with the hero.

5. Snipes's complexion, dark even among Black leading men, has presented a technical challenge for directors of photography unused to filming Black actors. See Dyer, 89–103.

6. Both *Blade* and *Blade II* feature scenes where vampire security guards armed with electric stun batons first overpower Blade, then continue to prod him even after he falls. To audiences in 1998 and 2002, these scenes evoked the video of LAPD officers beating Rodney King. The guards' cruelty makes Blade's subsequent massacre of the vampire forces all the more satisfying, especially in *Blade II*, where he uses their own stun batons against them.

7. Coates's wealth and politics also made him a safe choice. Cornel West writes, "When [Coates] honestly asks: 'How do you defy a power that insists on claiming you?', the answer should be clear: they claim you because you are silent on what is a threat to their order (especially Wall Street and war). [Coates's] conception of freedom is neoliberal. Racial groups are homogeneous and freedom is individualistic in his world. Classes don't exist and empires are nonexistent." If we accept West's assessment, then we can see why Marvel trusted Coates to write superhero comics and critique racism without, say, trying to unionize fellow comics writers.

8. For the classic elaboration of this thesis, see Walter Rodney's *How Europe Underdeveloped Africa*.

9. Strangely, the film never imagines that the king might need to safeguard the herb against distribution or replication. When the villain temporarily assumes the throne, planning to distribute Wakandan weapons and technology, he does not plan to distribute the herb. Instead he orders it burned.

10. Despite the central importance of vibranium to the film's conflict, we see nothing of mining except a seemingly automated ore train. Like most blockbuster films, *Black Panther* spares little time depicting human beings as productive or caregiving workers. Although the film briefly shows slaves awaiting the Middle Passage, it does not show slaves at work, and it shows present-day Wakandan workers hardly at all. When the Princess Shuri gives T'Challa a tour of the Design Group, the camera tracks her and her brother in walk-and-talk shots, while behind them, nameless Wakandan technicians assemble gadgets just out of focus in the background.

11. He grieves the way some fans might grieve for the conspicuous absence of Storm, T'Challa's longtime love interest in the comics; but Storm belongs to the X-Men, and in early 2018, the X-Men film rights still belonged to 20th Century Fox. When *Black Panther* appeared in theaters, Disney had only recently placed a bid of $52.4 million to buy the competitor. See Castillo.

12. Public Enemy's "Caught, Can We Get a Witness?" from *It Takes a Nation of Millions to Hold Us Back*, imagines Chuck D on trial for sampling other records. Rejecting the charge, D responds that he "found this mineral that I call a beat / paid zero / I packed my load cause it's better than gold." Like writers hunting for a metaphor to convey the great commercial value

of duopoly publications, D treats other musicians' work as a resource awaiting his work of discovery and refinement. But where "Caught" makes a hero of the MC seeking to raise Black consciousness, talk of the duopoly's "mining" makes heroes of executives and investors.

13. In no case I have found does a writer who uses this metaphor treat the "mining" as a form of labor, entailing human skill and sweat, or requiring managers and security guards to discipline the miners.

14. In the *Fantastic Four* comics of the 1960s where Wakanda first appeared, Klaw and his mercenary army attempt to conquer Wakanda for its vibranium.

15. See, e.g., Edward Burnett Tylor's *Primitive Culture* (1871), Lewis H. Morgan's *Ancient Society* (1877), or Friedrich Engels's *Origin of the Family, Private Property and the State* (1884). All would have recognized the Wakandans as the most "civilized" nation on Earth, despite their use of branding as punishment.

16. The Nazis considered Aryans both different from and superior to Slavs, which led the Nazis to enslave, displace, and kill Slavs. This baffles many American-style racists, who see whiteness as an obvious and eternal unity that the Nazis somehow failed to grasp. See my article "Lovecraft Fandom(s): Racism, Denial, and White Nationalism."

17. The film deodorizes some of these fantasies. For example, although the film has M'Baku wear an ape mask, it omits this villain's name from the comics, Man-Ape, as well Man-Ape's bathing in the blood of a sacred white gorilla to gain his superpowers.

18. See, e.g., coverage by *Middle East Eye* (Abu Sneineh) or United Press International (Sakelaris), or the US Treasury Department's announcement of sanctions against the Tiger Squad ("Treasury Sanctions").

19. Mainland China delivered the largest share of the film's international gross, $105 million.

20. Much as the film as a whole takes care to flatter the sensitivities of the absolute monarchy of Saudi Arabia, this line reflects the film's concern for the sensitivities of the Communist Party of China. By naming Hong Kong, the line recalls Beijing's repeated equation of dissent, once legal in Hong Kong, with sedition, either urged or funded by foreign enemies of China. The mainland city of Guangzhou would make a better candidate for Killmonger's subversion, since it had a large community of African migrant workers in the 2010s. But a cell of foreign agents in Guangzhou would imply that the party-state's security apparatus had failed, and no film that seeks mainland Chinese distribution can entertain such a possibility.

WORKS CITED

Aaker, David A. *Building Strong Brands*. Free Press, 1996.
"About." *Motion Picture Industry Pension and Health Plans*, 2021, https://www.mpiphp.org/home/aboutmpi.
"About Zorro Productions." *Zorro Productions Inc.*, https://www.zorro.com/about/. Accessed 6 Mar. 2020.
Abu Sneineh, Mustafa. "Revealed: The Saudi Death Squad MBS Uses to Silence Dissent." *Middle East Eye*, 23 Oct. 2018, http://www.middleeasteye.net/news/revealed-saudi-death-squad-mbs-uses-silence-dissent.
Acuna, Kirsten. "Why These Two Characters Are Allowed to Appear in Both the *X-Men* and *Avengers* Movies." *Yahoo! Finance*, 1 May 2015, http://finance.yahoo.com/news/why-two-characters-allowed-appear-172409947.html.
Adlakha, Siddhant. "Christopher Nolan's *The Dark Knight* Plummets into Real-World Terror." *IGN*, 31 Aug. 2020, https://www.ign.com/articles/christopher-nolan-the-dark-knight-war-on-terror.
Aizenman, Nurith. "Is Wonder Woman Suited to Be a U.N. Ambassador?" *NPR.Org*, 20 Oct. 2016, https://www.npr.org/sections/goatsandsoda/2016/10/20/498569053/is-wonder-woman-suited-to-be-a-u-n-ambassador.
Allen, Joe. "Batman's War of Terror." *CounterPunch.Org*, 2 Aug. 2008, https://www.counterpunch.org/2008/08/02/batman-s-war-of-terror/.
Al-Mahadin, Salam. "Wonder Woman: Goddess of Fictional and Actual Wars." *Journal of Middle East Women's Studies*, vol. 14, no. 2, July 2018, pp. 246–51, https://doi.org/10.1215/15525864-6680374.
Amdur, Meredith. "Marvel Sees Big Stock Gains." *Variety*, 10 Oct. 2003, https://variety.com/2003/biz/news/marvel-sees-big-stock-gains-1117893720/.
Anders, Charlie Jane. "Where Would Superheroes Be without 9/11?" *Gizmodo*, 7 Sept. 2011, https://gizmodo.com/where-would-superheroes-be-without-9-11-5837450.
Andrae, Thomas. "Kane, Bob, and Bill Finger." *Icons of the American Comic Book: From Captain America to Wonder Woman*, edited by Randy Duncan and Matthew J. Smith, vol. 1, Greenwood, 2013, pp. 383–92.
Annett, Evan. "Star Wars Day: What's Going on Today in a Galaxy Not So Far, Far Away." *Globe and Mail*, 4 May 2015, https://www.theglobeandmail.com/arts/film/star-wars-day-whats-going-on-today-in-a-galaxy-not-so-far-far-away/article24236432/.
"Anti-Piracy." *Motion Picture Association of America*, 12 Apr. 2006, https://web.archive.org/web/20060412164537/http://www.mpaa.org/piracy.asp.
Armbrust, Roger. "SAG Responded Immediately to Screener Ban." *Back Stage*, vol. 44, no. 50, 12 Dec. 2003, pp. 5, 44.

Asbell, Matthew D., and Danielle Weitzman. "It Started with a Mouse: TTAB Reverses Refusal of Application by Me and the Mouse Travel." *World Trademark Review*, 1 June 2017, https://www.worldtrademarkreview.com/enforcement-and-litigation/it-started-mouse-ttab-reverses-refusal-application-me-and-mouse.

"The Batman Chronicles, Vol. 1." *DC*, 9 Mar. 2012, https://www.dccomics.com/graphic-novels/the-batman-chronicles-2005/the-batman-chronicles-vol-1.

"Be HIP at the Movies." *Intellectual Property Office of Singapore*, 24 Sept. 2008, https://web.archive.org/web/20080924044120/http://www1.ipos.gov.sg/main/newsroom/media_rel/mediarelease1_270704.html.

Benton, Mike. *The Comic Book in America: An Illustrated History*. Taylor Publishing, 1993.

Bilton, Nick. "Masked Protesters Aid Time Warner's Bottom Line." *New York Times*, 29 Aug. 2011, p. B4.

"Black Hawk Download; Moving beyond Music, Pirates Use New Tools to Turn the Net into an Illicit Video Club." *New York Times*, 17 Jan. 2002, http://www.proquest.com/nytimes/docview/2231318874/abstract/B566564786524D87PQ/1.

"Black Panther." *Box Office Mojo*, https://www.boxofficemojo.com/title/tt1825683/. Accessed 3 Aug. 2021.

"Black Panther Movie Now." *Facebook*, 18 Sept. 2014, https://www.facebook.com/blackpanthermovienow/about/?ref=page_internal.

"Blade." *Box Office Mojo*, https://www.boxofficemojo.com/release/rl2403829249/weekend/. Accessed 1 Apr. 2021.

Blickley, Leigh. "10 Years Ago, Screenwriters Went on Strike and Changed Television Forever." *HuffPost*, 12 Feb. 2018, https://www.huffpost.com/entry/10-years-ago-screenwriters-went-on-strike-and-changed-television-forever_n_5a7b3544e4b08dfc92ff2b32.

Boichel, Bill. "Batman: Commodity as Myth." *The Many Lives of the Batman: Critical Approaches to a Superhero and His Media*, edited by Roberta E. Pearson and William Uricchio, Routledge, 1991, pp. 4–17.

Bond, Paul. "Disney to Buy Marvel for $4 Billion." *Hollywood Reporter*, 31 Aug. 2009, https://www.hollywoodreporter.com/news/disney-buy-marvel-4-billion-88259.

Bordwell, David. "Aesthetics in Action: Kungfu, Gunplay, and Cinematic Expressivity." *At Full Speed: Hong Kong Cinema in a Borderless World*, edited by Esther C. M. Yau, University of Minnesota Press, 2001, pp. 73–93.

Bordwell, David. "An Excessively Obvious Cinema." *The Classical Hollywood Cinema: Film Style and Mode of Production to 1960*, edited by David Bordwell et al., Columbia University Press, 1985, pp. 3–11.

Boucher, Geoff. "Avi Arad: From 'Blade' to 'Morbius,' Three Decades of Mining Marvel." *Deadline*, 20 Mar. 2019, https://deadline.com/2019/03/avi-arad-marvel-blade-spider-man-morbius-toys-1202576569/.

Boxer, Sarah. "Bob Kane, 83, the Cartoonist Who Created 'Batman,' Is Dead." *New York Times*, 7 Nov. 1998, p. A13.

Boyle, Kirk. "'Children of Men' and 'I Am Legend': The Disaster-Capitalism Complex Hits Hollywood." *Jump Cut: A Review of Contemporary Media*, vol. 51, Spring 2009, https://www.ejumpcut.org/archive/jc51.2009/ChildrenMenLegend/.

Boym, Svetlana. *The Future of Nostalgia*. Basic Books, 2001.

Braun, Kathryn A., Rhiannon Loftus, and Elizabeth F. Loftus. "Make My Memory: How Advertising Can Change Our Memories of the Past." *Psychology and Marketing*, vol. 19, no. 1, Jan. 2002, pp. 1–23.

Brevoort, Tom. "New Brevoort Formspring." *Tumblr*, 31 July 2014, http://brevoortformspring.tumblr.com/post/93403610623/so-i-will-ask-a-different-question-why-isnt.

Breznican, Anthony. "The One and Only Wonder Woman." *Entertainment Weekly: The Ultimate Guide to Wonder Woman*, 2017, pp. 4–5.
Brief of Screen Actors Guild–American Federation of Television and Radio Artists, Directors Guild of America, Inc., and Writers Guild of America, West, Inc., as Amici Curiae in Support of Petitioners, 13 June 2014, https://www.scribd.com/document/231022584/Kirby-v-Marvel-Guilds-Amicus-Brief-Final.
Brody, Richard. "'Rogue One' Reviewed: Is It Time to Abandon the 'Star Wars' Franchise?" *New Yorker*, 13 Dec. 2016, https://www.newyorker.com/culture/richard-brody/rogue-one-reviewed-is-it-time-to-abandon-the-star-wars-franchise.
Brooker, Will. *Batman Unmasked: Analyzing a Cultural Icon*. Continuum.
Brooker, Will. *Hunting the Dark Knight: Twenty-First Century Batman*. I. B. Tauris, 2012.
Brown, Jeffrey A. *The Modern Superhero in Film and Television*. Routledge, 2017.
Brown, Wendy. *Undoing the Demos: Neoliberalism's Stealth Revolution*. Zone Books, 2015.
Budd, Mike, and Max H. Kirsch, editors. *Rethinking Disney: Private Control, Public Dimensions*. Wesleyan University Press, 2005.
Burke, Liam. *The Comic Book Film Adaptation*. University Press of Mississippi, 2015.
Burr, Ty. "Comic Movies." *Entertainment Weekly*, 19 Apr. 1996, https://web.archive.org/web/20141018203620/http://www.ew.com/ew/article/0%2C%2C292190%2C00.html.
Busiek, Kurt. "Marvel and Jack Kirby Family Settle Long-Running Legal Dispute." *Comic Book Resources*, 27 Sept. 2014, http://community.comicbookresources.com/showthread.php?19301-Marvel-amp-Jack-Kirby-Family-Settle-Long-Running-Legal-Dispute&p=552712&viewfull=1#post552712.
Busiek, Kurt. "Through the Mail Slot." *Busiek.Com*, 8 Nov. 2010, http://busiek.com/site/tag/wonder-woman/.
Cabell v. Zorro Productions Inc., et al. 5:15-cv-00771-EJD, 11 May 2018. *law.justia.com*, https://law.justia.com/cases/federal/district-courts/california/candce/5:2015cv00771/284927/234/.
Captain America: Civil War Official Super Bowl TV Spot (2016)—Chris Evans Movie HD. Directed by Movieclips Trailers, 2016. *YouTube*, https://www.youtube.com/watch?v=xZVd2unfoFk.
Captain America: First Avenger (2011): Kevin Feige Sound Bite. Paramount Pictures and Marvel Entertainment, 2011. *YouTube*, https://www.youtube.com/watch?v=dEw5rv5V4DE.
"Captain Marvel, Serial Number 72283349." *Trademark Electronic Search System, United States Patent and Trademark Office*, https://www.uspto.gov/trademarks-application-process/search-trademark-database. Accessed 20 July 2017.
"Captain Marvel, Serial Number 87893616." *Trademark Electronic Search System, United States Patent and Trademark Office*, 25 Apr. 2018, https://tmsearch.uspto.gov/bin/showfield?f=doc&state=4810:tvkn6r.2.2.
"Captain Marvel, Serial Number 87893623." *Trademark Electronic Search System, United States Patent and Trademark Office*, 25 Apr. 2018, https://tmsearch.uspto.gov/bin/showfield?f=doc&state=4808:5vve7a.2.1.
"Captain Marvel, Serial Number 87893635." *Trademark Electronic Search System, United States Patent and Trademark Office*, 25 Apr. 2018, https://tmsearch.uspto.gov/bin/showfield?f=doc&state=4808:5vve7a.2.1.
"Captain Marvel, Serial Number 87893646." *Trademark Electronic Search System, United States Patent and Trademark Office*, 25 Apr. 2018, https://tmsearch.uspto.gov/bin/showfield?f=doc&state=4808:5vve7a.2.1.
"Captain Marvel, Serial Number 87893652." *Trademark Electronic Search System, United States Patent and Trademark Office*, 25 Apr. 2018, https://tmsearch.uspto.gov/bin/showfield?f=doc&state=4810:tvkn6r.2.5.

"Captain Marvel, Serial Number 87893658." *Trademark Electronic Search System, United States Patent and Trademark Office*, 25 Apr. 2018, https://tmsearch.uspto.gov/bin/showfield?f=doc&state=4808:5vve7a.2.1.

Carmody, Tim. "Synergy Killed the Fantastic Four." *The Verge*, 19 Jan. 2016, https://www.theverge.com/2016/1/19/10790450/marvel-secret-wars-comics-heroes-goodbye-fantastic-four.

Carpenter, Greg. "On Canons, Critics, Consensus, and Comics, Part 2." *Sequart Organization*, 13 Jan. 2014, http://sequart.org/magazine/38725/on-canons-critics-consensus-and-comics-part-2/.

Castillo, Michelle. "Disney to Buy 21st Century Fox Assets in a Deal Worth More Than $52 Billion in Stock." *CNBC*, 14 Dec. 2017, https://www.cnbc.com/2017/12/14/disney-to-buy-21st-century-fox-assets.html.

"Charlton Comics: A Brief History." *Connecticut Historical Society*, 2004, https://web.archive.org/web/20080412061537/http://www.chs.org/comics/charlton.htm.

Christensen, Jerome. *America's Corporate Art: The Studio Authorship of Hollywood Motion Pictures*. Stanford University Press, 2012.

Christensen, Jerome. "The Time Warner Conspiracy: JFK, Batman, and the Manager Theory of Hollywood Film." *Critical Inquiry*, vol. 28, no. 3, Spring 2002, pp. 591–617.

"Citizens United v. Federal Election Commission." *U.S.*, vol. 558, no. 08-205, 21 Jan. 2010, p. 310, https://www.law.cornell.edu/supct/html/08-205.ZO.html.

The Civil War Begins—1st Trailer for Marvel's Captain America: Civil War. Directed by Marvel Entertainment, 2015. *YouTube*, https://www.youtube.com/watch?v=43NWzay3W4s.

Claremont, Chris. "Nerdist Comics Panel #5." *Nerdist*, 7 June 2014, http://nerdist.com/nerdist-comics-panel-58-chris-claremont/.

Clark, Andrew. "Disney Buys Marvel Entertainment." *The Guardian*, 31 Aug. 2009, https://www.theguardian.com/business/2009/aug/31/disney-marvel-buy-out.

Clark, Krystal. "An Unsung Hero: How Blade Helped Save the Comic-Book Movie." *SYFY Wire*, 12 Mar. 2014, https://www.syfy.com/syfywire/an-unsung-hero-how-blade-helped-save-the-comic-book-movie.

Claverie, Ezra. "Ambiguous Mr. Fox: Black Actors and Interest Convergence in the Superhero Film." *Journal of American Culture*, vol. 40, no. 2, 2017, pp. 155–68. *Wiley Online Library*, https://doi.org/10.1111/jacc.12712.

Claverie, Ezra. "Folklore, Fakelore, Scholars, and Shills: Superheroes as 'Myth.'" *Journal of Popular Culture*, vol. 52, no. 2, Oct. 2019, pp. 976–98.

Claverie, Ezra. "From Off-Brand to Franchise: 'Watchmen' as Advertisement." *Jump Cut: A Review of Contemporary Media*, vol. 58, spring 2018, p. 5.

Claverie, Ezra. "Lovecraft Fandom(s): Racism, Denial, and White Nationalism." *Intensities: The Journal of Cult Media*, Winter 2013, pp. 80–110.

Claverie, Ezra. "Storm and the Angels of History: Blackness and Star Image in the X-Men Films." *Journal of American Culture*, vol. 42, no. 1, 2019, pp. 55–69. *Wiley Online Library*, https://doi.org/10.1111/jacc.12974.

Coggan, Devan. *Wonder Woman 75th Anniversary: Lynda Carter, Gal Gadot Reflect at the U.N.*, 21 Oct. 2016, http://ew.com/article/2016/10/21/lynda-carter-gal-gadot-wonder-woman-united-nations-ambassador/.

Coogan, Peter. "The Definition of the Superhero: From Hercules to Superman." *Super/Heroes: From Hercules to Superman*, edited by Wendy Haslem et al., New Academia Publishing, 2007, pp. 21–36.

Coombe, Rosemary J. *The Cultural Life of Intellectual Properties: Authorship, Appropriation, and the Law*. Duke University Press, 1998.

Copyright Act of 1976. 94-553 90 Stat. 2541, 19 Oct. 1976, https://www.copyright.gov/history/pl94-553.pdf.

Cornet, Roth. "Marvel Head Says Fans Want Black Panther and Captain Marvel." *IGN*, 21 Aug. 2014, https://www.ign.com/articles/2014/08/21/marvel-head-says-fans-want-black-panther-and-captain-marvel.

Cotta Vaz, Mark. *Empire of the Superheroes: America's Comic Book Creators and the Making of a Billion-Dollar Industry*. University of Texas Press, 2021.

"Creator Spotlight: Jack Kirby." *Marvel Entertainment*, 2017, https://www.marvel.com/comics/discover/801/jack-kirby.

Davis, Brandon. "Wolverine 3 Targeting R Rating." *Comicbook.Com*, 16 Feb. 2016, http://comicbook.com/2016/02/16/wolverine-3-targeting-r-rating/.

"DC Celebrates Wonder Woman Day with Massive Global Event on Saturday, June 3." *DC Comics*, 15 May 2017, https://www.dccomics.com/blog/2017/05/15/dc-celebrates-wonder-woman-day-with-massive-global-event-on-saturday-june-3.

"DC Comics v. Towle." *F. Supp. 3d*, vol. 802, 13-55484, 23 Sept. 2015, p. 1012, https://law.justia.com/cases/federal/appellate-courts/ca9/13-55484/13-55484-2015-09-23.html.

"DeadPool / Black Panther Back in Red & Black." *Kickstarter*, https://www.kickstarter.com/projects/818699830/deadpool-black-panther-back-in-red-and-black. Accessed 12 July 2021.

"DeadPool / Black Panther: The Gauntlet." *Kickstarter*, https://www.kickstarter.com/projects/818699830/deadpool-black-panther-the-gauntlet. Accessed 12 July 2021.

Decherney, Peter. *Hollywood's Copyright Wars: From Edison to the Internet*. Columbia University Press, 2012.

"Detective Comics Inc. v. Bruns Publications Inc., et al." *F.2d*, vol. 111, no. 203, 29 Apr. 1940, p. 432, https://law.justia.com/cases/federal/appellate-courts/F2/111/432/1503080/.

Dittmer, Jason. *Captain America and the Nationalist Superhero: Metaphors, Narratives, and Geopolitics*. Temple University Press, 2013.

Dockterman, Eliana. "Why Black Panther's Debut in *Captain America: Civil War* Is So Important." *Time*, 5 May 2016, https://time.com/4314966/black-panther-marvel-captain-america/.

Dockterman, Eliana. "Wonder Woman Breaks Through." *Time*, 26 Dec. 2016, http://time.com/4606107/wonder-woman-breaks-through/.

"Domestic Yearly Box Office." *Box Office Mojo*, https://www.boxofficemojo.com/year/. Accessed 23 Mar. 2023.

Donini, Andrea. "The Dark Knight: An Allegory of 9/11 and the War on Terror." *Hypercritic*, 3 Feb. 2021, https://hypercritic.org/collection/christopher-nolan-the-dark-knight-an-allegory-of-9-11-and-the-war-on-terror-2008-review/.

Downey, Mark. "Christian Identity: What Is It?" *Kinsman Redeemer Ministries*, 6 Nov. 2011, http://kinsmanredeemer.com/identity.htm.

Drucker, Peter F. *The Practice of Management*. Harper & Row, 1954.

Du Bois, Peter C. "Superman, Batman—and Ivanhoe: Comic Books Have Become Both Profitable and Respectable." *Barron's National Business and Financial Weekly*, 18 Sept. 1961, p. 9+.

Eco, Umberto. "The Myth of Superman." *Diacritics*, translated by Natalie Chilton, vol. 2, no. 1, Spring 1972, pp. 14–22.

Epstein, Edward Jay. *The Hollywood Economist: The Hidden Financial Reality behind the Movies*. Melville House, 2010.

Faithful, George. "Dark of the World, Shine on Us: The Redemption of Blackness in Ryan Coogler's *Black Panther*." *Religions*, vol. 9, no. 10, https://doi.org/doi.org/10.3390/rel9100304.

Fawaz, Ramzi. *The New Mutants: Superheroes and the Radical Imagination of American Comics.* New York University Press, 2016.

"Fawkes, Serial Number 78052947." *Trademark Electronic Search System, United States Patent and Trademark Office,* 13 Mar. 2001, https://tmsearch.uspto.gov/bin/showfield?f=doc&state=4810:zptrj2.5.2.

Feblowitz, Joshua C. "The Hero We Create: 9/11 and the Reinvention of Batman." *Inquiries Journal,* vol. 1, no. 12, 2009, http://www.inquiriesjournal.com/articles/104/the-hero-we-create-911-the-reinvention-of-batman.

Federman, Wayne. "What Reagan Did for Hollywood." *The Atlantic,* 14 Nov. 2011, https://www.theatlantic.com/entertainment/archive/2011/11/what-reagan-did-for-hollywood/248391/.

Fields, Barbara Jeanne. "Slavery, Race and Ideology in the United States of America." *New Left Review,* vol. 181, June 1990, pp. 95–118.

"Film Box Office Grosses." *Variety,* 7 Mar. 2017, p. 22.

Fingeroth, Danny. *A Marvelous Life: The Amazing Story of Stan Lee.* St. Martin's Press, 2019.

Fisher, Mark. "Gothic Oedipus: Subjectivity and Capitalism in Christopher Nolan's *Batman Begins.*" *ImageTexT: Interdisciplinary Comics Studies,* vol. 2, no. 2, http://www.english.ufl.edu/imagetext/archives/v2_2/fisher/. Accessed 31 July 2017.

"5 Things You Need to Know about Residuals." *Media Services,* 14 Nov. 2013, https://www.mediaservices.com/blog/five-things-you-need-to-know-about-residuals/.

Fjellman, Stephen M. *Vinyl Leaves: Walt Disney World and America.* Westview Press, 1992, http://ezproxy.library.nyu.edu:2287/view/work/bibliographic_entity%7Cbibliographic_details%7C1683435#page/276/mode/1/chapter/bibliographic_entity|document|1683470.

Fleming, Michael. "Hoffman on the 'Radio'; Col Deal for Cohen." *Variety,* 28 Oct. 1999, https://variety.com/1999/voices/columns/hoffman-on-the-radio-col-deal-for-cohen-1117757475/.

Fleming, Michael. "A Mania for Marvel." *Variety,* 14 Apr. 1997, https://variety.com/1997/voices/columns/a-mania-for-marvel-1117434784/.

Flinn, Tom. "'Suicide Squad' Plummets, but Still Wins." *ICv2,* 14 Aug. 2016, https://icv2.com/articles/reviews/view/35265/suicide-squad-plummets-but-still-wins.

Ford, Rebecca, and Lacey Rose. "100 Days That Changed Hollywood: The Writers Strike, 10 Years Later." *Hollywood Reporter,* 17 May 2018, https://www.hollywoodreporter.com/movies/movie-features/100-days-changed-hollywood-writers-strike-10-year-1111860/.

Fox, Gardner. "The Batman Meets Doctor Death." *The Batman Chronicles,* vol. 1, DC Comics, 2005, pp. 17–27.

Fox, Gardner. "The Batman Wars against the Dirigible of Doom." *Detective Comics #33,* November 1939. *The Batman Chronicles,* vol. 1, DC Comics, pp. 62–73.

Fox, Gardner. "Frenchy Blake's Jewel Gang." *The Batman Chronicles,* vol. 1, DC Comics, 2005, pp. 10–16.

Fox, Gardner. "The Return of Doctor Death." *The Batman Chronicles,* vol. 1, DC Comics, 2005, pp. 28–38.

Fradley, Martin. "What Do You Believe In? Film Scholarship and the Cultural Politics of the *Dark Knight* Franchise." *Film Quarterly,* vol. 66, no. 3, Spring 2013, pp. 15–27, https://doi.org/10.1525/fq.2013.66.3.15.

Frase, Peter. *Four Futures: Life after Capitalism.* Verso, 2016.

"Frederick Warne & Co. Inc. v. Book Sales Inc." *F. Supp.,* vol. 481, 78 Civ. 2375, 19 Dec. 1979, p. 1191, https://law.justia.com/cases/federal/district-courts/FSupp/481/1191/2397442/.

Frye, Northrop. "Archetypal Criticism: Theory of Myths." *Anatomy of Criticism: Four Essays,* Princeton University Press, 2000, pp. 131–239.

Furman, Phyllis. "Perelman's Tangled Web." *Crain's New York Business,* 28 May 1997, pp. 1, 40–44.

Gabler, Neal. *Walt Disney: The Triumph of the American Imagination.* Knopf, 2006.

Gaines, Jane. "Superman, Television, and the Protective Strength of the Trademark Chapter Seven." *Contested Culture: The Image, the Voice, and the Law*, University of North Carolina Press, 1991, pp. 208–27.

Gardner, Eriq. "Hollywood Guilds Want Supreme Court to Hear Marvel Characters Dispute." *Hollywood Reporter*, 23 June 2014, https://www.hollywoodreporter.com/thr-esq/hollywood-guilds-want-supreme-court-714104.

Gardner, Eriq. "'Zorro' Trademark Declared Invalid in Europe." *Hollywood Reporter*, 6 July 2015, https://www.hollywoodreporter.com/thr-esq/zorro-trademark-declared-invalid-europe-806823.

"Gary Friedrich Enterprises LLC v. Marvel Characters Inc." *F.3d*, vol. 716, 12-893-cv, 11 June 2013, p. 302, https://casetext.com/case/gary-friedrich-enterprises-llc-v-marvel-characters-inc.

Gates, Henry Louis, Jr. "Segregation in the Armed Forces during World War II." *The African Americans: Many Rivers to Cross*, 14 Jan. 2013, http://www.pbs.org/wnet/african-americans-many-rivers-to-cross/history/what-was-black-americas-double-war/.

Ginsburg, Jane C. "A Tale of Two Copyrights: Literary Property in Revolutionary France and America." *Tulane Law Review*, vol. 64, no. 5, 1990, pp. 991–1031.

Gliberman, Owen. "Logan." *Variety*, 21 Feb. 2017.

Goldstein, Patrick. "Hollywood's Slipped Discs." *The Guardian*, 22 May 2009, http://www.theguardian.com/film/2009/may/22/falling-dvd-sales.

Gordon, Ian. *Superman: The Persistence of an American Icon*. Rutgers University Press, 2017.

Goulart, Ron. "Captain America and the Super-Patriots." *Comics Buyer's Guide*, no. 22, April 1988, pp. 36–39.

Graeber, David. *Bullshit Jobs: A Theory*. Simon & Schuster, 2018.

Gray, Brandon. "'Spider-Man' Takes Box Office on the Ultimate Spin: $114.8 Million." *Box Office Mojo*, 6 May 2002, https://www.boxofficemojo.com/article/ed1651770372/.

Gray, Brandon. "Weekend Box Office." *Box Office Mojo*, 17 July 2000, https://www.boxofficemojo.com/article/ed2171864068/.

Gray, Jonathan. *Show Sold Separately: Promos, Spoilers, and Other Media Paratexts*. New York University Press, 2010.

Gray, Mackenzie. *The Rush, Shaw TV*, 19 June 2003, https://www.youtube.com/watch?v=XGasQcUukvM.

Greenwald, Marilyn S. *The Secret of the Hardy Boys: Leslie McFarlane and the Stratemeyer Syndicate*, Ohio University Press, 2004. bobcat.library.nyu.edu, http://proxy.library.nyu.edu/login?url=https://ebookcentral.proquest.com/lib/nyulibrary-ebooks/detail.action?docID=3026868.

Groth, Gary. "Jack Kirby Interview." *Comics Journal*, no. 134, Feb. 1990, http://www.tcj.com/jack-kirby-interview/.

Guerrasio, Jason. "'Suicide Squad' Is Not Getting a China Release and Will Take a Huge Blow in Global Box Office." *Business Insider*, 5 Aug. 2016, http://www.businessinsider.com/suicide-squad-likely-banned-in-china-global-box-office-2016-8.

Gustines, George Gene. "Ta-Nehisi Coates to Write Black Panther Comic for Marvel," *New York Times*, 22 Sept. 2015, http://www.proquest.com/nytimes/docview/1718093430/abstract/E5932FAF24DB4413PQ/1.

Gutis, Philip S. "Turning Superheroes into Super Sales." *New York Times*, 6 Jan. 1985, p. 6. ProQuest Historical Newspapers.

Hajdu, David. *The Ten-Cent Plague: The Great Comic-Book Scare and How It Changed America*. Farrar, Straus and Giroux, 2008.

Hassler-Forest, Dan. *Capitalist Superheroes: Caped Crusaders in the Neoliberal Age*. Zero Books, 2012.

Hayde, Michael J. *Flights of Fantasy: The Unauthorized but True Story of Radio and TV's Adventures of Superman*. BearManor Media, 2009.

Herbert, Frank. *Chapterhouse: Dune*. Ace Books, 1987.

Hesmondhalgh, David. "Exploitation and Media Labor." *The Routledge Companion to Labor and Media*, Routledge, 2015, pp. 30–39.

Higgins, Scott. *Matinee Melodrama: Playing with Formula in the Sound Serial*. Rutgers University Press, 2016.

"H9952." *Congressional Record, Government Printing Office*, 7 Oct. 1998, https://www.govinfo.gov/content/pkg/CREC-1998-10-07/pdf/CREC-1998-10-07-pt1-PgH9946.pdf.

"Holy Hera! DC Just Declared June 3 'Wonder Woman Day,' Massive Global Celebrations Planned." *Women You Should Know*, 24 May 2017, http://womenyoushouldknow.net/holy-hera-dc-just-declared-june-3-wonder-woman-day-massive-global-celebrations-planned/.

Home Recording of Copyrighted Works: Hearing on H.R. 4783, H.R. 4794, H.R. 4808, H.R. 5250, H.R. 5488, and H.R. 5705. US Government Printing Office, 1983.

Horrocks, Dylan. "Sketch a Day (Cartoonist Week): Jack Kirby." *Hicksville Comics*, 15 Mar. 2013, http://hicksvillecomics.com/1702.

House, Meredith Annan. "Marvel v. Kirby: A Clash of Comic Book Titans in the Work Made for Hire Arena." *Berkeley Technology Law Journal*, vol. 30, no. 4, pp. 933–64.

Howe, Sean. "Avengers Assemble! How Marvel Went from a Hollywood Also-Ran to Mastermind of a $1 Billion Franchise." *Slate*, 28 Sept. 2012, https://slate.com/business/2012/09/marvel-comics-and-the-movies-the-business-story-behind-the-avengers.html.

Howe, Sean. *Marvel Comics: The Untold Story*. HarperCollins, 2012.

In re Me and the Mouse Travel LLC, Serial No. 76717725, 21 Apr. 2017, http://ttabvue.uspto.gov/ttabvue/ttabvue-76717725-EXA-9.pdf.

International Copyright Piracy: A Growing Problem with Links to Organized Crime and Terrorism, 13 Mar. 2003, http://commdocs.house.gov/committees/judiciary/hju85643.000/hju85643_of.htm.

Ip, John. "The Dark Knight's War on Terrorism," *Ohio State Journal of Criminal Law*, no. 1, 2011, pp. 209–29.

James, C. L. R. *The Black Jacobins: Toussaint L'Ouverture and the San Domingo Revolution*, 2nd rev. ed., Vintage Books, 1963.

Jameson, Fredric. "Metacommentary." *PMLA*, vol. 86, no. 1, Jan. 1971, pp. 9–18.

Jameson, Fredric. *The Political Unconscious: Narrative as a Socially Symbolic Act*. Cornell University Press, 1981.

Jameson, Fredric. *Postmodernism, or the Cultural Logic of Late Capitalism*. Duke University Press, 1991.

Jaszi, Peter, and Martha Woodmansee. "Copyright in Transition." *A History of the Book in America*, edited by Carl F. Kaestle and Janice A. Radway, vol. 4, *Print in Motion: The Expansion of Publishing and Reading in the United States, 1880–1940*, University of North Carolina Press, 2009, pp. 90–101.

Jenkins, Henry. *Convergence Culture: Where Old and New Media Collide*. New York University Press, 2008.

"John Gertz." *Zorro Productions Inc.*, https://www.zorro.com/zorro-musical/talent-bios/john-gertz/. Accessed 6 Mar. 2020.

Johnson, Derek. "Cinematic Destiny: Marvel Studios and the Trade Stories of Industrial Convergence." *Cinema Journal*, vol. 52, no. 1, 2012, pp. 1–24.

Johnson, Derek. *Media Franchising: Creative License and Collaboration in the Culture Industries*. 2013.

Johnston, Rich. "Confirmed: Fantastic Four to Be Cancelled in 2015 with a Triple-Sized Issue 645, For Fantastic Fourever." *Bleeding Cool News and Rumors*, 5 Oct. 2014, https://bleeding

cool.com/comics/confirmed-fantastic-four-to-be-cancelled-in-2015-with-a-triple-sized-issue-645-as-january-kicks-off-fantastic-fourever/.

Jones, Gerard. *Men of Tomorrow: Geeks, Gangsters, and the Birth of the Comic Book*. Basic Books, 2004.

Jordan, Sean, and Edward Gross. "A Knight in Gotham." *Cinefantastique*, vol. 37, no. 4, July 2005, pp. 22–35.

"Juice." *Box Office Mojo*, https://www.boxofficemojo.com/release/rl2891810305/weekend/. Accessed 3 Oct. 2020.

Kamina, Pascal. *Film Copyright in the European Union*. Cambridge University Press, 2016.

Katz, Joey. "The Rewatch: Man of Steel." *Agnes Farta Weekly*, 17 June 2015, http://agnesweekly.weebly.com/blog/the-rewatch-man-of-steel.

Kay, Jeremy. "Independent Producers and MPAA Settle over Screeners." *Screen Daily*, 29 Mar. 2004, https://www.screendaily.com/independent-producers-and-mpaa-settle-over-screeners/4017985.article.

Kennedy, Mark. "Wonder Woman Named a Special UN Ambassador, Despite Protests." *CBC*, 21 Oct. 2016, https://www.cbc.ca/news/entertainment/wonder-woman-un-ambassador-1.3816155.

Kerstein, Benjamin. "Batman's War on Terror." *Azure*, vol. 34, no. 5769, Autumn 2008, https://azure.org.il/include/print.php?id=477.

Khanna, Derek. "The Conservative Case for Taking on the Copyright Lobby." *Business Insider*, 30 Apr. 2014, https://www.businessinsider.com/time-to-confront-the-copyright-lobby-2014-4.

Kidman, Shawna. *Comic Books Incorporated: How the Business of Comics Became the Business of Hollywood*. University of California Press, 2019.

Killian, Kyle. "Batman (and World War III) Begins: Hollywood Takes on Terror." *Journal of Feminist Family Therapy*, vol. 19, no. 1, 2007, pp. 77–82.

Kirby v. Marvel Characters Inc. 13-1178, *SCOTUSblog*, 21 Mar. 2014, https://www.scotusblog.com/case-files/cases/kirby-v-marvel-characters-incorporated/.

Kirkpatrick, David D. "Action-Hungry DVD Fans Sway Hollywood." *New York Times*, http://www.nytimes.com/2003/08/17/us/action-hungry-dvd-fans-sway-hollywood.html?pagewanted=all&src=pm. Accessed 11 Sept. 2013.

Kit, Borys. "Fox's Daredevil Rights on Verge of Reverting to Marvel as Ticking Clock Looms." *Hollywood Reporter*, 14 Aug. 2012, https://www.hollywoodreporter.com/tv/tv-features/daredevil-marvel-fox-comic-adaptation-sequel-361982/.

Klavan, Andrew. "What Bush and Batman Have in Common." *Wall Street Journal*, 25 July 2008, https://web.archive.org/web/20100218081413/http://online.wsj.com/public/article_print/SB121694247343482821.html.

Klein, Naomi. *The Shock Doctrine: The Rise of Disaster Capitalism*. Metropolitan Books, 2007.

Klemesrud, Judy. "Foundation to Aid Women over 40." *New York Times*, 7 Oct. 1981, http://www.nytimes.com/1981/10/07/garden/foundation-to-aid-women-over-40.html.

Kroll, Justin. "New Actresses Test for 'Batman vs. Superman' . . . as Wonder Woman?" *Variety*, 8 Nov. 2013, https://variety.com/2013/film/news/batman-superman-1200665552/.

Kroll, Justin. "'Wonder Woman' Gal Gadot Signs Three-Picture Deal with Warner Bros." *Variety*, 23 Jan. 2014, https://variety.com/2014/film/news/wonder-woman-gal-gadot-signs-three-picture-deal-with-warner-bros-1201067961/.

Kurtz, Leslie. "The Independent Lives of Fictional Characters." *Wisconsin Law Review*, June 1986, pp. 439–524.

Kusumi, Takashi, Ken Matsuda, and Eriko Sugimori. "The Effects of Aging on Nostalgia in Consumers' Advertising Processing." *Japanese Psychological Research*, vol. 52, no. 3, 2010, pp. 150–62.

Kutner, Max. "Why Critics Call Steven Mnuchin's Bank 'A Foreclosure Machine.'" *Newsweek*, 2 Dec. 2016, http://www.newsweek.com/donald-trump-steven-mnuchin-treasury-foreclosures-527810.

Lacan, Jacques. "Anamorphosis." *Four Fundamental Concepts of Psycho-Analysis*, Karnac, 2004, pp. 79–90.

Lang, Brent. "Ant-Man Shows Power and Limits of Marvel Brand." *Variety*, 19 July 2015, http://variety.com/2015/film/news/ant-man-box-office-marvel-1201543684/.

Lang, Brent. "United Nations Names Wonder Woman Honorary Ambassador." *Variety*, 21 Oct. 2016, https://variety.com/2016/film/news/wonder-woman-united-nations-ambassador-1201896751/.

Lang, Brent, and James Rainey. "Revenue Record for U.S. Box Office." *Variety*, 3 Jan. 2017, pp. 21–22.

Langshaw, Mark. "'Dark Knight Returns' Sales Surge 161%." *Digital Spy*, 13 Aug. 2013, http://www.digitalspy.com/comics/a506415/dark-knight-returns-sales-surge-following-comic-con-announcement/.

Lantagne, Stacey M. "Building a Better Mousetrap: Blocking Disney's Imperial Copyright Strategies." *Journal of Sports and Entertainment Law*, vol. 12, no. 1, 2021, pp. 141–74.

Lash, Scott, and Celia Lury. *Global Culture Industry*, Polity Press, 2007.

Leadbeater, Alex. "Logan's X-Men Comics and Eden Explained." *Screen Rant*, 5 Mar. 2017, http://screenrant.com/logan-wolverine-x-men-comics-eden-explained/.

Lee, Stan. *Secrets behind the Comics*. Famous Enterprises, 1947.

Lee, Timothy B. "15 Years Ago, Congress Kept Mickey Mouse Out of the Public Domain. Will They Do It Again?" *Washington Post*, 25 Oct. 2013, https://www.washingtonpost.com/news/the-switch/wp/2013/10/25/15-years-ago-congress-kept-mickey-mouse-out-of-the-public-domain-will-they-do-it-again/.

Lehu, Jean-Marc. *Branded Entertainment: Product Placement and Brand Strategy in the Entertainment Business*. Kogan Page, 2007.

Lent, John. "The Unfunny Tale of Labor and Cartooning in the US and around the World." *The Routledge Companion to Labor and Media*, edited by Richard Maxwell, Routledge, 2009, pp. 180–89.

Lepore, Jill. *The Secret History of Wonder Woman*. Knopf, 2014.

Li, Siu Leung. "Kung Fu: Negotiating Nationalism and Modernity." *Cultural Studies*, vol. 15, nos. 3–4, July 2001, pp. 515–42, https://doi.org/10.1080/095023800110046687.

Liptak, Andrew. "Marvel Is Rebooting Blade, with Mahershala Ali Set to Star." *The Verge*, 20 July 2019, https://www.theverge.com/2019/7/20/20702411/marvel-cinematic-universe-blade-reboot-mahershala-ali.

Littleton, Cynthia. "Justice Department Approves Disney's Acquisition of 21st Century Fox with Divestiture of Regional Sports Networks." *Variety*, 27 June 2018, https://variety.com/2018/biz/news/disney-21st-century-fox-justice-department-approval-1202859241/.

Loeb, Jeph. *Batman: The Long Halloween*. DC Comics, 1998.

Lopes, Paul. *Demanding Respect: The Evolution of the American Comic Book*. Temple University Press, 2009.

Loveland, Katherine E., et al. "Still Preoccupied with 1995: The Need to Belong and Preference for Nostalgic Products." *Journal of Consumer Research*, vol. 37, Oct. 2010, pp. 393–408.

Lubin, Gus. "It's Astonishing How Far Disney Is Going to Bury the X-Men." *Business Insider*, 6 Apr. 2015, http://www.businessinsider.com/its-astonishing-how-far-disney-is-going-to-bury-the-x-men-2015-4.

Lukács, Georg. "Reification and the Consciousness of the Proletariat." *History and Class Consciousness: Studies in Marxist Dialectics*, translated by Rodney Livingstone, Harvard University Press, 1971, pp. 83–222.

Lyman, Rick. "In a Weekend, 'Spider-Man' Jump-Starts the Summer." *New York Times*, 7 May 2002, https://www.nytimes.com/2002/05/07/business/in-a-weekend-spider-man-jump-starts-the-summer.html.

Lyons, Charles. "Warners Taps Alcott for Silver's 'Wonder.'" *Daily Variety*, 22 Jan. 2001, p. 64.
MacDonald, Heidi. "Miller's Double Noir: 'Sin City' and 'Batman Begins.'" *Publishers Weekly*, vol. 252, no. 10, 7 Mar. 2005, pp. 40+. Gale Academic OneFile.
"The Making of *Juice*." *Entertainment Weekly*, 24 Jan. 1992, https://ew.com/article/1992/01/24/making-juice/.
Malory, Sir Thomas. "The Noble Tale of the Sangreal." *Le Morte d'Arthur*, 1470 Caxton edition, Carleton University, https://carleton.ca/chum/wp-content/uploads/Malory-for-Hum3200.pdf. Accessed 16 Aug. 2015.
"Marvel Characters Inc. v. Simon." *F.3d*, vol. 310, 02-7221, 7 Nov. 2002, p. 280, https://caselaw.findlaw.com/us-2nd-circuit/1113903.html.
"Marvel Enterprises Settles Legal Dispute with Joe Simon concerning Captain America." *Business Wire*, 29 Sept. 2003, https://www.businesswire.com/news/home/20030929005081/en/Marvel-Enterprises-Settles-Legal-Dispute-Joe-Simon.
Marvel's Captain America: Civil War—Trailer 2. Directed by Marvel Entertainment, 2016. *YouTube*, https://www.youtube.com/watch?v=dKrVegVIoUs.
Marx, Karl. *Capital: A Critique of Political Economy*. Edited by Frederick Engels, translated by Samuel Moore and Edward Aveling, vol. 1, Modern Library, 1906.
Marx, Karl. *Capital: A Critique of Political Economy*. Edited by Frederick Engels, translated by I. Lasker, vol. 2, Lawrence & Wishart, 1970.
Marx, Karl. *The Grundrisse*. Translated by David McLellan, Harper & Row, 1971.
McCann, Erin. "U.N. Drops Wonder Woman as an Ambassador." *New York Times*, 13 Dec. 2016, https://www.nytimes.com/2016/12/13/world/un-wonder-woman-campaign.html.
McClintock, Pamela. "Marvel Touts Par's Hero Worship." *Variety*, 28 Apr. 2005.
McDonald, Paul. *Video and DVD Industries*. British Film Institute, 2007.
McGowan, Todd. "The Exceptional Darkness of *The Dark Knight*." *Jump Cut: A Review of Contemporary Media*, Spring 2009, https://www.ejumpcut.org/archive/jc51.2009/darkKnightKant/index.html.
McNary, Dave. "Box Office: 'Suicide Squad' Heads for Enormous $140 Million Opening Weekend." *Variety*, 5 Aug. 2016, variety.com/2016/film/news/box-office-suicide-squad-opening-weekend-will-smith-margot-robbie-1201831471/.
Meehan, Eileen R. "'Holy Commodity Fetish, Batman!': The Political Economy of a Commercial Intertext." *Many More Lives of the Batman: Critical Approaches to a Superhero and His Media*, edited by Roberta E. Pearson et al., British Film Institute, 2015, pp. 71–87.
Mendelson, Scott. "15 Years Ago, Batman, 'Star Wars' and Spielberg Confronted 9/11." *Forbes*, 29 June 2020, https://www.forbes.com/sites/scottmendelson/2020/06/29/15-years-ago-batman-star-wars-revenge-of-the-sith-and-steven-spielberg-tom-cruise-war-of-the-world-began-hollywood-obsession-with-911/.
"A Message to Our Readers: Introducing the Editorial Advisory Board." *More Fun Comics*, no. 72, Oct. 1941, n.p.
Michalowski, Raymond J., and Ronald C. Kramer. "State-Corporate Crime and Criminological Inquiry." *International Handbook of White-Collar and Corporate Crime*, Springer, 2007, pp. 200–219.
Mick, Jason. "Anti-piracy Ad Creators Fined for Stealing Musician's Work." *DailyTech*, 18 July 2012.
Millar, Kathleen. "Financing Terror." *U.S. Customs Today*, Nov. 2002, https://web.archive.org/web/20111023203500/http://www.cbp.gov/xp/CustomsToday/2002/November/interpol.xml.
Miller, Frank. *Batman: The Dark Knight Returns*. DC Comics, 1986.
Miller, Frank. *Batman: Year One*. DC Comics, 1987.
Miller, Toby, et al. *Global Hollywood 2*. British Film Institute, 2004.
Mitchell, Steve. "Slaughter of the Innocents." *Comics Buyer's Guide*, 17 May 1985, p. 40+.

Mokoena, Dikeledi A. "Black Panther and the Problem of the Black Radical." *Africology: The Journal of Pan African Studies*, vol. 11, no. 9, Aug. 2018, pp. 13–19.

"Monsanto Critics Denied U.S. Supreme Court Hearing on Seed Patents." *Reuters*, 13 Jan. 2014, https://www.reuters.com/article/us-usa-court-monsanto-idUSBREA0C10H20140113.

Moore, Jack. "'Wonder Woman' Faces a Ban in Lebanon Because It Stars Israeli Actor Gal Gadot." *Newsweek*, 31 May 2017, http://www.newsweek.com/wonder-woman-ban-lebanon-israeli-gal-gadot-617968.

Moore, Jack. "'Wonder Woman' Star Gal Gadot Has Israeli Cinema Named after Her." *Newsweek*, 16 Jan. 2018, http://www.newsweek.com/wonder-woman-star-gal-gadot-has-israeli-cinema-named-after-her-face-arab-782404.

Muehling, Darrel D. "The Relative Influence of Advertising-Evoked Personal and Historical Nostalgic Thoughts on Consumers' Brand Attitudes." *Journal of Marketing Communications*, vol. 19, no. 2, 2013, pp. 98–113.

Muehling, Darrel D., et al. "Exploring the Boundaries of Nostalgic Advertising Effects: A Consideration of Childhood Brand Exposure and Attachment on Consumers' Responses to Nostalgia-Themed Advertisements." *Journal of Advertising*, vol. 43, no. 1, pp. 73–84.

Munarriz, Rick. "5 Reasons Disney Is Buying Marvel." *Motley Fool*, 2 Sept. 2009, https://www.fool.com/investing/general/2009/09/02/5-reasons-disney-is-buying-marvel.aspx.

Nama, Adilifu. *Black Space: Imagining Race in Science Fiction Film*. University of Texas Press, 2008.

Nama, Adilifu. *Super Black: American Pop Culture and Black Superheroes*. University of Texas Press, 2011.

"National Comics Publications Inc. v. Fawcett Publications Inc., et al." *F.2d*, vol. 191, 30 Aug. 1951, p. 594, http://law.justia.com/cases/federal/appellate-courts/F2/191/594/91314/.

"New Jack City." *Box Office Mojo*, https://www.boxofficemojo.com/release/rl3613689345/weekend/. Accessed 1 Apr. 2021.

"Next Up: R-Rated X-Men Movie?" *Variety*, 7 Mar. 2017, p. 10.

Nolan, Christopher. "Christopher Nolan Says His Batman, Unlike the Marvel Cinematic Universe's Heroes, Doesn't Play Well with Others." Interview by Geoff Boucher, 2011. *Los Angeles Times*, https://www.latimes.com/la-et-mn-christopher-nolan-3-20081029-story.html.

North, Sterling. "A National Disgrace (and a Challenge to American Parents)." *Chicago Daily News*, 8 May 1940.

Order 81: Patent, Industrial Design, Undisclosed Information, Integrated Circuits, and Plant Variety Law. Coalition Provisional Authority [Iraq], 26 Apr. 2004, file:///Users/ec/Downloads/20040426_CPAORD_81_Patents_Law-2.pdf.

Ortner, Sherry B. "Studying Sideways: Ethnographic Access in Hollywood." *Production Studies: Cultural Studies of Media Industries*, edited by Vicki Mayer et al., Taylor & Francis Group, 2009, pp. 175–89.

Owoseje, Toyin. "Whoopi Goldberg Wants Disney to Build a Wakanda Theme Park." *CNN*, 31 Aug. 2020, https://www.cnn.com/2020/08/31/entertainment/whoopi-goldberg-disney-wakanda-theme-park-intl-scli/index.html.

Parker, Ryan, and Aaron Couch. "Wesley Snipes Reveals Untold Story behind His 'Black Panther' Film." *Hollywood Reporter*, 30 Jan. 2018, https://www.hollywoodreporter.com/movies/movie-news/black-panther-wesley-snipes-reveals-untold-story-behind-90s-film-1078868/.

Passas, Nikos. *Corruption in the Procurement Process/Outsourcing Government Functions: Issues, Case Studies, Implications*. Institute for Fraud Prevention, Feb. 2007.

Patten, Dominic. "Marvel and Jack Kirby Heirs Settle Legal Battle Ahead of Supreme Court Showdown." *Deadline*, 26 Sept. 2014, https://deadline.com/2014/09/jack-kirby-marvel-settlement-lawsuit-supreme-court-hearing-841711/.

"Piracy, n." *OED Online*, Oxford University Press, https://www.oed.com/view/Entry/144486. Accessed 20 Mar. 2022.

"Piracy and the Law." Motion Picture Association of America, 12 Apr. 2006, https://web.archive.org/web/20060413175607/http://www.mpaa.org/piracy_AndLaw.asp.

Piracy: It's a Crime. Federation against Copyright Theft, Motion Picture Association of America, and Intellectual Property Office of Singapore, 2004.

Poe, Edgar Allan. "The Purloined Letter." *The Fall of the House of Usher and Other Writings*, Penguin, 1844, pp. 330–49.

Pollard, Tom. *Hollywood 9/11: Superheroes, Supervillains, and Super Disasters*. Routledge, 2015, https://doi.org/10.4324/9781315634135.

Privacy and Piracy: The Paradox of Illegal File Sharing on Peer-to-Peer Networks and the Impact of Technology on the Entertainment Industry. US Government Printing Office, 30 Sept. 2003, https://www.govinfo.gov/content/pkg/CHRG-108shrg90239/html/CHRG-108shrg90239.htm.

Public Enemy. "Caught, Can We Get a Witness?" *It Takes a Nation of Millions to Hold Us Back*. Def Jam Recordings, 1988.

Puglise, Nicole. "Wonder Woman Announced as UN Ambassador amid Staff Protest." *The Guardian*, 21 Oct. 2016, http://www.theguardian.com/books/2016/oct/21/wonder-woman-un-ambassador-staff-protest.

Rathwell, Mark. "Interview with Kenneth Johnson." *The Incredible Hulk Television Series Page*, 2009, https://web.archive.org/web/20090106174931/http://www.incrediblehulktvseries.com/InterviewsAndArticles/Johnson_Interview.html.

Reconsider the Choice of Wonder Woman as the UN's Honorary Ambassador for the Empowerment of Women and Girls. Care2 Petitions, 2016, https://www.thepetitionsite.com/741/288/432/reconsider-the-choice-of-honorary-ambassador-for-the-empowerment-of-women-and-girls/.

Reed, Adolph. "Marx, Race, and Neoliberalism." *New Labor Forum*, vol. 22, no. 1, Jan. 2013, pp. 49–57, https://doi.org/10.1177/1095796012471637.

Reid, Calvin. "Graphic Novel Bestsellers." *Publishers Weekly*, vol. 255, no. 35, Sept. 2008, p. 18. Gale Academic OneFile.

Reid, Calvin. "Graphic Novel Bestsellers." *Publishers Weekly*, vol. 256, no. 5, Feb. 2009, p. 16. Gale Academic OneFile.

Reid, Calvin. "Graphic Novel Bestsellers." *Publishers Weekly*, vol. 257, no. 1, Jan. 2010, p. 13. Gale Academic OneFile.

Reid, Calvin. "Graphic Novel Bestsellers." *Publishers Weekly*, vol. 258, no. 37, Sept. 2011, p. 19. Gale Academic OneFile.

"Reign of Wakanda: Return of the Black Panther Series." *Kickstarter*, https://www.kickstarter.com/projects/shadovision/reign-of-wakanda-return-of-the-black-panther-serie. Accessed 12 July 2021.

"Report Piracy." *Motion Picture Association of America*, 12 Apr. 2006, https://web.archive.org/web/20060415004554/http://www.mpaa.org/ReportPiracy.asp.

Reynolds, Richard. *Superheroes: A Modern Mythology*. University Press of Mississippi, 1992.

Robbins, Trina. "Re-inventing Wonder Woman—Again!" *Hooded Utilitarian*, 30 Apr. 2012, http://www.hoodedutilitarian.com/2012/04/re-inventing-wonder-woman-again/.

Robinson, Cedric J. *Black Marxism: The Making of the Black Radical Tradition*. University of North Carolina Press, 2000.

Rohrer, Finlo. "Getting Inside a Downloader's Head." *BBC News Magazine*, 18 June 2009, http://news.bbc.co.uk/2/hi/uk_news/magazine/8106805.stm.

Ross, Alice. "One Less Woman in Politics: Wonder Woman Loses Job as UN Ambassador." *The Guardian*, 13 Dec. 2016, http://www.theguardian.com/world/2016/dec/12/wonder-woman-un-ambassador-gender-equality.

Roy, William G. *Socializing Capital: The Rise of the Large Industrial Corporation in America*. Princeton University Press, 1997.

Rozsa, Matthew. "The Sneaky Politics of 'Suicide Squad': A Popcorn Movie for the Prison-Industrial Complex Era." *Salon*, 6 Aug. 2016, http://www.salon.com/2016/08/05/the-sneaky-politics-of-suicide-squad-a-popcorn-movie-for-the-prison-industrial-complex-era/.

Rubin, Rebecca. "Ryan Coogler Pays Emotional Tribute to Chadwick Boseman: 'What an Incredible Mark He's Left for Us.'" *Variety*, 30 Aug. 2020, https://variety.com/2020/film/news/chadwick-boseman-death-ryan-coogler-tribute-black-panther-1234753958/.

Russell, Bradley, et al. "Marvel Phase 4 Recap: Everything That Happened after *Avengers: Endgame*." *Gamesradar*, 10 Nov. 2022, https://www.gamesradar.com/marvel-phase-4-leak-release-dates-new-mcu-movies-lineup/.

Sabin, Roger. "The Perils of Strip Mining." *Sight and Sound*, vol. 18, no. 8, Aug. 2008, pp. 24–27.

"Safeguarding Creativity." *Motion Picture Association*, https://www.motionpictures.org/what-we-do/safeguarding-creativity/. Accessed 13 Aug. 2021.

Sakelaris, Nicholas. "Saudi Prince Bin Salman Accepts Responsibility but Not Blame for Khashoggi Death." *UPI*, 26 Sept. 2019, https://www.upi.com/Top_News/World-News/2019/09/26/Saudi-Prince-bin-Salman-accepts-responsibility-but-not-blame-for-Khashoggi-death/6231569504880/.

Santo, Avi. "Batman versus the Green Hornet: The Merchandisable TV Text and the Paradox of Licensing in the Classical Network Era." *Cinema Journal*, vol. 49, no. 2, Winter 2010, pp. 63–85.

Santo, Avi. "The Lone Ranger and the Law: Legal Battles over Corporate Authorship and Intellectual Property Management, 1939–1942." *Critical Studies in Media Communication*, vol. 29, no. 3, Aug. 2012, pp. 185–201.

"Saudi Arabia to End 35-Year Cinema Ban with *Black Panther*." *Canadian Broadcasting Corporation*, 5 Apr. 2018, https://www.cbc.ca/news/entertainment/saudi-cinema-panther-1.4606037.

"Saudi Arabia's First Cinema in Over 35 Years Opens with *Black Panther*." *The Guardian*, 20 Apr. 2018, https://www.theguardian.com/world/2018/apr/20/saudi-arabias-first-cinema-in-over-35-years-opens-with-black-panther.

Schang, Gabrielle. "Gloria Steinem's CIA Connection: Radical Feminists Won't Be Ms.-Led." *Berkeley Barb*, 30 June 1975, pp. 8–9.

Schatz, Thomas. "New Hollywood, New Millennium." *Film Theory and Contemporary Hollywood Movies*, edited by Warren Buckland, Routledge, 2009, pp. 19–46.

Scola, Nancy. "Why Iraqi Farmers Might Prefer Death to Paul Bremer's Order 81." *Global Policy Forum*, 19 Sept. 2007, https://archive.globalpolicy.org/security/issues/iraq/attack/consequences/2007/0919iraqifarmers.htm.

Seitz, Matt Zoller. "Disney Is Quietly Placing Classic Fox Movies into Its Vault, and That's Worrying." *Vulture*, 24 Oct. 2019, https://medium.com/vulture-magazine/disney-is-quietly-placing-classic-fox-movies-into-its-vault-and-thats-worrying-ac26bb7ccbfc.

Seneca, Lucius Annaeus. "The Pumpkinification of Claudius the God." *Anger, Mercy, Revenge*, translated by Martha Nussbaum, University of Chicago Press, 2010, pp. 215–36.

Sengupta, Somini. "U.N. Picks Powerful Feminist (Wonder Woman) for Visible Job (Mascot)." *New York Times*, 12 Oct. 2016, https://www.nytimes.com/2016/10/13/world/americas/wonder-woman-united-nations.html.

"76 Years of Wonder Woman." *Entertainment Weekly: The Ultimate Guide to Wonder Woman*, 2017, pp. 74–83.

Siegel, Jerry, and Joe Shuster. "Superman's Phony Manager." *The Superman Chronicles*, vol. 1, DC Comics, 2006, pp. 69–82.

Siegel, Tatiana. "Conservative Koch Brothers Are Secret Investors in 'Wonder Woman.'" *Hollywood Reporter*, https://www.hollywoodreporter.com/news/conservative-koch-brothers-are-secret-investors-wonder-woman-1027376. Accessed 22 June 2018.

Simon, Joe, and Jim Simon. *The Comic Book Makers*. Revised, Vanguard Productions, 2003.

Sinnreich, Aram. *The Piracy Crusade: How the Music Industry's War on Sharing Destroys Markets and Erodes Civil Liberties*. University of Massachusetts Press, 2013.

Slater, Shawn. "May the Fourth Be with You! Two New Star Wars–Themed Character Dining Experiences May 4–June 15 at Disney's Hollywood Studios." *Disney Parks Blog*, 28 March 2014, https://disneyparks.disney.go.com/blog/2014/03/may-the-fourth-be-with-you-two-new-star-wars-themed-character-dining-experiences-may-4-june-15-at-disneys-hollywood-studios/. Accessed 14 July 2018.

Smith, Sean, and Devin Gordon. "Hollywood Family Feud." *Newsweek*, vol. 142, no. 16, 20 Oct. 2003, p. 56.

Solon, Olivia. "Rights Group Fined for Not Paying Artist Royalties on Anti-piracy Ad." *Wired UK*, 10 July 2012, https://www.wired.co.uk/article/dutch-rights-group-fined-for-not-paying-royalties.

"Sony Pictures Entertainment v. Fireworks Enter. Group, 137 F. Supp. 2d 1177 (C.D. Cal. 2001)." *Justia Law*, https://law.justia.com/cases/federal/district-courts/FSupp2/137/1177/2472491/. Accessed 7 Mar. 2020.

"Sony Pictures v. Fireworks Entertainment." *F. Supp. 2d*, vol. 156, 01-0723 ABC, 16 July 2001, p. 1148, https://law.justia.com/cases/federal/district-courts/FSupp2/156/1148/2317943/.

Sperling, Nicole. "Calling All the Shots." *Entertainment Weekly: The Ultimate Guide to Wonder Woman*, 2017, pp. 40–43.

Stahl, Matt. "Privilege and Distinction in Production Worlds: Copyright, Collective Bargaining, and Working Conditions in Media Making." *Production Studies: Cultural Studies of Media Industries*, edited by Vicki Mayer et al., Taylor & Francis Group, 2009, pp. 54–67. *ProQuest Ebook Central*, http://ebookcentral.proquest.com/lib/nyulibrary-ebooks/detail.action?docID=446571.

"Star Wars: May the 4th Be with You." *Disney Parks Blog*, 4 May 2013, https://disneyparks.disney.go.com/let-the-memories-begin/limited-time-magic/star-wars-4th-be-with-you-hollywood-studios/?CMP=SOC-WDWFY12Q2FBDM0553.

"Steel." *Box Office Mojo*, https://www.boxofficemojo.com/release/rl4285761025/weekend/. Accessed 5 Apr. 2021.

Steel, Emily. "Netflix Refines Its DVD Business, Even as Streaming Unit Booms." *New York Times*, 26 July 2015, https://web.archive.org/web/20170621135707/https://www.nytimes.com/2015/07/27/business/while-its-streaming-service-booms-netflix-streamlines-old-business.html.

Stevens, J. Richard. *Captain America, Masculinity, and Violence: The Evolution of a National Icon*. Syracuse University Press, 2015.

"'A Stink Bucket of Disappointment': The Most Savage *Batman v Superman* Reviews." *The Guardian*, 29 Mar. 2016, https://www.theguardian.com/film/shortcuts/2016/mar/29/most-savage-batman-v-superman-dawn-justice-reviews.

Stuever, Hank. "Wonder Woman's Powers." *Washington Post*, 18 Apr. 2001, https://www.washingtonpost.com/archive/lifestyle/2001/04/18/wonder-womans-powers/1bd2c8f3-b240-41cd-85af-eff33b995389/.

Sundell, Abner. "How to Crash the Comics." *Writer's Digest Yearbook*, 1942, pp. 32–37, 68.

Thompson, Anne. "Academy Clamps Down on Oscar Screeners." *Inland Valley Daily Bulletin*, 29 Sept. 2003.

Thompson, E. P. *Whigs and Hunters: The Origin of the Black Act*. Harmondsworth: Penguin, 1990. *Internet Archive*, http://archive.org/details/whigshunters00epth.

Toh, Justine. "The Tools and the Toys of (the) War (on Terror): Consumer Desire, Military Fetish, and Regime Change in *Batman Begins*." *Reframing 9/11: Film, Popular Culture, and the "War on Terror,"* edited by Jeff Birkenstein et al., Continuum, 2010, pp. 127–39.

"Tracking Amazon: Batman Titles Rise." *Publishers Weekly*, 5 July 2012, https://www.publishersweekly.com/pw/by-topic/industry-news/publisher-news/article/52876-tracking-amazon-batman-titles-rise.html.

"Treasury Sanctions the Saudi Rapid Intervention Force and Former Deputy Head of Saudi Arabia's General Intelligence Presidency for Roles in the Murder of Journalist Jamal Khashoggi." *US Department of the Treasury*, 26 Feb. 2021, https://home.treasury.gov/news/press-releases/jy0038.

"TriStar Pictures Inc., et al., v. Del Taco Inc., et al." *1999 U.S. Dist*, CV 99-07655-DDP, 31 Aug. 1999, https://www.scribd.com/document/239326856/TriStar-vs-Del-Taco-1999.

Tryon, Chuck. *Reinventing Cinema: Movies in the Age of Media Convergence*. Rutgers University Press, 2009.

Twentieth Century Fox Film Corporation v. Marvel Enterprises Inc. US. 01-7983, 14 Jan. 2002, http://caselaw.findlaw.com/us-2nd-circuit/1136021.html.

2021 Notice of Annual Meeting of Shareholders and Proxy Statement. The Walt Disney Company, 19 Jan. 2021, https://thewaltdisneycompany.com/app/uploads/2021/01/2021-Proxy-Statement.pdf.

Tyler, Patrick E. "After the War, Rebuilding." *New York Times*, 27 May 2003, https://www.nytimes.com/2003/05/27/world/after-the-war-rebuilding-us-says-bank-credits-will-finance-sale-of-goods-to-iraq.html.

Ulin, Jeff. *The Business of Media Distribution: Monetizing Film, TV, and Video Content*. Focal Press, 2010.

United States, District Court for the Central District of California. *Siegel v. Warner Bros. Entertainment Inc*. Docket no. CV 04-08400-SGL, 8 Jul. 2009. United States, District Court for the Central District of California.

"UN Secretary-General Appoints Red from the Angry Birds as Honorary Ambassador for Green on the International Day of Happiness." *United Nations Sustainable Development*, 18 Mar. 2016, https://www.un.org/sustainabledevelopment/blog/2016/03/angrybirdshappyplanet/.

Vadakin. "Post No. 1658." *EyesSkyward*, 26 June 2013, http://www.eyesskyward.com/forum=/showthread.php?1750-Man-of-Steel-COMPLETE-SPOILERDiscussion&p=178829&viewfull=1.

Vaidhyanathan, Siva. *Copyrights and Copywrongs: The Rise of Intellectual Property and How It Threatens Creativity*. New York University Press, 2001.

Valenti, Jack. "It's Lights, Camera, Politics." *Los Angeles Times*, 6 Sept. 1996, https://www.latimes.com/archives/la-xpm-1996-09-06-me-41045-story.html.

van Dijk, Teun. "Discourse and the Denial of Racism." *Discourse and Society*, vol. 3, no. 1, 1992, pp. 87–118.

Vaughn, Stephen. *Freedom and Entertainment: Rating the Movies in an Age of New Media*. Cambridge University Press, 2006.

Vlessing, Etan. "ACTRA Talks Back On, but Digital Divide Gaping." *Hollywood Reporter*, 3 February 2007, https://www.hollywoodreporter.com/business/business-news/actra-talks-back-but-digital-129370/.

Voigt, Kevin. "China Firm Buys AMC to Form World's Largest Cinema Chain." *CNN*, 21 May 2012, https://www.cnn.com/2012/05/21/business/china-amc-wanda-theater/index.html.

Wagner, Holly J. "Judge Throws Out Screener Ban." *Video Store*, 14 Dec. 2003, p. 10.

Wagner, Rudolf G. "Lobby Literature: The Archaeology and Present Functions of Science Fiction in China." *After Mao: Chinese Literature and Society*, edited by J. C. Kinkley, Harvard University Asia Center, 1985, pp. 17–62.

Ward, David. "Sega Plays Marvel Video Game." *Hollywood Reporter*, 1 May 2008, https://www.hollywoodreporter.com/business/business-news/sega-plays-marvel-video-game-110713/.

Wasko, Janet. "Critiquing Hollywood: The Political Economy of Motion Pictures." *A Concise Handbook of Movie Industry Economics*, edited by Charles C. Moul, Cambridge University Press, 2005, pp. 5–31.

Wasko, Janet. *Understanding Disney: The Manufacture of Fantasy*. Polity Press, 2001.

Watkins, S. Craig. "Ghetto Reelness: Hollywood Film Production, Black Popular Culture, and the Ghetto Action Film Cycle." *Genre and Contemporary Hollywood*, edited by Steve Neale, British Film Institute, 2002, pp. 236–50.

"Who Piracy Hurts: Entertainment Industry." *Motion Picture Association of America*, 12 Apr. 2006, https://web.archive.org/web/20060412164537/http://www.mpaa.org/piracy.asp.

Winstead, Nick. "'As a Symbol I Can Be Incorruptible': How Christopher Nolan De-queered the Batman of Joel Schumacher." *Journal of Popular Culture*, vol. 48, no. 3, 2015, pp. 572–85, https://doi.org/10.1111/jpcu.12228.

Wolk, Douglas. "Distributors See Growth Potential." *Publishers Weekly*, vol. 247, no. 51, 18 Dec. 2000, p. 34. Gale Academic OneFile.

Wright, Bradford W. *Comic Book Nation: The Transformation of Youth Culture in America*. Johns Hopkins University Press, 2001.

Yang, Yingzhi. "'Logan' Tops China's Box Office despite Cuts by Censors." *Los Angeles Times*, 7 Mar. 2017, http://www.latimes.com/business/hollywood/la-fi-ct-china-box-office-20170307-story.html.

Ydstie, John. "Trump's Potential Treasury Secretary Headed a 'Foreclosure Machine.'" *National Public Radio*, 29 Nov. 2016, https://www.npr.org/2016/11/29/503755613/trumps-potential-treasury-secretary-headed-a-foreclosure-machine.

Young, Thomas. "'Nuff Said?" *Copyright Culture: A Law Blog*, 15 Sept. 2014, https://copyrightculture.wordpress.com/2014/09/15/nuff-said/.

Zakarin, Jordan. "How the Fake X-Men Comics in Logan Were Made." *Inverse*, 27 Feb. 2017, https://www.inverse.com/article/28381-logan-movie-fake-x-men-comics-wolverine.

Ziv, Stan. "'Wonder Woman' Will Be Screened in Jordan, Despite Controversy over Israeli Actress Gal Gadot." *Newsweek*, 15 June 2017, http://www.newsweek.com/wonder-woman-screened-jordan-despite-controversy-israeli-actress-gal-626384.

INDEX

20th Century Fox: R-rated superhero films, 135, 153, 156; X-Men film rights, 49–50, 107–8, 154–55, 162, 166; Zorro film rights, 74, 76
21st Century (production company), 64
100 Orders (Iraq), 60
3:10 to Yuma (1957 film), 163
3:10 to Yuma (2007 film), 163

ABC (American Broadcasting Company), 118
Abomination (character), 52–53
Action Comics, 12, 34–37, 68, 214n3
"Action Heroes" line, 150
adamantium (fictional metal), 184
Adventure Comics, 100
Adventures of Sharkboy and Lavagirl in 3-D, 8
Adventures of Superman (radio series), 15
Adventures of Superman (TV series), 13, 101
advisory boards, 115–16, 216n10
Afghanistan, Islamic Republic of, 60, 82
Afrofuturism. See *Black Panther* (film)
aging: in *Ant-Man*, 136, 144; of Batman, 89, 157–58; in duopoly films, 135; of Hugh Jackman, 163; in *Logan*, 156–58, 163; and nostalgic marketing, 144
alienation, 7, 21, 59, 79
allegorical reading: of Batman trilogy, 69; of *Black Panther*, 187, 201; of *Blade*, 176–77; of *Captain America: The First Avenger*, 99, 112–13; of *Logan*, 154, 167; as method, 6, 23–26, 67; of *Wonder Woman*, 99, 131
Alliance of Canadian Cinema, Television, and Radio Artists, 49
Alliance of Motion Picture and Television Producers, 49
All-Star Comics, 115

Ambassadors, The, 66
AMC Entertainment Holdings (Dalian Wanda subsidiary), 147, 195–96
anamorphosis, 66–67
Annan, Kofi, 78
Ant-Man (character): as father, 30, 136–39, 141–42, 148–49, 167; and nostalgia, 140–43, 144–46
Ant-Man (film), 135–49, 164–65, 168, 181, 217n1
apocalypse, 5–6, 41, 110, 135, 178–81
Ares, 128–33
authorship: corporate (legal fiction), 4, 14–15, 36, 67–68, 86, 201, 208; disputes over, 15, 53–54, 75, 80–81, 104, 109, 111
Avengers (characters), 105, 112, 146–47
Avengers (comic), 102, 145
Avengers (film), 60, 148
Avengers: Age of Ultron (film), 50, 145, 186
Avengers: Endgame (film), 201
Avengers: Infinity War (film), 7, 201
Azuquita, Camilo, 144

Ballard, J. G., 159
Bane (character), 71, 88–93, 198
Banner, Bruce (character), 51–53. See also Hulk (character)
Bat Bible, 71
Bat Whispers (film), 215n4
Batcave, 18, 72–73, 94
Batgirl, 71, 92
Batman (character): beginning of, 74–76, 80–81; as brand within fiction, 70, 83, 86–87, 90–91, 94; competing with other vigilantes, 76–77, 82–83, 84–86; and copying, 84–86, 90–91, 95–97, 215n7; entering public domain, 4, 208; franchise, 17–18,

72, 120, 131, 203; licensing, 12, 23, 215n7; relationship with guns, 85, 93–94, 97, 115, 216n10; "rules" of character, 71, 93, 97; in *Suicide Squad*, 150, 151–52; thefts committed by, 72, 78–79
Batman (1989 film), 17–18, 25, 120, 125, 173, 215n2, 215n6
Batman (comics magazine), 82
Batman (serial), 13
Batman (TV series), 53, 71, 118, 174
Batman: The Dark Knight Returns (comic book), 72, 77–78, 84, 89, 215n5, 216n10
Batman: The Long Halloween (comic book), 84, 188
Batman: The Movie, 215
Batman: Year One (comic book), 72–73, 77, 84, 188
Batman and Robin (film), 71, 92, 143, 173–74
Batman Begins (film), 30, 69; compared to other Nolan films, 72, 81; cross-promotion of comics, 77–78; isolation from other DC characters, 73; realist gestures, 78–80; relationship to Zorro films, 73–76
Batman Forever (film), 71
Batman v. Superman: Dawn of Justice (film), 58; anticopying melodrama, 58
Batman's use of guns, 97; cross-promotion of comics, 77; DC film franchise, 120, 123; "death" of Superman, 6; steep box-office decline, 148
Batmobile, 77–78, 83, 85, 216n14
Ben Hur case (*Kalem Co. v. Harper Bros.*), 40
Black action cinema, 172–74
Black characters, psychological depth of, 153
Black Lives Matter movement, 182
Black Panther (character): as absolute monarch, 195, 197–98; failed 1990s film, 202; failed Kickstarter campaigns, 181–82; promotion via *Captain America: Civil War*, 182–83; Ta-Nehisi Coates as celebrity writer, 182
Black Panther (film): Afrofuturism, 171, 184, 194, 203; as allegory of defense of IP, 186–89, 197–201; celebration of monarchy, 171, 189–90, 194–99, 202–3; distribution in Saudi Arabia, 171, 195–96; King T'Chaka, 184–86; King T'Challa, 171, 185–87, 193–94, 197–200, 203, 219nn10–11; "mining" as metaphor, 186–89, 219–20n12; references

to slave trade, 189, 200, 219n10; state violence, 186, 192–95; Ulysses Klaue, 184, 186–88, 190–95
Blade (character): creation "for Marvel Comics," 3; film rights, 171–72; revision of comics character, 174
Blade (film): as allegory of defense of IP, 178–81; bricolage of other genres, 3–4, 174–76; demonstration of duopoly characters' box-office potential, 7, 32, 134, 174, 176; licensing of character, 172; style, 170–71; as surprise hit, 4, 174
Blade: Trinity (film), 180–81
Blade II (film), 179–80, 219n6
Blake, John (character), 88–94. *See also* Robin, the Boy Wonder
Blankman (film), 8, 172
Blaxploitation films, 145, 172, 175
bondage (fetish), 115–17
Bono, Mary, 208–9
Bono, Sonny, 4, 208–9
bootlegging (media), 33–34, 40–41, 43–47, 51
Bordwell, David, 64, 185
"Borombon," 144, 218n5
Boseman, Chadwick, 182, 203–4
box office: 1940s characters in 2010s, 132; declines after opening weekend, 148, 153; dominance of duopoly films during 2010s, 11, 171, 188; mainland China, 220n19; records broken by duopoly films, 10, 108, 148, 153, 156, 176; and residuals, 9; R-rated duopoly films, 135, 156–57, 168; as selective disclosure of information, 26–29; share of studio profits, 9–10
brand (character as), 75, 80, 85; competition between, 86; corporate understanding of, 108, 113; differentiation within range, 97, 104, 150–51; immortality, 6, 93–94, 167; Jack Kirby as character, 201; management of self as, 69–70, 75, 80, 85–87, 92, 97, 118; as mask for capital, 34; in mise en scène, 64, 142–43; as movie protagonist, 62–68; off-brand superheroes, 5, 62, 68; promotion of, 123–27; revival of, 131; as source of licensing revenue, 35
brand (commercial term): as commercial property, 48; consumer perception of, 135, 139; cross-promotion and placement, 142–43, 144, 146–48, 203, 216n13;

hollowness of, 93–94, 97, 104; loyalty, 25, 140, 148; as means of deception, 19, 63, 140; as means of production, 62; mobility, 88; props as characters, 65, 82–83, 216n9; narrative brand, 19, 162, 167; range, 31, 69–70, 80, 92, 103

branding of human bodies: metaphorical, 161–62; as punishment, 152, 186–88, 192–93, 195, 200, 220n15; as sign of ownership, 177

Brando, Marlon, 56
Bremer, Paul, 61
Brevoort, Tom, 50
Brooker, Will, 70, 151
Brown, Michael, police killing of, 182
Bruns Publications, 16, 37
Bucky (character), 103, 114
Busiek, Kurt, 110, 119, 127
Business Wire, 108

Cadence Industries, 104
Cannon Films, 64, 102, 187, 208
capital: dependence on legal order, 13–14, 49, 107–10, 201, 207–9; expansion, 18, 67, 133; mobility, 87–88; necessity of labor, 18, 133, 201, 206–7; as precondition for production, 104–5; as relation between persons, 21–22, 59, 83

capital circulation: as encounter with living labor, 21, 189; as publicity for brand, 29, 69; requirement to maintain rights, 119–20; and social goods, 55

Captain America (character): cessations of publication, 102; challenges to publisher's control, 106–10; constitutive inconsistency, 103–4; entering public domain, 4; as fundraising tool, 99, 104–5, 112–14; revival, 102; supposed endurance as popular icon, 98; as wartime gimmick, 99–101

Captain America (serial), 13
Captain America (telefilm), 102
Captain America: Civil War (film), 141, 146–47, 153, 182–83, 187
Captain America: The First Avenger (film): allegory of hero as financial instrument, 111–14; parallels with *Wonder Woman*, 127, 129, 132; as part of Marvel franchise, 98–99; as revisionist history, 216–17n3 (chap. 4)*Captain America Comics*, 99–100, 107, 112–14

Captain America . . . Commie Smasher! (comics magazine), 102
Captain America II: Death Too Soon (telefilm), 102
Captain America's Weird Tales (comics magazine), 101
Captain Fearless, 116
Captain Marvel: *Captain Marvel* (Marvel Cinematic Universe film), 38–40; Fawcett/DC Comics character, 38; infringement lawsuit, 37–38; Marvel Comics character, 38; Marvel trademark filings, 39; *Shazam!* comic, 38; *Shazam!* film, 39–40; *Shazam!* TV series, 38
Carter, Lynda, 118, 123, 125–27
cash, 87, 132, 203
Cash, Johnny, 164–67
Catwoman (character), 88, 90, 93
Catwoman (film), 120, 125
Charlton Comics, 105, 149–50, 208. *See also* "Action Heroes" line
Christian Identity movement, 179
Claremont, Chris, 49–50
class, 22–25, 95, 133, 205, 219n7
Coalition Provisional Authority (Iraq), 60
Coates, Ta-Nehisi, 182–83, 219n7
Columbia Pictures (Sony subsidiary): *Batman* serial, 13; failed Black Panther film, 202; Spider-Man film rights, 64, 66, 108, 176; Zorro film rights, 74
comic books: as commodity, 3, 6, 17, 39, 101–2; licensing revenues, 5, 12–13, 101–2, 119; moral panics, 105, 114–16; and nostalgia, 142, 160–64; origin of platform, 11–12; promotion by film trailers, 77–78, 84, 89; publication to avoid copyright reversion, 119–22, 127, 132; reception, 160–62; sales, 84, 89, 118, 121, 142, 182; as simulacra, 163–64; subversive vs. dominant form, 16–17
Comics Code Authority, 46, 214n5
Communist Party of China, 24, 135, 168, 220n20
conglomeration: DC Comics's acquisition by Kinney National Service, 38, 213n6; duopoly as subsidiaries, 6, 104, 122, 131; Fox's acquisition by Disney, 50, 167; Lucasfilm as Disney subsidiary, 217n3 (chap. 4); Marvel's acquisition by Disney,

188; news outlets and cross-promotion, 26, 121, 125–27
continuity (comics term), 17
continuity capital (neologism): defined, 18–22; duopoly character as instance of, 34, 62; duopoly refusal to share, 50; as hoard, 189; idleness, 56–57, 91, 189; as means of production, 18–19, 56–57, 62, 119–20, 196; simulated, 163
Coogan, Peter, 7, 16
copying: in early US film industry, 40; imagined as theft, 41–48; popular attitudes toward, 8–9; superhero powers, 6–7, 32–34, 51–60, 136–38, 149, 179–80; within comics industry, 16, 37–38, 100, 116
copyright: acquisition of other publishers' catalogs, 38, 149–50; artist or writer control of, 207; copyright notice as incantation, 36; defined in United States Constitution, 213n1; idea vs. expression, 213n5; lobbyists, 41–49; monopoly rights, 4–5, 7–8, 19, 40, 46–48, 65, 197; vs. moral rights, 7; and originality, 16; reversion from corporate to human author, 119–22, 127, 132, 201; and scarcity, 56; term extension, 4, 21, 62, 65, 169, 201, 208–9; termination, 107–10, 208; as tool of class power, 22; transfer (*see* work made for hire)
Copyright Act of 1909, 13, 107
Copyright Act of 1976, 14, 107
Copyright Term Extension Act (CTEA), 4, 19, 62, 104, 146, 208–9
Cox, Brian, 159
cross-promotion, 9, 77–78, 84, 89, 119, 123–26, 144–48, 155
"Curse of Capistrano," 75

Dalian Wanda Group, 196
Dark Knight (film): Batmobile, 216n14; box-office, 10; character doubling, 87–88; critical acclaim, 70; cross-promotion of comics, 84; Joker, 84, 87–88, 95; misrecognition of fake Batmen, 84–87, 97; surveillance, 78
Dark Knight Rises (film), 69, 71, 88–94, 135, 157, 198; aging of Batman, 89, 157–58; avoidance of homoeroticism, 71, 93–94; Bane, 71, 88–93, 198; cross-promotion of comics, 89; ending of trilogy, 69; succession of Batman, 92–94
Darkman (film), 8
DC Comics: as Detective Comics, 16, 37, 54, 80, 82, 213n6; as National Allied Publishing, 11–14, 16, 35–38, 131, 149; as National Comics Publications, 38, 208, 213n6; as National Periodical Publications, 53, 99–101, 102, 105, 115–17
DC Comics, relationships with artists and writers: Bob Kane, 80–81; Frank Miller, 23; Alan Moore, 23; Jerry Siegel and estate of, 56–57; William Moulton Marston and estate of, 119–22, 115–16, 119–22, 127, 132. *See also* Siegel and Shuster: disputes with publisher
DC Comics v. Towle, 83
Deadpool (film), 68, 135, 150, 153–56, 168
Deadshot (character), 148–53, 167
Death of Superman (comics crossover), 58, 173
Detective Comics (magazine), 80, 82, 215n7
Detective Comics Inc. v. Bruns Publications Inc., et al., 16, 37
Diana of Themyscira (character), 99, 128–31. *See also* Wonder Woman (character)
Digital Millennium Copyright Act of 1998, 4
disaster capitalism, 61
Disintegration (album), 145
Disney. *See* Walt Disney Company
Disney, Walt, 35. *See also* Walt Disney Company
Disney+, 11
Disneyland, 114, 203
Doctor Strange (film), 145–46, 168, 218n6
Doomsday (character), 58, 215n12
Downey, Robert, Jr., 32, 59, 141
Dozier, William, 118
Dracula, 180–81
DVD (digital videodisc), 4, 9–10, 33, 43–46, 47–48, 51, 135

Eastwood, Clint, 41–42, 164
Eco, Umberto, 57, 205
Eisner, Will, 80
Eisner and Iger Studio, 14, 37
elders, care of, 134, 156–57
Empire Strikes Back (film), 146–47
Enchantress (character), 149
"Escape," 145

Escape from New York (film), 3, 95
ethnocentrism, 191
executives, 5–9, 16, 22–28, 55, 155, 187, 206, 219–20n12
exploitation, 8, 21–23, 60, 80, 105, 206
expropriation: as capitalist practice, 17, 19, 87, 191; as duopoly policy, 13–14, 23, 33, 105, 119, 188–89, 202, 204; of shareholding classes, 205, 208; by Siegel and Shuster, 215n11; through work-for-hire doctrine, 5, 8, 13

Fantastic Four (2005 film), 154–55
Fantastic Four (2015 film), 155
Fantastic Four (characters), 154, 196–97
Fantastic Four (comics magazine), 102, 155, 220n14
Fantastic Four: Rise of the Silver Surfer, 155
Faust, 73–74
Fawcett Publications, 16, 38–40, 115, 149
Feature Comics, 116
"Feels So Good," 146
Feige, Kevin, 28, 111, 181–82
Fiction House, 116
Fighting American, 101
file-sharing, 45
film rights: adamantium (fictional metal), 184; Blade, 171–72; Fantastic Four, 20, 154–55, 196–97; Quicksilver, 50; Scarlet Witch, 50; Spider-Man, 20, 64, 66, 108, 176; Steel, 173–74; X-Men, 49–50, 107–8, 154–55, 162, 166; Zorro, 74, 76
Finger, Bill, 74, 80–81, 215n4
Fireworks Productions, 65, 74–75
Flash (character), 4, 12, 126
Flash Gordon (comic strip), 81
Fox, Lucius (character), 78–79, 86, 88–91
Frankfurt, Peter, 171–72
Frase, Peter, 43, 67
freelance artists and studios, 5, 11–14, 21, 49, 110
Freeman, Morgan, 78–79, 153
Frost, Deacon (character), 3, 178–79, 192
Fruitvale Station, 189
Frye, Northrop, 206

Gadot, Gal, 122–24, 126–27
Gaines, Maxwell Charles, 11, 115–16
Gates, Bill, 133
Gaza Strip, 122
General Zod (character), 56–58, 130

genetically modified organisms (GMOs), 61, 165
Gertz, John, 75
ghost artists, 14, 80, 215n11
ghostwriters, 14, 215n11
gloves as proprietary design element: Batman, 82–83, 90; Mickey Mouse, 65, 216n9
Goldberg, Whoopi, 204
Goldman Sachs, 132
Goodman, Martin, 100–102, 104, 105–7, 216nn1–2
goon (media industry), 42, 43, 48, 68, 214n7
Gordon, Commissioner (character), 18, 84, 87, 93–94, 216n11
Gotham City, 69–71, 76–80, 82–84, 87–88, 90–91, 95, 96
Goyer, David, 73–74, 76, 176, 179–81
Graeber, David, 42
Grant, Oscar, police killing of, 189
Gray, Mackenzie, 56–57
Green Lantern, 12; film, 120
Guardians of the Galaxy, 150
Guy Fawkes mask, 96

Haggard, H. Rider, 183
Hamas, 122
Hammer, Justin (character), 59–60, 137
Hancock, 8
Hardy Boys series, 13
Harry Potter franchise, 8, 71
Hasbro, 147–48
Hays Office (Production Code Administration), 46, 207
Herbert, Frank, 213n9
hip-hop, 150, 151, 171, 173, 175–76, 184
Hollywood Reporter, 26, 110, 133
Holy Grail, 63. See also *Monty Python and the Holy Grail*
homoeroticism, 71, 93
Hong Kong: cinema of, 3, 175; as place, 84, 88, 199, 220n20
Howard the Duck (film), 3, 13
Hulk (2003 film), 30, 51
Hulk (character), 51–53, 58, 155
Human Torch, 4, 102, 196–97
Hunger Games franchise, 8, 125
Hydra (fictional organization), 104, 111–12, 114

"I Got No Strings," 145
Icahn, Carl, 132
ideology, 25
Image Comics, 172, 207
imperialism, 69, 185, 191, 198
Inception (film), 71, 87, 207, 215n8
Incredible Hulk (2008 film), 52–53, 54
Incredible Hulk (TV series), 13, 173
infringement (copyright or trademark): *Detective Comics Inc. v. Bruns Publications Inc.*, 37; Fireworks Productions, 65, 74–75; by gatekeepers, 42, 47; *National Comics Publications Inc. v. Fawcett Publications Inc.*, 37–38; threat of litigation, 5, 9, 16, 36, 40, 61, 67; *TriStar Pictures Inc., et al., v. Del Taco Inc., et al.*, 74; vigilante solutions, 9
Insomnia (film), 71–72
Intellectual Property Office of Singapore, 47–48, 60
intellectual property, inaccuracy of term, 19
Iraq, US invasion and occupation, 32–33, 60–62, 78, 82
Iron Man (character), 32, 58–62, 68, 146–47, 155, 181, 203
Iron Man (film), 10, 32, 68, 134, 137, 188
Iron Man II (film), 58–60, 137–38
Iron Man III (film), 60–62
Irons, John Henry (character), 173
Israel, State of, 122–23
Israel-Gaza War (2014), 122
It Aint Me Babe (comic book), 117
"It's a Small World (After All)," 144, 214n12

Jackman, Hugh, 155–56, 158, 163, 165
Jameson, Fredric, 23–24, 66, 159
Jameson, J. Jonah (character), 63–64, 67
Jenkins, Patty, 123, 125, 127
Jews in comics industry, 58, 99–100
Jimenez, Phil, 121
Johnson, Kenneth, 173–74
Joker (film), 70, 94–96
Jones, Quincy, 173
Jordan, Michael B., 196–97
Juice (film), 171–72
Justice League (film), 126
Justice League of America (comic), 102, 148

Kahn, Jenette, 22–23, 118–22, 131
Kamen, Herman, 35

Kane, Bob, 73–74, 80–81, 215n4
Kashoggi, Jamal, assassination of, 195–96
Kevlar, 78
Kickstarter, 181–82
Kidman, Shawna, 12, 16–17, 23, 36, 46, 64, 188
Killmonger (character), 187–90, 192–94, 196–200, 203, 220n20
King, Rodney, police beating of, 219n6
King Features Syndicate, 81
Kinney National Service, 38, 208, 213n6
Kirby, Jack: cocreation of Captain America, 100–101, 216n2; heirs' lawsuit against Marvel, 109–10, 132, 200–201; relationship with Timely Comics, 101–2; struggle over Captain America, 105–7; warning about duopoly, 22; as writer and artist of Black Panther comics, 183–84
Kirby v. Marvel Characters Inc., 109–10
Klaue, Ulysses (character). See *Black Panther* (film)
"Knightfall" (comics storyline), 89
Koch brothers, 133
kryptonite, 15, 215n11

Lacan, Jacques, 66
Lane, Lois, 35, 37, 207, 217n4 (chap. 4)
Lang, Scott (character), 135–39, 141–45. See also *Ant-Man* (film)
Larson, Stephen G. (judge), 214n10
Laura (clone of Wolverine), 157–58, 160–63, 167. See also *Logan*
League of Shadows, 76–77, 82–84, 88–92
Lebanon, 2006 Israeli invasion of, 122
Ledger, Heath, 151
Lee, Stan, 28, 38, 100, 102, 105–6
Legend of Wonder Woman, 119, 127
Legend of Zorro (film), 74–75
Leonardo da Vinci, 81
Lepore, Jill, 116–18
lèse-majesté, 193
Leto, Jared, 150–51
Levitz, Paul, 77
licensing: across media, 5, 10–11, 13, 15, 20, 22, 34, 38, 101–2, 165; as advertising, 12, 35–36; and authorship, 15, 34–37, 108, 110; basis of duopoly business model, 5, 8, 11–13, 16, 176, 188–89; compared with owning real estate, 35, 56, 119–20; as component of corporate "mania," 120; as

main source of duopoly profits, 5, 11, 22, 34–37, 108; of merchandise, 12, 34–36, 39, 96; as reason for character immortality, 167; relationship to fictional character's traits, 104; and R-rated films, 167–68, 176; "Superman's Phony Manager," 34–35; threat posed by loss of copyright, 34–37, 108, 110, 119

licensing revenue, 67, 110, 174; desired by artists and writers, 12, 22–23, 34–37, 207; fees as barrier to competitors, 39, 46, 174; from sale of film rights, 20, 49, 101–2, 108, 176

Liebowitz, Jack, 36, 53–56, 99–100

Lloyd, Alan, 96

Logan (film): adult problems, 155–57; child care, 157–58; depiction of aging, 157–58, 164; depiction of comic books, 160; depiction of protagonist death, 158–59, 167; drought as metaphor for inter-corporate relations, 154–55; elder care, 134, 156–57; elegiac marketing, 156, 160, 164–65; nostalgia, 154, 158–62, 164, 168; R rating, 135, 156–57; and western genre, 160–67

lost race fiction, 183–84

Lucasfilm (Disney subsidiary), 21, 147, 217n9 (chap. 3), 217n3 (chap. 4)

Luis (*Ant-Man* character), 144–45

Luthor, Lex (character), 51, 53–56, 58, 61

Magneto (character), 50

mainland China as theatrical market, 4, 168, 218n18, 220nn19–20

Mainline Publications, 101–5

Maisel, David, 68

management, 55–56, 70, 80, 87, 99, 123

Mangold, James, 154–55, 160, 163–64

"mania," corporate manufacture of, 120, 122–27, 182

Mark of Zorro (1920 film), 75–76

Mark of Zorro (1940 film), 73–74

Marston, Willam Moulton, 115–17, 119–22, 124, 127, 130, 131–32

martial arts film, 3, 174–75

Marvel Characters Inc. v. Simon, 106–8

Marvel Cinematic Universe, 132, 135–36, 145–48, 155, 186, 202–4

Marvel Comics: as Atlas Comics, 13, 216n1; characters, 3–4, 33, 38, 50, 66, 105–10, 188–89; in counterfactual timelines, 207–8; film rights, 20; as licensee, 147; manufacturing "mania," 182; many names of company, 13, 102, 112; name redacted in *Logan*, 163; Stan Lee as public face, 106; struggles with Kirby family, 105–7, 200–201; as Timely Comics, 13, 99–108, 112, 113, 131; work-for-hire practices, 14, 105–10, 200–201

Marvel Entertainment Group, 5, 39, 50, 104, 188

Marvel Studios, 10–11, 21, 28, 32, 38–40, 201–4; animated logo, 142; avoidance of mentioning adamantium, 184; Black sidekicks, 155; box-office dominance, 135, 148; independent financing of films, 10–11, 21, 68, 104–5, 134, 181, 188; marketing, 111; manufacturing "mania," 182–83; reacquisition of film rights, 52, 197; style of fight scenes, 185

Marvel Super Heroes (TV series), 102

Mask of Zorro (film), 65, 74–75

Mayer, Sheldon, 115

McCulley, Johnston, 73–76

Me and the Mouse Travel, 65

means of production, 17–19, 25, 62, 133, 153, 187, 198

Meehan, Eileen, 17, 28, 56, 120

Mefistofele, 72–74

Merrill Lynch, 21, 104

Merritt, Abraham, 183

Meteor Man (film), 8, 172

MGM, 10, 64, 207

Mickey Mouse, 4, 21, 35, 65, 140, 216n9

Miller, Frank, 23, 72–74, 84, 161, 188

mining. See under *Black Panther* (film)

Miss Israel pageant, 122

MLJ Publications, 100, 105

Mnuchin, Steven, 132, 133

monarchy, 171, 190–203

monopoly. See under copyright

Monsanto (Bayer AG subsidiary), 61

Monty Python and the Holy Grail, 194

Moore, Alan, 23, 150

moral rights doctrine, 7

More Fun Comics, 100, 115

Motion Picture Industry Pension and Health Plans, 15, 48–49

MPA (Motion Picture Association). See MPAA (Motion Picture Association of America)

MPAA (Motion Picture Association of America), 33, 41–48, 168
Ms. (magazine), 117–18, 120, 125

Nama, Adilifu, 171, 175
Nancy Drew series, 13
Nazis: in 1940s American comics, 99–100, 104, 116, 131; Aryan vs. white supremacy, 220n16; evil Kryptonians reimagined as, 57–58; originators of fictional "super-soldier" process, 111–12; as substitute for American racism, 179–81, 218n17
Nelson, Diane, 123
neoliberalism, 61, 83, 91, 219n7
New Line Cinema, 3, 170, 174, 182, 187, 202, 219n1
Nicholson, Jack, 151
N'Jobu, Prince (character), 184–86, 189, 193
Nolan, Christopher, 69–78, 81–91, 93–97
Nolan, Jonathan, 84, 94
Nomad (character), 103
Nomex, 78
North, Sterling, 114–15
nostalgia: as affective appeal in films, 140–48, 150–51, 154, 158, 167, 175; of characters, 94, 127, 135, 141–42, 153; and comics fandom, 3, 102, 117, 164; deceptive, 139–40; for franchises, 56, 104, 127, 131, 146–48, 158–60, 168; historical, 147; as magical solution, 161–62; as marketing appeal, 104, 127, 134–35, 139
nuclear weapons, 32, 71, 88, 91
NYU Shanghai (New York University Shanghai), 27

Oakland, California, 184, 189, 203
Objectivism, 62
Olsen, Jimmy (character), 214n4, 215n11
O'Neal, Shaquille, 173
OneWest, 132–33
open-source villainy, 94–96
Operation Reinhardt, 179
Order 81 (Iraq), 60–61, 215n13
organized crime, 43–47, 69, 76–77, 84–88, 174
Orgazmo (film), 8
originality, 9, 16, 70, 72–83
outsourcing, 70, 79–82, 215n11

Paramount Pictures, 147
parenting, 114–16, 135–48, 149–53, 157, 162–67

Parker, Peter (character), 63–64, 207
patent, 8, 19, 52, 61, 165, 213n5
Pennyworth, Alfred (character), 79, 89, 91
Perelman, Ron, 20–21, 132
Perlmutter, Ike, 132–33
Phoenix, Joaquin, 151
Pinocchio (film), 145–46
piracy: false equivalency of copying and stealing, 41, 47–48; media, 40–41; as metaphor for copying, 43–45, 67, 214n6
Piracy: It's a Crime (video), 47–48, 51
Prestige, The (film), 87, 215n8
Procter & Gamble, 11, 43
Production Code Administration (Hays Office), 46, 207
Professor X (character), 154, 156–60, 162, 164–65, 218n11, 218n14
Prometheus myth, 53, 55
public domain: enclosure, 62, 204; freedom of use, 40, 74, 75, 81, 180; freezing by copyright term extension, 4, 21, 104, 146, 169; and mythic characters, 40, 53; and serial characters, 213n2
Public Enemy, 184, 219n12
Punisher (character), 103
Punisher (film), 3
"Purloined Letter," 64
Pym, Hank (character), 136–39, 141, 144

QDE Entertainment, 173
Queen of Swords (TV series), 74
Quicksilver (character), 50
Quinn, Harley (character), 148–50

racism: ambiguous, 189–96; Hollywood's mapping onto Europe, 179–80; superficial treatment in blockbuster films, 170–71, 178, 185, 202; Ta-Nehisi Coates on, 182, 219n7. *See also* Nazis
Rand, Ayn, 59
Ra's al Ghul (character), 76–77
RatPac-Dune Entertainment, 133
Red Skull (character), 111
Redstockings, 120
Reeve, Christopher, 56
Reinhardt (character), 179
Republic Pictures, 13, 36, 38, 101
residuals (compensation), 9, 15, 48–49
Reynolds, Richard, 51, 205–6, 214n8

Rhodes, Lt. Col. James (character), 59–60. *See also* War Machine
Rietveldt, Melchior, 47
Robbins, Trina, 117, 119–20, 127
Robin, the Boy Wonder, 4, 71, 78, 92–94. *See also* Blake, John (character)
Rockwell, Sam, 58–59
Rogers, Steve (character), 99–100, 103–4, 111–14, 129
Rogue One: A Star Wars Story (film), 147, 217n3 (chap. 4)
romance comics, 101, 105
Romero, Caesar, 151
royalties, 5, 8, 15, 35, 47, 56, 100–101, 105, 116, 207; denoting licensing fees, 35; in job offer to Jack Kirby and Joe Simon, 100–101; negotiated by William Moulton Marston, 116; as payment into pension funds, 15, 48–49, 207; potential royalties as object of litigation, 56; unpaid by Timely Comics (Marvel), 105; unpaid for music used in *Piracy: It's a Crime*, 47; work-for-hire as means of avoiding payment of, 5, 8, 15

Santangelo, John, 149. *See also* Charlton Comics
SAPPRFT (State Administration of Press and Publication, Radio, Film, and Television), 168, 218n18
Saudi Arabia, Kingdom of: assassination of Jamal Kashoggi, 195–96; *Black Panther* screening, 31, 171, 195; cinema ban, 31, 171, 195; corporal punishment and execution, 195; monarchy, 220n20; Rapid Intervention Force (Tiger Squad), 195–96
savage (noun), 191–95, 200
scarcity, creation of: discontinuation of characters, 49–50, 154–55; Disney vaulting strategy, 50, 91; role of copyright in creating, 49–50, 55–56, 91
Scarecrow (character), 77–85
Scarlet Witch (character), 50
Screen Actors Guild-American Federation of Television and Radio Artists, 15, 46, 49, 109
screener (video), 46
secrecy in media industry, 10, 25–29
segregation, racial, 180, 216–17n3 (chap. 3)
September 11th, 5–6, 33, 43, 83
serials, theatrical, 13, 20, 38, 45, 101, 217n7

Shaft (film), 174
Shane (film), 160–63, 166–67
Shanghai, 27–28, 132, 214n12
shareholders, 12, 26–27, 55, 68, 108, 207
Sheena, Queen of the Jungle (character), 116, 117
Shield (character), 100–101
SHIELD (fictional organization), 136, 144
Shuri, Princess (character), 197–98, 201, 203, 219n10
Shuster, Joe, 54, 56, 80, 106, 207; ghost artists, 14, 207; illustrations, 80. *See also* Siegel and Shuster
Siegel, Jerry: dispute over Superboy, 37; scolding by Jack Liebowitz, 54; use of ghostwriters, 14. *See also* Siegel and Shuster
Siegel and Shuster: differences between original and later adaptations of Superman, 15; disputes with publisher, 35–37, 56, 106, 214n3, 214n10; as expropriators of ghost artists and ghostwriters, 215n11; hopes to license character, 12, 35–36; transfer of Superman copyright to publisher, 12; unauthorized interview with *Cleveland Plain Dealer*, 53–54
Siegel v. Warner Bros. Entertainment Inc., 56, 214n10
Simmons, J. K., 63–64
Singleton, John, 202
Sky High, 8
slavery, 58, 154, 180, 189, 200, 219n10, 220n16
Smith, Will, 148–53
Snipes, Wesley, 170, 174–75
Snow White, 96
Snyder, Zack, 57–58
Sony, 65–66, 74–76, 146, 176
Spawn, 172–73
Specials, The, 8
Spider-Man (character): entering public domain, 208; film rights, 64, 66, 108, 176; as means of nostalgic address, 146–47; in New York Stock Exchange, 20; as part of Marvel's 1960s revival, 155; succession of villains, 216n15
Spider-Man (film): box office record, 108, 176; caricature of licensing, 63–64; film rights and development, 64, 66, 108, 176; product placement, 66–67; role in establishing duopoly in Hollywood, 63–64

Star Wars franchise, 8, 126, 146–47, 217n9 (chap. 3), 217n3 (chap. 4), 218n7
Stark, Tony (character), 32, 58–62, 141, 201
Steamboat Willie, 21, 44
Steel (character), 173–74
Steel (film), 173–74, 219n4
Stewart, Sir Patrick, 160
Stratemeyer Syndicate, 13
Stryker, Col. William (character), 159
Sub-Mariner (character), 101–2
succession: kings, 171, 184–85, 193–95; superheroes, 92–94, 157, 162–63; villains, 216n15
Suicide Squad, 135, 148–53, 167–68, 218n8
Super, 8
Super Friends, 119, 127
Superboy, 37
Superman (character): accretion of franchise by artists and writers, 14–15; alternate universe versions, 206–8; altruism, 68; chevron, 64; cloning, 51; in DC film franchise, 120, 122, 126, 131; "death," 58, 173; entering public domain, 4, 169; excision from Nolan Batman films, 73; as franchise, 174, 214n4, 215n11; infringement lawsuits, 16, 37–38, 40; initial avoidance of World War II, 99–100; Kryptonian technology, 54–56; licensing revenues, 23, 34–37, 102; "The Myth of Superman," 205–6; popularity, 12, 80–81, 101, 117, 120; relationship with Lois Lane, 207, 217n4 (chap. 4); struggles over copyright, 35–37, 56, 106, 214n3, 214n10; role in establishing comics industry and superhero genre, 12, 80–81; style of violence, 116, 130; as vessel for character library, 56–58, 130–31. See also *Adventures of Superman* (radio series); *Adventures of Superman* (TV series); *Man of Steel*; Siegel and Shuster
Superman (film), 13, 53, 55, 56, 139
Superman, Inc., 35–37
Superman Returns (film), 53–56, 61, 217n4 (chap. 4)
surplus value, 16, 56, 67, 133
"symbol" rhetoric (Batman franchise), 70, 73, 93–97

Talia al Ghul (character), 88, 92
Tarzan (character), 35
T'Chaka, King (character). See Black Panther (character)

T'Challa, King (character). See Black Panther (character)
termination of copyright, 107–10, 208
Terminator franchise, 141
Thanos (character), 201
Thomas the Tank Engine, 142
Thor (character), 181, 217n1
Tiger Squad. See Saudi Arabia, Kingdom of
Time Warner. See Warner Bros. (studio)
Toxic Avenger, 8
trademark: character, 29, 64–67, 68, 99, 121, 142–43, 216n16; character element as, 65, 82–83, 216n9; effects on perception, 63; key to licensing, 5, 23, 35; in popular consciousness, 8; infringement and litigation, 9, 74–76; prevention of competition, 38–39, 62, 94; necessary originality, 80, 90; relationship to labor, 20, 126; and rent-seeking, 63, 67; unlimited duration, 65; within fiction, 7, 34, 69–70, 73, 84–87
Trademark Trial and Appeal Board, 65, 82, 216n9
trailers, film, 45, 47, 84, 145–47, 164, 182–83
Transformers franchise, 8, 147–48, 151
Traue, Antje, 57
Trevor, Steve (character), 128–30
TriStar Pictures Inc., et al., v. Del Taco Inc., et al., 74

Ultimate Guide to Wonder Woman, 126–27
Unbreakable, 8
Uncle Tom's Cabin, 178
Unforgiven, 164
Union Station, St. Louis, 3
United Nations, 78, 123–25
United States Patent and Trademark Office, 39, 86
United States Senate Subcommittee on Juvenile Delinquency, 105

V for Vendetta, 96
Valenti, Jack, 41–46, 48, 209, 214n7
Van Dyne, Hope (character), 136, 138
Vanko, Ivan (character), 59–60
Variety, 104, 105, 108, 121–22, 143, 156–57
vaulting (exhibition strategy), 50
vibranium (fictional metal), 183–87, 192–93, 196–200, 219n10, 220n14
videocassette recorder (VCR), 41–43

Vietnam War, 60
villain as protagonist, 51, 206

Walk the Line, 164
Wall Street (film), 141
Walt Disney Company: acquisition of Fox, 50, 167, 196–97, 219n11; acquisition of Marvel, 5, 10, 109, 155, 188, 200; alternate histories, 207–8; astroturfing fan culture, 217n9; competitor of Warner Bros., 62, 123, 131, 132; dependence on copyrights, 109–10; enclosure of public domain, 204; expansion-as-capitulation, 196; as licensor, 13; lobbying to extend copyright, 4, 21, 62, 213n1; management of brands, 113, 135, 188; nostalgic marketing, 141, 143–48, 217n3 (chap. 3), 218n7; ownership of Marvel, 104; secrecy, 27–28; shareholders, 25–27, 55, 132; theme parks, 114, 140, 144, 203, 204, 214n12; trademarks, 65, 96, 140; vaulting (exhibition strategy), 50
War Machine, 146
War on Terror, 29, 61, 69
Warner Bros. (studio): acquisition of DC Comics, 5; acquisition of New Line Cinema, 219n1; anti-screener initiative, 46; character as range brand, 69; competitor of TriStar (Sony), 74; competitor of Walt Disney Company, 62, 123, 131, 132, 148; conglomerate subsidiary, 22, 25, 77, 84, 216n13; copyrights, 18, 37–39, 55–56, 58, 62, 110, 119; cross-promotion via news outlets, 121, 125–26; differentiation of within range brands, 149–51; as distributor, 173; gangster films, 130; management of franchises, 89, 92, 94, 122, 131–32, 150; manufacture of "mania" and event films, 120, 122–27, 174; pioneering home video retail, 9; preoccupation with branding, 70, 215n8; promotion of Wonder Woman, 117–20, 123, 127; and scarcity, 55–56; secrecy, 26; trademarks, 96
Warner Bros. Discovery (conglomerate), 5, 25
Wasko, Janet, 26, 34, 62, 181
Wayne, Bruce (character): aging, 89, 157–58; as brand manager, 69–71, 73–74, 78–80, 82–83, 87–88, 216n14; as criminal, 78–79, 82, 87–88; "death," 71–72, 89, 92, 216n11; murder of parents, 18, 72–73, 152; as proprietor, 72, 78; and realism, 72, 79, 86; refusal to share, 72, 90–91
Wayne, Thomas (character), 76, 83
Wayne Enterprises (fictional company), 70, 76–84, 87–92
Wayne Manor, 18, 72, 79, 92, 94
WCI (Warner Communications, Inc.), 17, 26, 118–19, 208
Wertham, Fredric, 93
West, Cornel, 219n7
western (genre), 101, 158, 160–64, 218n12
Wheeler-Nicholson, Malcolm, 11–12, 213n5
White, Michael Jai, 172–73
White, Perry (character), 214n4, 215n11
Whiz Comics, 38, 40, 100
Wolverine (character): aging, 157–58, 164; amnesia, 159–60; as antihero, 103; "death," 158, 167; metal bones, 184; powers, 155, 157–58, 164–65; suffering, 155–56, 164–65, 218n15; violence, 162–63
Wolverine (film), 154, 156
Wonder Comics, 37
Wonder Man, 37
Wonder Woman (character): copyright reversion clause, 119–22, 127, 132; entering public domain, 4; fandom, 117–18; as instrument, 127–31; licensing, 12, 23, 117–18; manufactured "mania," 120, 122–27; and *Ms.* magazine, 117–18, 120, 125; origin, 114–17; popularity, 98; protest against UN Honorary Ambassadorship, 124; violence, 130; as UN Honorary Ambassador for the Empowerment of Women and Girls, 123–25. *See also* Marston, Willam Moulton
Wonder Woman (film): as allegory of corporate self-congratulation, 98–99; development, 121–23; parallels with Captain America, 127–29, 131–32; promotion, 120, 122–27
Wonder Woman (TV series), 118, 125, 127, 130
Wonder Woman: A "Ms." Book, 118
Wonder Woman Day, 126
Wonder Woman Foundation, 118
Wonder Women of History, 117
work made for hire: as category of work, 9–11, 13, 18, 66, 109–10, 133, 162; at duopoly, 14, 105–10, 200–201, 214n3; expropriation of artists and writers, 5, 8, 12–14, 21, 29, 49; legal doctrine, 12–14; means of avoiding

payment of royalties, 5, 8, 15, 29; in radio, 215n11
workers: below the line (Hollywood), 10, 48–49; ethnography of, 27–28; expropriation of, 17, 19, 87, 133, 187, 191; fans as unpaid workers, 126; invisibility in Hollywood blockbusters, 33, 59–60, 70, 79, 219n10; nonunionized, 15–16, 110, 207–8; opposition to management, 17, 21, 25, 43, 201; unionized, 9, 15, 21, 46, 48–49, 109–10, 207–8
World War I, 45, 128
World War II, 98, 99–105, 128, 216–17n3 (chap. 3)
Writers Guild of America, 49, 109
"wrong hands" metaphors, 7, 90, 138, 178, 197

X2: X-Men United (film), 30, 154, 165
X3: The Last Stand (film), 154
X-24 (character), 158–59, 165, 167, 218n14
Xavier, Charles. *See* Professor X (character)
X-Men (comic), 49–50, 107, 158, 160, 162–64, 166
X-Men (film), 49, 108, 154, 156, 159, 176
X-Men franchise, 150, 154–62, 165, 167–68, 218n17
X-Men: Days of Future Past (film), 50, 154
X-Men Origins: Wolverine (film), 154, 156, 159, 218n16

Young Romance, 105

Zeus, 40, 53, 129
Zorro, 65, 71, 72–76, 216n16
Zorro, the Gay Blade (film), 75, 216n16
ZPI (Zorro Productions Incorporated), 75, 216n16

ABOUT THE AUTHOR

Photo courtesy of the editor

Ezra Claverie has a GED from the Missouri Department of Elementary and Secondary Education and a PhD in English from the University of Illinois, Urbana-Champaign. For eight years he taught as a nontenured professor at New York University Shanghai, until the zero-COVID lockdowns of 2022 convinced him to change careers. He now writes full-time for Washington University in Saint Louis, his hometown.

www.ingramcontent.com/pod-product-compliance
Lightning Source LLC
Chambersburg PA
CBHW022005220426
43663CB00007B/967